Introduction to International Relations and Religion

We work with leading authors to develop the strongest educational materials in international relations, bringing cutting-edge thinking and best learning practice to a global market.

Under a range of well-known imprints, including Longman, we craft high quality print and electronic publications which help readers to understand and apply their content, whether studying or at work.

To find out more about the complete range of our publishing, please visit us on the World Wide Web at: www.pearsoned.co.uk

Introduction to International Relations and Religion

Jeffrey Haynes

Harlow, England • London • New York • Boston • San Francisco • Toronto
Sydney • Tokyo • Singapore • Hong Kong • Seoul • Taipei • New Delhi
Cape Town • Madrid • Mexico City • Amsterdam • Munich • Paris • Milan

PEARSON EDUCATION LIMITED

Edinburgh Gate
Harlow
Essex CM20 2JE
England
and Associated Companies throughout the world
Visit us on the World Wide Web at: www.pearsoned.co.uk

First published 2007

ISBN: 978-1-4058-2474-3

British Library Cataloguing-in-Publication Data
A catalogue record for this book is available from the British Library

Library of Congress Cataloging-in-Publication Data
A catalog record for this book is available from the Library of Congress
10 9 8 7 6 5 4 3 2 1
10 09 08 07

Typeset in 9/13.5pt Stone Serif by 35
Printed and bound in Malaysia

The publisher's policy is to use paper manufactured from sustainable forests.

Contents

Acknowledgements

We are grateful to the following for permission to reproduce copyright material:

Table 6.1 from Old madness. New methods. Revival of religious terrorism begs for broader U.S. policy, republished with permission of Rand Corporation from *Rand Review Vol. 22 No. 2*, (Hoffman, B. 1998-9), permission conveyed through Copyright Clearance Center, Inc.; Table 8.1 from The chosen nation: the influence of religion on US foreign policy in *Policy Brief No. 37*, The Carnegie Endowment for International Peace, (Judis, J. 2005); Tables 9.1, 9.2 and 9.3 from Islamic extremism: common concern for Muslim and western publics in *Pew Global Attitudes Project*, July 2005, copyright the Pew Research Center; Table 10.1 from *Islamic NGOs in Africa: the promise and peril of Islamic voluntarism*, Centre of African Studies, University of Copenhagen (Salih, M. A. Mohamed 2002), Professor Mohamed Salih's permission conveyed through University of Copenhagen.

In some instances we have been unable to trace the owners of copyright material and we would appreciate any information that would enable us to do so.

PART ONE

Religion and international relations: theory and analysis

CHAPTER 1

Introduction

A variety of religious actors are now involved in various significant ways in international relations. For many observers, this is new and unexpected: until recently, it appeared that religious actors could safely be ignored in international relations because they appeared to be collectively insignificant (Petito and Hatzopoulos, 2003; Fox and Sandler, 2004). Now, however, many governments, analysts and observers would agree that things have changed in various ways. This book examines religion's involvement in current international relations.

We approach this issue as follows. The first section of the book, comprising the current chapter and the following one, discusses theoretical and analytical concepts related to the issue of religion and international relations. In Chapter 2, we examine how various theories of International Relations[1] analyse the impact of religion on international relations, with particular focus on the notion of 'soft power' because of its relevance for understanding how religion can influence social and political issues (Nye, 1990, 2004). The analytical insights offered by the concept of soft power inform several later chapters, especially in the third section of the book, Chapters 8–13, which collectively focus on specific regions and countries. Before that, in the book's second section, Chapters 3–7, we focus upon several important contemporary issues in international relations, which are associated with the idea of a widespread religious resurgence: globalization, transnational religious actors, religious fundamentalism, international order and conflict, and conflict resolution and peacebuilding. The third section, Chapters 8–13, examines various kinds of religious actors in international relations on a regional basis, focusing upon: the United States of America, Europe, Africa, The Middle East, South Asia and Pacific Asia. Chapter 14, the concluding chapter, summarizes the main points made in the book.

This chapter examines several controversies in the study of religion and international relations, including: the issue of a 'clash of civilizations' between the 'West' and the 'Muslim world', a topic commonly associated with the US academic Samuel Huntington; the impact of secularization and secularism on the involvement of religion in international relations; definitions of key terms used in the book; basic beliefs of the religions on which we focus: Buddhism, Christianity, Confucianism, Hinduism, Islam and Judaism; and, finally, the influence of what many see as a widespread, current religious resurgence, affecting how we understand and account for religion's involvement in international relations.

Religion and international relations: Huntington and the 'clash of civilizations'

While it is difficult to single out an event that would on its own explain the current focus on religion and international relations, it is impossible to ignore Samuel Huntington's (1993, 1996) influential yet controversial argument about 'the clash of civilizations'. According to Huntington, the West's security, and by extension global order, is under attack from international Islamic militancy. For some, Huntington's thesis was given credence by the emergence of overtly anti-Western Islamist regimes in Afghanistan and Sudan in the 1990s, the sustained attempt to do so contemporaneously in Algeria, the events of September 11, 2001 ('9/11') and subsequent bomb attacks in Madrid, London, and elsewhere, and the US-led invasions of Afghanistan (2001) and Iraq (2003). Around the world, societies responded to both 9/11 and subsequent US retaliation in broadly religious and cultural terms. On the one hand, Western governments, including those of Britain, Italy and Spain, strongly supported the American people and their president. On the other hand, many 'ordinary' Muslims – although not necessarily their governments – appeared to view the events rather differently: acknowledging the undesirability of the loss of thousands of innocent people as a consequence of a terrorist outrage, for some Muslims 9/11 also represented an attempt to 'fight back' against what some saw as a globally destructive state: the USA (and by extension the 'West' more generally) (Dolan, 2005). In addition, many Muslims regarded punitive US-led actions against both Afghanistan and Iraq as unjust, designed unfairly to 'punish' fellow believers for 9/11 – a tragic event over which they had no control (Shlapentokh et al., 2005).

Huntington and the 'Clash of Civilizations'

The US academic, Samuel Huntington, first presented his 'clash of civilizations' thesis in an article published in 1993, followed by a book in 1996. Huntington claims that in the post-Cold War era most conflicts will be between several civilizations that are significantly informed by religion, including 'Islamic' and 'Confucian' countries. In particular, the new fight is between the (Christian) 'West' and the Muslim – especially Arab – world. Huntington avers that the 'Christian', democratic West finds itself in conflict especially with radical Islam, a political movement seeking to reform politics towards Islamic interpretations, united by antipathy to the West, inspired by anti-democratic religious and cultural dogma, and collectively focused ideologically in 'Islamism' or 'Islamic fundamentalism'. It is regarded as a key threat to international – especially Western – security and stability.

Critics of Huntington's argument note that it is one thing to argue that various brands of political Islam have qualitatively different perspectives on liberal democracy compared to Western models, but quite another to claim that Muslim states en masse want conflict with the West. This is because there are many 'Islams' – some 'moderate' some less so; only the malevolent or misinformed, critics contend, would blame on all Muslims recent terrorist attacks characterized by 'Islamic terrorism'. Secondly, the 9/11 atrocities – as well as subsequent bomb outrages in Bali (Indonesia), Istanbul, London, Madrid and elsewhere – were not carried out by a state or group of states or at their behest, but by al-Qaeda, an international terrorist organization. Despite energetic US attempts, no definitive proof was ever found to link the regime of Saddam Hussein in Iraq with either Osama bin Laden or al-Qaeda.

Thirdly, the idea of civilizational conflict is problematic because it is very difficult to identify clearly territorial boundaries to civilizations, and virtually impossible to perceive them as acting as coherent units. Further, Huntington's image of 'clashing civilizations' is said to focus too closely on an undifferentiated category – 'civilization' – and place insufficient emphasis on various trends, conflicts and disagreements within cultures. Finally, cultures may not be seen usefully as closed systems of essentialist values. It is implausible to understand the world as comprising a strictly limited number of cultures, each with unique core sets of beliefs. Here, the influence of globalization is to be noted as it leads to more channels, pressures and agents through which various norms are diffused, and interact.

Finally, the image of 'clashing civilizations' is said to ignore the very important sense in which radical Islamist revolt and al-Qaeda terrorism is primarily aimed *internally* at corrupt and 'un-Islamic' governments in Muslim countries – from Morocco in the west to Indonesia in the east. In recent years,

(Continued)

the genesis of numerous Islamist groups is linked to governmental policy failures – not to the encouragement of Osama bin Laden. This suggests that contemporary Islamist resurgence has its foundations in widespread popular Muslim disillusionment at slow or non-existent progress as well as growing disgust with corrupt and unrepresentative governments. Such perceptions are not helped when such regimes refuse to open up political systems to become more representative.

No doubt, al-Qaeda, the author of 9/11, envisaged such Muslim reactions to the 9/11 outrage (Haynes, 2005c). Its purpose was of course to wreak terrible destruction on the USA – but that was not all. In addition, al-Qaeda wished to create a global media spectacle, to show the mass of 'downtrodden ordinary Muslims' that bin Laden personally – already for some Muslims a hero following anti-Soviet exploits in Afghanistan in the late 1980s – and al-Qaeda collectively acted on *their* behalf. Thus, around the world, 'ordinary' Muslims were an important target audience for the highly visual spectacle of the destruction of the Twin Towers and the contemporaneous attack on the Pentagon. For bin Laden and al-Qaeda a key goal of 9/11 was to grab the attention of ordinary (Sunni) Muslims, to encourage them to make connections between the attacks and widespread Muslim resentment against the USA. Prior to 9/11 this was already simmering as a result, *inter alia*, of the US-led invasion of Iraq in 1990–91 and the American government's unwavering support both for Israel's resolutely harsh treatment of the Palestinians and many unelected rulers in the Muslim world.

However, even if such areas of specific concern to many Muslims were speedily resolved, it may be that associated resentment and antipathy towards the USA and by extension the West would not necessarily dissipate speedily. This is because, rather than there being only a finite list of specific issues, potentially resolvable via negotiation and compromise, there are also sources of antipathy and disquiet that go much deeper and are as a result more problematic to resolve. Thus even if solutions for specific sources of complaint were quickly found, it would not necessarily deal fully with all sources of Muslim anger. This may be because, as Hurrell notes, it 'seems plausible that much [Muslim] resentment has to do with the far-reaching and corrosive encroachments of modernization, westernization and globalization' (Hurrell, 2002: 197).

Among such factors can be noted attempts by the US and other Western governments and international organizations – notably the European

Union – to spread and disseminate secular models of democracy in the Muslim world. Some Muslims see this as a foreign 'imposition' of unacceptable policies and programmes that are culturally, religiously and socially inappropriate, because they appear to legitimize suppression of local, traditional, religiously-informed, socio-political authorities and practices. It is perceived as a policy of *forced* secularization whose purpose is to reduce or even eliminate religion's political significance, especially that of political parties inspired by Islam, such as the Front Islamique de Salut in Algeria and the Welfare Party in Turkey. Their respective secular governments in the 1990s banned both parties. For some Muslims, the implication is that religion-inspired political parties are excluded from political competition, unable to compete for power. This may suggest, not only to those inspired by political Islam – that is, 'Islamists' or 'Islamic fundamentalists' – but also to many 'ordinary' Muslims, that the West's claim – to represent neutrality, justice and democracy – is problematic (Roy, 2004). In sum, recent focus on relations between the West and the Muslim world highlights that religion's role in both politics and international relations is now impossible to ignore.

In this book, we are interested in two broad categories of international actors informed by religious concerns: *states* and *non-state actors*. First, various states – including the governments of Iran and Saudi Arabia, both of which are theocracies[2] – have foreign policies that would purport to be guided, ultimately, by Islamic precepts. There is also the government of the United States, whose external concerns under the presidency of George W. Bush (2001–2009) are sometimes expressed in terms of Christian imagery (Dolan, 2005; Philips, 2006), and the Bharatiya Janata Party government in India (1996–2004) that sought to develop a foreign policy, especially in relation to its regional rival, Pakistan, with a focus related to 'Hindu fundamentalist' aspirations. Secondly, there are numerous non-state, religious transnational actors.[3] Such actors include, but are not restricted to, various kinds of ('moderate' and 'extremist') Islamic entities and Christian (especially Roman Catholic and Protestant) groups. Taken together, both state and non-state religious actors represent an important religious dimension to international relations.

Religion, secularization and secularism

The Iranian revolution of 1979 was a highly significant event in focusing attention on religious actors in international relations. Prior to this epochal event, religion was widely seen as rather insignificant in international relations, a lack of concern that at least in part derived from the prominence of secular international security issues during the Cold War (Almond et al., 2003). Underpinning such a view were two widely accepted assumptions in Western social science: (1) rationality and secularity go hand in hand, and (2) 'modern', political, economic and social systems are found in societies that have modernized via a process of secularization that publicly marginalizes or 'privatizes' religion (Casanova, 1994). In short, the secular cannot be viewed as a successor to religion, or be seen as on the side of the rational. It is a category with a multilayered history, related to major premises of modernity, democracy, and the concept of human rights.

Majid Tehranian on modernization, development and secularization

Theories of modernization and development have been largely grounded on secularist assumptions. From Marx to Freud and Parsons, industrial society has been assumed to be the graveyard of religious faith. Marx called religion 'an opiate of the masses', a false consciousness which will be banished from the historical stage by the rise of the proletariat's true, class consciousness, a socialist revolution, and the construction of a secular, rational, and scientific communist society. Similarly, Freud considered religion as an 'illusion', catering to the infantile impulses of helplessness and need for protection that will be replaced by the growth of adult personality assuming rational consciousness and social responsibility. In a like manner, Parsons and a whole generation of postwar positivist social scientists also continued to propose that modernization correlates positively with structural–functional differentiation, secularization, and political participation (Tehranian, 1997).

Secularization implies a significant diminishing of religious concerns in everyday life, a unidirectional process, whereby societies move from a sacred condition to an increasingly areligious state – until the sacred eventually becomes socially and politically marginal. According to what became known as 'secularization theory', both religion and piety are destined *universally* to become 'only' private matters; consequently, religion would no longer be an important public actor. Shupe points out that, 'the demystification of religion inherent in the classic secularization paradigm posits a gradual, persistent, unbroken erosion of religious influence in urban industrial societies' (Shupe, 1990: 19). Such was secularization theory's claim to universalism that, according to the sociologist José Casanova, it 'may be the only theory which was able to attain a truly paradigmatic status within the modern social sciences' (Casanova, 1994: 17). This was partly because some of the leading figures in nineteenth- and twentieth-century social science – including, Emile Durkheim, Max Weber, Karl Marx, Auguste Comte, Sigmund Freud, Talcott Parsons, and Herbert Spencer – all maintained that secularization is an integral facet of modernization, a global trend of relevance everywhere as societies modernized. They 'all believed that religion would gradually fade in importance and cease to be significant with the advent of industrial society. The belief that religion was dying became the conventional wisdom in the social sciences during most of the twentieth century' (Norris and Inglehart, 2004: 3). As modernization extended its grip, so the argument went, religion would everywhere be 'privatized', losing its grip on culture, becoming a purely personal matter. Thus religion would no longer be a *collective* force with significant mobilizing potential for social change. In short, secularization, Donald Eugene Smith proclaimed, was 'the most fundamental structural and ideological change in the process of political development' (Smith, 1970: 6). It was thought a one-way street: societies gradually – but inexorably – move away from being focused around the sacred and a concern with the divine to a situation characterized by significant diminution of religious power and authority.

Secularism

Secularism is the state or quality of being *secular*, the end result of a process of *secularization*. Secularism is a term that was for a long time associated in much Western social science with terms like 'worldly' and 'temporal', lacking reference to a transcendent order involving a divine being, such as God or gods.

Secularism is normatively characterized by both universalist pretensions and a claim to superiority over each and every set of religious ideas. In order to dominate ideologically, secularism requires religious ideas to be publicly marginalized. It seeks to do this by marking out the domain of the 'secular', characterizing it with normatively desirable attributes, such as, tolerance, common sense, justice, rational argument, the public interest and public authority.

The secularization thesis was a core assumption of Western social sciences for decades, including in the decades immediately following the Second World War. It animated two highly significant sets of ideas: modernization theory in the 1950s and early 1960s, and dependency theory in the late 1960s and early 1970s. Both schools of thought maintained – or rather implicitly accepted the then conventional wisdom, then at its most unchallenged – that the course of both international relations and of integrated nation-states necessarily lay squarely in secular participatory politics. In an example of theory guiding 'real world' politics, many political leaders – especially in the developing world, vast areas of which were then emerging from colonial rule – worked from a key premise. It was that sometimes, irrespective of their own religious beliefs and cultural affiliations, they must for ideological reasons *necessarily* remain neutral in respect of entanglements stemming from particularist religious and cultural claims *if* they wanted to build successful nation-states and conduct flourishing international relations. Not to do so would serve both to encourage dogmatism and reduce tolerance ('isn't this what "history" tells us?', they queried) and as a result be antipathetic to the development of viable nation-states, democracy and the smooth running of the (secular) international system. As Juergensmeyer notes, 'secular nationalism was thought to be not only natural but also universally applicable and morally right' (Juergensmeyer, 1993: 27). In sum, as a consequence of the global advance of secular, centralized states from the seventeenth century via colonialism and an international system from which religion was from the eighteenth century expunged – because of its demonstrable 'bad influence', reflected in numerous religious war between Christians, on the one hand, and between Muslims and Christians, on the other – religion was relegated to the category of a potentially dangerous but actually rather minor issue that must not be allowed to intrude on the search for domestic national unity and international political stability and progress. Before examining what the apparent resurgence of religion implies for our understanding of international relations, it is necessary to define and discuss two key terms used in the book: 'international relations' and 'religion'.

Defining and explaining key terms: 'international relations' and 'religion'

International relations

'Narrow' definitions of international relations focus primarily upon relations between the world's governments, represented by senior politicians – such as, Britain's Foreign Secretary, Margaret Beckett, or Condoleezza Rice, the US Secretary of State – whose job it is to try to put into effect their government's foreign policies and external programmes. A more inclusive definition, one that is adopted in this book, understands international relations as both more comprehensive and interdisciplinary. This 'broad' understanding of international relations not only engages with subject matter drawn from various fields of study but also includes a focus on both state and non-state actors. The following subject areas inform the broad version:

- **Economics** is given a key focus in a specific area of international relations, known as International Political Economy (IPE), it involves the politics of international economic relationships. These include: trade and financial relations between states; and North–South development issues, including international debt and economic dependency.

- **Politics** within the subject matter of international relations includes, on the one hand, political relations between states and, on the other, various international organizations, such as, the United Nations, the European Union and the Organization of the Islamic Conference.

- **Security studies** is a traditional issue in international relations, originally focusing on war, peace and diplomacy, but now covering 'new' areas, including economic, environmental and anti-terrorism security.

- **History** informs international relations by making clear the main events in the past that inform and influence the present.

Religion

According to Huntington, 'In the modern world, religion is central, perhaps *the* central, force that motivates and mobilizes people . . .' (Huntington, 1996: 27). But *defining* religion is very difficult. Marty (2000) begins his discussion of religion by listing 17 different definitions, before commenting that 'Scholars will never agree on the definition of religion'. Marty does not himself attempt to offer a precise meaning of the term but instead identifies several 'phenomena that help describe what we're talking about'. He lists five features of religion that 'help point to and put boundaries around the term'. For Marty (2000: 11–14), religion:

- focuses our 'ultimate concern'
- builds community
- appeals to myth and symbol
- is enforced through rites and ceremonies
- demands certain behaviour from its adherents.

From this we can see that religion can be thought of as (1) a system of beliefs and practices – often but not necessarily related to an ultimate being or beings, or to the supernatural and/or (2) that which is sacred in a society – that is, ultimate beliefs and practices which are inviolate (Aquaviva, 1979). For purposes of social investigation, religion may be approached (1) from the perspective of a body of ideas and outlooks – that is, as theology and ethical code; (2) as a type of formal organization – that is, the ecclesiastical 'church', or (3) as a social group – that is, religious groups and movements. There are two basic ways that religion can affect the world: by what it *says* and by what it *does*. The former relates to religion's doctrine or theology, the latter to its importance as a social phenomenon and mark of identity, that works through a variety of modes of institutionalization, including church–state relations, civil society and political society.

It is important to distinguish between religion at the individual and group levels, because only the latter is normally of importance in international relations; although as we shall see, some individual religious figures, such as Pope John Paul II, can significantly influence outcomes in international relations. 'From an individualist perspective, religion may be thought of as "a set of symbolic forms and acts that relates man (sic) to the ultimate conditions of his existence'" (Bellah, 1964: 359). This is religion's *private*, spiritual side. We are, however, primarily concerned in this book with *group* religiosity, whose claims and pretensions are very often to some degree political. For Ramet, there is no such thing as a religion without consequences for value systems (Ramet, 1995: 64). Group religiosity is a matter of collective solidarities and of inter-group interactions. Sometimes this focuses on cooperation with other groups; sometimes on tension and conflict, concerned either with shared or contested images of the sacred, or on cultural and class concerns. To complicate matters, however, such influences may well operate differently and with 'different temporalities for the same theologically defined religion in different parts of the world' (Moyser, 1991: 11).

Basic beliefs of Buddhism, Christianity, Confucianism, Hinduism, Islam and Judaism

To understand how and why many religious traditions and movements are involved in international relations, it is useful to become aware of some of the basics of their belief systems, as they will inform what religious actors actually do. We examine the basic beliefs of several religious traditions upon which we focus in this book: Buddhism, Christianity, Confucianism, Hinduism, Islam and Judaism. Our focus is on these 'world religions' because most of the significant actors in contemporary international relations come from these faiths.

There is potential for religions to act in international relations in ways that increase chances of cooperation, conflict resolution and peacebuilding. For example, with regard to Islam, 'Islam has a direct impact on the way that peace is conceptualized and the way that conflicts are resolved in Islamic societies, as it embodies and elaborates upon its highest morals, ethical principles and ideals of social harmony . . .' (Bouta et al., 2005: 11). The Dalai Lama, leader of Tibetan Buddhism living in exile in India as a result of China's takeover of the country, has remarked that 'Every religion emphasizes human improvement, love, respect for others, sharing other people's suffering. On these lines every religion had more or less the same viewpoint and the same goal' (quoted in Hirohita, 2002). Gopin suggests that it is very likely that all religions have developed laws and ideas that provide civilization with cultural commitments to critical peace-related values. These include: empathy, an openness to and even love for strangers, the suppression of unbridled ego and acquisitiveness, human rights, unilateral gestures of forgiveness and humility, interpersonal repentance and the acceptance of responsibility of past error as a means of reconciliation, and the drive for social justice (Gopin, 2000: 13). On the other hand, religious involvement in international relations is also sometimes characterized by competition and conflict.

Buddhism

Buddhism is both a philosophy and moral practice. Its purpose is to work towards the relief of suffering in existence by ridding oneself of desire. In the early 2000s, there were an estimated 350 million Buddhists, divided into three main schools: Mahayana (56 per cent), Theravada (38 per cent) and Vajrayana (6 per cent). Rather than a religion as such, Buddhism is often regarded as a philosophy based on the teachings of the Buddha, Siddhartha Gautama (in the Sanskrit form, Siddhattha Gotama in the Pāli form). He lived between approximately 563 and 483 BCE. Buddhism began in India, and gradually spread throughout Asia to Central Asia, Tibet, Sri Lanka and South-East Asia, as well as to China, Mongolia, Korea, and Japan in East Asia. At the current time, several Asian countries have majority Buddhist populations: Thailand (95 per cent), Cambodia (90 per cent), Myanmar (88 per cent), Bhutan (75 per cent), Sri Lanka (70 per cent), Tibet (a region of China, 65 per cent), Laos (60 per cent), Vietnam (55 per cent). Other Asian countries with significant Buddhist populations include: Japan (50 per cent) and Taiwan (43 per cent). Overall, there were more than 380 million Buddhists in the world in 2005 (http://www.buddhanet.net/e-learning/history/bstatt10.htm).

While there are very large differences between different Buddhist schools of thought, they all share an overall purpose and aim: to liberate the individual from suffering (*dukkha*). While some interpretations stress stirring the practitioner to the awareness of *anatta* (egolessness, the absence of a permanent or substantial self) and the achievement of enlightenment and nirvana, others (such as the 'Tathagatagarbha' sutras) promote the idea that the practitioner should seek to purify him/herself of both mental and moral defilements that are a key aspect of the 'worldly self' and as a result break through to an understanding of the indwelling 'Buddha-Principle' ('Buddha-nature'), also termed the 'True Self', and thus become transformed into a Buddha. Other Buddhist interpretations beseech bodhisattvas (that is, enlightened beings who, out of compassion, forego nirvana, or heaven, in order to save others) for a favourable rebirth. Others, however, do none of these things. Most, if not all, Buddhist schools also encourage followers to undertake both good and wholesome actions, and consequently not do bad and harmful actions.

Christianity

Christianity is a faith with foundations in the teachings of Jesus, regarded by Christians as the Son of God. Jesus is the second component of a Trinity, comprising God the Father, Jesus the Son, and the Holy Spirit. Christians believe that Jesus' life on earth, his crucifixion, resurrection, and subsequent ascension to heaven are signs not only of God's love for humankind but also his forgiveness of human sins. Christianity also includes a belief that through faith in Jesus individuals may attain salvation and eternal life. These teachings are contained within the Bible, especially the New Testament, although Christians accept also the Old Testament as sacred and authoritative scripture.

The ethics of Christianity draw to a large extent from the Jewish tradition as presented in the Old Testament, notably the Ten Commandments. There is, however, some difference of interpretation between them as a result of the practice and teachings of Jesus. Christianity can be further defined generally through its concern with the practice of corporate worship and certain rites. These include the use of sacraments – including the traditional seven rites that were instituted by Jesus and recorded in the New Testament and that confer sanctifying grace (in the Eastern Orthodox, Roman Catholic, and some other Western Christian churches) – and in most other Western Christian churches, by two rites: baptism and the Eucharist, instituted by Jesus to confer sanctifying grace.

There were an estimated 2.1 billion Christians in 2005 (Center for the Study of Global Christianity, 2006), found in probably every country but with major populations found in Europe, the Americas, Africa and parts of Asia.

Confucianism

Confucianism is a religious and philosophical system that developed from the writings attributed to the Chinese philosopher Confucius (the latinized version of Kung Fu-tzu (that is, Master Kung), who was a teacher in China (*c*.551–479 BCE). Confucianism focuses mostly upon the relationships between individuals, between individuals and their families, and finally between individuals and general society. Confucianism profoundly influenced the traditional culture of China and countries that came under Chinese influence, including Korea. Confucianism places a high value on learning and stresses family relationships, and is the name given by Westerners to a large body of Chinese scholarly works, which the Chinese refer to as 'the scholarly tradition'. Historically, Confucianism has been culturally and politically influential in several East and South-East Asian countries, including China, Hong Kong, Japan, Singapore, Taiwan, and Vietnam. It has long been an important influence in Chinese and Chinese-influenced attitudes towards life, suggesting patterns of living and standards of social value, while providing a backdrop to Chinese political theories and institutions. Key teachings are concerned with principles of good conduct, practical wisdom, and 'proper' social relationships. Recently, Confucianism has aroused interest among Western scholars because the ideas it represents are widely regarded as an important component of the concept of 'Asian values'. Various Asian countries including China, Korea, Japan and Singapore have cultures strongly influenced by Confucianism.

Hinduism

Hinduism is the Western term for the religious beliefs and practices of the vast majority of the people of India. One of the oldest living religions in the world, Hinduism is unique among the world religions in that it had no single founder but grew over a period of 4,000 years in syncretism with the religious and cultural movements of the Indian subcontinent. Hinduism is composed of innumerable sects and has no well-defined ecclesiastical organization. Its two most general features are the caste system and acceptance of the Veda – that is, the oldest and most authoritative Hindu sacred texts, composed in Sanskrit and gathered into four collections – as the most sacred scriptures.

Hinduism's salient characteristics include an ancient mythology, an absence of recorded history (or 'founder'), a cyclical notion of time, a pantheism that infuses divinity into the world around, an immanentist[4] relationship between people and divinity, a priestly class, and a tolerance of diverse paths to the ultimate ('god'). Its sacral language is Sanskrit, which came to India about 5,000 years ago along with the Aryans, who came from Central Asia. It is a varied corpus, comprising religion, philosophy, and cultural practice that are both indigenous to and prevalent in India. The faith is characterized by a belief in rebirth and a supreme being that can take many forms and types, by the perception that contrasting theories are all aspects of an eternal truth, and by its followers' pursuit of liberation from earthly evils.

Of the total global Hindu population of more than 870 million (Center for the Study of Global Christianity, 2006), about 94 per cent (818 million) live in India. Other countries with a significant Hindu population include: Nepal (22.5m.), Bangladesh (14.4m.), Indonesia (4.3m.), Pakistan (3.3m.), Sri Lanka (3m.), Malaysia (1.5m.), Mauritius (600,000), Bhutan (560,000), Fiji (300,000), and Guyana (270,000). In addition, the Indonesian islands of Bali, Java, Sulawesi, Sumatra, and Borneo all have significant native Hindu populations.

Islam

There were an estimated 1.3 billion Muslims in the word in 2005 (Center for the Study of Global Christianity, 2006). Like Christians, Muslims are found in probably every country in the world with major populations throughout the Middle East, Africa and parts of Asia.

The origins of Islam are found in an allegiance to Allah, articulated by his prophet Muhammad (c.570–632 CE). Muhammad was born in Mecca (in present day Saudi Arabia) and over a period of 23 years received revelations from an angel (Jibreel, or Gabriel), who Muhammad believed was relaying the word of Allah. For Muslims, Muhammad was the last in a series of prophets, including Abraham, Moses and Jesus, who refined and restated the message of Allah. After Muhammad's death in 632, Muslims divided into two strands, Shia and Sunni. The Shi'ites are followers of the caliph (that is, leader of an Islamic polity, regarded as a successor of Muhammad and by tradition always male) Abu Bakr and those who supported Muhammad's closest relative, his son-in-law, Ali ibn Abi Talib. Overall, Shi'ites place more emphasis on the guiding role of the caliph. The Sunni, on the other hand, is the majority sect within Islam, followers of the *custom* of the caliphate rather than an individual caliph, such as Ali. The Shia–Sunni division still persists, although both share most of the customs of the religion. About 90 per cent of the world's Muslims are Sunni and about 10 per cent Shia.

Shias and Sunnis share five fundamental beliefs:

- *Shahada* (profession of faith in the uniqueness of Allah and the centrality of Muhammad as his prophet)
- *Salat* (formal worship or prayer)
- *Zakat* (giving of alms for the poor, assessed on all adult Muslims as 2.5 per cent of capital assets once a year)
- *Hajj* (pilgrimage to Mecca, which every Muslim should undertake at least once in their lifetime; the annual hajj takes place during the last 10 days of the 12th lunar month every year)
- *Sawm* (fasting during Ramadan, the holy ninth month of the lunar year)

Judaism

Judaism is a term with several distinct meanings: (1) the Jews' monotheistic religion, with origins going back to Abraham and with spiritual and ethical principles mainly contained in the Hebrew scriptures and the Talmud; (2) compliance with the Jewish religion's traditional ceremonies and rites; (3) the Jews' religious, cultural and social practices and beliefs; and (4) the people or community identified as Jews. There were over 15 million Jews worldwide in 2005 (Center for the Study of Global Christianity, 2006), many living in Israel among its population of more than six million people.

All these aspects of Judaism have an essential shared characteristic: belief in one God who created the universe and continues to rule it. The God who created the world revealed himself to the Israelites at Mount Sinai. The content of that revelation makes up the Jewish holy book, the Torah, with God's will for humankind stated in his commandments. In Judaism, a second major concept is that of the covenant, or agreement, between God and the Jewish people. The covenant worked like this: Jews would acknowledge God, agreeing to obey his laws and in turn God would acknowledge the Jews as his 'chosen people'.

Jews believe that goodness and obedience will be rewarded and sin punished by God's judgement after death. Then at the end of times, God will send his Messiah to redeem the Jews and deliver them to their Promised Land. Although all forms of Judaism come from the Torah, Judaism is mainly derived from the rabbinic movement during the first centuries of the Christian era. At the turn of the third century, the rabbis (Jewish sages), produced the *Mishnah*, the earliest document of rabbinic literature.

Conclusion

We conclude this section by noting that all six religious traditions we examine bring together an array of beliefs and understandings. Partly as a result, to try to bring together the spheres of religion and international relations and to discern and interpret significant patterns and trends is not a simple task. But, in attempting it, three points should be emphasized. First, there is something of a distinction to be drawn between looking at the relationship in terms of the impact of religion on international relations, and that of international relations on religion. At the same time, they are interactive: effects of one stimulate and are stimulated by the other. As we are broadly concerned with how *power* is exercised in international relations and the way(s) in which religion is involved, then the relationship between religion and international relations is both dialectical and interactive: each shapes and influences the other. Both causal directions need to be held in view.

Secondly, *all* religions are both creative and constantly changing; consequently their relationships with other religious – as well as secular – actors may vary over time. The nature of the relationship between religion and secular power may suddenly – and unexpectedly – change. For example, in Iran in the late 1970s, and in Eastern Europe, Latin America and Africa in the 1980s and 1990s, leading religious institutions and figures shifted – apparently abruptly – from support to opposition of incumbent authoritarian regimes. This led in Muslim Iran to a theocracy, while in Eastern Europe, Latin America and Africa religious actors, notably Roman Catholic figures, were in the forefront of moves towards popular, democratically elected governments. Later, during the 1990s and early 2000s, religious actors from numerous faiths became involved in both domestic and international attempts to resolve conflicts and build peace (Bouta et el., 2005).

In sum, religions may not have a fixed, immovable position on various issues. This is because what is judged to be religiously appropriate for some believers may not be seen like that for others. In addition, religious understandings and meanings are affected by the broader context within which believers live. In this book we are concerned with two interactive issues: (1) how religious belief or affiliation can affect outcomes in international relations, and (2) how specific international contexts and factors affect what religious actors do. This points to the analytical importance of a range of state and non-state actors and of interactions between domestic and international spheres in order to explain and account for outcomes in international relations that involve religious actors. I take the view that heuristically it is useful to dichotomize such actors' international involvement. On the one hand, especially since the end of the Cold War in the late 1980s, there have been a number of national and international conflicts with roots in religious, cultural and ethnic divisions. On the other hand, religion is also an increasingly important source of cooperation, often focusing upon conflict resolution and peacebuilding, as well as human and social development.

Religious resurgence and international relations

Anybody who had predicted '30 years ago that the 20th century would end with a resurgence of religion, with great new cathedrals, mosques, and temples rising up, with the symbols and songs of faith everywhere apparent, would, in most circles, have been derided' (Woollacott, 1995). Such claims would have been treated with scepticism because by this time, for nearly 200 years, secularization theorists had claimed that religion must inevitably decline in the modern world. As already noted, secularization theory held that – through a combination of technological advancement and associated undermining of traditional cultures – religion would decline and we would live, according to Harvey Cox, in a 'secular city'. Cox, an influential secularization theorist in the 1960s, reversed himself in *Religion in the Secular City* (1984). He declared that the future of religion now lay in religious grassroots movements, including religious fundamentalism, Pentecostalism and liberation theology.

In addition, it is often claimed, something totally unexpected has happened: a near-global religious resurgence with important ramifications for international relations (Moghadam, 2003; Petito and Hatzopoulos, 2003; Thomas, 2005) Much current evidence suggests *not* that religion's influence is declining in line with the claims of secularization theory but rather that its social and, in some cases, political influence is growing in many parts of the world. Others contend, however, that religious decline is not simply a sociological myth, because modernization has caused religion to change in such ways that it has often lost its social significance (Bruce, 2002). As Bruce argues, 'Individualism, diversity and egalitarianism in the context of liberal democracy undermine the authority of religious beliefs', making belief in God a personal option rather than a compelling necessity. As a result, 'religion diminishes in social significance, becomes increasingly privatized, and loses personal salience except where it finds work to do other than relating individuals to the supernatural' (Bruce, 2002: 30).

In contrast, an eminent sociologist of religion, Peter Berger – like Harvey Cox, also once an important proponent of the secularization thesis – contends that 'far from being in decline in the modern world, religion is actually

experiencing a resurgence'. Consequently, 'the assumption we live in a secularized world is false . . . . The world today is as furiously religious as it ever
was' (Berger, 1999: 3). According to Berger, the process of 'modernization' did
not weaken religion, but actually strengthened it. As a result, rather than declining in significance, in much of the world religion is every bit as significant
as it ever was, reinforcing the idea of a widespread 'religious resurgence'.

Peter Berger on religious resurgence

Like Harvey Cox, Peter Berger (1999) argues that religious movements have not
adapted to secular culture merely in order to survive, but instead have successfully developed their own identities and retained a focus on the supernatural in
their beliefs and practices. Today, numerous religious actors are interested in
and have an impact upon key areas of concern for politics and international relations, including: economic development, war and peace, human rights and
social justice. Berger also points to various countries and regions with clear evidence of interaction of religion and politics. These include the *USA*, especially
the continuing vitality of the Christian Right, the evangelical revival in various
countries in *Latin America*, the new religious emphasis in post-Communist *Central and Eastern Europe*, the reported renaissance of Islam in the *Middle East*, and
evidence that in many countries in *Africa* and *Asia*, various religious practices
and beliefs thrive. In response to Berger's claims, Norris and Ingelhart comment
that 'some of these reported phenomena may have been overstated, but the
simplistic assumption that religion was everywhere in decline, common in earlier decades, had become implausible to even the casual observer (Norris and
Ingelhart, 2004: 215–16).

Only in Western Europe is there evidence of a continued waning in the
public importance of religion. But even here there has been a shift in the institutional location of religion, not secularization per se (Davie, 2002). In
other words, Western European *societies* may have become more secular but
individuals mostly have not. How to explain this seeming paradox? Religion's decline is often measured by falling income levels for mainstream
Protestant and Catholic churches, declining ordinations of religious professionals, diminishing church attendance, and falling popular observance of
church-dictated codes of personal behaviour on, *inter alia*, conventions regarding sexuality, reproduction and marriage. Overall, these trends point to
'a process of decline in the social significance of religion' in Western Europe
(Wilson, 1992: 198). In Europe, institutional Christianity has lost many of

the functions it once fulfilled for other social institutions. Once it provided legitimacy for secular authority in a number of ways. It not only endorsed public policy while sustaining with 'a battery of threats and blandishments the agencies of social control', but also claimed to be the only font of 'true' learning (Wilson, 1992: 200). Christianity was also largely responsible in many regional countries for socializing the young and sponsoring a range of recreational activities. Signs of religious decline have long been observed in the northern segment of the region, but over the last three or four decades they have also been increasingly clear in the predominantly Catholic south. For example, both Italy and Spain have experienced rapid decline in church-related religion – blamed by Catholic conservatives on the liberalizing effects of the second Vatican Council ('Vatican II', 1962–5). However, the fact that there has also been a similar decline in orthodox Greece rather undermines the conservatives' claims regarding Vatican II (Moore, 1989).

But while such facts are not seriously in dispute, recent works on the sociology of religion concerned with several highly secular societies in Europe – including, France, Britain, and Scandinavia – point out that 'secularization' may not be the right term to apply to what has happened. This is because there is much evidence that religious belief survives, most of it Christian, despite widespread alienation from mainline churches. Grace Davie (2002) suggests that an important distinction can be drawn between 'belonging' and 'believing' in Western Europe. She contends that in Western Europe, traditional, that is, Christian, religious institutions have generally lost some public influence, while at the same time religious beliefs and practices continue to be important in the lives of millions of Europeans. Sometimes this takes the form of new or renewed religious expressions, with associated increments of religious fervour, often focused in what Berger (1999) refers to as religious grassroots movements.

Grace Davie on religious belief in Western Europe

Grace Davie (2000, 2002) argues that in Britain the shrinking number of people attending church services has not been accompanied by a widespread decline in religious beliefs. She also claims that similar patterns can be observed overall in Western Europe. Davie concludes that overall Western Europeans are 'unchurched' populations, not simply secular. She makes this claim because, as she observes, while there has been a marked falling-off in religious attendance (especially in the Protestant north) this has not resulted, yet, in the renunciation of religious belief.

Some mainstream religious institutions – such as, the Anglican and Roman Catholic churches in Britain and Catholic bishops in the USA – are significant voices in relation to various issues, including: economic development, war and peace, human rights and social justice. In Britain, both the Anglican and Roman Catholic churches re-emerged as significant social and political actors in the 1990s. Building on a tradition established during the premiership of Margaret Thatcher (1979–90), the publication in October 1996 of the Roman Catholic Church's 13,000-word pamphlet, *The Common Good and the Catholic Church's Social Teaching*, was an important intervention in the political debate between the Labour and Conservative parties in the run-up to the May 1997 general election. Politicians, especially of the latter party, saw it as an endorsement of Labour's policies. Six months later, in April 1997, eleven churches collectively published a further report entitled, *Unemployment and the Future of Work*, an outspoken attack on the inability of the main parties in Britain to focus upon the amelioration of the suffering of the underprivileged. The report accused them of putting tax cuts before solutions to poverty and unemployment in the battle for victory in Britain's May 1997 general election.

Centrally concerned with social and political issues, both *The Common Good* and *Unemployment and the Future of Work* were manifestations of the contemporary process of repoliticization of hitherto increasingly private religious and moral spheres in England. Together, the reports represented an attempt to re-establish ethical norms of behaviour and activities in public and political spheres and to present a political case for so doing. In the publications, the churches endorsed what were clearly political goals, expressing opposition to the dualism between religion and politics, and arguing that the concerns of social justice were, in fact, not only scripturally rooted, but also wedded to the defence of liberal democracy, pluralism and the market economy. In short, the central issue for the churches was the degree to which the consumerist version of politics should be modified or balanced by the social dimension.

However, it is not only churches in Britain that are concerned with social and political issues. Numerous religious organizations and institutions around the world also share a desire to change their societies in a direction where religious standards would be of greater significance. In pursuit of such objectives, they use a variety of tactics and methods: some, like the British churches noted above, lobby, protest and publish reports at the level of civil society; others seek desired changes via political society – for example, in the USA the Religious Right (sometimes known as the Christian Right) regularly endorses electoral candidates with the most 'pro-religion' policies, such as

George W. Bush in 2000 and 2004, while also increasingly having an influential voice in foreign policy, for example, in relation to US policy in Iraq post-2003 (Haynes 2005b; Phillips 2006).

In addition, the US Catholic Bishops Conference has had an important voice in the nuclear debate in the USA. In general, US Catholics, comprising about 28 per cent of Americans, hold a significant position in a keen cultural and political struggle with the Religious Right. However, political divisions between ordinary Catholics are reflected in their leaders' political pronouncements. On the one hand, bishops' pastoral letters on nuclear arms and the economy have given ammunition to social gospel liberals, while, on the other, anti-abortion pronouncements and support for public accommodation of faith tend to buoy cultural conservatives. The overall point is twofold: (1) American Catholicism's pluralism helps to shape and constrain the Church's political influence, and (2) the Church has a significant voice in a number of public debates related to a number of economic, political and social issues. Overall, the examples noted above in relation to Christian churches in Britain and the USA suggest that such religious actors seek to increase their public significance in relation to a number of political, social and economic issues.

What encourages religious actors to enter political, social and economic debates? Berger maintains that what they have in common is (1) a critique of secularity, because (2) human 'existence bereft of transcendence is an impoverished and finally untenable condition'. He argues that a human desire for transcendence – that is, a state of being or existence above and beyond the limits of material experience – is an integral part of the human psyche, and secularity – that is, the condition or quality of being secular – does not allow for this necessary sense of transcendence (Berger, 1999: 4). Without a sense of transcendence, he asserts, life for many people is unsatisfactorily empty. However, many people now appear to reject some established institutional forms of religion, and the search for transcendence may be expressed in membership of grassroots religious movements.

The overall sense of emptiness of modern life, of which the search for transcendence is a characteristic, is captured for many people in the concept of the 'postmodern condition'. The term 'postmodernism' is said to have been invented by a French philosopher, J.-F. Lyotard (1979). Postmodernism decisively reflects the end of belief in the Enlightenment project in two key ways: (1) assumptions of universal progress based on reason, and (2) the 'modern Promethean myth of humanity's mastery of its destiny and capacity for resolution of all its problems' (Watson, 1994: 150).[5] For Lyotard, postmodernism is centrally concerned with 'incredulity toward meta-narratives', that is, rejection of absolute, unquestionable ways of speaking truth. It reflects an undermining of the certainties by which many people, especially in the West, have hitherto lived for decades – which may help to explain popular support for various grassroots religious movements.

For many people, disaffection with the scientific rationalism of Western thought is a consequence of secularity (Berger, 1999). Overall, the 'postmodern condition' offers opportunities for various religious actors to pursue a public role in a variety of areas, including social justice, encouraged by widespread feelings of economic, social, and political instability. This reflects the exigencies of an epoch that De Gruchy identifies as 'turbulent, traumatic and dislocating, yet also . . . potentially creative' (De Gruchy, 1995: 5). One of the most important aspects of postmodernism is the cultural/interpretative dimension, with various religious 'fundamentalisms' a key manifestation, as well as the Religious Right in the United States, the evangelical revival in Latin America and various expressions of Islamism (Cox, 1984; Ahmed, 1992; Simpson, 1992; Berger, 1999). In addition, as a result of the communications revolution that characterizes globalization, more and often better sources of information are widely available, encouraging many people, for example in Eastern Europe during the declining years of the Communist era, to demand their rights, including religious freedoms (Ahmed, 1992: 129).

Conclusion

The belief that all societies would inevitably secularize along a linear path as they modernized was wrong. Instead, the combined impact of modernization (involving urbanization, industrialization and swift technological developments) – coupled with a growing lack of faith in secular ideologies – left many people with feelings of loss rather than achievement. Undermining 'traditional' value systems and allocating opportunities in highly unequal ways within and among nations, secularization helped produce in many people a deep sense of alienation, helping to stimulate for some a search for identity to give life meaning and purpose; many people found what they wanted in various religious expressions, including grassroots religious movements. In addition, the rise of global consumerist culture led to expressions of aversion, sometimes focused in the concerns of religious groups. The overall result was a wave of resurgent religious expressions, with far-reaching implications for social integration, political stability and, in some cases, regional and international peace and security. In sum, religious resurgence is occurring in a variety of countries with differing political and ideological systems, at various levels of economic development, and with diverse religious traditions. But all have been subject to the destabilizing pressures of state-directed pursuit of modernization and secularization; in other words, all are experiencing to some degree the postmodern condition – characterized by a lack of clarity and certainty about the future direction of society.

Resurgent religion does not only relate to personal beliefs but also leads to a desire to grapple with social, economic and political issues. 'Because it is so reliable a source of emotion, religion is a recurring source of social-movement framing. Religion provides ready-made symbols, rituals, and solidarities that can be accessed and appropriated by movement leaders' (Tarrow, 1998: 112). Such religious actors are found in many different faiths and sects, yet share a key characteristic: a desire to change domestic, and in many cases international, arrangements in order to increase religion's influence. They adopt various tactics to try to achieve their goals. Some protest, lobby, or otherwise encourage decision makers; others focus reform intentions through the ballot box or via civil society; still others, a tiny minority, even resort to political violence to pursue their objectives. Overall, numerous religious actors of various kinds seek to engage in current political, economic and social debates, in both domestic and international contexts. The forms these interventions take will be examined in forthcoming chapters.

Notes

1   According to Chris Brown, the discipline of 'International Relations' is the study of 'international relations' (Brown, 2001: 1)

2   A theocracy is a government ruled by or subject to religious authority.

3   Transnational actors are cross-border non-state actors. Examples of secular transnational entities are Greenpeace International and Amnesty International, various global financial activities, global science research, global environmental concerns. In fact, the term encompasses any entity or activity that 'transcends' national boundaries and in which state governments do not play the most important or even a significant role (Keohane and Nye, 1972).

4   Immanentism refers to something existing in the realm of the material universe and/or human consciousness.

5   For a discussion of postmodernism and Christianity, see Simpson (1992) and in relation to Islam see Ahmed (1992)

Questions

1   What is 'secularization'? How does it affect the relationship between religion and politics?

2   Why are religious actors often overlooked in international relations theory?

3   How does globalization facilitate the development of transnational religious actors?

4   Does 9/11 imply that 'Islam' and 'the West' are incompatible?

Bibliography

Ahmed, A. (1992) *Postmodernism and Islam: Predicament and Promise*, London: Routledge.

Almond, G., Appleby, R. Scott and Sivan, E. (2003) *Strong Religion: The Rise of Fundamentalisms Around the World*, Chicago and London: University of Chicago Press.

Aquaviva, S. (1979) *The Decline of the Sacred in Industrial Society*, Oxford: Blackwell.

Bellah, R. (1964) 'Religious evolution', *American Sociological Review*, 29, pp. 358–74.

Berger, P. (1999) (ed.) *The Desecularization of the World: Resurgent Religion and World Politics*, Grand Rapids/Washington, DC: William B. Eerdmans/Ethics and Public Policy Center.

Bouta, T., Kadayifci-Orellana, S. Ayse and Abu-Nimer, M. (2005) *Faith-Based Peace-Building: Mapping and Analysis of Christian, Muslim and Multi-Faith Actors*, The Hague: Netherlands Institute of International Relations.

Brown, C. (2001) *Understanding International Relations*, 2nd edn, Basingstoke: Palgrave.

Brown, C. (2005) *Understanding International Relations*, 3rd edn, Basingstoke: Palgrave.

Bruce, S. (2002) *God Is Dead: Secularization in the West*, Oxford: Blackwell.

Casanova, J. (1994) *Public Religions in the Modern World*, Chicago and London: University of Chicago Press.

Center for the Study of Global Christianity (2006) Available at: http://www.gcts.edu/ockenga/globalchristianity/ Accessed 1 April 2006.

Cox, H. (1984) *Religion in the Secular City: Toward a Postmodern Theology*, New York: Simon and Schuster.

Davie, G. (2000) *Religion in Modern Europe*, Oxford: Oxford University Press.

Davie, G. (2002) *Europe: The Exceptional Case. Parameters of Faith in the Modern World*, London: Darton, Longman and Todd.

De Gruchy, J. (1995) *Christianity and Democracy: A Theology For a Just World Order*, Cambridge: Cambridge University Press.

Dolan, C. (2005) *In War We Trust: The Bush Doctrine and the Pursuit of Just War*, Aldershot: Ashgate.

Fox, J. and Sandler, S. (2004) *Bringing Religion into International Relations*, Basingstoke: Palgrave Macmillan.

Gopin, M. (2000) *Between Eden and Armageddon: The Future of World Religions, Violence and Peacemaking*, New York and London: Oxford University Press.

Hasenclever, A. and Ritberger, V. (2003) 'Does religion make a difference? Theoretical approaches to the impact of faith on political conflict', in F. Petito and P. Hatzopoulos (eds) *Religion in International Relations: The Return from Exile*, New York: Palgrave, pp. 107–46.

Haynes, J. (1998) *Religion in Global Politics*, Harlow: Longman,

Haynes, J. (2005a) *Comparative Politics in a Globalizing World*, Cambridge: Polity.

Haynes, J. (2005b) 'Religion and International Relations after "9/11"', *Democratization*, 12(3), pp. 398–413.

Haynes, J. (2005c) 'Al-Qaeda: ideology and action', *Critical Review of International Social and Political Philosophy*, 8(2), pp. 177–91.

Hirohita, M. (2002) 'Muslims and Buddhists dialogue', Unitarian Universalist Fellowship of Frankfurt, 10 November. Available at http://www.uufrankfurt.de/MuslimsBuddhists021110.htm Accessed 28 March 2006.

Huntington, S. (1993) 'The clash of civilisations?', *Foreign Affairs*, 72 (3), pp. 22–49.

Huntington, S. (1996) *The Clash of Civilizations*, New York: Simon and Schuster.

Hurrell, A. (2002) '"There are no rules" (George W. Bush): international order after September 11', *International Relations*, 16 (2), pp. 185–204.

Juergensmeyer, M. (1993) *The New Cold War? Religious Nationalism Confronts the Secular State*, Berkeley: University of California Press.

Keohane, R. and Nye, J. (1972) *Transnational Relations and World Politics*, Cambridge, MA: Harvard University Press.

Kubálková, V. (2003) 'Toward an international political theology', in F. Petito and P. Hatzopoulos (eds) *Religion in International Relations: The Return from Exile*, New York: Palgrave, pp. 79–105.

Lyotard, J.-F. (1979) *The Post-Modern Condition: A Report on Knowledge*, Manchester: Manchester University Press.

Marty, M., with J. Moore (2000) *Politics, Religion and the Common Good: Advancing a Distinctly American Conversation About Religion's Role in Our Shared Life*, San Francisco: Josey-Bass Publishers.

Miles, J. (2004) 'Religion and American foreign policy', *Survival*, 46, 1, pp. 23–37.

Moghadam, A. (2003) 'A Global Resurgence of Religion?'. Paper written as part of the third Weatherhead Initiative project, 'Religion in Global Politics', Harvard University, Cambridge, Massachusetts.

Moore, P. (1989) 'Greece', in S. Mews (ed.), *Religion in Politics: A World Guide*, Harlow: Longman, p. 88.

Moyser, G. (1991) 'Politics and religion in the modern world: an overview', in G. Moyser (ed.), *Politics and Religion in the Modern World*, London: Routledge, pp. 1–27.

Norris, P. and Inglehart, R. (2004) *Sacred and Secular: Religion and Politics Worldwide*, Cambridge: Cambridge University Press.

Nye, J. (1990) *Bound to Lead: The Changing Nature of American Power*, New York: Basic Books.

Nye, J. (2004) *Soft Power: The Means to Success in World Politics*, Washington, DC: Public Affairs.

Petito, F. and Hatzopoulos, P. (eds) (2003) *Religion in International Relations: The Return from Exile*, New York: Palgrave.

Philips, K. (2006) *American Theocracy*, New York: Viking.

Ramet, S. (1995) 'Spheres of religio-political interaction: social order, nationalism, and gender relations', in S. Ramet (ed.), *Render unto Caesar: The Religious Sphere in World Politics*, Lanham, MA: The American University Press, pp. 51–70.

Roy, O. (2004) *Globalised Islam: The Search for a New Ummah*, London: C. Hurst and Co.

Shlapentokh, V., Woods, J. and Shiraev, E. (eds) (2005) *America. Sovereign Defender or Cowboy Nation?*, Aldershot, and Burlington, VT: Ashgate.

Shupe, A. (1990) 'The stubborn persistence of religion in the global arena', in E. Sahliyeh (ed.), *Religious Resurgence and Politics in the Contemporary World*, Albany: State University of New York Press, pp. 17–26.

Simpson, J. (1992) 'Fundamentalism in America revisited: the fading of modernity as a source of symbolic capital', in B. Misztal and A. Shupe (eds), *Religion and Politics in Comparative Perspective: Revival of Religious Fundamentalism in East and West*, Westport and London: Praeger, pp. 10–27.

Smith, D. E. (1970) *Religion and Political Development*, Boston, MA: Little Brown.

Tarrow, S. (1998) *Power in Movement: Social Movements and Contentious Politics*, 2nd edn, Cambridge: Cambridge University Press.

Tehranian, M. (1997) 'Religious resurgence in global perspective', *Economic and Political Weekly* (New Delhi), 32 (50), December 13–19.

Thomas, S. (2003) 'Taking religious and cultural pluralism seriously: the global resurgence of religion and the transformation of international society,' in F. Petito and P. Hatzopoulos (eds) *Religion in International Relations: The Return from Exile*, New York: Palgrave, pp. 21–54.

Thomas, S. (2005) *The Global Transformation of Religion and the Transformation of International Relations: The Struggle for the Soul of the Twenty-First Century*, New York/Basingstoke: Palgrave Macmillan.

Watson, M. (1994) 'Christianity and the green option in the new Europe', in J. Fulton and P. Gee (eds), *Religion in Contemporary Europe*, Baltimore, MD: Penguin, pp. 19–41.

Wilson, B. (1992) 'Reflections on a many sided controversy', in S. Bruce (ed.), *Religion and Modernization*, Oxford: Clarendon Press, pp. 195–210.

Woollacott, M. 1995. 'Keeping our faith in belief', *The Guardian*, 23 December.

Further reading

P. Berger (ed.), *The Desecularization of the World. Resurgent Religion and World Politics*, Ethics and Public Policy Center, 1999. This volume challenges the belief that the world is increasingly secular, showing that while modernization does have secularizing effects, it also provokes a reaction that more often strengthens religion.

P. Beyer, *Religion and Globalization*, Sage, 1994. Beyer's book is a useful survey of transborder religious interactions in the context of globalization.

J. Casanova, *Public Religions in the Modern World*, University of Chicago Press, 1994. Casanova makes the case that religious 'deprivatization' is a key development marking the political 'return' of religion to the public realm.

J. Haynes, *Religion in Global Politics*, Longman, 1998. Haynes offers a global survey of the interaction of religion and politics.

S. Huntington, *The Clash of Civilizations*, Simon and Schuster, 1996. Huntington's articulation of his controversial thesis – that the world is poised to enter an era of 'civilizational clashes' between Islam and Christianity – has been much debated, especially since 9/11.

M. Juergensmeyer, *The New Cold War? Religious Nationalism Confronts the Secular State*, University of California Press, 1993. Examining similar ground to that of Huntington, Juergensmeyer focuses upon the extent to which religious ideologies have replaced secular ones as a key source of international conflict.

R. Mainuddin (ed.), *Religion and Politics in the Develoing World: Explosive Interactions*, Ashgate, 2002. This book examines a number of key religio-political interactions in the developing world.

P. Norris and R. Ingelhart, *Sacred and Secular: Religion and Politics Worldwide*, Cambridge University Press, 2004. This book develops a theory of secularization and existential security and compares it against survey evidence from almost 80 societies worldwide.

'Religion, culture, and international conflict after September 11. A conversation with Samuel P. Huntington', Ethics and Public Policy Center, 'Center Conversations', no. 14, June 2002. Available at: http:www.eppc.org.publications/pubID.1537/pub_detail.asp) This 'conversation' between Huntington and an assortment of US journalists from June 2002 offers insights into the nature and characteristics of his 'clash of civilizations' thesis.

F. Volpi, *Islam and Democracy: The Failure of Dialogue in Algeria*, Pluto, 2003. Volpi's monograph is a well-researched account of the failure of religious and political actors in Algeria to arrive at a modus vivendi during the civil war of the 1990s that led to more than 100,000 deaths.

D. Westerlund (ed.), *Questioning the Secular State: The Worldwide Resurgence of Religion in Politics*, Hurst, 1996. Westerlund examines the question of a global religious resurgence.

L. Woodhead and P. Heelas (eds), *Religion in Modern Times*, Blackwell, 2000. This is a very useful survey of the contemporary position of religion in political and social contexts.

CHAPTER 2

Religion, soft power and international relations

Religion, secularization and international relations after the Treaty of Westphalia

Before the development of increasingly secular international relations, religion was a key source of competition and sometimes conflict in many parts of the world, including Europe. By the time of the Treaty of Westphalia (1648), such religious activity was an established aspect of European conflict, discord and instability, involving rival religious faiths (both *intra-Christian*, including Protestant and Roman Catholic and Greek Orthodox and Roman Catholic, and *Christianity* versus *Islam*). Over time, however, religion's significance for international relations appeared to decline significantly, linked to the development of politically centralized, increasingly secular states – initially in Western Europe and then via colonialism to much of the rest of the world.

This was reflected in two related processes – modernization and secularization. These interrelated concepts carried a shared assumption for international relations analysis: sovereign states are *the* key actors in international relations, characterized by a key attribute: state sovereignty, and a fundamental principle: international non-intervention. Gradually these notions became embedded in international thinking, manifested in what are known as the 'four pillars' of the Westphalian system. In sum, the Treaty of Westphalia was 'a structure of political authority that was forged centuries ago by a sharply secularizing set of events and that has endured in its secular guise ever since' (Philpott, 2002: 79). Its overall impact was to remove religion as a justification for war. As the salience of religion for international relations declined, it was widely believed that two related developments – secular modernization and the rise of science and rationality – would combine to put relentless pressure on religious faith, resulting in its steady decay and the emergence around the world of decidedly secular polities and societies.

The 'four pillars' of the Westphalian system of international relations

- States are the sole legitimate actor in the international system.

- Governments do not seek to change relations between religion and politics in foreign countries.

- Religious authorities legitimately exercise few, if any, domestic temporal functions, and even fewer transnationally.

- Separation between church and state – that is, the main manifestation respectively of religious and political power – meant that governments did not normally vigorously promote the welfare of one religion over others.

As we saw in Chapter 1, this view has undergone revision, with some seeing a near-global religious resurgence, with only Western Europe not conforming to the trend (Berger, 1999; Stark and Fink, 2000). This has refocused attention on the 'secularization thesis', which has undergone sustained and continuing challenge. Those now attempting to defend the continued veracity of the secularization thesis, such as Bruce (2002), often interpret

> evidence of burgeoning religiosity in many contemporary political events to mean that we are witnessing merely a fundamentalist, antimodernist backlash against science, industrialization, and liberal Western values . . . typically explained away as an isolated exception to unremitting trends of secularization and seldom recognized as part of a larger global phenomenon. (Sahliyeh 1990: 19)

As the quotation suggests, proponents of the secularization thesis typically perceive the impact of religion on politics – and by extension international relations – as normatively 'anti-modern', typically associated with the often-pejorative concept of 'religious fundamentalism' (Marty and Appleby, 1993). The problem, however, is that to restrict our understanding of religious actors in international relations to such a view means that we would miss important issues that do not fit into the anti-modernist and fundamentalist conception. For example, the Israel–Palestinian conflict – neither anti-modernist nor fundamentalist in orientation – focuses primarily on territorial issues, a concern explicitly linked in recent years with various religious and cultural issues, including who controls holy places of great importance for both Judaism and Islam. In addition, the Iranian revolution

(1979) is sometimes regarded as both anti-modernist and fundamentalist in direction, yet its ramifications for international relations include a more general concern with the role of Islam as a revolutionary actor in the service of Iran's foreign policy, a focus that goes way beyond a narrow concern with the revolution's explicitly religious fundamentalist connotations. A third example is provided by the Roman Catholic Church, which played a leading role in the 1980s and 1990s in relation to democratic transitions in various parts of the world, including Southern Europe, Latin America, Eastern Europe, sub-Saharan Africa and East Asia. There was nothing anti-modern or fundamentalist about this development. A final example comes from the 11 September 2001 ('9/11', New York and Pentagon attacks), 11 March 2003 ('3/11', Madrid bombings) and 7 July 2005 ('7/7', London bombings) outrages perpetuated by various Islamist terrorists against governments and populations in the USA, Spain and Britain. To see these incidents as merely an anti-modernist and fundamentalist reaction against secularization misses several important points. The bombings collectively raise the question about the ideological assumptions and goals of their perpetrators, given that most of the dead, especially on 9/11, were not Christians or Jews, but Muslims. What were the bombers trying to achieve? What were their ideological assumptions and goals? To dismiss them as simply anti-modernist and as advocates of Islamic fundamentalism leaves us with a narrow focus that does not take into account other important concerns, including the impact of globalization and of Western, pro-Israel foreign policies.

In addition, various religious actors have taken the view that involvement in politics is essential as a part of their ethics. For example, several religious individuals, including Pope John Paul II (1920–2005) and Archbishops Desmond Tutu (b. 1931) and Óscar Arnulfo Romero y Galdámez (1917–80), were individually and centrally involved in recent human rights campaigns. This is not a new phenomenon: for example, religious actors were centrally involved in the Abolitionist anti-slavery movement in the nineteenth century, the civil rights struggle in the USA in the 1960s, and the anti-apartheid movement in relation to South Africa, concluding with democratization in 1994.

The overall point is that there are now numerous religious actors in international relations, with various concerns that go beyond a narrow focus on religious fundamentalism and anti-modernism. Some encourage cooperation, 'interreligious dialogue and greater religious engagement around questions of international development and conflict resolution' (Banchoff, 2005). Others are more concerned with competition, and occasionally conflict, in relation both to other religious traditions and various secular actors.

Both areas of concern – cooperation and conflict – will be kept in view in the chapters that follow.

Categories of religious actors in international relations

It is useful to identify and briefly describe two key sets of religious actors in international relations. They are:

■ State-related religious actors

■ Non-state religious actors

State-related religious actors are closely linked to but conceptually distinct from governments. Certain countries, for example, the USA, India, Iran and Saudi Arabia, have sets of religious actors with close relationships with government. The result, as we shall see in later chapters, is that such religious actors can sometimes influence foreign policies. *Non-state religious actors* of various kinds comprise the second category. They are religious individuals or movements that act in both domestic and international contexts, often engaging with other faith traditions in their concern with various global issues, including conflict resolution and human development. As Banchoff (2005:1) notes,

> The formation and contestation of more global religious identities has both reflective and ethical dimensions. On the one hand it entails wrestling with the implications of religious pluralism for received understandings of truth. This involves communication and dialogue across religious traditions. On the other hand, more global identities encourage a reframing of received ethical commitments to peace and justice as transnational, and not just local or national imperatives. This broader ethical horizon increasingly informs religious engagement and collaboration around global issues including peaceful conflict resolution and social development.

Religious actors and international relations

State-related religious actors are closely linked to certain governments. Notable examples include the governments of the USA, India, Iran and Saudi Arabia, although others governments at various times have been influenced by religious actors, for example, the government of Israel, as well as a 'quasi-government', that of the Palestinian National Authority that administers the Gaza Strip and portions of the West Bank of the River Jordan. When a government has foreign policies that are significantly influenced by religious concerns, it implies that significant domestic religious actors are able to influence what government does in relation to the country's international relations.

(Continued)

> There are numerous *non-state religious actors* active in international relations, from several religious traditions. They are defined as religious individuals or movements that, drawing on religious traditions, act in international relations. They may engage with other faith traditions in shared concerns with various global issues, including conflict resolution and human development, or they may encounter other religious entities in ways that are more characterized by competition or conflict.

Despite a variety of objectives in international relations, non-state religious actors generally wish to inaugurate, embed and develop interactions with like-minded groups either domestically and/or internationally. This process is likely to be characterized by transmission and receipt of inter-personal and inter-group exchanges of information, ideas, personnel and/or money. Such interactions are facilitated when religious actors take advantage of globalization, where previously significant barriers to communication have considerably diminished. Overall, globalization serves to facilitate not only national but also regional, continental and, in some cases, global networks

This chapter focuses upon the following: the fundamental norms of international relations as enshrined in the Treaty of Westphalia (1648), which included: state restraint in religious matters, encouraging the belief that international relations discourse is predominantly secular; two general categories of religious actors in international relations: state-related and non-state religious actors; examination of the 'English School' of international relations, primarily concerned with the importance of international society and associated norms, values and institutions; the variable influence of globalization on international society, including the idea of multicultural international relations; and, finally, the issue of 'soft' power, which both state-related and non-state religious actors utilize in order to try to influence international relations.

The English School and international society

Emerging as an academic discipline after the First World War, most international relations analyses initially reflected the view that religion was usually of little analytical importance in explaining international outcomes. Consequently, religion was normally afforded little attention or emphasis, especially in the USA, where the approach known as Realism achieved prominence. Realism is based on three fundamental premises:

- States' foreign policies have two main goals: accumulate both material goods and as much power[1] as possible.

- All states share similar international motivations and goals. Because of perceived unity of purpose, what goes on within state policy-making processes and structures can be safely placed in a 'black box' – and ignored.

- The international system is a chaotic, self-help system, characterized by competition, conflict and cooperation.

In Britain, another key centre of international relations enquiry, analysis took a different turn. In the 1950s, the 'English School' approach emerged, focusing on the evolution and operation of what it referred to as 'international society'. The English School gained its name because most of its key figures, while not necessarily English by birth, worked in English universities, including the London School of Economics and Political Science, and Oxford and Cambridge universities. Key names associated with the English School include: Martin Wight, Hedley Bull, R.J. Vincent, James Mayall, Robert Jackson, Barry Buzan, Tim Dunne and Nicholas J. Wheeler. According to Buzan, 'The English School can be thought of as an established body of both theoretical and empirical work' (Buzan, 2004: 6). What primarily distinguishes the English School from Realist approaches is its concern with both morality and culture. This leads to a distinctive approach to the study of international relations, emphasizing problems of coexistence, cooperation, and conflict, especially in the relations between sovereign states (Jackson and Owens, 2005: 46; Brown, 2005: 51).

The idea of international society involves 'relations between politically organized human groupings, which occupy distinctive territories and enjoy and exercise a measure of independence from each other' (Jackson and Owens, 2005: 46). Thus conceptually the idea of 'international society' stresses a network of 'autonomous political communities' – typically, states – that are autonomous of any higher juridical authority. For Hedley Bull, a founder of the English School, the 'starting point of international relations is the existence of states, or independent political communities, each of which possesses a government and asserts sovereignty in relation to a particular portion of the earth's surface and a particular segment of the human population' (Bull, 1977: 8). Thus for Bull, the main focus of study of IR is the 'world of states' not sub-state entities – such as ethnic or religious communities – nor universal categories, such as 'humanity'.

International society and the international system

It is a key premise of the English School approach that when states interact regularly and systematically they do not merely form an international *system* – that is, a purely functional arrangement for mutual benefit – but comprise an international *society*. An international society differs from an international system by virtue of the fact that the former is a 'norm-governed relationship whose members accept that they have at least limited responsibilities towards one another and to the society as a whole. These responsibilities are summarised in the traditional practices of international law and diplomacy' (Brown, 2005: 51).

Recent interest in the roles of religion in international relations raises an important theoretical question in relation to the English School approach: is an international society possible in a multicultural and multi-religious international environment? For Brown, it makes sense to think of the idea of international society as 'an occasionally idealized conceptualization of the norms of the old, pre-1914 European states system' (Brown, 2005: 51). If this is right, can such a conception of 'international society' be a satisfactory starting point when we bear in mind that most existing states are not European? It might be that the old – that is, pre-First World War – international order functioned relatively well because of a quite high level of cultural homogeneity among the members of international society. This may have been in part because Europeans have a mutual history informed by common Graeco-Roman cultural origins. This relationship was not, however, always peaceful: many historical relationships between European states were intermittently or regularly based on competition and sometimes conflict between, for example, followers of the (Greek) Orthodox and (Roman) Catholic churches or between Protestant and Catholic interpretations of Christianity. How much more likely now is the potential for competition and perhaps conflict, given that the normative basis for international society – based on shared religious and cultural underpinnings of Europe – has given way to international relations comprising not only Christian-rooted conceptions but also others deriving from, for example, Islam, Hinduism, Confucianism, Buddhism, Judaism, and so on?

Several points are relevant here. First, some have suggested potential for competition and conflict emanating from differing conceptions of international society. For example, the Harvard academic, Samuel Huntington, has controversially focused on a real or imagined 'clash of civilizations', asking whether the post-Cold War conflict between 'the West' and 'Islam' has now replaced the ideological confrontation of the Cold War as the biggest source of international rivalry and antagonism. Huntington's views have been regarded with interest within the US foreign policy community. Some at least accept the view that after the Cold War 'Islamic fundamentalism' has replaced Communism as the main threat facing the United States (Halper and Clarke, 2004; Dolan, 2005). In addition, a former NATO secretary-general Willy Claes (*The Guardian,* 3 February 1995) has stated that

> Muslim fundamentalism is at least as dangerous as communism once was. Please do not underestimate this risk . . . at the conclusion of this age it is a serious threat, because it represents terrorism, religious fanaticism and exploitation of social and economic justice. . . . NATO is much more than a military alliance. It has committed itself to defending basic principles of civilisation that bind North America and Western Europe.

In sum, thinking about the influence of religion on perceptions of international society, we can note both theoretical and practical foreign policy issues.

The second point is that the idea of international society must now be seen in relation to the multifaceted phenomenon of globalization. Often associated with metaphors like 'the hollowed out state' and 'a borderless world', globalization is said to be changing economic, political and cultural arrangements and configurations both within and between countries. The result is erosion of what was previously seen as the nation-state's impenetrable 'hard' boundaries and a consequent diminution of governments' ability to control domestic environments. The implication is that globalization reduces the power of the nation-state to make definitive decisions regarding its own future. The 'globalization thesis' is, however, at odds with several traditional, embedded assumptions of international relations analysis. These include an understanding that the world comprises: (1) confined political territories governed by national – sovereign – states, (2) nation-states, and (3) national economies. These have long been regarded, respectively, as the 'natural' units of international relations analysis, while the globalization thesis implies that these long-standing arrangements are in the process of being transcended. Finally, rejection of state-centric international relations highlights the significance both of various kinds of non-state actors as well as transnational networks, including those based on religious concerns, for an understanding of contemporary international relations. Taken together, these concerns may undermine the concept of international society as traditionally understood.

Thirdly, there is the significance of cultural factors in international relations to take into account. According to Murden, this dimension 'appeared to be reaffirmed amid the reorganization of world politics that followed the end of the cold war and the release of new waves of globalization' (Murden, 2005: 539). Saurin argues that culture has become a potent political force threatening the basis of the current fragmented state system and its structures of supporting nationalism. This is because, he argues, 'culture avoids being located and tied down to any definable physical space' (Saurin, 1995: 256). However, and somewhat paradoxically, nationalism and ethnic awareness are also cultural components transmitted around the globe, becoming both a globalized *and* a globalizing phenomenon. One of the main causes of contemporary ethnic and religious conflict in many countries is said to be such groups' awareness of what other groups around the world are doing, and with this knowledge seeking to emulate counterparts' struggles for greater power (Juergensmeyer, 2000). Overall, cultural globalization is a central facet in many sociological interpretations of globalization, especially when the issue of religion is assessed. Sometimes, for example, notions such as 'Westernization' and 'Americanization' are juxtaposed with others, including 'Islamic fundamentalism' or 'Asian values'. Much theorizing about globalization has focused on such cultural issues, said to be encouraged by the global spread of identical consumer goods and an American(ized) culture (Thomas, 2005). Disseminated primarily by US-based transnational corporations, Americanization is believed to subvert local cultures, not only encouraging people to become 'consumers' but also to buy American goods and services. Together, the 'media revolution' and the growth of consumerism are thought to help erode particularistic cultures and values, replacing them with an Americanized 'global culture' of Disney, McDonald's, Coca-Cola, and Starbucks. For Benjamin Barber, post-Cold War international relations are primarily characterized by 'Jihad vs. McWorld' – that is, 'the forces of particular religious tribalisms and the universal, economic, ecological, and commercial forces of "globalism"' (Barber, 1992).

In sum, globalization is significant for an understanding of international society.

Globalization and international society

Globalization is significant for an understanding of international society for two main reasons. First, globalization facilitates the transmission of both material and non-material factors, and religious actors may seek to use opportunities to spread messages, funds and personnel. Second, as our case studies in the second half of the book show, the domestic social and political impact of religion is always contoured by particular social and political circumstances in individual countries and these factors will influence the transnational focus of religious actors. Under the conditions of globalization, state policy makers must attempt to cope with the demands both of domestic political actors, while simultaneously dealing with external developments that can influence domestic outcomes. As a result of globalization, all states, both 'weak' and 'strong', experience increasing 'porousness' of national borders. This leads to increased complexity requiring policy makers to deal routinely with external inputs when making and executing policy both at home and abroad.

'Soft power' and international relations

How do religious actors affect outcomes in international relations? While their goals vary, they will typically attempt to achieve objectives through the application of what the American international relations expert Joseph Nye calls 'soft power'. The concept of 'soft power' refers to the capability of a political body, often but not necessarily a state, to influence what other entities do through direct or indirect, often cultural or ideological, influence and encouragement. Nye first used the term in his 1990 book, *Bound to Lead: The Changing Nature of American Power*, and further developed the concept in a later volume: *Soft Power: The Means to Success in World Politics* (2004a). While its value as a descriptive theory has been questioned (Webber and Smith, 2002: 42–3, 45), the usefulness of the concept of soft power is now widely accepted in international relations analysis.

The idea of soft power works from the premise that certain attributes – such as, culture, values and ideas – represent different, not necessarily lesser, forms of influence, compared to 'hard' power – that is, more direct, more forceful measures typically involving armed force or economic coercion. For some international relations analysts, especially those associated with the school of thought known as Realism, a country's power is best regarded as a quantitative measure derived from its various material attributes, including gross national product (GNP), military capability and natural resources.

However, seeking to measure a country's potential hard-power assets is not necessarily a good guide to understanding whether it will achieve foreign policy goals. The problem is that even when a country seems to have sufficient relevant material assets 'to get the job done' *and* the will to use them, this does not always translate into success. For example, the USA was not able to achieve its main goal in the Vietnam War (1954–75) – to prevent a Communist regime taking power – nor, so far, a secular, pro-Western regime built on democratic foundations in post-Saddam Iraq. More generally, US foreign policy in the Middle East after 9/11, in relation to both post-Taliban Afghanistan and Iraq, has sought to apply hard power with only limited success.

Joseph Nye on power

The basic concept of power is the ability to influence others to get them to do what you want. There are three major ways to do that: one is to threaten them with sticks; the second is to pay them with carrots; the third is to attract them or co-opt them, so that they want what you want. If you can get others to be attracted, to want what you want, it costs you much less in carrots and sticks (Nye, 2004b).

'Soft' power is a 'third way' of achieving objectives; it is not sticks or carrots. Nye argues that soft power is more than influence, since influence can also rest on the hard power of (military or diplomatic) threats or (economic) payments. On the other hand, while soft power is not entirely synonymous with cultural power, it is the case that 'exporting cultural goods that hold attraction for other countries can communicate values and influence those societies' (Nye, 2005) – for example, the USA exporting democracy during the 'third wave of democracy' in the 1980s and 1990s (Haynes, 2001).

Economic strength is usually not soft power. This is because responding to an economic incentive or sanction is not the same as aligning politically with a cause that is admired or respected. We can see this in relation to the influence of foreign aid donors, collectively of great importance in encouraging some economically poor authoritarian regimes to democratize in the 1980s and 1990s. This followed significant oil price rises in the 1970s and associated international indebtedness, when the ability of many such regimes to maintain adequate programmes of political and economic development dropped sharply in the 1980s and 1990s. The result was that it became increasingly difficult, especially for many developing countries without oil, for them to balance their budgets. Many became increasingly dependent on loans and aid from the West. Aid donors argued that the situation would be remedied by democratization, part of a general process of improving governance. Increasingly, the continuity of foreign aid was made dependent on aid-hungry regimes agreeing to democratize. In this way, many economically poor, authoritarian regimes were strongly encouraged to shift to democracy. In addition, in a linked move, Western governments encouraged the installation of market-based economic programmes to the extent that they were 'intrinsic' to democratic openings in economically impoverished Africa and Central America (Joseph, 1998: 10; Karl, 1995: 77). In short, external encouragement to democratize, linked to the supply of aid and loans, was often of major significance for poor countries – but it was not soft power, and overt economic leverage was used.

Soft power is not necessarily humane. For example, soft-power activism of various significant political figures, including the Indian nationalist, Mohandas 'Mahatma' Gandhi (1869–1948), the US civil rights leader, Martin Luther King (1929–68), and the anti-apartheid activist, Nelson Mandela (b. 1918), was informed by universal humanist ideas, while those of others, including the German Nazi leader, Adolph Hitler (1889–1945), the Russian Communist head, Josef Stalin (1879–1953), and the mastermind of the 9/11 attacks, Osama bin Laden (b. 1957), are said to be reliant on twisting people's minds (Nye, 2004c). This suggests that the exercise of soft power not only does not rely on persuasion or the capacity to convince people by argument but also is a sign of an ability to attract, and attraction often leads to acceptance of associated ideas. As Nye (2004c, emphasis added) puts it,

> If I am persuaded to go along with your purposes without any explicit threat or exchange taking place – in short, if my behavior is determined by an observable but intangible attraction – soft power is at work. *Soft power uses a different type of currency – not force, not money – to engender cooperation. It uses an attraction to shared values, and the justness and duty of contributing to the achievement of those values.*

Religion may be a form of soft power. We can see this in relation to the post-9/11 'war on terror', when competing conceptions of soft power have vied for supremacy, and religious values are central to this competition. Lacking an influential soft-power, hearts-and-minds policy that would demonstrably persuade all Muslims not to follow extremist groups who encourage violence, US foreign policy found it very difficult to convince Muslims that its objectives in Iraq are not simply self-serving. In addition, both 'extremist' and 'moderate' Islamic ideas and movements have competed post-9/11 for the support of ordinary Muslims by offering differing soft-power visions. Casanova (2005), Voll (2006) and Appleby (2006) have identified competing Muslim 'transnational advocacy networks' (TANs) with both 'extremist' and 'moderate' world-views. In general, TANs are networks of 'relevant actors working internationally on an issue . . . bound together by shared values, a common discourse, and dense exchange of information and services' (Keck and Sikkink, 1998).

Liberal internationalism and transnational actors

A theory of international relations – known as liberal internationalism – takes into account transnational advocacy networks (TANs) in seeking to explain outcomes in international relations. Liberal internationalism is based on four key premises:

- International stability and order require building and upholding appropriately consensual international institutions and norms.

- Building and sustaining relevant international institutions and norms are core aspects of an international society aiming to bring 'peace and prosperity to all'.

- To achieve this goal, it is necessary to discover, cultivate and implement shared values that help achieve this aim.

- States are no longer *automatically* the primary actor in world politics in every context and in relation to every issue (Burchill, 2005: 64–6).

The liberal internationalist view notes several distinct forms of influence, with Keohane and Nye's (1977) typology of world politics as 'complex interdependence' often the starting point. This is a 'multiple issues' agenda encouraging government decision makers – once concerned 'only' with 'domestic' issues, for example, energy, telecommunications, food, agriculture and the natural environment – to take external actors into account. This not only presents organizational difficulties in coordinating the work of different branches of government but also 'generates political problems as a proliferation of newly created policy coalitions seek to influence policy' (Webber and Smith, 2002: 63–4). In short, there are now multiple channels of contact linking states and societies, both within and between countries, and in some cases this includes various religious actors that may impact upon both policy-making and execution through their ability to wield soft power. Overall, liberal internationalists recognize the potential and in some cases actual importance of religious actors in international relations, in relation to specific issues and outcomes. Such analyses also recognize

(Continued)

the ability of soft power under certain circumstances to be influential in relation to international outcomes.

The numbers of transnational non-state actors grew from a few thousand
in the early 1970s to an estimated 25,000 'active' organizations in the early
2000s (Anheier and Themudo, 2002: 195). While many are secular in orientation a large number are religious. Collectively, transnational religious networks can be influential motivators of, as well as participants in, conflict; they
can also be independently significant in promoting various normatively 'progressive' objectives, including: peace, inter-group understanding, cooperation
and human development.

Religious actors and the exercise of soft power in international relations

Non-state religious actors

We are concerned in this book with six major religious traditions and movements that we identify as the 'world religions' – Buddhism, Christianity,
Confucianism, Hinduism, Islam and Judaism – and their involvement in international relations, especially since the end of the Cold War in 1989. It is
important to note that there are potentially important differences between
the religious traditions in terms of the extent of their networks that will obviously affect the extent and focus of their followers' international interactions and involvement. For example, while the main strands of Islam, Sunni
and Shia, as well as various expressions of Christianity, including Roman
Catholicism and Protestantism, have tens of millions of followers in numerous countries with often extensive cross-border links, more geographically
specific religious traditions, such as Hinduism (mostly concentrated in
India), Theravada Buddhism (South-East Asia) and Confucianism (East Asia)
have little in the way of such interactions that are relevant to an understanding of current international relations.

More generally, until recently international relations literature on
transnationalism devoted little concentrated attention to religious phenomena. This is because transnational linkages and penetration were often
studied primarily to assess their impact on questions of political and economic
security. The conventional security bias of much of the transnational literature
helps explain the lack of sustained focus on religious actors. Until the recent
focus on, *inter alia*, transnational Islamic and Christian actors (Rudolph
and Piscatori, 1997), in general religious actors were regarded as interesting

phenomena, although remote from central questions affecting states and state power in international politics. Now, however, it is widely accepted that various religious actors can not only directly affect the *internal* politics of states and thus qualify state power, as conventionally understood, but also have significant ramifications for international relations.

Transnational ideas and 'soft power'

It is useful to see religious traditions and movements with ability to influence outcomes in international relations not unique as actors but instead fitting into a pattern that also includes secular transnational actors of various kinds. This is because both secular and religious transnational entities reflect the power of soft power in relation to their adherents. In other words, transnational ideas urge a transnational course of action on adherents, typically containing a coherent set of symbols, such as the Bible, the Quran, or *The Communist Manifesto*, and leading prophets (Jesus, Mohammed or Marx).

Transnational ideas can be examined as a form of 'soft power' in world politics, that is, attractive ideas that can be contrasted with 'hard' power (military or economic muscle). Soft power is the ability to set the political agenda, determine both the vocabulary of political debate, or the language in which the political discourse is conducted. Transnational ideas, such as Zionism, Pan-Africanism, Pan-Arabism, Afro-Asian solidarity, and various conceptions of Islamism,[2] as well as changing international norms and values, such as anti-colonialism, anti-imperialism, anti-racism, national self-determination, and environmentalism, can contribute to a transnational actor's soft-power resources. This is because people in many countries adhere to such ideas, believing that the norms and values they represent should influence international outcomes.

It is important to bear in mind that transnational actors do not control territory, and thus are deprived of a key hard-power resource. However, some liberation movements for example, the Palestine Liberation Organization, do represent a widely held principle – in this case, national self-determination for the Palestinian people – and enjoy the loyalty of most Palestinians, despite the fact that they live in territories for the most part under the control of existing states, such as Israel or Jordan. The Vatican is another example of a religious entity wielding considerable soft power: it represents the Roman Catholic Church and commands the attention (if not always the allegiance) of Catholics in various countries around the world. On the other hand, the

Organization of the Islamic Conference (OIC) projects 'Islamic interests' in world politics, although its soft power is blunted because there are various states in the OIC, including Saudi Arabia and Iran, vying for leadership. In sum, religious transnational actors have the support of sympathetic individuals and sub-national groups that promote a range of concerns and values internationally. Some transnational religious actors – al-Qaeda is an obvious example because of the events of September 11, 2001 – can have a greater impact on the world stage and receive more foreign policy attention from the great powers than many 'weak' states in the international system.

Taken together the thousands of extant transnational non-state actors, both secular and religious, are collectively conceptualized in international relations as comprising 'transnational' or 'global' civil society (Glasius et al., 2006).[3] The concept has three main components. First, like domestic civil society, transnational civil society (TCS) encompasses various, principally non-state, groups with social and/or political goals; groups overtly connected to the state, as well as profit-seeking private entities, such as transnational corporations, are conceptually excluded. Secondly, such groups interact with each other across state boundaries and are not overtly manipulated by governments, although they might have links. Thirdly, TCS takes a variety of forms; many are secular in orientation, for example, an international non-governmental organization with constituent groups in a number of countries, such as Amnesty International or Human Rights Watch, or an organization with a presence in various countries, such as the National Democratic Institute or the National Endowment for Democracy (Gagnon, 2002: 215–16; Adamson, 2002: 191–2). Others are specifically concerned with religious issues, for example, the Roman Catholic lay organization, Opus Dei.

Transnational civil society and globalization

Transnational civil society (TCS) forms an important aspect of the globalization thesis as it challenges the notion that states are always the dominant political and economic actors in both domestic and international contexts. Distinct from the insular concerns of states and most political parties, the 'cosmopolitan' focus of TCS concentrates on direct relationships between people in various countries. The growth of transnational interactions as a result of globalization leads to growing spread and interchange of ideas and information between groups within TCS. Lipschutz defines TCS as 'the self-conscious constructions of networks of knowledge and action, by decentred, local actors, that cross the reified boundaries of space as

(Continued)

though they were not there' (Lipschutz, 1992: 390). Thus TCS comprises groups and organizations in different countries that work together to create dedicated cross-border communities that: (1) pursue common goals via regional or global campaigns, and (2) encourage the development of goal-focused transnational coalitions. Overall, TCS seeks the goal of better, more ethical standards of international governance by providing potential for direct links between individuals and groups in different countries, and some constituent groups draw on various religious traditions and understandings.

Attina (1989: 350–1, emphases added) notes that

transnationalism is not just a matter of individuals and masses who feel conscious of being primary international subjects as they are entitled to civil, political, economic, social and cultural rights by positive international law. In the world system these subjects form *the international social layer* which claims primacy over the diplomatic layer. Today the chances of *social transnationalism* reside in INGOs whose members cross states and assert 'pan-human' interests such as the promotion of human rights, environmental ecology, [and] international development co-operation.

In this view, international society is an agglomeration of different issue areas, including: democracy, human rights, development, and environmental protection. What Attina calls *social transnationalism* refers to the multiple linkages between individuals and groups in different societies yet concerned broadly with the same issues, creating what he labels the *international social layer*. This is a line of contacts between societies operating and underpinning the formal world of supposedly independent states.

Two key questions can be asked about TCS:

- *Why* does TCS exist?
- *How* does TCS influence international outcomes?

TCS networks exist because their constituents aim for certain goals based on shared conceptions of the public good, sometimes known as 'cosmopolitanism' (Held, 1999). Such networks are bound together not primarily by self-interest but by shared values, such as a normative belief in the desirability of democracy, human development, international debt relief for poor countries, or the desirability of extending religious networks.

In relation to the second question, we can note that a main function of domestic civil society is to try to check the power of the state (Haynes, 2001). Of course there is no world government analogous to those of domestic governments within individual countries. Unlike domestic civil society, transnational civil society is not *territorially* fixed, but comprises a field of action whose parameters can readily change to suit the requirements of new issues and changing circumstances. In sum, TCS seeks to influence international outcomes by using networks of like-minded individuals to focus on shared concerns and encourage decision makers, whether domestically or internationally based, to make the 'right' decisions.

In sum, transnational linkages focused in TCS help develop networks of diversity and plurality, taking advantage of new communication technologies, that facilitates the growth of regional or global social networks. The increase in cross-border links between such groups is facilitated by the global communications revolution. The overall significance of TCS for international relations is that many people, both secular and religious and not confined to a single country, all hold similar notions about something and work collectively to achieve objectives.

State-related religious actors

All states have foreign policies ostensibly directed towards achieving a set of national interests and specific goals. A state's foreign policy must be flexible enough to follow the changing contours and dynamics of international politics, while simultaneously preserving and promoting national interests. It is widely agreed that any country's domestic environment has a major role in shaping its foreign policy. For Frankel (1963), foreign policy is to a large extent a reflection of a country's domestic milieu, its needs, priorities, strengths and weaknesses. This suggests that a state's foreign policy is influenced by certain 'objective' conditions – such as, history, geography, socio-economic conditions, and culture – that interact with the changing dynamics of international politics. For a country to enjoy a successful foreign policy, it is necessary to achieve a balance between domestic and external dimensions. In sum, foreign policies of all countries are, to some degree, a product of and interaction between (1) a country's overall power indices (including, geo-strategic location, economic wealth and health, military strength, and domestic political stability), and (2) the prevailing international environment.

Only a few governments have foreign policies and more generally international relations ostensibly or significantly motivated by religion. Below we shall look briefly at the governments of the USA, India, Saudi Arabia and Iran, before focusing upon them more fully in the relevant chapters in the second half of the book concerned with individual countries and regions.

How and under what circumstances might domestic religious actors influence a state's foreign policy? To answer this question, a useful starting point is to note that as 'religion plays an important role in politics in certain parts of the world' then it is likely that there will be 'greater prominence of religious organizations in society and politics' in some countries compared to others (Telhami, 2004: 71). Secondly, ability of religious actors to translate *potential* ability into *actual* influence on state foreign policies will depend to some degree on whether they can access and thus potentially influence foreign policy decision-making processes. Thirdly, religious actors' ability to influence foreign policy is also linked to ability to influence policy in other ways. For example, the USA has a democratic system with accessible decision-making structures and processes, potentially offering actors – both religious and secular – clear opportunities to influence policy-making, both domestic and foreign (Hudson, 2005: 295–7). However, the idea that religious actors must 'get the ear of government' directly is a very limited and traditional understanding of influence. Overall, as Walt and Mearsheimer note, 'interest groups can lobby elected representatives and members of the executive branch, make campaign contributions, vote in elections, try to mould public opinion etc.' (Walt and Mearsheimer, 2006: 6).

It is important to note, however, that religions are not just run-of-the-mill lobby groups. There are in addition key aspects of influence that are indirect but nevertheless help construct the mindset that engages with such issues: What questions are raised? What issues are of concern? What terms are used? How they are thought about? And even if a religious actor gets access to formal decision-making structures and processes it does not *guarantee* their ability significantly to influence either policy formation or execution. To have a profound policy impact, it is necessary in build relations with key players in both society and politics, as well as to foster good relations with influential print and electronic media. Overall, religious actors' ability to influence state foreign policies is likely to be greatest when, as in the USA after 9/11, there was pronounced ideological empathy between key religious groups and secular power holders – that is, when they wield soft power. In this context, we can note, first, post-9/11 the influence of the Religious Right in relation to US foreign policy in the Middle East. Leading figures – such as Gary Bauer, Jerry Falwell, Ralph Reed, Pat Robertson, Dick Armey and Tom DeLay – enjoyed close personal relationships both with President George W. Bush and several of his close confidantes, such as John Bolton, Robert Bartley, William Bennett, Jeane Kirkpatrick and George Will (Walt and Mearsheimer, 2006: 6). Secondly, there is a wider coalition – involving Christian conservatives, main line Protestants,

Catholics, Jews, and others – successfully using its soft power to encourage successive US governments under both Bill Clinton and George W. Bush to pass various laws – the International Religious Freedom Act (1998), the Trafficking Victims Protection Act (2000), the Sudan Peace Act (2002), and the North Korea Human Rights Act (2004) – that collectively focus upon social welfare and human rights issues as a focal point of US foreign policy. We shall examine this issue in more detail in Chapter 8, dealing with religion and international relations in the context of the USA.

India provides a second example. It highlights attempts by religious actors – in this case, Hindu fundamentalists – to influence foreign policy through articulation of soft power in relation to India's chief regional rival, Pakistan, and the issue of the status of Kashmir. Like the USA, India is another established democracy with governmental decision makers open to a variety of non-state actors seeking to influence both domestic and foreign policies. In relation to (Hindu) India's long-running conflict with (Muslim) Pakistan over Kashmir, we can note the influence of Hindu actors in recent years on foreign policy, especially in successive governing coalitions from the mid-1990s to the mid-2000s when the government was dominated by the 'Hindu fundamentalist' Bharatiya Janata Party (BJP).

Achieving independence in 1947 from British colonial rule, India was ruled for the next 30 years by the secular Congress Party. During this time, India's foreign policy was characterized by moderation and pragmatism, with four main goals (Katalya, 2004):

- dialogue with Pakistan
- expansion of trade and investment relations with China
- strengthening ties with Russia, Japan, the European Union and the United States
- attempts to help construct the leading regional organization, the South Asian Association for Regional Cooperation.

The end of the Cold War in 1989 and the deepening of globalization coincided with the rise to power of the BJP. What impact was there on foreign policy and India's international relations more generally? MacFarquhar (2003) avers that the BJP's foreign policy shifted India's focus from moderation, pragmatism and non-alignment to a focus on 'Islamist terrorism' and the threat it posed to India. This implied a more abrasive stance in relation to Pakistan, said to be the sponsor of 'anti-Indian', Muslim terror groups who sought to wrest Muslim-majority Kashmir from Indian control. The BJP government also 'criticized nonalignment and advocated a more vigorous use of India's power to defend national interests from erosion at the hands of Pakistan and China. The BJP also favored the overt acquisition of nuclear weapons' (Federal Research Division of the Library of Congress, 1995).

Given the BJP-led attempt to reorientate India's foreign policy, it might be expected that when it became the dominant party in government from the mid-1990s it would try to use the opportunity to change emphatically India's foreign policy and international relations. Thirumalai claims that, following the BJP's ascent to power, 'the role of religion in India's foreign policy cannot be exaggerated. Hindus claim to be the most tolerant of all religious groups. But this claim has been continuously shattered, resulting in certain adverse reactions among various nations'. For Thirumalai (2001) this was because

> India has to come to grapple with the fact that Hinduism is more or less a single nation religion, whereas Islam, Christianity and Buddhism are religions practiced and encouraged in many and diverse nations. The view the practitioners of other religions hold regarding Hinduism and Hindus certainly influences the foreign policy of these nations towards India. India's insistence on its secular credentials may be appreciated in the academic circles all over the world, but India continues to be a Hindu-majority nation, a Hindu nation, in the minds of lay Christians, Muslims, and Buddhists all over the world. The foreign policy formulations of other nations do not fail to recognize that India is a Hindu nation, despite India's claims to the contrary.

For Marshall, perceptions of India as a Hindu nation were reinforced as a result of Hindu extremism and terrorism in the 1990s. Globally, however, especially since 9/11, there was much attention paid to Islamic extremism and terrorism but relatively little overt concern with what some commentators saw as violent trends in Hindu extremism, supported by 'allies in the Indian government, which until mid-2004 was led by the BJP' (Marshall, 2004). Instead, a political focus of Hindu nationalism was given attention. Bidwai suggests that 'if the ideologues of India's Hindu-supremacist Bharatiya Janata Party and key policy-makers in the coalition government it leads in New Delhi had their way, they would bring into being just such an alliance or "Axis of Virtue" against "global terrorism"', involving the governments of India, USA, and Israel (Bidwai, 2003). India's then National Security Adviser Brajesh Mishra advanced the 'Axis of Virtue' proposal on 8 May 2003 in Washington. Mishra was addressing the American Jewish Committee (AJC) at an event where there were also many US Congressmen and women present. Mishra emphasized his desire to help fashion an 'alliance of free societies involved in combating' the scourge of terrorism. Apart from the fact that the USA, Israel and India were all 'advanced democracies', each 'had been a significant target of terrorism. They have to jointly face the same ugly face of modern-day terrorism'. The proposed 'Axis of Virtue' would seek to 'take on international terrorism in a holistic and focused manner . . . to ensure that the global campaign . . . is pursued to its logical conclusion, and does not run out of steam because of other preoccupations. We owe this commitment to our future generations' (Mishra, quoted in Embassy of India, 2003). A month later, also in Washington, Deputy Prime Minister Lal Krishna Advani spoke in glowing terms about the proposal. He stressed 'similarities' between India and the USA, calling them 'natural democracies'. He praised the relationship 'developing between our two countries [that is, India and the USA], which is powerfully reflected' in President Bush's latest National Security Strategy document. Obliquely referring to Pakistan, he added, 'it is not an alliance of convenience. It is a principled relationship' (Advani, quoted in Bidwai, 2003). According to Bidwai, 'The BJP's ideology admires people like [the then Israeli prime minister, Ariel] Sharon for their machismo and ferocious jingoism. It sees Hindus and Jews (plus Christians) as "strategic allies" against Islam and Confucianism. Absurd and unethical as it is, this "clash-of-civilisations" idea has many takers on India's Hindu Right'. Overall, according to Bidwai (2003), there were three main reasons why the BJP wished to move India closer to Israel and its ideology of Zionism:

■ a wish to build closer relations with Israel's main ally, the USA, and thus try to isolate Pakistan;
■ shared 'Islamophobia' and anti-Arabism;
■ shared commitment to an aggressive and dynamic nationalism.

In conclusion, the soft power of Hindu fundamentalism was reflected both in the political ideology of the BJP and in a shift in India's foreign policy in the mid-1990s from moderation, pragmatism and non-alignment to a concern with 'Islamic terrorism' and 'clash of civilizations' that led to a change in foreign policy to build closer alliances with the United States and Israel.

A third example of the influence of religious actors in relation to foreign policy is the case of Saudi Arabia. For decades Saudi foreign policy has been based on ostensibly religious considerations. The Muslim country's government was fervently and consistently opposed both to Jewish Israel and the atheist Soviet Union, while also promoting Islam in various ways around the world. We can see the hand of hard power in operation here: following the onset of oil prosperity in the 1970s, the government donated large sums of money – millions of US dollars annually – to support the spread of Islam in various ways, including the building of mosques and the printing and distribution of numerous copies of the Quran. In addition, Saudi Arabia serves as the chief patron of the Muslim duty to make a pilgrimage to Mecca, expanding arrangements to house and transport the millions of pilgrims who visit Mecca from all over the world. Saudi contributions also played a major role in the World Muslim League, a religious-propagation agency founded in 1962 with headquarters in Mecca. Finally, Saudi Arabia is also highly influential in the Organization of the Islamic Conference (OIC), a multinational grouping of Muslim countries that periodically organizes summit conferences of government leaders.

We can see the influence of religious soft power in Saudi Arabia's foreign policy, notably a purist strand of Islam, known as Wahhabiya. Its influence is reflected in the fact that the country is run as a theocracy, under the aegis of the king. *Shariah* (Muslim) law is the law of the land and Islamists have access to the levers of power. At the same time, Saudi Arabia's foreign policy has not only reflected Islam's socio-political dominance: like every other state, Saudi Arabia has important security goals unconnected to religious objectives. As evidenced by the fear of invasion by Iraq at the time of the first Persian Gulf War in 1990–91 when Iraq invaded Kuwait and seemingly threatened Saudi Arabia, the kingdom's leaders recognize that the country's security is best protected by its alliance with the USA. As a result, Saudi Arabia seeks to balance both religious and secular security goals in its foreign policy. To avoid what might have been unacceptable levels of conflict with the USA, the ruler of Saudi Arabia, King Abdullah, sought to block the support of his rival, Prince Nayef, for al-Qaeda and other radical Islamist organizations. Fear of offending Washington also prevented a Saudi/OIC stand against US sanctions on Iran for its alleged attempt to acquire nuclear weapons and against Pakistan for its, until now, development of the sole nuclear capacity in the Muslim world. In addition, once Washington began to question Saudi Arabia's strategic loyalty on the basis of its responses to 9/11, US attacks on the regime's anti-democratic practices and policies and cultural differences between the two countries suddenly became both apparent and relevant to their relationship. Overall, the case of Saudi Arabia shows that although religious actors, including Prince Nayef, seek to influence foreign policy, albeit in competition with others such as the King, their influence is not guaranteed to be the most significant.

The Islamic Republic of Iran is another example of a government whose foreign policies are influenced by religious issues and actors. Like Saudi Arabia, Iran is a theocracy strongly influenced by Islam (in Iran's case, Shia Islam, contrasted with the rival Sunni articulation, religiously dominant in Saudi Arabia). Few nations today have so clearly articulated as post-revolution Iran an official religion-based ideology and view of the state as an instrument of that ideology.

But Iran's foreign policies and activities are characterized not only by a clearly religious dimension, but also by a discrepancy between the country's theocratic ideology and policies dictated by its secular security interests. Overall propagation of (Shia) Islam and advancing the cause of other Muslim peoples are aspects of Tehran's foreign policy activity that rise and fall depending on the views of the government of the day and the influence on policy-making of key religious personnel (Afrasiabi and Maleki, 2003).

According to Sarioghalam, 'Iran's foreign policy is shaped, not mainly by international forces, but by a series of intense post-revolutionary debates inside Iran regarding religion, ideology, and the necessity of engagement with the West and specifically the United States' (Sarioghalam, 2001: 1). When the material interests of the state have conflicted with commitments to 'Islamic solidarity', Tehran has usually given preference to secular security and economic considerations. Indeed, Iran often uses religion to pursue material state interests as a way of contending with neighbouring regimes or trying to force changes in their policies. For example, it promotes Islamic radicals and anti-regime movements when official relations with a Muslim country are poor, such as with Uzbekistan or Azerbaijan, but does not work to undermine secular Muslim regimes such as Turkmenistan if that regime's relations with Tehran are good.

Kemp (2005) notes a particular context where Iran's religious soft power is influential – in relation to its neighbour, Iraq. Iran is 90 per cent Shi'ite and Iraq is between 60 and 65 per cent Shi'ite, while about one-third of Iraqis are Sunnis. These factors have facilitated the ability of Iran to achieve considerable power and influence in Iraq since the fall of Saddam Hussein in March 2003. During 2003–06, Iran actively supported the position of the United States in supporting elections in Iraq. The main reason was that by the use of its cultural and religious soft power Iran had a practical way to try to facilitate the political dominance of Iraq's Shi'ite majority and, as a result, the government hoped to achieve an influential position in relation to the country's political future. The post-2003 position contrasts with the approach Iran adopted in the immediate aftermath of the 1979 revolution when the government focused efforts on hard-power strategies, for example, seeking to export the revolution 'through the funding of Shiite resistance groups'. Now, however, 'current circumstances encourage Iran to use soft power to help create some sort of Islamic government in Iraq' (Kemp, 2005: 6).

Overall, Iran is likely to continue to promote democratic structures and processes in Iraq, as a strategy to help consolidate a strong Shi'ite voice in Iraq's government. On the one hand, Iran is likely to seek to continue to use its soft power as a key short- and medium-term means to try to facilitate its main objectives in Iraq: political stability and an accretion of Iran's influence.

On the other hand, Iran's involvement in Iraq is also part of a long-term strategy that involves exercise of both soft and hard power. Since 2003 Iran has opted for intervention through primarily soft power and religious ties, but it could choose to be a more significant and active (and violent) player should its strategic interests be challenged. 'Iran's capacity, capability, and will to influence events in Iraq are high in terms of both hard power and soft power' (Kemp, 2005: 7).

Conclusion

In terms of state-related religious power, our examples – the USA, India, Saudi Arabia and Iran – collectively underline 'that religion's greatest influence on the international system is through its significant influence on domestic politics. It is a motivating force that guides many policy makers' (Fox and Sandler, 2004: 168). To understand and account for the influence of religious actors on foreign policy in relation to the USA, India, Saudi Arabia and Iran, we saw that their wielding of soft power is the best – actually, the *only* way – to influence foreign policy. We also learnt that while it is obviously important for religious actors directly to get the ear of government through various available mechanisms, both formal and informal, in order to have a chance of their preferred policies being put into effect, there are also additional means, including: trying to mould public opinion through the media, demonstrations, or via think tanks, that might be used. In sum, religious actors may try to influence outcomes in international relations by encouraging states to adopt foreign policies that they believe are most in tune with their religious values and goals. We shall examine this issue further in later chapters.

We also saw that there is another category of religious actors, non-state religious actors, who attempt to influence international relations through a focus on transnational civil society. Transnational religious networks have received growing attention since the end of the Cold War in 1989, but the ability of such actors to influence outcomes in international relations is variable. The influence on international relations of transnational religious actors forms the focus of Chapter 5.

In sum, we saw in this chapter that both state-related and non-state religious actors can be of significance for outcomes in international relations. Overall, four main points were made in the chapter:

- State foreign policies can be motivated or significantly influenced by religious actors.
- Domestic religious actors can cross state borders and become internationally significant.

- These transnational religious phenomena use various strategies to try to achieve their goals.
- Religious norms and values can affect international relations in various ways.

Notes

1 As we shall see below, there are various forms of power, notably 'hard' (for example, military and economic influence) and 'soft' power (Nye, 1990, 2004a).

2 Islamism relates to religious faith, principles, or the general cause of Islam, and can take both 'moderate' and 'extremist' forms.

3 I use the term 'transnational civil society' rather than 'global civil society' as the latter term implies a universal reach that may be lacking in such networks.

Questions

1 Why did religion diminish in importance in international relations from the eighteenth century?

2 What are non-state religious actors and how do they try to influenc outcomes in international relations?

3 Does globalization facilitate the development of transnational religious actors? If so, how?

4 What is 'soft power' and how does it influence religious actors' behaviour in international relations?

5 Do religious actors encourage governments to adopt policies they prefer in the USA, India, Saudi Arabia, and Iran? If so, what tactics do they use?

Bibliography

Adamson, F. (2002) 'International democracy assistance in Uzbekistan and Kyrgyzstan: building civil society from the outside?', in S. Mendelson and J. Glenn (eds) *The Power and Limits of NGOs: A Critical Look at Building Democracy in Eastern Europe and Eurasia*, New York: Columbia University Press, pp. 177–206.

Afrasiabi, K. and Maleki, A. (2003) 'Iran's foreign policy after September 11', *The Brown Journal of World Affairs*, 9(2), pp. 255–65. Available at: http://www.watsoninstitute.org/bjwa/archive/9.2/Iran/Afrasiabi.pdf Accessed 6 January 2006.

Anheier, H. and Themudo, N. (2002) 'Organisational forms of global civil society: implications of going global', in M. Glasius, M. Kaldor and H. Anheier (eds), *Global Civil Society 2002*, Oxford: Oxford University Press, pp. 191–216.

Appleby, R. Scott (2006) 'Building sustainable peace: the roles of local and transnational religious actors'. Paper presented at the conference on 'The New Religious Pluralism in World Politics', Berkley Center for Religion, Peace and World Affairs, Georgetown University, 16–17 March.

Attina, A. (1989) 'The study of international relations in Italy', in H. Dyer and L. Mangasarian (eds), *The Study of International Relations: The State of the Art*, Basingstoke: Macmillan, pp. 344–57.

Banchoff, T. (2005) 'Thematic Paper, August 5, 2005', prepared as background material for 'Conference on The New Religious Pluralism in World Politics', 16–17 March 2006, Berkley Center for Religion, Peace and World Affairs, Georgetown University. Available at: http://siteresources.worldbank.org/DEVDIALOGUE/Resources/GeorgeTown.doc Accessed 7 April 2006.

Barber, B. (1992) 'Jihad vs. McWorld', *The Atlantic Monthly*, March, pp. 53–63.

Berger, P. (1999) (ed.) *The Desecularization of the World: Resurgent Religion and World Politics*, Grand Rapids/Washington, DC: William B. Eerdmans/Ethics and Public Policy Center.

Bidwai, P. (2003) 'Critical moment for India', *Frontline*, 20(13), 21 June. Available at: http://www.tni.org/archives/bidwai/critical.htm Accessed 6 September 2005.

Brown, C., with Ainley, K. (2005) *Understanding International Relations*, 3rd edn, Basingstoke: Palgrave Macmillan.

Bruce, S. (2002) *God Is Dead: Secularization in the West*, Oxford: Blackwell.

Bull, H. (1977) *The Anarchical Society*, London: Macmillan.

Burchill, S. (2005) 'Liberalism', in S. Burchill et al., *Theories of International Relations*, 3rd edn, Basingstoke: Palgrave Macmillan.

Buzan, B. (2004) *From International to World Society?: English School Theory and the Social Structure of Globalisation*, Cambridge: Cambridge University Press.

Casanova, J. (1994) *Public Religions in the Modern World*, Chicago and London: University of Chicago Press.

Casanova, J. (2005) 'Catholic and Muslim politics in comparative perspective', *Taiwan Journal of Democracy*, 1(2), pp. 89–108.

Dolan, C. (2005) *In War We Trust: The Bush Doctrine and the Pursuit of Just War*, Aldershot: Ashgate.

Embassy of India (2003) 'Address by Shri Brajesh Mishra, National Security Advisor of India at the American Jewish Committee Annual Dinner', 8 May 2003. Available at: http://www.indianembassy.org/indusrel/2003/nsa_ajc_may_8_03.htm Accessed 6 September 2005.

Federal Research Division of the Library of Congress (1995) 'India: the role of political and interest groups'. Country Studies Series. Available at: http://www.country-data.com/cgi-bin/query/r-6130.html Accessed 9 January 2005.

Fox, J. and Sandler, S. (2004) *Bringing Religion into International Relations*, Basingstoke: Palgrave Macmillan.

Frankel, J. (1963) *The Making of Foreign Policy*, London: Oxford University Press.

Gagnon, V.-P. (2002) 'International NGOs in Bosnia-Herzegovina: attempting to build civil society', in S. Mendelson and J. Glenn (eds) *The Power and Limits of NGOs: A Critical Look at Building Democracy in Eastern Europe and Eurasia*, New York: Columbia University Press, pp. 207–31.

Glasius, M., Kaldor, M. and Anheier, H. (eds) (2006) *Global Civil Society 2005/6*, London, Thousand Oaks, New Delhi: Sage.

Halper, S. and Clarke, J. (2004) *America alone: The Neo-Conservatives and the Global Order*, Cambridge: Cambridge University Press.

Haynes, J. (2001) *Democracy in the Developing World*, Cambridge: Polity.

Held, D. (1999) 'The transformation of political community: rethinking democracy in the context of globalization', in I. Shapiro and C. Hacker-Cordón (eds), *Democracy's Edges*, Cambridge: Polity, pp. 84–111.

Hudson, M. (2005) 'The United States in the Middle East', in L. Fawcett (ed.), *International Relations of the Middle East*, Oxford: Oxford University Press, pp. 283–305.

Huntington, S. (1993) 'The clash of civilizations?', *Foreign Affairs*, 72(3), pp. 22–49.

Huntington, S. (1996) *The Clash of Civilizations*, New York: Simon and Schuster.

Hurrell, A. (2002) '"There are no rules" (George W. Bush): international order after September 11', *International Relations*, 16(2), pp. 185–204.

Jackson, R. and Owens, P. (2005) 'The evolution of international society', in J. Baylis and S. Smith (eds), *The Globalization of World Politics*, 3rd edn, Oxford: Oxford University Press, pp. 45–62.

Joseph, R. (1998) 'Africa, 1990–97: from abertura to closure', *Journal of Democracy*, 9(2), pp. 3–17.

Juergensmeyer, M. (1993) *The New Cold War? Religious Nationalism Confronts the Secular State*, Berkeley: University of California Press.

Juergensmeyer, M. (2000) *Terror in the Mind of God: The Global Rise of Religious Violence*, Berkeley: University of California Press.

Karl, T. (1995) 'The hybrid regimes of Central America', *Journal of Democracy*, 6(3), pp. 72–86.

Katyala, K. (2004) 'Issues and trends in Indian elections', *South Asian Journal*, 5 (July–September). Available at: http://www.southasianmedia.net/Magazine/Journal/previousissues5.htm Accessed 9 January 2006.

Keck, M. and Sikkink, K. (1998) 'Transnational advocacy networks in the movement society', in D. Meyer and S. Tarrow (eds), *The Social Movement Society*, Lanham, MD: Rowman and Littlefield, pp. 217–38.

Kemp, G. (2005) 'Iran and Iraq: the Shia connection, soft power, and the nuclear connection', Washington, DC: United States Institute of Peace.

Keohane, R. and Nye, J. (1977) *Power and Interdependence: World Politics in Transition*, New York: Little Brown.

Lipschutz, R. (1992) 'Reconstructing world politics: the emergence of global civil society', *Millennium*, 21(3), pp. 389–420.

MacFarquhar, L. (2003) 'Letter from India: the strongman', *The New Yorker*, 26 May, pp. 50–57.

Marshall, P. (2004) 'Hinduism and terror', *First Things: A Monthly Journal of Religion and Public Life*, June 1. Available at: http://www.freedomhouse.org/religion/country/india/Hinduism%20and%20Terror.htm Accessed 1 September 2005.

Marty, M. and Appleby, R. Scott (1993) 'Introduction' in Marty and Scott Appleby (eds), *Fundamentalism and the State: Remaking Polities, Economies, and Militance*, Chicago: University of Chicago Press, pp. 1–9,

Murden, S. (2005) 'Culture in world affairs', in J. Baylis and S. Smith (eds), *The Globalization of World Politics*, 3rd edn, Oxford: Oxford University Press, pp. 45–62.

Norris, P. and Inglehart, R. (2004) *Sacred and Secular: Religion and Politics Worldwide*, Cambridge: Cambridge University Press.

Nye, J. (1990) *Bound to Lead: The Changing Nature of American Power*, New York: Basic Books.

Nye, J. (2004a) *Soft Power: The Means to Success in World Politics*, Washington, DC: Public Affairs.

Nye, J. (2004b) 'Edited transcript, 04/13/04 Carnegie Council Books for Breakfast' (Nye discussing *Soft Power: The Means to Success in World Politics* with Joanne Myers). Available at: http://www.carnegiecouncil.org/viewMedia. php/prmTemplateID/8/prmID/4466 Accessed 10 April 2006.

Nye, R. (2004c) 'The benefits of soft power', *Harvard Business School Working Knowledge*, 2 August. Available at: http://hbswk.hbs.edu/item. jhtml?id=4290&t=globalization Accessed 10 April 2006.

Nye, J. (2005) 'Think Again: Soft Power'. Yale Global Online. Available at: http://yaleglobal.yale.edu/display.article?id=7059 Accessed 5 May 2006.

Petito, F. and Hatzopoulos, P. (2003) *Religion in International Relations: The Return from Exile*, New York: Palgrave.

Philpott, D. (2002) 'The challenge of September 11 to secularism in international relations', *World Politics* 55 (October), pp. 66–95.

Rudolph, S. and Piscatori, J. (eds) (1997) *Transnational Religion and Fading States*, Boulder, CO: Westview.

Sahliyeh, E. (1990) 'Religious resurgence and political modernization', in E. Sahliyeh (ed.), *Religious Resurgence and Politics in the Contemporary World*, Albany: State University of New York Press, pp. 1–16.

Sarioghalam, M. (2001) 'Iran's Foreign Policy and US–Iranian Relations. A summary of remarks by Dr. Mahmood Sarioghalam, National university of Iran, at the Middle East Institute, February 5, 2001'. Available at: http://209.196.144.55/html/b-sarioghalam.html Accessed 6 January 2006.

Saurin, J. (1995) 'The end of international relations?', in J. Macmillan and A. Linklater (eds), *Boundaries in Question: New Directions in International Relations*, London: Pinter, pp. 244–61.

Stark, R. and Fink, R. (2000) *Acts of Faith: Explaining the Human Side of Religion*, Berkeley: University of California Press.

Telhami, S. (2004) 'Between faith and ethics', in J. B. Hehir, M. Walzer, L. Richardson, S. Telhami, C. Krauthammer and J. Lindsay, *Liberty and Power: A Dialogue on Religion and U.S. Foreign Policy in an Unjust World*, Washington, DC: Brookings Institution Press, pp. 71–84.

Thirumalai, M. S. (2001) 'Language and culture in India's foreign policy – Part 1', *Language in India: Strength for Today and Bright Hope for Tomorrow*, 1(3) (May). Available at: http://www.languageinindia.com/ may2001/foreign.html Accessed 31 August 2005.

Thomas, S. (2005) *The Global Transformation of Religion and the Transformation of International Relations: The Struggle for the Soul of the Twenty-First Century*, New York/Basingstoke: Palgrave Macmillan.

Voll, J. (2006) 'Trans-state Muslim movements in an era of soft power'. Paper presented at the conference on 'The New Religious Pluralism in World Politics', Berkley Center for Religion, Peace and World Affairs, Georgetown University, 16–17 March.

Walt, S. and Mearsheimer, J. (2006) 'The Israeli lobby and U.S. foreign policy', *The London Review of Books*, 28(6), 23 March. Available: at www.lrb.co.uk Accessed 6 April 2006.

Webber, M. and Smith, M. (eds) (2002) *Foreign Policy in a Transformed World*, Harlow: Pearson Education.

Further reading

P. Berger (ed.), *The Desecularization of the World: Resurgent Religion and World Politics*, Ethics and Public Policy Center, 1999. This volume challenges the belief that the world is increasingly secular, showing that while modernization does have secularizing effects, it also provokes a reaction that more often strengthens religion.

S. Huntington, *The Clash of Civilizations*, Simon and Schuster, 1996. Huntington's articulation of his controversial thesis – that the world is poised to enter an era of 'civilizational clashes' between Islam and Christianity – has been much debated, especially since 9/11.

M. Juergensmeyer, *The New Cold War? Religious Nationalism Confronts the Secular State*, University of California Press, 1993. Examining similar ground to that of Huntington, Juergensmeyer focuses upon the extent to which religious ideologies have replaced secular ones as a key source of international conflict.

M. Juergensmeyer, *Terror in the Mind of God: The Global Rise of Religious Violence*, University of California Press, 2003. This book not only documents the global rise of religious terrorism but also seeks to understand the 'odd attraction of religion and violence'. Juergensmeyer bases his study on scholarly sources, media accounts and personal interviews with convicted terrorists.

P. Norris and R. Ingelhart, *Sacred and Secular: Religion and Politics Worldwide*, Cambridge University Press, 2004. This book develops a theory of secularization and existential security and compares it against survey evidence from almost 80 societies worldwide.

J. Nye, *Bound to Lead: The Changing Nature of American Power*, Basic Books, 1990. Nye's book is a blend of policy analysis and academic theory. He first explores the very concepts of power and decline before analysing the position of the USA relative to major competitors.

J. Nye, *Soft Power: The Means to Success in World Politics*, Public Affairs, 2004. Nye analyses the shortcomings of unilateralism and reliance solely on military power in confronting the threat posed by Islamic extremists. He contends that post-9/11, US foreign policy goals will best be delivered through a combination of 'hard' and 'soft' power.

S. Thomas, *The Global Resurgence of Religion and the Transformation of International Relations: The Struggle for the Soul of the Twenty-First Century*, Palgrave Macmillan, 2005. According to Thomas, the current global resurgence of religion is more wide-ranging than a clash of civilizations driven by religious extremism, terrorism, or fundamentalism. It also represents a near-global cultural and religious shift that challenges our interpretation of the modern world, as a variety of social and religious groups struggle to find alternative paths to modernity. This book examines what this means for the key concepts and theories of international relations – international conflict and cooperation, diplomacy, the promotion of civil society, democracy, nation-building, and economic development – and how it is influencing them.

PART TWO

Religion and international relations: contemporary issues

CHAPTER 3

Religion and globalization

T his chapter focuses on the relationship between religion and globalization. Its main purpose is to provide an overview of their association and how it impacts more generally on international relations. In the first section we examine the concept of globalization, identifying and discussing key aspects. In the second section, we consider how globalization affects religion and religious values. The third section assesses specific aspects of the relationship between religion and globalization, highlighting challenges and opportunities. It focuses on ideas, experiences, practices and two sets of issues that engage many religious actors at the global level: social development and human rights, and conflict and conflict resolution. In sum, the chapter seeks to:

- assess how globalization affects religious actors' involvement in international relations;
- understand the reactions of religions and religious believers to globalization.

What is globalization?

The first task is to understand what globalization *is*. There are numerous definitions of globalization. Many focus on the idea that globalization is a continuing means by which the world is more and more characterized by common activity, emphasizing in particular how many highly important aspects of life – including wars, crime, trade and culture – are becoming increasingly globally interrelated. This implies that globalization is also a matter of a change in consciousness, with people from various spheres, including business, religion, sport, politics and many other activities, thinking and acting in the context of what many would regard as an increasingly 'globalized' world. One result is that 'territoriality' – a term signifying a close connection or limitation with reference to a particular geographic area or country – now has less significance than it once did. Thus globalization suggests greatly increased interdependence, involving both states and non-states: what happens in one part of the world affects others. Overall, then, globalization encompasses the idea that humankind is currently experiencing a 'historically unique *increase of scale* to a global interdependency among people and nations'. It is characterized by (1) rapid integration of the world economy, (2) innovations and growth in international electronic communications, and (3) increasing 'political and cultural awareness of the global interdependency of humanity' (Warburg, 2001).

Globalization controversies

Globalization is a topical, controversial and at times violent issue. For example, in recent years, concerned by the perceived socio-economic impact of transnational business corporations and more generally of the effects of an increasingly globalized capitalism, anti-globalization protesters have periodically fought police, especially at regular Group of Eight (G8) summits (Held and McGrew, 2002: 56–9).[1] In addition, the attacks on the World Trade Center in New York and the Pentagon in Washington on 11 September 2001 certainly had global ramifications, as they served to afford religion 'a high place on the agendas of those concerned with globalization. Yet, the issues and the ways of responding are far from clear' (Society for the Scientific Study of Religion, 2001).

Before turning to the explicit issue of religion's interaction with globalization, it will be useful to examine when globalization started and what its key aspects are.

When did globalization begin?

Many analysts point to the importance of the past two decades – that is, the post-Cold War period – for an understanding of the impact of globalization on current international relations (Baylis and Smith, 2005). Many would also acknowledge, however, that globalization has deep historical roots, accepting the idea that it began in Europe in the 1500s and encompassing three inter-related political, economic and technological processes (Clark, 1997).

Globalization in historical perspective

1. *Development of an international states system* from the sixteenth century stimulated by the geographical spread of European influence and subsequent colonization of the Americas, Asia and Africa. This extension of European political control and influence resulted in forms of government around the globe, whether presidential, monarchical or neo-Marxist, based on Western models.

2. *Growth and spread of a world capitalist economy* from the sixteenth century dividing the globe into economically 'developed' and 'underdeveloped' areas. This process served to internationalize production, produced a universal division of labour and led to huge increases in international economic interactions.

3. *Effects of technological and industrial revolutions* in the eighteenth, nineteenth and twentieth centuries. Also global in scope, these revolutions significantly influenced patterns of industrialization, communications and technological development around the world, facilitating the spread of the political and economic factors referred to in points (1) and (2).

While it is appropriate to perceive of globalization as a continuous, historically based, multifaceted process, it is important to note that there have been periods when it has been especially speedy. For example, its pace increased from around 1870 until the start of the First World War in 1914. This was partly because during those four decades, 'all parts of the world began to feel the impact of the international economy, and for the first time in history it was possible to have instant long-distance communication (telegraph, radio) between people' (Warburg, 2001). After the Second World War, the speed, density and international impact of globalization expanded again, as it did once more after the Cold War came to an end in 1989 (Clark, 2005). According to Keohane, the overall impact of these processes of globalization resulted in an end-state that he calls 'globalism'. For Keohane, globalism is 'a state of the world involving networks of interdependence at multicontinental distances, linked through flows of capital and goods, information and ideas, people and force, as well as environmentally and biologically relevant substances' (Keohane, 2002: 31). Thus *globalism* refers to the reality of being interconnected, while *globalization* denotes the speed at which these connections grow, or diminish. Overall, the concept of globalism 'seeks to . . .

understand all the inter-connections of the modern world – and to high-light patterns that underlie (and explain) them' (Nye, 2002).

Technological, political, economic and cultural globalization

It is clear that globalization is a wide-ranging phenomenon, albeit often perceived primarily in economic terms. But this is by no means the whole story. To understand important current interactions between religion and globalization, we need to take into account not only economic but also technological, political, and cultural aspects of globalization. Consider the following:

> The various definitions of globalization in social science all converge on the no-tion that, as a result of technological and social change, human activities across re-gions and continents are increasingly being linked together (Keohane, 2002: 31).

> Spatial reorganisation of production, the interpenetration of industries across borders, the spread of financial markets, the diffusion of identical consumer goods to distant countries, massive transfers of population within the South as well as from the South and the East to the West, resultant conflicts between im-migrant and established communities in formerly tight-knit neighbourhoods, an emerging worldwide preference for democracy. A rubric for varied phenomena, the concept of globalisation interrelates multiple levels of analysis (Mittelman, 1994: 429).

> The term 'globalization' has come to be emotionally charged in public discourse. For some, it implies the promise of an international civil society, conducive to a new era of peace and democratization. For others, it implies the threat of an American economic and political hegemony, with its cultural consequence being a homogenized world resembling a sort of metastasized Disneyland (charmingly called a 'cultural Chernobyl' by a French government official) (Berger, 2002: 1).

These quotations collectively emphasize that globalization is a contro-versial and multifaceted process underpinned by significant intensification of global interconnectedness. They point to the idea that globalization im-plies diminution of the significance of territorial boundaries and, theoreti-cally, state-dominated structures and processes. They also emphasize that there are different dimensions to globalization that can usefully be broken down for analytical purposes into technological, political, economic and cultural aspects. Next we examine these four aspects of globalization to help understand how they can encourage various religious actors into global involvement in relation to a number of issues, including social development and human rights, as well as conflict and conflict resolution.

Technological globalization

Woods on technological globalization

The technological revolution is a [key] aspect of globalisation, describing the effect of new electronic communication which permits firms and other actors to operate globally with much less regard for location, distance, and border (Woods, 2001: 290).

There is a parallel between the global conditions of a century or more ago and those prevailing now: both periods were characterized by extensive and intensive technological, political, economic and cultural changes. But there is an important difference between the world of a hundred years ago and that of today: now there is an astonishing reduction in costs of global communications and transportation and easy access to them for millions of people, especially in the richer, more developed countries. Two specific aspects of technological globalization – the internet and electronic communications revolutions – have transformed beyond recognition the ability of individuals, groups, communities, organizations and governments to communicate, easily and speedily, with each other (Smith, 2002: 177). In 2004, there were more than 850 million internet users worldwide (http://www.geohive.com/charts/charts.php?xml=ec_inet&xsl=ec_inet_top1), implying that around 15 per cent of the global population of approximately six billion people is linked in this way. The consequence is that 'new IT-driven media such as email, the Web and chat rooms present a wide range of opportunities due to their global reach. Technological change, information revolution, and global communications thus enhance the visibility of a variety of once unknown, marginal, illegal, unpopular and unorthodox groups' (Dartnell, 2001: 1).

The overall implication is that numerous national and transnational groups – religious and secular, legitimate and illegitimate – can and do use the circumstances offered by technological globalization to enhance the spread of their networks and to exchange ideas, information, personnel and financial assets. Various religious movements and organizations seek to benefit from technological globalization, with such actors enjoying ability to 'talk' directly to each other across international boundaries, frequently be-yond state control. For example, Protestant evangelization in Latin America seeks to benefit from the circumstances provided by technological globaliza-tion, linking mission efforts to new technologies and new market penetra-tions (Spickard, 2001). In addition, the ability of important transnational terrorist groups, such as al-Qaeda, to proselytize and organize around the world is directly linked to their capacity to profit from what has become a global communications network (Haynes, 2005b; Gunaratna, 2006).

Political globalization

According to Held and McGrew (2002), two fundamental transformations have shaped the constitution of contemporary political life. We have already noted the first of these: development of territorially based political commu-nities, that is, states, initially in Europe and then primarily via colonization to the rest of the world. The second development is more recent but poten-tially equally significant, explicitly linked to the impact of globalization. It is the emergence and development of non-territorial based political enti-ties that, while by no means replacing the first in overall importance, have resulted in a disjuncture in the formerly absolute connection between polit-ical power and geography.

Political globalization and intergovernmental organizations

There is an emerging system of multilayered global and regional governance, reflected in the growth of intergovernmental organizations (IGOs) at both regional and global levels. Whereas in the early years of the twentieth century there were less than 40, by its end there were about 250, a near seven-fold in-crease, supplying important global or regional collective goods (Willetts, 2001: 357). Only internationally recognized states can be members of IGOs. Reflect-ing the upsurge in globalization following the Second World War, most were founded after 1945, although some functional bodies were established earlier, for example, the International Telecommunications Union was established nearly a century earlier, in 1865. Several IGOs inaugurated after the Second World War – for example, the United Nations (UN), North Atlantic Treaty Or-ganization (NATO), EU, and the Organization of the Islamic Conference (OIC) – have multiple tasks, including security, welfare and human rights goals (Haynes, 2005a: 102).

Some developed states, including many in Europe and North America, belong to dozens or even hundreds of IGOs, implying myriad contexts whereby the latter can theoretically influence domestic policy-making and outcomes (Hague and Harrop, 2001: 49). For states, IGO membership implies trying to preserve their formal sovereignty while at the same time being committed to particular policy-making options because of their IGO commitments. The overall impact is to institutionalize an often complex process of political coordination involving not only states but also various non-states – including intergovernmental and transnational actors, both public and private – which work together in pursuit of collective goals via the implementation of global or transnational rules, aiming to manage and resolve cross-border problems. According to Held and McGrew, the IGO system 'is scarred by enormous inequalities of power, and remains a product of the inter-state system. But it has, nevertheless, created the infrastructure of a global polity and new arenas through which globalization itself is promoted, contested or regulated. It has also instigated new forms of multilateral, regional and transnational politics' (http://www.polity.co.uk/global/executiv.htm#Territorial).

As well as an internationalization of the state implied by the growth of numerous IGOs, there is also a remarkable transnationalization of political activity focused in the development of thousands of international non-governmental organizations (INGOs). From a few hundred in the early twentieth century, the number of INGOs has grown, especially over the past 30 years, to reach around 25,000 now (Willetts, 2001: 357; Anheier and The-mudo, 2002: 195). INGOs are cross-border bodies, such as Amnesty International, Greenpeace International and the Roman Catholic Church, whose members are individuals or private groups drawn from more than one country. The chief theoretical assumptions concerning INGOs are that: (1) states are not the only important cross-border actors in international politics, and (2) INGOs can be politically significant.

Some INGOs seek to change state policy more proactively in a variety of political areas. However, their influence is not assured but depends on two main factors: (1) how skilful they are in infiltrating national policy-making processes, and (2) the extent to which a targeted government is receptive to them. Their effectiveness may be augmented when groups of transnational actors link up – for example, in pursuit of political, religious, gender-orientated or developmental goals – to encourage popular pressure for domestic change. This can lead to the development of 'transnational citizen groups' (TCGs).

Partly a function of the global communications revolution, the chief consequence of TCGs is regional or global spread and interchange of ideas and information. To understand the social dynamics of TCGs, it is useful to perceive the international system as an agglomeration of various issue areas – for example, political, religious, environmental, human rights, gender and development concerns – organized under the rubric of 'social transnationalism'. This is facilitated by multiple linkages between individuals and groups interested in the same goals but separated by large physical distances. Cross-border exchanges of experiences and information and shift of funds not only facilitate development of TCG strategies but also can lead to national, regional and/or global campaigns (Haynes, 2005a: 105). However, whether the collection of TCGs constitutes the infrastructure of a transnational civil society remains questionable.

Finally, there has been an important change in the scope and content of international law. After the Second World War, public opinion moved decisively against the doctrine that international law only involved states. Henceforward, both single persons and groups became recognized as subjects of international law. It is now generally accepted, for example, that persons as individuals are subjects of international law on the basis of such documents as the Charters of the Nuremberg and Tokyo War Crimes Tribunals, the Universal Declaration of Human Rights (1948), the Covenant on Civil and Political Rights (1966), and the European Convention on Human Rights (1950). Opinion also moved at this time against the doctrine that international law is only, or even primarily, about political and strategic (that is, *state*) affairs. Instead, it was now perceived, international law was in fact concerned progressively with orchestrating and regulating economic, social and environmental matters.

Consequently, the traditional legal doctrine that the only true source of international law is the consent of states was fundamentally challenged after the Second World War. Today, a number of sources of international law jostle for recognition. These include the traditional sources such as international conventions or treaties that are recognized by states; international custom or practice which provides evidence of an accepted set of rules; and the underlying principles of law recognized by 'civilized nations'. They also include the 'will of the international community', expressed through the UN, most recently in relation to Iraq's alleged 'weapons of mass destruction', which can assume the 'status of law' or which can become the 'basis of international legal obligation' under certain circumstances. The last represents a break in principle with the requirement of individual state consent in the making of international rules and responsibilities.

In conclusion, as a result of globalization, states and their citizens have become progressively involved in and affected by extensive networks and layers of regional and global governance. The ramification is that they are subject to new sources of authority, that function above, below and alongside national governments. The characteristics of this contemporary political globalization pose a significant challenge to the traditional, Westphalian-orientated perception of political life, with states no longer the exclusive wielders of political authority. In conclusion, contemporary political globalization implies that neither political space nor political community are necessarily or exclusively territorially linked and, as a result, national governments are not the only political authorities in charge of their own well-being and that of their citizens. Note, however, that this does not imply that national governments and national sovereignty are being overtaken by the various agents of political globalization; many states still retain much power.

Economic globalization

How geographically extensive is economic globalization? Hirst and Thompson (1999) argue that economic globalization is not global but actually a 'triangular' phenomenon, principally involving three regions and countries: North America, Western Europe and Japan. The implication is that economic globalization affects economically marginal regions, such as sub-Saharan Africa and Central Asia to a much lesser degree. On the other hand, as Schulz et al. (2001) contend, the effects of economic globalization, especially extensive neo-liberal economic development programmes, have affected billions of people around the world, especially in economically marginal regions, where many countries have felt the full rigours of such policies and, in many cases, evince generally negative attitudes towards them and their socio-economic effects.

What is economic globalization?

Mittelman breaks down the concept of economic globalization into three main components: (1) 'the spatial reorganization of production', (2) 'the interpenetration of industries across borders', (3) and the worldwide 'spread of financial markets' (Mittelman, 1994: 429). This, in turn, has various – political and social, as well as economic – connotations for people around the world, such as recurrent fears over the stability of the multilateral trading order and the impact on jobs of the sales of national assets to foreigners consequent to privatizations of formerly state-owned assets.

The current phase of economic globalization was facilitated by the demise of the Soviet bloc. Whereas the USSR had developed, since the late 1940s, a parallel non-capitalist economic system, its demise favoured increased movement of capital, labour and goods across national boundaries while also encouraging increased international economic competition and cooperation. Economic changes were also reflected in transformation of production systems and labour markets, and a general weakening of the power of organized labour to pressurize governments to enforce labour standards, such as minimum wage legislation. There is much agreement, however, that the already weak economic position of many poor people worsened as a result of economic globalization, especially the impact of neo-liberal economic policies in numerous developing countries in the 1990s and early 2000s (Held and McGrew, 2002).

The International Monetary Fund (IMF) and the World Bank are key agents, centrally involved in disseminating a particular form of economic globalization that aims to stimulate globally beneficial economic and developmental outcomes. The IMF has three main aims: to institutionalize economic globalization, to ensure greater mobility of capital across borders, and to encourage states, especially in the developing world, to move towards balanced budgets. The overall purpose is, on the one hand, to provide the potential for general growth and prosperity and, on the other, to increase provision of social services for the poor. However, the IMF would also admit that while the *potential* benefits from economic globalization are clear, there is also the possibility for destabilizing risks in those countries unwilling or unable to benefit from what the Fund sees as the dynamic forces that characterize economic globalization, such as transnational corporations and their attendant investment power (Haynes, 2005c).

Structural adjustment programmes (SAPs) were the IMF's chosen vehicle to deliver beneficial economic and developmental outcomes; they were adopted in numerous developing countries, especially in the 1980s and 1990s. Critics contend, however, that far from encouraging and stimulating beneficial economic growth and developmental outcomes, a more common outcome was that SAPs led to reductions in welfare programmes that disadvantaged the poor (Haynes, 2001).

Both the IMF and its partner organization, the World Bank, acquired increased economic and developmental influence in numerous countries as a result of their sponsorship of SAPs. Their critics allege that the reform programmes typically failed to kick-start economic development, and recent research, including from the World Bank, backs this up. Research shows that: (1) poverty has actually grown in recent years, (2) most economic 'progress' has occurred in a small number of countries (some of them with large populations and unusual appeal for foreign investors), and (3) even in successful cases many people are actually no better off, and may actually be poorer, than they were previously (World Bank, 2003).

In short, there is a global economy, with individual economies increasingly interacting with others, which has the (unintended) effect of helping create even greater social differences and social polarization than before. This perception has not only helped generate secular political protest movements that in some cases were transnationally orientated but has also led to an increased involvement of numerous religious agents around the pursuit of what they regard as enhanced economic and developmental justice for the developing world.

Cultural globalization

For Seabrook (2004),

> Globalization is a declaration of war upon all other cultures ... Cultural, social and religious disruptions are inseparable spectral companions of economic globalization in the attempt of the leaders of the globalizing world to colonize the whole planet in their own image.

Radhakrishnan (2004. 1403) contends that in his view the 'major religions of the world are being used as purveyors of the globalisation agenda and this is often accompanied by an unprecedented flow of funds into the third world'. The consequences include:

> the transmogrification of traditional religions and belief systems; the beginnings of the disintegration of the traditional social fabrics and shared norms by consumerisms, cyber-culture, newfangled religions and changing work ethics and work rhythms; the fast spreading anomie forcing an ever increasing number of individuals to fall back upon the easily accessible pretentious religious banalities, and attributing to religion the creation and acceleration of extremist, fundamentalist and terrorist tendencies in the third world countries.

It is likely that both Seabrook and Radhakrishnan would regard 'cultural globalization' as a synonym for 'Americanization' or perhaps more generally 'Westernization'. In such views, cultural globalization is widely associated with global dissemination of identical consumer goods and associated dissemination of American-style consumer culture that result in erosion or destruction of particularistic cultures and values and their replacement by a drab and uniform Americanized culture of Disney, McDonald's, Coca-Cola,

Microsoft and Starbucks. Spread by predominantly US-based transnational corporations and media networks, Americanization is seen to subvert non-Western, local cultures by also encouraging people to buy American goods and services. Some developing countries – especially in Asia and the Muslim world – have sought to meet the perceived onslaught of Americanization by articulating defiantly anti-individualistic world-views: popularized via a focus on 'Asian values' and/or Islamism. Taken together – as they sometimes are (Huntington, 1996) – 'Asian values' and Islamism are said to represent a significant challenge to Western-style cultural globalization. Another interpretation, however, is to see such ripostes as a manifestation of a desire to protect indigenous cultures and local preferences in the face of an aggressively projected Americanized global culture that undermines deep-rooted communal values (Haynes, 2005a: 170–3).

Robertson and 'glocalization'

Cultural globalization involves movements of ideas, information, images and people, the main carriers of and transporters of ideas and information. Examples include the movement of religions or the diffusion of scientific knowledge (Nye, 2002). Many believe that globalization leads to a situation characterized by cultural homogenization, that is, where local cultures are destroyed by the intrusion of a universal global culture. On the other hand, despite such fears, 'localism' has not died in the current globalized age. Roland Robertson (1995) uses the term 'glocalization' (GLObal loCALIZATION) to describe what he sees as the globalized world's increasing *heterogeneity*, that is, increasingly pronounced cultural differences.

Cultural globalization was high on the international agenda as a result of the events of September 11, 2001 and the attacks on the World Trade Center and the Pentagon. Many people in the Middle East and parts of Asia saw them as a protest against Western (and particularly American) trade and military power (Juergensmeyer, 2005). But some also saw the attacks more generally as a protest against Western attempts to globalize its culture, that is, to impose a particular set of values and attitudes on the rest of the world. As a result, issues of cultural globalization are sometimes linked to human rights issues. Many people in the West would no doubt be unhappy at the ways that, for example in some Muslim countries, women are socially and religiously compelled to live their lives hidden from public view. On the other hand, many Muslims would regard Western ways as seeking aggressively to undermine the structures of society and family life, in particular undermining values of respect and obedience to family, especially male, authority. In addition, rightly or wrongly, 'Western culture' is seen to disparage sexuality and to degrade both family life and females. Moreover, what is especially offensive to many Muslims is the perception that Western, especially American, culture is being forced upon them via commercialism and various media, including advertising, films and television. In response, Muslims may look to religious vehicles to help them deflect or otherwise deal with this cultural onslaught, a pernicious influence judged to be a key contributor to the erosion of family life and, more generally, the key components of both culture and community. These concerns can lead to people responding in various, including extreme, ways. Standpoints can easily become polarized with, on the one hand, Muslim religious and community values and, on the other Western individualistic values, including equal rights for all individuals regardless of their gender.

In summary, the key points of the section are:

- Globalization is a historical phenomenon whose pace and impact increased during the twentieth century.

- Contemporary globalization is characterized by: *technological globalization* that enables various constituencies to build local, national, regional and global networks; development of international and transnational sources of *political globalization* that do not replace the state but instead provide new layers and networks of political action; *economic globalization* with perceived malign effects on the poor, especially in the developing world; and *cultural globalization* which some contend is based on 'American' or 'Western' individual values.

Globalization: challenges and opportunities for religion

Most international relations analysts would probably agree that globalization is an important phenomenon. But there is little agreement regarding precisely *how* globalization changes our understanding of international relations – beyond the general idea that the core of globalization implies increasing interdependence between states and peoples, with what happens in one part of the world affecting what happens elsewhere. Instead, there are numerous debates about globalization and its impact, and such exchanges are often polarized, sometimes rather simplistically conducted along the lines of 'Is globalization a "good" or a "bad" thing?' For example, in reference to the latter interpretation, some see the term 'globalization' as nothing more than a cover for a thoroughly malign – and comprehensive – Westernizing process. In this view, globalization is inherently undesirable, a process whereby Western – especially American – capitalism and culture seek to dominate the world. As a result, it is believed, the Western world is kept rich at the expense of the poverty of many non-Western parts of the world. This is possible because, many contend, Western interests determine trading terms, interest rates and dominance of highly mechanized production, via its control of important international institutions, such as the World Trade Organization (Held and McGrew, 2002).

An alternative view of globalization is to emphasize that it offers enhanced opportunities for international cooperation in relation to various issues, including social development and human rights, as well as conflict resolution and peacebuilding. Globalization is seen to enhance the chances of international cooperation to resolve a range of economic, developmental, social, political, environmental, gender, and human rights concerns and injustices. In particular, the end of the Cold War was seen to offer an unprecedented opportunity for collective efforts involving both states and non-state actors to deal with a range of global concerns. For many, progress would be enhanced by bottom-up contributions from local groups and grassroots organizations around the world, including various religious organizations and movements.

In sum, globalization in both views is a multifaceted process of change, universally affecting states, local communities, industrial companies and individuals. Religious organizations and movements are not exempted from its influence and, as a result, like other social agents, such religious entities participate in and are affected by globalization. Current academic discussions of religion and globalization – with important voices like Roland Robertson (1995), Peter Beyer (1994) and James Spickard (2001, 2003) – mainly concentrate on the trends towards cultural pluralism and how religious organizations respond to this development. Some react positively, by accepting or even endorsing pluralism, such as 'some Christian ecumenical movements or the Baha'is. Other groups emphasize the differences and confront the non-believers in an attempt to preserve their particular values from being eroded by globalization. So-called fundamentalist Christian, Muslim, and Jewish movements are well-known examples' (Warburg, 2001). In sum, there is growing awareness in international research of the importance of religion as a transnational actor in the context of globalization.

Overall, the relationship between religion and globalization is character-ized by tension between forces that lead on the one hand to *integration* in globalization and on the other hand to *resistance* to it. In this context 'inte-gration' refers to religious processes that both promote and follow from pro-cesses of globalization. The concept of 'resistance' implies the opposite trend: explicit or implicit criticism of and mobilization against some or all processes of global change manifested in globalization. Both integration and resistance can be seen in relation to religious resources that generally repre-sent various expressions of soft power. Several authors have noted religion's soft power in relation to contemporary international relations. For Ferguson (2003), it is important not to underestimate

> the power of ideology and religion – which certainly has proved more enduring than the power of the Red Army. Indeed, there are those who would say that, after Mikhail Gorbachev and Ronald Reagan, no one did more to bring down communism in Eastern Europe than John Paul II. Faith, then, is perhaps as im-portant a component of power as material resources.

Reychler on religion as a source of soft power

According to Reychler, the growing impact of religious discourses on interna-tional relations is a response to a 'world where many governments and interna-tional organizations are suffering from a legitimacy deficit. . . . Religion is a major source of soft power. It will, to a greater extent, be used or misused by religions and governmental organizations to pursue their interests. It is there-fore important to develop a more profound understanding of the basic as-sumption underlying the different religions and the ways in which people adhering to them see their interests. It would also be very useful to identify ele-ments of communality between the major religions' (Reychler, 1997).

Also emphasizing the idea that religious organizations and movements often enjoy more legitimacy than some governments and international organizations, Juergensmeyer contends that, in particular, 'radical reli-gious ideologies have become the vehicles for a variety of rebellions against authority that are linked with myriad social, cultural, and political grievances' (Juergensmeyer, 2005).

Overall, Ellis and ter Haar (2004: 2) highlight four, not necessarily discrete, areas that not only generally emphasize the significance of religion in the context of contemporary globalization but also point to the actual or potential soft power of religious organizations to influence outcomes in the ways they prefer. They are:

- Ideas
- Experiences
- Practices
- Organizations.

Ideas

Most religions traditionally comprise the ideas, beliefs and practices of a particular community. That is, religions have provided what Peter Berger (1969) calls a 'sacred canopy', enabling followers to make sense of their world. Beyer (2003) explains that there were once many individual and different societies around the world, each with its own set of practices, some of which today we would call religious. As a result, religious ideas can be seen as 'the major organizing principles for explaining the world and defining ethical life' (Kurtz, 1995: 3). Now, however, circumstances of globalization dramatically undermine the notion that all members of a society must necessarily hold the same ideas in relation to religion, because globalization encourages the idea that religion is a matter of individual choice. At the present time, many religions compete for individuals' attention and there is what is known as a 'global marketplace of religion' (Bruce, 2003). The consequence is that the spread of various, sometimes competing, religious ideas leads to a situation where the once relatively autonomous sacred canopy is increasingly regarded as an artefact of the past. This process may be met with resistance, 'countered by the revival of more localised practices in the form of religious fundamentalist and other protest movements' (Kurtz, 1995: 99).

Experiences

There is a dynamic and dialectic connection between globalization and religion. Globalization may lead individuals and groups to increased self-reflection, as a result of the experiences they encounter following two simultaneous developments. On the one hand, cultural, religious and social differences between people have sometimes become increasingly visible as a result of globalization. On the other hand, many people also experience direct or indirect pressure towards increased homogenization and 'free' religious competition. This creates a field of tension where the value of religious belonging as identity-forming becomes more important while at the same time it is rapidly changing. This is because globalization facilitates the transmission of both non-material factors – ideas, information and beliefs – as well as material ones. Many religious actors seek to use any available opportunities to disseminate their religious ideas in various ways. Secondly, what religions do within a country is affected by social, political and economic experiences, and these in turn may well be affected by globalization. As Berger notes, in some cases – for example, in relation to manifestations of Islamism (or 'Islamic fundamentalism') – this is a challenge that is seen to emanate from attempts to impose 'an emerging global culture, most of it of Western and indeed American provenance, penetrating the rest of the world on both elite and popular levels. The response from the target societies is then seen as occurring on a scale between acceptance and rejection, with in-between positions of coexistence and synthesis' (Berger, 2002: 1).

Practices

Religious ideas and traditions are often connected intimately to specific cultures, but this is not to imply that they are static. On the contrary, religious traditions are generally dynamic, changing as they encounter each other. As a result, there are no 'pure', unadulterated religious traditions preserved intact over long periods of time until now (Kurtz, 1995: 98). This implies that religious practices differ, even within the same religious traditions. Thus there may be various – associated but different – versions of the same religious tradition encompassing different groups, for example, dissimilar social groups and classes (Haynes, 1996). Put another way, the 'sacred canopy' has generally not been uniform and religious practices vary from place to place and culture to culture, even among those ostensibly following the same religious tradition. As with ideas and experiences, the impact of globalization is likely to be to make religious practice even more diverse.

Organizations

Turning to the relationship between religious organizations and globalization, we can note that ideas, experiences and practices – all affected by globalization – serve to encourage the former to adopt new or renewed agendas. This enables them to look beyond local or national contexts to regional or international environments in relation to various issues. While such expressions differ widely, we can identify two main areas of interest and engagement – encouraged by globalization – that collectively involve numerous religious organizations from many of the world religions: (1) social development and human rights, and (2) conflict and conflict resolution.

Social development and human rights

We saw above that images of globalization often focus on its economic and, by extension, social, character and ramifications. This includes the economic range and clout of transnational corporations and a perception that they are taking economic power from governments, and thus from citizens and their efforts to control their own fates (Haynes, 2005a). We also noted widely perceived downsides to economic globalization, especially the apparent mass impoverishment of already poor people, particularly in the developing world. These circumstances have led to a focus from numerous religious organizations seeking to ameliorate social and human rights imbalances perceived to be exacerbated by economic globalization. Acting alone or together, there is a collective concern with social, developmental and human rights dimensions of the impact of economic globalization. This is manifested in various ways, including: new religious fundamentalisms, support for anti-globalization activities, such as anti-World Trade Organization protests and North/South economic justice efforts (Spickard, 2001). Collectively, these reactions underline that religious responses to globalization now often include a stress on social interests that go way beyond the confines of what might be called 'church life'.

Alkire (2006) emphasizes that, in relation to social development and human rights, ideas of desirable outcomes expressed by religious organizations and more generally by faith perspectives may well differ significantly from those advanced by non-religious economic development models, for example, those advanced by the IMF or the World Bank. This is because from a general religious perspective, development programmes and policies appear to be 'one-eyed giants' which 'analyse, prescribe and act *as if* man could live by bread alone, *as if* human destiny could be stripped to its material dimensions alone' (Goulet, 1980, quoted in Alkire, 2006).

We can also note rather similar objections to non-religious developmental programmes and policies emanating from individual religious perspectives. For example, writing from an Islamic viewpoint, Seyyed Hussein Nasr focuses on the link between modernization and development, and emphasizes how important it is for them to be concerned with religion. For him, development without such a concern will fatally distract Muslims from what is their true – that is, religious – nature and, as a result, seriously undermine their chances of living appropriately (Nasr, 1975). Secondly, recent Roman Catholic social teachings, especially those since the encyclical of Pope Paul VI *Populorum Progressio*, have consistently articulated what might be called a faith-based view of development (1967; http://www.vatican.va/holy_father/paul_vi/encyclicals/documents/hf_p-vi_enc_26031967_populorum_en.html). This emphasizes the contributions of 'spiritual disciplines and of ethical action to a person's "vocation to human fulfillment", addressed alongside contributions made by markets, public policy, and poverty reduction' (Alkire, 2006). Another articulation of concern about the goals and purpose of human development from a Catholic perspective is to found in liberation theologies. Their emphasis is to criticize structural injustice through a demand for increased religious engagement in political and economic institutions as the only realistic way of ensuring just development processes and outcomes. A Peruvian priest, Gustavo Gutierrez, famously articulated liberation theology in his *A Theology of Liberation: History, Politics and Salvation* (1973). Representatives of other religious faiths, including Judaism and Buddhism, have also advanced similar kinds of development interpretations to that of Gutierrez, underlining that religious faiths tend to work from similar positions in relation to some social development issues. In addition, distinct liberation theologies have also been articulated by other major faiths. For example, various popular books have also explicated a similar people-centred development perspective, such as, Bernardo Kliksberg's *Social Justice: A Jewish Perspective* (2003) and Sivaraksa and Ginsburg's *Seeds of Peace* (1992), from a Buddhist perspective.

In addition to that emanating from specific faiths, there are also recent examples of interfaith religious involvement in social development issues. A key example in this regard is the World Faiths Development Dialogue (WFDD), an initiative that sought to map areas of convergence among religious faiths' visions of development agendas, with a focus on: relationships of service and solidarity, harmony with the earth, and the vital but limited contribution of material progress (World Faiths Development Dialogue, 1999).

In a speech delivered in June 2005, a senior World Bank figure, Katherine Marshall, emphasized that the Bank did not believe 'that religion and socio-economic development belong to different spheres and are best cast in separate roles – even separate dramas'. Her observation was based on recognition that around the world many religious organizations and development agencies share similar concerns: how to improve (1) the lot of materially poor people, (2) the societal position of those suffering from social exclusion, and (3) unfulfilled human potential in the context of glaring developmental polarization within and between countries, partly as a result of the impact of globalization (Marshall, 2005). Marshall's speech emphasized that while religion has often in the past been understood by the Bank as 'otherworldly' and 'world-denying', it is now accepted that religion can significantly contribute to developmental goals in the developing world, not least because issues of right and wrong and social and economic justice are central to the teachings of all the world religions (that is, Buddhism, Christianity, Hinduism, Islam and Judaism).

Reflecting such concerns, periodic 'leaders' meetings' have been convened to pursue avenues to address these issues. In their book, *Millennium Challenges for Development and Faith Institutions* (2003), Marshall and March report on a meeting in Canterbury, England in October 2002, hosted by Jim Wolfensohn and George Carey. The purpose of the meeting was to bring together an important group of leaders 'from the world's faith communities, key development organisations, and from the worlds of entertainment, philanthropy and the private sector'. Linked to the Millennium Development Goals (MDGs) announced in 2000, common themes included poverty, HIV/AIDS, gender, conflict, and social justice. Another common theme was the dualistic impact of globalization, with its differential impact on rich and poor countries. Participants accepted that poverty, HIV/AIDS, conflict, gender concerns, international trade and global politics explicitly link all the world's countries and peoples, rich and poor, into a global community. This sense of oneness highlighted the urgency of developing shared responsibility and partnership to deal with collective problems facing humanity. The overall conclusion was that more needed to be done to move from expressions of solidarity in the face of shared problems to the realization of practical plans involving collaboration between the worlds of faith, and development in confronting major development issues (Marshall and March, 2003).

The Millennium Development Goals (MDGs)

Eight MDGs were announced in 2000:

- Eradicate extreme poverty and hunger
- Achieve universal primary education

(Continued)

- Promote gender equality and empower women

- Reduce child mortality

- Improve maternal health

- Combat HIV/AIDS, malaria, and other diseases

- Ensure environmental sustainability

- Develop a global partnership for development (http://www.development goals.org/)

Shared concern with poverty and social development encourages closer links between faith-based organizations and development agencies, such as the World Bank. Cognisant of the polarizing impact of economic globalization, this common ground links them to what might be an emerging global consensus underpinning the pursuit of the MDGs.

In conclusion, the international community recently set itself the challenge of a renewed onslaught on poverty and related dimensions of human deprivation in the developing world. This concern was reflected in the announcement of the Millennium Development Goals, declared in September 2000, with a deadline of 2015 to achieve their objectives.

Conflict and conflict resolution

The second issue linked to globalization that has particularly attracted the attention of various religious actors in recent years is conflict and conflict resolution. A starting point to analysis in this regard is to note that globalization both highlights and encourages religious pluralism. Some religions, especially Judaism, Christianity and Islam (sometimes known as the 'religions of the book', because in each case their authority emanates principally from sacred texts – actually, similar texts) claim what Kurtz calls 'exclusive accounts of the nature of reality', that is only *their* beliefs are regarded as *true* beliefs (Kurtz, 1995: 238).

Religious exclusivist truths

Exclusivist truth claims can be a serious challenge to religious toleration and diversity, essential to our coexistence in a globalized world. On the other hand, most religious traditions have within them beliefs that can make a contribution to a multicultural world. For example, from within Christianity comes the

(Continued)

> idea of non-violence, a key attribute of Jesus, the religion's founder, who insisted that all people are children of God, and that the test of one's relationship with God is whether one loves one's enemies and brings good news to the poor. As St Paul said, 'There is no Jew or Greek, servant or free, male or female: because you are all one in Jesus Christ' (Galatians, 3: 28)

Globalization results in increased interaction between people and communities. This implies not only that encounters between different religious traditions are increasingly common but also that in some cases they are not harmonious. Sometimes, the result is what Kurtz labels 'culture wars' (Kurtz, 1995: 168). Kurtz contends that this is because, as already noted, various religious world-views encourage different allegiances and standards in relation to various areas, including the family, law, education and politics. Increasingly, it appears, conflicts between people, ethnic groups, classes, and nations are framed in religious terms. Such religious conflicts seem often to 'take on "larger-than-life" proportions as the struggle of good against evil' (Kurtz, 1995: 170).

This contention seems to be borne out when we focus upon the issue of religious involvement in current conflicts. For example, stability and prosperity in the Middle East is a pivotal goal, central to achievement of peace and the elimination of poverty. The Middle East is particularly emblematic in this regard as it is the birthplace of the three monotheistic religions (Christianity, Islam, and Judaism), with a legacy not only of shared wisdom but also of conflict – a complex relationship that impacts on countries as far away as Indonesia and the United States. A key to peace in the region may well be achievement of significant collaborative efforts among different religious bodies, which along with external religious and secular organizations, for example from Europe and the United States, may through collaborative efforts work towards developing a new model of peace and cooperation to enable the Middle East to escape from what many see as an endless cycle of religious-based conflict. This emphasizes the fact that religion may be intimately connected, not only in the Middle East, *both* to international conflicts and their prolongation *and* to attempts at reconciliation of such conflicts. In other words, in relation to many international conflicts, religion can play a significant, even a fundamental role, contributing to conflicts in various ways, including how they are intensified, channeled or reconciled.

The role of religion is also emphasized in other violent conflicts and nationalistic currents in Asia (notably India/Pakistan) and Africa (for example, Sudan and Nigeria). In addition, for example, in relation to al-Qaeda, on the one hand, and the civil war in Sri Lanka, on the other, that has seen numerous examples of (Hindu) Tamil suicide bombers against the (Buddhist) Sinhalese, it is also a key component in some examples of terrorism. The influence of religion can also be seen in a third context of international conflict: nationalist struggles against Russian domination, for example, in Chechnya, which employs Islam as a key source of identity differentiating the Chechens from the Russians.

In sum, religion is becoming more and more important on the international political scene. Many international conflicts have religious roots and religion is driving both hatred and violence. Hans Kung, an eminent Roman Catholic theologian, claims (quoted in Smock 2004) that

> the most fanatical, the cruelest political struggles are those that have been colored, inspired, and legitimized by religion. To say this is not to reduce all political conflicts to religious ones, but to take seriously the fact that religions share in the responsibility for bringing peace to our torn and warring world.

We noted in Chapter 1 Samuel Huntington's concerns of a serious 'civilizational' threat to global order after the Cold War, emanating from competing 'civilizations', that is, the 'West' (especially North America and Western Europe) with its democratic and Judaeo-Christian values and political cultures, supposedly emphasizing tolerance, belief in moderation, and societal consensus, opposed by a bloc of allegedly 'anti-democratic', primarily Muslim countries, believed by Huntington to be in collusion to threaten Western security.

The problem, however, is that such 'civilizations' are not as single-minded, undivided and uniform as Huntington seems to believe. Instead, within all of the so-called great 'civilizations', there is much dispute over definitions, concerns and aims. This is as true of the Islamic world as it is of the USA; as Said asks rhetorically, 'What is the real America'? Is it the mid-Western world of the moralistic Christian fundamentalists and televangelists? Or is it the gay communities of San Francisco and New York?' (Said, 1995: 32). Moreover, *within* 'civilizations', new voices – often focused among the young and alienated – emerge periodically, demanding real changes, arguing that the dominant values and ideals are wrong. The point, as Said notes, is that the battle is not necessarily *between* civilizations but *within* them. For example, to many Western analysts Islam is perceived monolithically as *dar-Islam*, the house of Islam. The rest of the world is understood as 'the house of war', meaning that Islam is at war with everything outside it. But this by no means describes current realities within Muslim societies where there are energetic debates over the question of what Islam is and how it should be expressed in modern societies. In short, there is a battle over the definition of Islam and who or which type represents the voice of 'authentic' Muslims.

But discord within Muslim communities is not new. Throughout Islamic history, critics of the status quo have periodically emerged against what they perceive as unjust rule (Ayubi, 1999). Contemporary Islamists characterize themselves as the 'just' struggling against the 'unjust' that is, their political rulers and allies, the Islamic establishment. The goal of the 'just' historically was to create popular consultative mechanisms so a ruler would be open to popular pressure and, consequently, compelled to act to settle social problems brought to him by his subjects. But this concept of consultation (*shura*) should not be equated with the Western notion of liberal democracy – implying popular sovereignty. In Islam, sovereignty resides with Allah alone, not any person or group of people. Thus Islamists oppose Western interpretations of democracy, because they are seen as negating Allah's authority.

The issue of differing views within Islam, regarding what is the appropriate form of the faith and how best to pursue it, is also currently replicated in other religious traditions. Overall, the impact of globalization is to emphasize how futile it is to expect to find religions as monolithic, unchanging, undivided expressions of faith. Instead it underlines that all religious traditions comprise a variety of views.

It is important to bear this in mind when we seek to examine the role of religion in relation to international conflict under the circumstances of globalization. We have noted that religion is often implicated in domestic and international conflicts. On the other hand, it is important not to overestimate religion's potential for and involvement in large-scale violence and conflict if that implies ignoring or underestimating its involvement and potential as a significant source of conflict resolution and peacebuilding. It is important to recognize that, especially in recent years, numerous religious individuals, movements and organizations have been actively involved in attempts to end conflicts and to foster post-conflict reconciliation between formerly warring parties (Bouta et al., 2005). This emphasizes that various religions collectively play a key role in international relations and diplomacy by helping to resolve conflicts and build peace. For David Smock (2004), Vice President of USIP's Center for Mediation and Conflict Resolution, Huntington's 'clash of civilizations' thesis oversimplifies causal interconnections between religion and conflict, in particular by disregarding important alternate variables, including the numerous attempts from a variety of religious traditions to help resolve conflicts and build peace. When successful, religion's role in helping resolve conflicts is a crucial component in wider issues of human development because, as Ellis and ter Haar note: 'Peace is a precondition for human development. Religious ideas of various provenance – indigenous religions as well as world religions – play an important role in *legitimising or discouraging violence*' (Ellis and ter Haar, 2004; my emphasis).

Conclusion

Key questions remain, however, in relation to how the world's religions can help build and sustain peaceful coexistence and enhance social development in circumstances where, encouraged by globalization, increasingly multi-faith societies must deal with a world suffering from what appears to be growing strife and economic disparity. How can religious individuals and organizations advocate successfully reconciliation and fairness in a world characterized by what appears to be growing polarization between rich and poor? It may be that religious organizations that try to resolve conflicts and build peace between conflicting groups are likely to be most successful when they (1) have an international reach, and (2) systematically emphasize peace and avoidance of the use of force (Bouta et al., 2005). We saw in the first chapter that all the world religions broadly share a theological and spiritual set of values that, theoretically, should facilitate their efforts in this regard. But conflict resolution and peacebuilding efforts are more likely to be successful when there are already existing good relations between religions as this will be the key to a positive input from them in relation to conflict resolution.

The circumstances of contemporary globalization that we have noted in this chapter encompass technological, political, economic and cultural dimensions. We have noted on the one hand that in some cases religion has been and still is used to justify violence while, on the other, from religious traditions have also come a growing number of anti-violence social reform movements seeking to build a globalization that is more concerned with social-development issues. Religious traditions are currently being used around the world as vehicles for protest, especially in relation to what are perceived as the detrimental effects of globalization. We have also noted, however, that another side of religion's involvement in current international relations in the wake of contemporary globalization are various attempts to help end conflicts and bring greater harmony and cooperation.

Note

1   The Group of Eight (G8) is an international organization that was officially established in 1985. Its purpose is to facilitate economic cooperation
among the world's largest industrial nations, among which 'summit
meetings' of member states began over thirty years ago, in 1975. G8
members are: Canada, France, Germany, Italy, Japan, the United Kingdom and the United States. G8's remit is to discuss and coordinate
members' actions on economic and commercial matters and to work to
aid other states' economies. The leaders of the G8 states meet annually
in member countries. Anti-globalization protesters regard the G8 as little
more than 'a rich man's club', meeting periodically in order to plot how
to dominate the world through self-interested capitalist policies (Held
and McGrew, 2002: 75–6). (Although not an original member of the G7,
with the recent incorporation of Russia into the organization the group
is now known as G8.)

Questions

1   Is it accurate to describe contemporary international relations as a global environment where religious actors are of little consequence?

2   Why did religion diminish in importance in international relations
from the eighteenth century, only to reappear in significance in recent
years in the wake of deepening globalization?

3   It is often said that the contemporary religious resurgence impacts
upon international political outcomes. How does globalization encourage this development?

4   Does globalization facilitate the growth and spread of transnational
religious actors?

5   'Globalization aids growth and influence of transnational networks of
religious actors. This is because they can feed off each other's ideas and
perhaps aid each other with funds, while forming bodies whose main
priority is the well-being and advance of a specific transnational religious community.' Discuss.

Bibliography

Alkire, S. (2006) 'Religion and development', in D. Clark (ed.), *The Elgar
Companion to Development Studies*, London: Elgar, pp. 305–19.

Anheier, H. and Themudo, N. (2002) 'Organisational forms of global civil
society: implications of going global', in M. Glasius, M. Kaldor and

H. Anheier (eds), *Global Civil Society 2002*, Oxford: Oxford University Press, pp. 191–216.

Ayubi, N. (1999) 'The politics of Islam in the Middle East', in J. Haynes (ed.), *Religion, Globalization and Political Culture in the Third World*, Basingstoke: Macmillan, pp. 71–92.

Baylis, J. and Smith, S. (eds) (2005) *The Globalization of World Politics: An Introduction to International relations*, 3rd edn, Oxford: Oxford University Press.

Berger, P. (1969) *The Sacred Canopy: Elements of a Sociological Theory of Religion*, New York: Anchor.

Berger, P. (2002) 'Introduction: the cultural dynamics of globalization', in P. Berger and S. Huntington (eds), *Many Globalizations: Cultural Diversity in the Contemporary World*, New York: Oxford University Press, pp. 1–15.

Beyer, P. (1994) *Religion and Globalization*, London: Sage.

Beyer, P. (2003) 'Constitutional privilege and constituting pluralism: Religious freedom in national, global, and legal context', *Journal for the Scientific Study of Religion*, 42, 3, pp. 333-9.

Bouta, T., Kadayifci-Orellana, S. Ayse and Abu-Nimer, M. (2005) *Faith-Based Peace-Building: Mapping and Analysis of Christian, Muslim and Multi-faith Actors*, The Hague: Netherlands Institute of International Relations.

Bruce, S. (2003) *Politics and Religion*, Cambridge: Polity.

Clark, I. (1997) *Globalisation and Fragmentation*, Oxford: Oxford University Press.

Clark, I. (2005) 'Globalisation and the post-cold war order', in J. Baylis and S. Smith (eds), *The Globalization of World Politics: An Introduction to International Relations*, 3rd edn, Oxford: Oxford University Press, pp. 727–42.

Dartnell, M (2001) 'From action directe to pax electronica: context and method in the analysis of anti-government groups'. Paper presented at the conference, 'Trajectories of Terrorist Violence in Europe', Minda de Gunzburg Center for European Studies, Harvard University, 10 March.

Ellis, S. and ter Haar, G. (2004) *Religion and Development in Africa*. Background paper prepared for the Commission for Africa.

Ferguson, N. (2003) 'What is power?', Hoover Digest, No. 2. Available at: http://www.hooverdigest.org/032/ferguson.html Accessed 14 April 2006.

Goulet, D. (1980) 'Development experts: the one-eyed giants', *World Development*, 8, pp. 481–93.

Gunaratna, R. (2006) 'On the nature of religious terrorism', in J. Haynes (ed.), *The Politics of Religion: A Survey*, London: Routledge, pp. 83–91.

Gutierrez, G. (1973) *A Theology of Liberation: History, Politics and Salvation*, New York: Orbis Books.

Hague, R. and Harrop, M. (2001) *Comparative Government and Politics: An Introduction*, 5th edn, Basingstoke: Palgrave.

Haynes, J. (1996) *Religion and Politics in Africa*, London: Zed.

Haynes, J. (2001) *Democracy in the Developing World: Africa, Asia, Latin America and the Middle East*, Cambridge: Polity.

Haynes, J. (2005a) *Comparative Politics in a Globalizing World*, Cambridge: Polity.

Haynes, J. (2005b) 'Al-Qaeda: ideology and action', *Critical Review of International Social and Political Philosophy*, 8(2), pp. 177–91.

Haynes, J. (ed.) (2005c) *Palgrave Advances in Development Studies*, Basingstoke: Palgrave Macmillan.

Held, D. and McGrew, A. (2002) *Globalization/Anti-Globalization*, Cambridge: Polity.

Hirst, P. and Thompson. G. (1999) *Globalization in Question: The International Economy and the Possibilities of Governance*, 2nd edn, Cambridge: Polity Press.

Huntington, S. (1996) *The Clash of Civilizations*, New York: Simon and Schuster.

Juergensmeyer, M. (2005) 'Religion in the new global order'. Available at: http://www.maxwell.syr.edu/moynihan/programs/sac/paper%20pdfs/marks%20paper.pdf Accessed 18 April 2006.

Keohane, R. (2002) 'The globalization of informal violence, theories of world politics, and the "liberalism of fear"', *Dialog-IO*, Spring, pp. 29–43.

Kliksberg, B. (2003) *Social Justice: A Jewish Perspective*, New York: Gefen Publishing House.

Kurtz, L. (1995) *Gods in the Global Village*, Thousand Oaks, CA: Pine Forge Press.

Marshall, K. (2005) 'Religious faith and development: rethinking development debates'. Paper presented at the 'Religious NGOs and International Development Conference', Oslo, Norway, 7 April.

Marshall, K. and March, R. (2003) *Millennium Challenges for Development and Faith Institutions*, Washington, DC: The World Bank.

Mittelman, J. (1994) 'The globalisation challenge surviving at the margins', *Third World Quarterly*, 15(3), pp. 427–41.

Nasr, S. H. (1975) *Islam and the Plight of Modern Man*, London: Longman.

Nye, J. (2002) 'Globalism versus globalization', *The Globalist* ('The daily on-line magazine on the global economy, politics and culture'), 15 April. Available at: http://www.theglobalist.com/StoryId.aspx?StoryId=2392 Accessed 13 April 2006.

Radhakrishnan, P. (2004) 'Religion under globalisation', *Economic and Political Weekly*, 27 March, pp. 1403–11.

Reychler, L. (1997) 'Religion and conflict', *The International Journal of Peace Studies*, 2, 1. Available at: http://www.gmu.edu/academic/ijps/vol2_1/Reyschler.htm Accessed 14 April 2006.

Robertson, R. (1995) 'Glocalization: Time–space and homogeneity–heterogeneity', in M. Featherstone et al. (eds), *Global Modernities*, London: Sage, pp. 25–44.

Said, E. (1995) 'What is Islam?', *New Statesman and Society*, 10 February, pp. 32–4.

Schulz, M., Söderbaum, F. and Öjendal, J. (eds) (2001) *Regionalization in a Globalizing World: A Comparative Perspective on Forms, Actors and Processes*, London: Zed Books.

Seabrook, J. (2004) 'Localizing cultures', *Korea Herald*, 13 January. Available at: http://www.globalpolicy.org/globaliz/cultural/2004/0113jeremyseabrook.htm Accessed 18 April 2006.

Sivaraksa, S. and Ginsburg, T. (eds) (1992) *Seeds of Peace: A Buddhist Vision for Renewing Society*, Berkeley, CA: Parallax Press.

Smith, S. (2002) 'The end of the unipolar moment? September 11 and the future of world order', *International Relations*, 16(2), pp. 171–83.

Smock, D. (2004) 'Divine intervention: regional reconciliation through faith', *Religion*, 25(4), pp. 32–40.

Society for the Scientific Study of Religion (2001) Proceedings of a symposium on 'Religion and globalisation' at the conference of the Society for the Scientific Study of Religion, Ohio, USA, October. Available at: http://www.cra.org.au/pages/00000061.cgi Accessed 19 April 2006.

Spickard, J. (2001) 'Tribes and cities: towards an Islamic sociology of religion', *Social Compass*, 48, pp. 103–116.

Spickard, J. (2003) 'What is happening to religion? Six sociological narratives'. Unpublished manuscript, available at: http://www.ku.dk/
Satsning/Religion/indhold/publikationer/working_papers/what_is_hap
pened.PDF Accessed 14 April 2006.

Warburg, M. (2001) 'Religious organisations in a global world: a comparative perspective', University of Copenhagen, Denmark. Paper presented at the 2001 international conference, 'The Spiritual Supermarket:
Religious Pluralism in the 21st Century', 19–22 April, London School
of Economics, Houghton Street, London WC2A 2AE.

Willetts, P. (2001) 'Transnational actors and international organizations in
global politics', in J. Baylis and S. Smith (eds), *The Globalization of
World Politics: An Introduction to International Relations*, Oxford: Oxford
University Press, pp. 356–83.

Woods, N. (2001) *The Political Economy of Globalization*, Basingstoke: Palgrave.

World Bank (2003) *Breaking the Conflict Trap: Civil War and Development Policy*, New York: World Bank.

World Faiths Development Dialogue (1999) *Poverty and Development: An
Inter-faith Perspective*. Available at: http://www.wfdd.org.uk/documents/
publications/poverty_development_english.pdf Accessed 2 March
2006.

Further reading

P. Berger, *The Sacred Canopy*, Anchor, 1969. This is an important contribution to the sociology of religion. It provides an analysis that clarifies
the often ironic interaction between religion and society. Berger writes
in a particularly concise and lucid style.

P. Beyer, *Religion and Globalization*, Sage, 1994. Beyer examines the issue of
what role religion plays in a globalized society. His book examines the
interaction between religion and worldwide social and cultural
change. He examines major theories of global change and discusses
ways in which such change impinges on contemporary religious practice, meaning, and influence. He explores some of the key issues confronting religion today, including religion as culture, pure and applied
religion, privatized and publicly influential religion, and liberal versus
conservative religion.

G. Gutierrez, *A Theology of Liberation: History, Politics and Salvation*, Orbis
Books, 1973. This is the first and probably the most important book

written on liberation theology that followed the Vatican II (1960–65) and the Medellin (1968) conferences. The book is not an easy one to read as it challenges many readers both by its level of abstraction and by some of the jargon employed. However, for anyone interested in the interaction of religion and politics this book is a 'must read'!

L. Kurtz, *Gods in the Global Village*, Pine Forge Press, 1995. Lester Kurtz provides readers with many of the necessary tools to understand religious life in today's globalized world. First he considers the plentiful global interconnections among beliefs and believers (as well as among those who oppose them), and secondly by introducing students to the fundamentals of each of the world religions: Hinduism, Buddhism, Judaism, Christianity, and Islam. This book is both provocative and informative, likely to encourage re-examination of some of our conventional understandings about the role of religion in the contemporary world.

K. Marshall and R. March, *Millennium Challenges for Development and Faith Institutions*, The World Bank, 2003. This book traces the development of the World Bank's concern with religious organizations as a key component of its current development strategy that for the first time recognizes religion's potential importance in this regard. The book focuses primarily on a meeting in Canterbury, England in October 2002, hosted by former World Bank president Jim Wolfensohn and the then Archbishop of Canterbury, Dr George Carey. The meeting brought together an important group of leaders from the world's faith communities, as well as others from development and other organizations. The assembled figures examined the impact of globalization on the world's poor, especially highlighting: poverty, HIV/AIDS, conflict, gender concerns, international trade and global politics – issues that bind the world's countries and peoples into a global community, underscoring the urgency of shared responsibility and partnership.

CHAPTER 4

Religion and international order: historical and contemporary issues

The collapse of first Soviet Communism in the early 1990s and the twin World Trade Towers on September 11th 2001, has led to a resurgence of interest in culture and identity in international relations. In particular, religion, which had hitherto been an overlooked element in international relations, has moved center stage. (Shani, 2002: 15)

I t is suggested that, in recent years, there have been a number of challenges to international order emanating from various entities, including 'Islamic extremists' and those 'excluded' from the benefits of globalization; sometimes they are the same people (Lieven, 2001). The 'excluded' include 'those numerous social and ethnic groups who, for whatever reasons of culture, history and geography, are unable to take part in the world banquet'. Lieven identifies the Muslim world as 'the greatest victim' in this regard, and as a result Islamic extremist 'pathologies [assume] their greatest and more dangerous forms' (Lieven, 2001: 19). These concerns highlight more generally how various 'identity' issues, including those linked to religion, have in many cases become significant for international order issues after the Cold War, especially when linked to the polarizing economic and developmental impact of globalization on people and communities around the world. The context is also informed by the end of the Cold War: cessation of the four-decades-long battle for supremacy between competing secular ideological visions – Communism and liberal democracy/capitalism – that ended with a near-global collapse in the efficacy of the former and a growing, but by no means universal, acceptance of the desirability of the latter. Two key issues in this regard are: (1) How has international order changed as a result of globalization and the end of the Cold War? and (2) How is this change to be interpreted in relation to the impact of religion on international relations? This chapter examines the relationship of religion to international order, examining developments in both historical and contemporary contexts.

Encouraged both by the fall of Soviet Communism in the early 1990s and by the events of 9/11 a decade later (Shani, 2002), a renewed concern with religion in international relations has occurred among diverse cultures and religious faiths, in different countries with uneven levels of economic development. For many observers and analysts, reinsertion of religion into international relations was unexpected (Fox, 2001), not least because it challenged conventional wisdom about the nature and long-term, historical impact on societies of political development, modernization, and secularization. It did this by calling into question a core presumption in much Western social science thinking: modernization of societies and polities, *invariably* significant and expanding secularization, with religion largely excluded from the public realm, becoming both marginalized and 'privatized'. However, as we have already seen in earlier chapters, there are many recent examples of religious *deprivatization* in both domestic and international contexts; many have political impacts and some, for example Islamic extremism focused in international terrorism, clearly affect international order.

What is 'international order'?

'International order' can be thought of usefully as a regime[1] based on the more or less consensual acceptance of common values, norms – including the body of international law – and institutions that enforce it. This combination of actors, rules, mechanisms and understandings works to manage the coexistence and interdependence of states. Opinions about the current involvement of religion in international relations and its impact on international order tend to be polarized. On the one hand, reinjection of religion into international relations is seen to present increased challenges to international order, especially from extremist Islamist organizations such as al-Qaeda (Shani, 2002). On the other hand, some religious actors are seen to advance international order, for example the Roman Catholic Church's encouragement to democratize affecting authoritarian governments in Latin America, Africa and Eastern Europe in the 1980s and 1990s, or the role of the Organization of the Islamic Conference in promoting dialogue and cooperation between Muslim and Western governments.

(Continued)

> Other actors may be viewed more ambiguously, such as states like China that, in emphasizing cultural characteristics rooted in Neo-Confucianism, appear to promote a 'non-Western' perspective which potentially highlights different conceptions of international order (Ommerborn, n.d.).

Thinking of international order, the issue of international conflict is never very far away. A focus on current international order would note that various aspects of international conflict have significantly changed in recent years, with frequent involvement of religious, ethnic and cultural actors. Change in this regard is manifested in various ways. First, there are now fewer *inter*state wars, yet significant numbers of *intra*state conflicts; all affect international order. The 2005 *Human Security Report* notes that:

- The number of armed conflicts declined by over 40 per cent between 1992 and 2005. The deadliest conflicts (those with 1,000 or more battle deaths) fell even more dramatically – by 80 per cent.

- The number of international crises, often precursors of war, fell by more than 70 per cent between 1981 and 2001.

- International wars – that is, conflicts between countries – are less common now than in many previous eras; they now constitute less than 5 per cent of all armed conflicts.

Secondly, there are significant numbers of serious conflicts within countries, and many involve religious, cultural and/or ethnic actors. While numbers of international wars and war deaths have declined in recent years, some 60 armed conflicts raged around the globe in 2005; over 70 per cent were classified as *communal* wars, that is, conflicts characterized significantly by religious, cultural and/or ethnic factors and combatants (*Human Security Report*, 2005).

Finally, the *Human Security Report* (2005) emphasized that a new and growing threat to international order comes from transnational religious terrorist groups, notably al-Qaeda. As the Report notes:

> International terrorism is the only form of political violence that appears to be getting worse. Some datasets have shown an overall decline in international terrorist incidents of all types since the early 1980s, but the most recent statistics

suggest a dramatic increase in the number of high-casualty attacks since the September 11 attacks on the US in 2001. *The annual death toll from international terrorist attacks is, however, only a tiny fraction of annual war death toll* ('Overview', *Human Security Report*, 2005, my emphasis).

Although the number of annual deaths from 'international terrorist attacks' is, according to the 2005 *Human Security Report*, only 'a tiny fraction' compared to overall war deaths in any one year, it is important to note that the number of deaths due to this source has been swiftly rising in recent years. The US State Department's annual report on global terrorism for 2005 stated that there were 11,111 attacks that caused 14,602 deaths in 2005. Those figures can be contrasted with earlier State Department reports from 2003 and 2004. In the former year, there were 208 terrorist attacks causing 625 deaths; in 2004 there were 3,168 attacks resulting in 1,907 deaths. Thus, comparing 2005 to the previous year, there was a more than seven-fold increase in those killed as a result of international terrorist attacks; most such fatalities were linked to the consequences of US-led invasions of Afghanistan (2001) and Iraq (2003), including the increases in deaths attributed to religious and sectarian extremists, especially in the latter country (http://www.latimes.com/news/nationworld/nation/la-na-terror29apr29,1,4616593.story?coll=la-headlines-nation&ctrack=1&cset=true). The significant recent increase in numbers of deaths as a result of international terrorist attacks, coupled with the fact that US personnel are often in the firing line in both Afghanistan and Iraq, has led to the present era being dubbed 'the age of global terrorism' (Ervin, 2006).

In sum, international religious terrorists fundamentally deny (1) the legitimacy of the secular international state system, as well as (2) foundational norms, values and institutions upon which contemporary international order is based (Milton-Edwards, 2006).

This chapter is structured as follow. First, we examine theoretical approaches to international order in international relations theory. Secondly, we consider how international order after the Treaty of Westphalia developed according to a more general trend of secularization, helping produce broadly consensual foundations: international law, diplomacy and the balance of power. Over time, this led to what is often known as 'international society'; and the question is to what extent various religious actors undermine or strengthen this consensus. To focus upon this issue, the final section of the chapter looks at international order after the end of the Cold

War when, in combination with factors associated with globalization, religious actors of various kinds have been noted for their significance.

International order and international relations

The period from the Treaty of Westphalia in 1648 saw the development of three fundamental cornerstones of international order:

- the balance of power
- international law, and
- international diplomacy.

Each of the three elements was mutually reinforcing, and together they were foundations of the present-day situation of complex interactions between the world's nearly 200 states and the numerous significant non-state actors, both secular and religious, including: multinational corporations, nationalist movements, such as the Palestinian Liberation Organization, and transnational religious organizations, including the Roman Catholic Church, various expressions of Protestant evangelicalism and a number of Islamic movements.

To comprehend the bases of contemporary international order, we need to start by understanding its historical foundations, from the time of the Treaty of Westphalia. They are especially important because they were both the fundamentals and dynamism of a secular and secularizing state system based on a vital principle: unchallenged predominance of state sovereignty. The principle evolved over time from the seventeenth century, with different stages of development. As time went on, an increasing number of issues were identified as global in scope and, as a result, states sought to develop collective, consensual outlooks and strategies. Examples include the successful fight against slavery in the nineteenth century and later and more general improvements in human rights, including the principle of gender equality, as well as the fight against nuclear weapons proliferation and environmental degradation and destruction. Yet while states and important non-state actors in international relations, such as the United Nations and the European Union, widely acknowledge various threats to international order, this does not imply that they always agree on how to deal with them.

The issue of international order – how to maintain and strengthen it – received particular attention after the Cold War, in the context of globalization (Haynes, 2005a). Many observers and analysts of international relations perceive that a key impact of globalization on international relations is to undermine the international state system, so that it is now in decline (Held and McGrew, 2002). This is characterized by: withdrawal of the state or at least a reduction in its authority in various issue areas, including economic concerns, and the emergence of new realms with only minimal state involvement (such as, cyberspace and the internet), as well as 'the rise of non-state actors showing signs of successfully influencing states' policies, and taking over subject areas that the state largely ignored or mishandled' (Mendelsohn, 2005: 50). Despite such concerns, however, there is no consensus on the extent to which such issues collectively represent a new and significant threat to international order. On the one hand, many important, non-state, transnational actors accept the desirability of strong international order, albeit one increasingly characterized by improved human rights, democracy and developmental outcomes. For example, various Christian churches, including but not limited to the Roman Catholic Church, have pursued such agendas in recent years, key components of a global coalition of forces working towards the aim of developing a functional world society based on such values (Thomas, 2005). Others would prefer different values to triumph, for example, the creation of a global *ummah* (Muslim community) or an international order featuring community-orientated values, rather than individualistic values (Haynes, 2005b). Challenges to international order are said to emanate from 'violent non-state actors', including religious terrorist organizations. Such actors emphatically do not accept 'the legitimacy of the state system and the foundations on which the society of states is based. Such actors may also try to advance an alternative order' (Mendelsohn, 2005: 50).

Contending theoretical approaches to international order

Realists rely on the balance of power for order, liberal internationalism relies on international law, regimes and organizations, and the neo-Marxist view sees international political processes as expressions of underlying class conflicts on a global scale.

Realists 'emphasise how hegemonic powers, such as the United States, have an important role in establishing and maintaining order in the international

system, stressing that the international structure of power shapes the character of the political order' (Bull, 1977). For Realists, the state is always the
most important actor in international relations because there is no higher
authority; international organizations are regarded as always subservient to
the state. The global system is a global *state* system grounded in competition, conflict and cooperation. States must rely upon their own resources to
achieve the power they need to thrive, even if they are prepared, as most
are, to collaborate with others to achieve general goals. Serious conflict is
not the usual status of the international system because peace is maintained
through local and/or global balances of power. A variant of Realism, neo-Re-
alism, emphasizes how hegemonic powers, such as the United States, have
an important role in establishing and maintaining order in the international system and stresses that the structure of power in the international system
shapes the character of the political order. In sum, Realist analysis places
great stress on the significance of hard power (especially, military and economic power) as they believe that states must ultimately rely on their own
efforts to achieve their goals.

In contrast, the liberal internationalist paradigm begins from the
premise that the state is no longer automatically the primary actor in
world politics. The recent increase in numbers of various kinds of
'transnational actors' – a 'transnational actor' is any non-governmental
actor from one country that has relations with any actor from another
country or with an international organization – underlines such actors'
significance (Haynes, 2005a). What all transnational actors have in common is a significant degree of independence from any state or group of
states' control. Indeed, for liberal internationalists, the state itself is not
regarded as a unitary actor. Rather, it consists of a body of bureaucratic organizations and institutions that might well interact with each other
transnationally, for example, in the context of the EU or the UN (Hague
and Harrop, 2001). The global system is perceived as an aggregate of different issue areas, such as trade, finance, energy, human rights, democracy
and ecology, in which domestic and international policy processes increasingly interact or merge. Management of global interdependencies is
carried out through processes of bargaining, negotiation and consensus
seeking. Thus, international order is not maintained by a 'balance of
power', as Realists contend, but by consensual acceptance of common values, norms and international law. In other words, international order is in
place because most states and prominent non-state actors have a shared,
vested interest in this state of affairs.

In the neo-Marxist view, political processes at the global level are viewed primarily as expressions of underlying class conflicts on a global scale. Unlike Realists, neo-Marxists do not conceive of global order as based upon the structure of military and economic state power, nor sustained by networks of interdependence as do liberal internationalists. One of the dominant characteristics of the global order for neo-Marxists is the structural differentiation of the world into core, peripheral and semi-peripheral centres of economic power. While, traditionally, this was regarded as the division between the 'North', 'South' and the communist Eastern bloc, the emergence in the 1980s of the East Asian Newly Industrializing Countries (South Korea, Taiwan, Singapore, Hong Kong) and the demise of Soviet-dominated Eastern Europe in the early 1990s undermined comprehensively the simple (and increasingly simplistic) three-way international economic division. In short, for neo-Marxists, global order is preserved through the power of the leading capitalist states, in collusion with international organizations, such as the United Nations, multinational corporations, and international regimes that collectively strive to legitimate a global diffusion of a dominant ideology of liberalism and Western-type modernization.

As we saw in Chapter 2, adherents of what is known as the 'English School of international relations' were so named because its leading figures were, while not necessarily English by nationality, mostly based in several English universities, including Oxford, Cambridge and the London School of Economics. Influential figures within the English School include Hedley Bull, James Mayall, Adam Watson, Martin Wight and Robert Jackson. For the English School international order is maintained by a *shared conception of international society*. This is the idea that the world's states form an *international society* – not 'just' an international *system* – whose constituent parts interact and are bound together by the pursuit and protection of common interests, values, rules, and institutions. What principally distinguishes the English School from Realist approaches in particular is a major concern with both morality and culture. The consequence is that the English School's distinctive approach to the study of international relations emphasizes problems of coexistence, cooperation, and conflict, especially in relations between sovereign states, the main focus of the approach (Jackson and Owens, 2005: 46; Brown, 2005: 51). Overall, the English School is especially concerned with various issues associated with order and justice concerns in an anarchical international society. These include: international institutions, rules, norms and practices collectively concerned with such goals and the tensions that exist between them.

Order and justice concerns within countries

Order and justice concerns are not only a concern for international relations analysis, as they also occur in all domestic political and social systems, whatever their ideological and historical bases. Questions concerned with order and justice are raised in all societies. Typically, issues include: how to prevent or deal with serious crime; how to ensure the supremacy of the ballot box in political processes; and how to ensure that transport infrastructures are able to ensure easy movement of people in towns and cities. Means adopted within countries to deal with such concerns typically feature a mix of laws, police forces, and democratic political institutions; they are all examples of means adopted by states throughout the world to try to promote order in often pluralist societies like Britain or Germany. Justice is also a concern, one that is perhaps more problematic to resolve, not least because justice is a subjective term leading to complex and difficult questions and answers. For example, how to ensure a reasonably equitable distribution of resources within a society, how to guarantee that all citizens enjoy equal treatment under the law, how to be certain that all children receive comparable education. These are all examples of various issues, connected to justice concerns, that occur in most, if not all, societies. In Britain, taxation (its level and purpose), welfare provision (who should get it and why), as well as rules, such as *habeas corpus*, and the funding levels of state schools, are examples of topics intimately concerned with societal and state desire to promote justice among citizens. Within a country, issues of both order and justice significantly depend on what governments do, and the power and authority they can muster and project.

At the international level there is no 'world government' with powers and authority commensurate with what many governments, especially in the developed world, wield domestically within countries. Thus, in relations between states, in the absence of a definitive global authority, many issues connected to order and justice, while not by any means absent, are notoriously difficult to resolve. Such concerns include problems of war and peace and of disparities of wealth; they may well be even more extreme *among* states than *within* them. A key concern for the English School of international relations is to consider how the 'international community' – that is, the collectivity of states and other important non-state international actors – seeks to address order and justice issues without the benefit of a world government. There is a concern here with historical evolution of what might be called 'international governance' – that is, collective attempts, usually via individual states or groups of states, with various goals, centring on regulation of particular issues in international relations through various mechanisms, including: agreements between significant states, international institutions, including the UN and EU, as well as various kinds of legal arrangements; all centre on a range of issues-informed questions of order and justice.

For the English School, *consensual* acceptance of international society's common values, norms, international law and various institutions collectively underpin, and enforce, international order. For the English School, issues to do with international order focus on the following:

- Most, especially 'Western', state and non-state actors share common values, norms and beliefs.

- International political structures and processes that defend international order involve both state and non-state actors: political leaders, authorities, institutions, organizations and movements.

- These state and non-state actors have a vested interest in perpetuating international order, as for them it implies both stability and desirable continuity.

- Together these actors establish and collectively enforce and defend their preferred rules as a way to defend their common values in international relations (Jackson and Owens, 2005: 46; Clark, 2005: 730).

In addition, as Bull contends, there are three sets of rules – constitutional normative principles, 'rules of coexistence', and rules governing cooperation among states – that together comprise the core components of international order (Bull, 1977: 67–70). According to Bull, five key institutions underpin these rules: the Balance of Power, International Law, Diplomacy, War, and the Great Powers. Note, however, that since Bull was writing about this issue in the 1970s, some of the institutions he mentions appear to be less influential than three decades ago – for example, the great powers and the balance of power – or have changed their complexion (diplomacy; now the importance of multilateral diplomacy is often noted). On the other hand, there is still much agreement that international law is a key institution helping to maintain international order.

Hedley Bull, international law and international order

For Hedley Bull, a major voice in the English School (albeit he was actually an Australian!), international law is 'the body of rules which binds states and other agents in world politics in their relations with one another and is considered to have the status of law' (Bull, 1977: 127). In this view international law functions as a key pillar of international order. It does this by distinguishing the idea of a *society* of sovereign states as the ultimate normative principle of humankind's international political organization and sets out substantive rules of coexistence that substantively link them. However, in Bull's view and era – the Cold War – the main threats to international order were from secular Communist states, including the USSR, Cuba and China, which wanted to change the international rules of the game in their favour.

Over time, the principle of state sovereignty in international society has been sustained by two important conditions: first, the absence of transnational ideologies that fundamentally compete with states and nations for people's political loyalties; second, the existence of a common set of values, especially at the state level, that engenders an element of respect for other states. Does the reintroduction of religion and culture, as a significant type of transnational idea in international relations, seriously weaken these two 'pillars' of the Westphalian system? This form of challenge comes from new, or newly significant, transnational allegiances that may challenge popular allegiance to the state by focusing on politically significant alternative, and often incompatible, beliefs and values. As a result, they may not sit well alongside established Westphalian principles of international order. This is especially the case if these beliefs and values reject and hence undermine the basic rules on which post-Westphalian international order was founded and the institutions that seek to maintain it.

■ Such challenges can manifest themselves in the rejection of the state as the main political unit in world affairs – the rejection of the principle that leaders of states are autonomous in their ability to deal with other such leaders and, additionally, pursue an independent foreign policy. Negation of the principle that states are the sole actors that can legitimately use force is also significant, as is non-acceptance of restrictions on the use of force (for example, civilians are not legally targets of war).

- A second way in which a violent non-state actor can challenge the values of international society is by undermining state – society relations through not accepting the ability of states to fulfil a basic governmental responsibility to their citizens: general security – for example, by the use of weapons of mass destruction.

- A third means by which a violent non-state actor may undermine international society is by provoking an overreaction by the internationally dominant power that, as a consequence, results in the demise of an accepted code of conduct for states' behaviour in general and for the dominant power in particular. 'This can be done by magnifying the conflict between the dual roles of a hegemon's as systemic leader and great power, provoking it to act in accordance with the latter at the expense of the former' (Mendelsohn, 2005: 53).

In order to locate the current relationship of religious and cultural actors to international-order issues, in the next section we trace the secularization of international order over time since the Treaty of Westphalia.

Secularization of international order

The international legal system that has dominated the way in which humans have ordered international politics since the seventeenth century is European in origin. For the most part, it dates from the Treaty of Westphalia of 1648, one of the most important points marking off the medieval from the modern period in European and international history. Note, however, that like many recognized historical benchmarks, the Treaty of Westphalia is as much a convenient reference point as the key source of a new normative system. It is clear, however, that the Treaty was influential in helping to create the foundations of a new European – and from the mid-twentieth century truly global – system from the ruins of the political structures and the idealized rationale for them – Christendom – that existed in Europe for a millennium prior to the Treaty.

The Treaty was created and signed in Europe by leaders representing two sets of transnational religious belligerents: Catholics and Protestants. This outcome followed the last and most devastating of the great wars of religion (the Thirty Years War) that had raged in Europe for more than a hundred years prior to 1648. While the causes and trajectory of the conflict itself are complex, its results were clear enough: huge numbers of civilian casualties – between one-third and a half of the populations of many areas in Europe perished – and massive destruction of property, as well as famines and widespread disease. The result was the eclipse of the medieval structures that had sought but failed to promote the common good and the unrestrained contest for power of individual, mostly religious actors.

From the chaos came a revolutionary change in the way European states tried to order their mutual relations. In fact, the state system they created more than three centuries ago actually looks rather familiar to us; as a result, Westphalia's revolutionary quality may not be immediately apparent. The Westphalia treaties (there were actually two) created the basis for a decentralized system of sovereign and legally equal nation-states that had never previously existed. From that time, the reality of decentralized, scattered power has been regarded as the legitimate mode of organization, first for the European and later the global system. The 1,000-year-old dream of a form of 'Christian unity' ('Christendom'), albeit restricted to Europe, the 'known' world at the time, was henceforth recognized as both outmoded and unworkable. This was primarily because of the immutable division in Christianity between Catholics and Protestants; in addition, references to 'the shared values of Christendom' were no longer adequate or effective as a legitimizing ideal governing the behaviour of Europe's increasingly secular heads of state. However, the de facto separateness that replaced it could only be made legitimate through insistence that fragmentation of authority carried with it a new concept and set of organizing values: sovereign equality of states, where individual rulers had *absolute* authority within their own domains.

Once Europe's rulers had established the principle of sovereign equality, they went on to develop a modus vivendi (way of living) known as the balance of power. This was a key instrument and method in establishing and maintaining international order right up until the First World War. The notion of the balance of power is a simple one, although it has many meanings. I am using it in the present context to refer to a regime whereby states collaborate with each other to maintain their independence against threats from those who would seek systemic dominance, such as France's Napoleon Bonaparte at the beginning of the nineteenth century or Germany's Adolph Hitler in the mid-twentieth. Napoleon's aggression resulted in the formation of a defensive alliance – involving, among others, Britain and Prussia (the forerunner of Germany) – acting collectively to defeat Napoleon's bid for overall control of the international system. Later, the Second World War (1939–45) was another example of the balance of power mechanism in action: this time the European democracies, aided by the USA, joined together not only to defeat Hitler's dreams of a 1,000-year Reich but also the associated bids for more power from Japan and Italy.

These examples indicate that serious threats to international order during the nineteenth and twentieth centuries triggered defensive coalitions to combat them. But they were ad hoc, temporary alliances that fragmented once the threat to international order that had led to their formation was removed. In other words, the balance of power was a temporary arrangement, a short-lived unity to defeat a common aggressor. It was not intended to prevent *all* conflicts from breaking out: it was not a *formal* mechanism to safeguard international order, like the institutional innovations – the League of Nations and the United Nations – in the twentieth century. Instead, the purpose of the balance of power was to protect and defend international order, to safeguard state sovereignty and independence and, by extension, the state system itself.

The balance of power and international order

During the eighteenth and nineteenth centuries, four prerequisites were necessary for the balance of power to work successfully:

- A multiplicity of sovereign actors and the absence of a single systemic authority

- Relatively equally distributed power among the sovereign units

- Continuous but controlled competition among the sovereign units (states) for scarce resources: territory, trading opportunities, and influence

- Collective acceptance among the constituent units that the status quo was mutually beneficial and desirable.

In particular, the period between 1815 (date of the Congress of Vienna ending the Napoleonic wars) and 1914 (First World War) is often referred to as the 'golden age of the balance of power'. This is partly because, over this hundred-year period, the political significance of religion in international relations steadily diminished, as nationalism emerged and developed into the dominant organizing ideology. This led to a secular international system underpinned by the expansion of mercantilism – the control of international trade by national governments – that paved the way for the current era of 'free trade'. Over time, albeit gradually, absolute monarchies in Europe were replaced by less absolutist, more democratic, forms of government. This was also the period of 'limited war', when conflicts between states, while numerous, were often rather ritualized and limited in intensity and scope. Rarely were civilian populations seriously affected during such conflicts, and religion was a diminishing cause of war. These circumstances led to an international environment where, for a century (1815–1914), international wars were avoided, in part because of the ability of the balance of power to encourage peaceful resolutions to occasional conflicts.

The main ideological characteristic of the second half of the seventeenth and eighteenth centuries was the development of the so-called 'corporate mentality' of the various aristocracies of the European countries. European elites found that they had much more in common with each other than with the 'ordinary' people of their countries; their claims to power were invariably based on secular, not religious, principles. The period from the second half of the seventeenth until the end of the eighteenth century was, as a result of these factors, a period of relative political and economic homogeneity in Europe. There were no fundamental variations between the leaders' philosophies or among European political structures. There was no ideological challenge to international order until the French Revolution (1789) – rallying cry: 'Liberty, Equality, Fraternity' – radically destabilized international order, just as the Russian Revolution did a century later in 1917.

Over time, the analogy was made between the mutual position and conditions of states in the emerging international system and that of individuals within societies. While there was international anarchy – that is, no overarching world government to wield authority and power – there *was* a mutually reinforcing set of bonds, values, norms and institutions that linked the members of the international system. In short, there was what is known as a 'society of states', that is a group of similarly constituted states that regulated their mutual relations through broadly comparable domestic institutions – governments – in areas of mutual interests, principally areas of diplomacy and trade. Gradually states began to accept that warfare should only legitimately be used for purposes of self-defence, righting an injury, or for upholding the fundamental outlines of the state system and its norms, values and laws.

The balance of power was a key force for international stability and regularization of interactions between states. The second component of the international system leading to an institutionalization of international order that also developed at this time was the international diplomatic system. While the concept was not new (regular, official contacts between rulers and governments were known in ancient China, Egypt and India), the emerging institution of diplomacy helped to bolster, embed and develop international norms, values and rules. Initially diplomacy simply involved delivery of messages and warnings, pleading of causes and transfer of gifts or tribute. Later, envoys became negotiators, not merely messengers. A permanent system of diplomatic interaction was established in the eighteenth and nineteenth centuries, over time developing into one of the cornerstones of the international system in general and international order in particular. An increasingly professional diplomatic corps became agents of the state sent abroad for purposes of negotiation, reporting and intelligence work. Diplomats reported regularly to their home government and, in the process, bureaucratized foreign ministries began to emerge. What this underlines is that governments, all governments, needed regular contact with others, and rules to govern such interaction.

In sum, from the mid-seventeenth century European governments agreed to follow specific rules of conduct governing their diplomatic and commercial interactions, even, as we shall see, in relation to fighting wars. It also underlines that for states to stick to internationally agreed rules of conduct is actually a highly rational course of action, as they shared a collective goal: maintenance and development of international order.

A third change was also important for the development of international order: the concept and practice of international law, including the important concept of 'just war'. This was very significant for international relations because it pointed to the notion that restraints in fighting war are morally justified; many such restraints were rooted in religious, especially Christian, strictures. Over two centuries from the early sixteenth century, several figures, including Francisco de Vitoria (1486–1546), Francisco de Suarez (1548–1617), Hugo Grotius (1583–1645), Samuel Pufendorf (1632–94), Christian von Wolff (1679–1754), and Emmerich de Vattell (1714–1767), were collectively important in advancing the concept of 'just war' – that is, a regime that seeks to place moral restraints on warfare by establishing criteria for determining *when* and *how* to wage war justly.

During the twentieth century the concept of just war underwent a revival. This was closely linked to two issues: the invention of nuclear weaponry in the early 1940s and American involvement in the Vietnam War two decades later. Reflecting on such concerns, several important books were produced, including *Just and Unjust Wars* (1977) by Michael Walzer, *The Ethics of War* (1979) by Barrie Paskins and Michael Dockrill, *Ethics, Killing, and War* (1995) by Richard Norman, and *War and International Justice* (2001) by Brian Orend.

At the beginning of the twenty-first century, scholars again turned their attention to just war following the 9/11 terrorist attacks on the USA. After

September 11, 2001 and the subsequent US-directed wars in Afghanistan and Iraq, many people, including large numbers of Americans, turned to the just war tradition for moral guidance. Discussions of what constitutes a morally justifiable war can be found in many religious traditions, including that of Christianity. However, while some parts of the Bible suggest concerns with ethical behaviour in war and concepts of its just cause, it was St Thomas Aquinas who gave the most systematic exposition of just war theory in the Christian tradition. In the *Summa Theologicae* Aquinas presents the general outline of what became known as 'just war theory', focusing on two issues: (1) when is war justified? and (2) kinds of activity permissible in war. Aquinas's thoughts become the model for later scholars and jurists, including those noted above, to expand. Post-9/11 debate in the United States drew primarily on classic just war theory, with its origins in Christian theology and natural law theory. This focus not only underlines that just war theory has a long history, it also highlights more generally the involvement of various religious actors in post-Cold War conceptions of international order, especially in relation to globalization (Buzan, 2004; Clark, 2005).

In conclusion, the period from the Treaty of Westphalia saw the development of three fundamental cornerstones of international order: balance of power, international law and diplomacy. They were mutually reinforcing, laying the foundations of the present-day situation of complex interactions between the world's nearly 200 states and myriad significant non-state actors, such as multinational corporations, nationalist movements, such as the Palestinian Liberation Organization, and transnational religious organizations, like the Roman Catholic Church.

Religion and international order after the Cold War

After the Cold War ended in 1989, there appeared to be a window of opportunity to establish the contours of a new, post-conflict consensual framework for international order, primarily based on the dissemination of Western values and norms. In 1990 the then US president, George H. W. Bush, spoke confidently about the birth of a 'new world order' following the collapse of the Soviet Union and its Communist empire. For President Bush Snr, international order would henceforward be focused upon international law and organizations, including the United Nations. When his son, George W. Bush, came to power a decade later, the US focus had shifted to the desirability of global acceptance and pursuit of liberal democracy, human rights and capitalism as interactive routes to universal prosperity and enhanced human development and progress; this period also coincided with what many perceived as enhanced impact of globalization, notably for development polarization and creation of growing numbers of what Lieven (2001) calls the 'excluded'. President George H. W. Bush's optimism had, however, already been dashed: the first Gulf War (1990–9) and later US setbacks in the 1990s in, *inter alia*, Somalia and Haiti, suggested that a post-Cold War vision of consensual international order would be very difficult to attain. Realists such as Charles Krauthammer (2004) argued that the USA must try to build and maintain an international order *on its own hegemonic terms, via unilateralism,* to strive for a qualitatively *better* world order on the USA's own terms.

Following the end of the Cold War in 1989, religion and culture emerged as significant factors in relation to international order (Lapid and Kratochwil, 1996). The deepening of globalization from this time, as well as the related technological revolution facilitated their impact with demonstrable effects upon international order. We saw in Chapter 3 that globalization involves increased focus on links and interactions between both states and societies which together comprise what might be called the global system. Note, however, that while global interconnections existed for centuries, in the past their impact was comparatively minor, often amounting to little more than trade routes or select military and naval operations that only affected certain towns, rural centres and territories.

It is important to observe not only the globalizing effects of religion but also that religious conflicts that took place long ago can still have resonance hundreds of years later (Milton-Edwards, 2006). For example, hundreds of years ago, both Christianity and Islam expanded to become world religions, conveying their associated civilizations around the globe via colonization, conquest and the expansion of global trade. In the sixteenth and seventeenth centuries, during a period of sustained expansion of the international system, contending religious beliefs provided the chief motor for international conflicts and the main threat to international peace and security. But the development of the global state system after the Treaty of Westphalia in 1648 (which ended the religious wars in Europe between Catholics and Protestants) was largely reflected in the history of clashing nationalisms, with numerous national groups actively seeking their own states.

During the twentieth century, the rise of those supremely secular ideologies – Communism and Fascism – stimulated challenges to international order that ultimately led to the Second World War. At this time, there was a process of global ideological differentiation, deepening after the War, when the defeat of Fascism led to the emergence of liberal democracy as the dominant but not yet global ideology. During the Cold War (*c.*1948–89) one set of secular ideas – Communism – was pitched against another – liberal democracy and its economic counterpart, capitalism – in a struggle for dominance, which culminated in the collapse of Soviet-style Communism and associated political systems throughout Central and Eastern Europe in 1989–91.

The fall of the Soviet empire was due, in part, to the impact of processes of globalization that served to end the USSR's self-imposed isolation from the Western world. The collapse of Eastern Europe's Communist systems was facilitated by increasingly widely available methods of interpersonal communications, such as the telephone, the internet, email, and fax. The result was that, as Beyer put it, we now live in 'a globalizing social reality, one in which previously effective barriers to communication no longer exist' (Beyer, 1994: 1). Development of both domestic and transnational religious communities, many with political/social/economic concerns, was greatly enhanced by the rapid increase in interpersonal and inter-group communications. It facilitated the ability of religious communities to spread their messages, to link up with like-minded groups, with geographical distance no longer an insuperable barrier. As a result, links between religious actors both *in* and *between* countries have multiplied in recent years, as have their international concerns, many of which are linked to globalization and its perceived impact on order and justice issues (Rudolph and Piscatori, 1997; Haynes, 2005a).

Various kinds of concerns can be noted. For example, the Roman Catholic Church is often noted as an especially influential transnational actor, with a major influence during the 1980s and 1990s on democratization outcomes and human rights more generally in various parts of the world including Eastern Europe, Latin America and sub-Saharan Africa. Other religious actors, including some religious terrorist organizations, notably al-Qaeda, had a quite different impact on international relations, as it was a central focus of the US-led 'war on terror' after 9/11. This enables us to conclude that a combination of circumstances – focusing upon the end of the Cold War and its effects upon international relations, as well as the multifaceted impact of globalization – have encouraged various religious groups to focus upon international order concerns. Such a focus not only reflects the increased importance of various religious traditions and beliefs to international relations but also highlights how what are primarily domestic issues can 'spill over' to become regional or international threats to international order. For example, the Palestinian Islamist group Hamas confronts Israel over land in a conflict that has become increasingly informed by polarized religious and cultural positions. This conflict illustrates how domestic and international political issues can feed off each other to present significant challenges to international order, with religious values and norms of central concern.

After the Cold War, to what extent are religious belief systems associated with specific political ideologies? In some cases, existence of a connection is not difficult to demonstrate. Close links exist, for example, in India between Hindu chauvinism (or 'fundamentalism') and ultra-nationalism, between Jewish and Christian fundamentalism and political conservatism, in Israel and the USA respectively, and between some of Thailand's new Buddhist movements and demands for a more just social, political and economic order. More generally, around the world, many religious groups now regularly express views on various issues, including:

- what they believe should constitute appropriate government and economic systems
- the preferred nature of a country's interstate relations, and
- what social mores, customs and manners should predominate.

Many religious groups with political aims endeavour to achieve their objectives by extending their operations from the domestic to the international field of action. And this can impact upon international order. For example, the Iranian revolution of 1979 helped to stimulate an increase in expressions of radical Islam, both in relation to domestic 'non-Islamic' governments, especially in the Middle East, as well as encouraging a perception that 'Islamic fundamentalism' was a real threat to Western security and international order (Ayubi, 1999). In addition, during the first Gulf war (1990–91) the aggression of Muslim Iraq against a key Western ally, Kuwait, crystallized for many the threat to international order posed by Islam, with its different norms, values and beliefs compared to Western perceptions.

More recently, transnational Islamic terrorist organizations such as al-Qaeda both emphatically reject and seek to undermine basic rules on which post-Westphalian international order is founded, as well as key institutions that underpin it, including the United Nations (Haynes, 2005b). Such manifestations of religious involvement in international relations significantly challenge Westphalian values, not least because they offer a competing logic to the sovereignty-based state system and popular allegiance to it (Rudolph and Piscatori, 1997: 12). As Mendelsohn notes, religious challenges can manifest themselves in various ways. This is because a religious source of authority is believed by its followers to be divine and thus higher than the authority of the state. Both states and sets of religious beliefs share the same constituency, and so religious people need to balance key aspects of their identity: both religious and secular national concerns. But when the two appear to be in competition, religious people may choose between one of two competing sets of values, because they feel that they 'cannot obey a state law that contradicts "higher" religious imperatives' (Mendelsohn, 2005: 54).

We can also note, however, that it is not only non-state religious actors that articulate and pursue sets of religious goals; we also saw in Chapter 2 that some states – including those of the USA, India, Iran, and Saudi Arabia – also do in various ways, although there is no clear result in terms of international order issues. In addition, whereas religious terrorism emanating from the likes of al-Qaeda is a direct and sustained onslaught on international order, we can also note that various countries in East Asia (such as, China, Vietnam and Singapore) have state policies explicitly or implicitly influenced by Confucianist norms, beliefs and values. Like al-Qaeda and other violent Islamist organizations, such countries are responding to what they see as an international order that, facilitated by globalization, appears to attack their national cultural values. Kurth contends that 'this process has been led by the United States'. The influence of the USA in this regard is underpinned by three factors: it is the only remaining superpower, it has a 'high-technology economy' and it regards its values as universally applicable. Since the end of the Cold War, the USA has sought to spread its values by 'systematically pressing to remove any national barriers to the free movement of capital, goods, and services' (Kurth, 1999). The USA has sought to achieve this via its influence in global financial institutions, such as the International Monetary Fund, the World Bank and the World Trade Organization. Economic and political values are mutually reinforcing, privileging individualistic economic, political and human rights interpretations. The Confucian countries do not necessarily share these goals, especially in relation to individualistic political and human rights goals.

As a result, the principal sources of resistance to an international order championed by the USA and its core allies come from two of the world's great religious and cultural traditions: Islam and Confucianism; the former pursues its own values and norms, as does the latter in relation to the promotion of 'Asian values'. Samuel Huntington (1993) helped to focus attention on their anti-US stance in his influential essay on 'the clash of civilizations'. However, as Thomas (1999) points out, there is a conceptual problem in relation to how the impact of religion on international order might usefully be examined: is it an aspect of different cultures, civilizations, ideational communities, or as stand-alone transnational ideas in international relations? Huntington's argument carries within it a vital, fundamental postulation that all these approaches acknowledge: no matter how the categories are described, they carry a key assumption – the post-Cold War world is a time and place where the most important challenges to international order will come from groups defined in religious and cultural terms. This is because civilizational and/or cultural differences are said by Huntington to be both fundamental and permanent. 'Even more than ethnicity, religion discriminates sharply and exclusively among people' (Huntington, 1993: 27). He also contends that 'differences between civilisations are not only real; they are basic, they differentiate people by history, language, and religion. . . . they are far more fundamental than differences among political ideologies and political regimes' (ibid: 25).

Conclusion

We can draw the following conclusions from our discussion in this chapter. First, the contemporary visibility of religious actors in international relations calls into question a hitherto basic tenet of Western social sciences: modernization goes hand in hand with secularization and, as a result, religion is privatized, that is, socially and politically marginalized. Secondly, certain events and developments – especially the 1979 Iranian revolution, the first Gulf War of 1990–91, 9/11 and the development of 'anti-Western' 'Asian values' – collectively emphasize the propensity of religion to affect international order, built on secular processes of modernization and development over time. Thirdly, from the seventeenth century to the twentieth, international order developed increasingly institutional procedures and mechanisms, while the public role of religion declined. Recently, however, religion and culture have returned to international relations, with ramifications for international order. Fourthly, this in turn was linked to political, social and economic upheavals that have occurred following the end of the Cold War, the collapse of the Soviet Union and associated Eastern European Communist systems, and the onset of a deepening phase of globalization. Finally, as the forces of change have swept across the globe, affecting both developed and underdeveloped worlds, large numbers of people seem to have become unconvinced by the secular values that underpin international order, and have done for centuries. Instead, many believe that they can most effectively pursue their goals through membership of religious groups or movements, a development with both domestic and international ramifications. According to Huntington, this has encouraged real or perceived differences between civilizational/cultural groups to become politically salient.

He also claims that conflict between such groups will be both more prolonged and more violent than the secular conflicts of the Cold War, with serious impacts on international order (Huntington, 1993: 25). As a result, according to Thomas, 'in so far as it is a component of civilisational or ideational conflict, [religion] undermines the possibility of international society' (Thomas, 1999: 32). In the next chapter, we turn our attention to various religious non-state transnational actors – in particular the Roman Catholic Church and the Organization of the Islamic Conference – in order to assess their impact on international order and the development of international society.

Note

1   In international relations a regime is, according to Krasner, a set 'of implicit or explicit principles, norms, rules, and decision making procedures around which actors' expectations converge in a given area of international relations' (Krasner, 1983: 2). Such areas include: human rights, human and social development, and democratization and democracy.

Questions

1   'A global resurgence of religion is increasingly impacting upon international political outcomes, facilitated by the processes of globalization and encouraged by the communications revolution.' Discuss.

2   What was the overall impact of religion upon international order in the historical past?

3   To what extent did the end of the Cold War in 1989 change how religion engaged with international-order issues?

4   What is the relationship between globalization and international order?

5   Can war ever be justified?

Bibliography

Ayubi, N. (1999) 'The politics of Islam in the Middle East with special reference to Egypt, Iran and Saudi Arabia', in J. Haynes (ed.), *Religion, Globalization and Political Culture in the Third World,* Basingstoke: Macmillan, pp. 71–92.

Beyer, P. (1994) *Religion and Globalization*, London: Sage.

Brown, C. (2005) *Understanding International Relations*, 3rd edn, Basingstoke: Palgrave.

Bull, H. (1977) *The Anarchical Society*, London: Macmillan.

Buzan, B. (2004) *From International to World Society? English School Theory and the Social Structure of Globalisation*, Cambridge: Cambridge University Press.

Clark, I. (2005) 'Globalization and the post-Cold War order', in J. Baylis and S. Smith (eds), *The Globalization of World Politics: An Introduction to International Relations*, 3rd edn, Oxford: Oxford University Press, pp. 727–42.

Ervin, Kent C. (2006) 'Terrorism's soft targets', *The Washington Post*, 7 May. Available at: http://www.washingtonpost.com/wp-dyn/content/article/2006/05/05/AR2006050501754.html Accessed 10 May 2006.

Fox, J. (2001) 'Religion as an overlooked element of international relations', *International Studies Review*, 3(2), pp. 53–73.

Hague, R. and Harrop, M. (2001) *Comparative Government and Politics: An Introduction*, 5th edn, Basingstoke: Palgrave.

Haynes, J. (2005a) *Comparative Politics in a Globalizing World*, Cambridge: Polity.

Haynes, J. (ed.) (2005b) *Palgrave Advances in Development Studies*, Basingstoke: Palgrave Macmillan.

Held, D. and McGrew, A. (2002) *Globalization/Anti-Globalization*, Cambridge: Polity.

Human Security Report (2005), Oxford: Oxford University Press.

Huntington, S. (1993) 'The clash of civilizations?', *Foreign Affairs*, 72(3), pp. 22–49.

Jackson, R. and Owens, P. (2005) 'The evolution of international society', in J. Baylis and S. Smith (eds), *The Globalization of World Politics: An Introduction to International Relations*, 3rd edn, Oxford: Oxford University Press, pp. 45–62.

Krasner, S. (ed.) (1983) *International Regimes*, Ithaca, NY: Cornell University Press.

Krauthammer, C. (2004) 'When unilateralism is right and just', in J. B. Hehir, M. Walzer, L. Richardson, S. Telhami, C. Krauthammer and J. Lindsay, *Liberty and Power: A Dialogue on Religion and U.S. Foreign Policy in an Unjust World*, Washington, DC: Brookings Institution Press, pp. 95–99.

Kurth, J. (1999) 'Religion and globalization'. The Templeton Lecture on Religion and World Affairs, *Foreign Policy Research Institute Wire*, Vol. 7, No. 7. Available at: http://www.fpri.org/fpriwire/0707.199905.kurth.religionglobalization.html Accessed 18 March 2004.

Lapid, Y. and Kratochwil, F. (1996) *The Return of Culture and Identity in International Relations Theory*, Boulder, CO: Lynne Rienner.

Lieven, A. (2001) 'Strategy for terror', *Prospect,* Issue 67, pp. 19–23.

Mendelsohn, B. (2005) 'Sovereignty under attack: the international society meets the Al Qaeda network', *Review of International Studies*, 31, pp. 45–68

Milton-Edwards, B. (2006) *Islam and Violence in the Modern Era*, Basingstoke: Palgrave.

Norman, R. (1995) *Ethics, Killing, and War*, Cambridge: Cambridge University Press.

Ommerborn, W. (n.d., probably 2003) 'The importance of universal principles in Confucianism and the problems connected to Jiang Qing's concept of political Confucianism and his theory of particular principles'. Available at: http://www.eko-haus.de/menzius/universal.htm#_ftnref3]%20 Accessed 16 January 2006.

Orend, B. (2001) *War and International Justice*, Waterloo, Ontario: Wilfrid Laurier University Press.

Paskins, B. and Dockrill, M. (1979) *The Ethics of War*, London: Duckworth.

Rudolph, S. and Piscatori, J. (eds) (1997) *Transnational Religion and Fading States*, Boulder, CO: Westview.

Shani, G. (2002) ' "A revolt against the west": politicized religion and the international order. A comparison of the Islamic *Umma* and the Sikh *Qaum*', *Ritsumeikan Annual Review of International Studies*, Volume 1, pp. 15–31.

Thomas, S. (1999) 'Religion and international society', in J. Haynes (ed.), *Religion, Globalization and Political Culture in the Third World,* Basingstoke: Macmillan, pp. 28–44.

Thomas, S. (2005) *The Global Resurgence of Religion and the Transformation of International Relations: The Struggle for the Soul of the Twenty-First Century*, New York and Basingstoke: Palgrave Macmillan.

Walzer, M. (1977) *Just and Unjust Wars*, New York: Perseus Books.

Further reading

H. Bull, *The Anarchical Society: A Study of Order in World Politics*, Macmillan, 1977. This book is widely regarded as Bull's most systematic and fundamental work. He explores three main questions: What is the nature of order in world politics? How is it maintained in the contemporary state system? What alternative paths to world order are feasible and desirable? According to Bull, the system of sovereign states is not in decline and far from being an obstacle to world order is actually its essential foundation.

B. Buzan, *From International to World Society? English School Theory and the Social Structure of Globalisation*, Cambridge University Press, 2004. Buzan offers a bracing critique and reappraisal of the English School approach. He begins with the often neglected concept of world society, focusing on the international society tradition and constructivism. He then develops a new theoretical framework that can be used to address globalization as a complex political interplay among state and non-state actors.

Y. Lapid and F. Kratochwil (eds) *The Return of Culture and Identity in International Relations Theory*, Lynne Rienner, 1996. In an examination of cultural change in the post-Cold War era, this work addresses a series of questions covering topics such as the lack of interest in culture and identity in IR theory, and the case for rethinking the contemporary theoretical reach of the concepts.

R. Norman, *Ethics, Killing, and War*, Cambridge University Press, 1995. Norman examines key questions in relation to just war: Can war ever be justified? Why is it wrong to kill? He provides practical examples, such as the 1990–91 Gulf War and the Falklands War in 1982 to show that, while moral philosophy can offer no easy answers, it is a worthwhile enterprise which sheds light on many pressing contemporary problems. A combination of lucid exposition and original argument makes this the ideal introduction to both the particular debate about the ethics of killing and war, and the fundamental issues of moral philosophy itself.

B. Orend, *War and International Justice*, Wilfrid Laurier University Press, 2001. Brian Orend contends in this book that Immanuel Kant's theory of international justice not only accommodates just war's traditional understanding of the morality of war, but improves it. The main strengths of Orend's book lie in its clear writing, theoretical analysis, and insightful interpretation of Kant's theory of international justice as well as his views on the morality of war.

M. Walzer, *Just and Unjust War*, Perseus Books, 1977. This classic work examines not only the issues surrounding military theory, war crimes and the spoils of war, from the Athenian attack on Melos to the My Lai massacre, but also a variety of conflicts in order to understand exactly why, according to Walzer, 'the argument about war and justice is still a political and moral necessity'.

CHAPTER 5

Religion and international order: transnational religious actors

The aim of this chapter is to look at transnational religious non-state actors in the context of international order. We saw in the previous chapter that the concept of international order centres on two themes: (1) more or less consensual international acceptance of common values and norms, including the body of international law, and (2) development of institutions geared to preserve and develop international order. The combination of structures and processes – involving various actors, rules, mechanisms and understandings – serves overall to manage the coexistence and interdependence of state and non-state actors in the context of 'international society'. In the literature, there is no consensus about the impact of transnational religious actors on international order, although there is generally acceptance that various religious actors can influence international order outcomes in various ways (Rudoph and Piscatori, 1997; Thomas, 2005; Petito and Hatzopoulos, 2003; Carlson and Owens, 2003).

It is, however, clear that some religious actors present significant challenges to international order, especially extremist Islamist organizations, such as al-Qaeda, the key focus of the post-9/11 US-directed 'war on terror' (Shani, 2002). The post-9/11 focus on al-Qaeda has more generally reignited the debate on the 'clash of civilizations' controversy, while at the same time serving to obscure the emergence of what many regard as a new transnational religious landscape marked by both interreligious conflict *and* cooperation, and involving a number of broadly human rights and development issues (Rudolph and Piscatori, 1997; Thomas, 2005;

Bouta et al., 2005). Informing this development are the circumstances we discussed in Chapter 4, especially the impact of globalization and the accompanying communications revolution. This is a key factor in encouraging recent and continuing dynamic growth of transnational networks of religious actors (Rudolph and Piscatori, 1997; Florini, 2000). In addition, over the past two decades or so, global migration patterns have also helped spawn more active transnational religious communities (Willetts, 2005). The overall result is a new religious pluralism that has impacted upon international relations in two key ways. First, there has been an emergence of what Spickard calls 'global religious identities' that may lead to increasing interreligious dialogues, involving greater religious engagement around various issues, including international development, conflict resolution, and transitional justice (Spickard, 2003). On the other hand, this globalizing environment is also said in some cases to encourage greater, often more intense, interreligious competition, for example between Muslims and Christians in Nigeria and Uganda (Bouta et al., 2005; Juergensmeyer, 2005; Haynes, 1996).

The contention of this chapter is that the dynamics of the new religious pluralism influence the global political landscape, with significant impacts upon international order. To provide evidence for the claim that (1) transnational religious actors are increasingly influential in international relations and (2) what they do is important for international order, we focus on three sets of transnational religious actors in the second half of the chapter: American evangelical Protestants, the Roman Catholic Church, and the Organization of the Islamic Conference. According to Kristoff (2002), American evangelical Protestants are the 'new internationalists', having developed a wide post-Cold War international agenda focusing on improving development, health, and religious freedom, especially in the developing world. This claim is, however, contested (Mitchell, 2003). Similarly, the Roman Catholic Church has also sought to develop its transnational influence in recent years, especially by encouraging numerous authoritarian governments – in Latin America, Africa and Eastern Europe – to democratize and inaugurate improved human-rights regimes. Finally, the Organization of the Islamic Conference, an international Muslim organization with both religious and political concerns, was established in 1969 to promote dialogue and cooperation between Muslim and Western governments. In sum, these three sets of actors all wish to see the spread and development of certain values and norms, with potential impact on international order.

Transnational actors and soft power

Each of these transnational religious actors aims to spread their influence by the establishment and development of cross-border networks, focusing on increasing acceptance. They aim to spread influence by the application of 'soft power'. We noted earlier that the concept of soft power is closely associated with the American international relations expert, Joseph Nye (Nye, 2004). Soft power is the power of attractive ideas to persuade individuals or groups to act in a certain way, in pursuit of identifiable goals. Soft power can be conceptually contrasted with the notion of 'hard power', that is military or economic influence, which is more about leverage or coercion. Note that not all sources of transnational soft power are religious. Important transnational secular sources of soft power include:

- *Communism* (Karl Marx and Frederick Engels' *Communist Manifesto* was published in 1848. The ideology that developed from it – Marxism – was until the demise of the Soviet Union in 1991 an important source of transnational soft power)

- *Zionism* (the notion that Jews should return to and live in Israel. Zionists believe that Israel is the Jews' 'promised land')[1]

- *Pan-Africanism* (a general term for various movements in Africa that have as their common goal the political unity of all Africans, who had been unjustly divided into nation-states by European colonialism)

- *Pan-Arabism* (a similarly general term for the modern movement for political unification among the Arab nations of the Middle East)

- *'Afro-Asian solidarity'* (a 'Third-Worldist' ideology emphasizing the perceived shared developmental and political goals and values of post-colonial Africans and Asians).

These secular transnational ideas emerged and developed in response to changing international circumstances during the nineteenth and, especially, twentieth centuries. Since the Second World War in particular, various concerns, including anti-colonialism, anti-imperialism, anti-racism, national self-determination, and environmentalism, have encouraged the creation and development of transnational networks (Florini, 2000; Keck and Sikkink, 1998). Such ideas represent soft power in international relations because they appeal to large numbers of people around the world who, by virtue of their collective effort, may seek to influence outcomes in the directions they would like to see. Success or failure does not necessarily depend on their ability to link up with state power. As Thomas puts it: 'Transnational actors represent – or are seen to represent by individuals and groups in the international community – ideas whose time has come, ideas which increasingly shape the values and norms of the international system' (Thomas, 1999: 30). In sum, transnational ideas, both religious and secular, can help set and mould international agendas. They do this by adding to the lexicon and vocabulary of debate; and in some cases they are a source of soft power in international relations, informing the ideas and development of what is known as transnational civil society.

Transnational civil society

We saw in Chapter 2 that most theories of international relations are premised on the analytical centrality of the state, although all would accept that in some contexts non-state actors can also be of significance (Sullivan, 2002; Burchill et al., 2005). For example, in the 1970s there was widespread recognition of the importance of the Organization of Petroleum Exporting Countries (OPEC) for international economic and political outcomes. From this time, more generally, states were no longer necessarily seen as the only key actors in international relations. A focus on other non-state actors – including transnational corporations and various international organizations, such as the European Union – also emphasized growing political and economic significance of transnational actors (Florini, 2000; Willetts, 2005). One particular strand of international relations theory – referred to variously as liberalism, liberal internationalism or liberal institutionalism – sees international relations as an aggregate of different issue areas. These include: trade, finance, energy, human rights, democracy, and the natural environment; these are all contexts where domestic and international policy processes are seen to merge and interact. Management of the result – growing global interdependencies – is understood to be carried out at various levels via processes characterized by bargaining, negotiation and consensus-seeking, processes that often involve both state and non-state actors (Burchill, 2005). In this view, international order is not maintained, as the Realists would have it, by the 'balance of power'. Instead, it comes about as the result of a more or less consensual acceptance of common values, norms and the legitimacy of international legal frameworks focused in an 'international society' (Buzan, 2004; Jackson and Owens, 2005).

Cosmopolitanism

The idea that all of humanity belongs to a single 'moral community' with important sets of shared values is reflected in the notion of 'cosmopolitanism' (Beck, 2005). This idea is contrasted with divisive ideologies, such as patriotism and nationalism. The idea of cosmopolitanism may extend to a physical entity: some sort of global administration or world government, perhaps reflected in an extension of powers for the United Nations. Or it may less grandiosely refer to more inclusive relationships between nations or individuals of different nations that have shared moral, economic, and political ideals and goals. As the Cold War came to an end in the late 1980s, the 'cosmopolitan world-view' emerged in order to try to make sense of global events and changes (Held, 2003). In sum, cosmopolitanism puts transnationally-orientated groups with shared values at the centre of analysis, while overall stressing the importance of various non-state actors for outcomes in international relations in the context of 'global' or 'transnational' civil society.[2]

How best to characterize transnational civil society? While there are various views expressed in the literature, most would agree that transnational civil society is a separate concept, linked to but different from domestic civil society (Willetts, 2005). The key point is that the overall concern of domestic civil societies – that is, the group of non-state organizations, interest groups and associations, such as trade unions, professional associations, further and higher education students, religious bodies and the media – is to maintain a check on the power of the state (Stepan, 1988). The idea of *transnational* civil society is that it seeks to undertake broadly the same job as *domestic* civil society *but at the international* level. For Lipschutz, transnational civil society is 'the self-conscious constructions of networks of knowledge and action, by decentred, local actors, that cross the reified boundaries of space as though they were not there' (Lipschutz, 1992: 390). The outcome of such transnational interactions is what Attina refers to as a 'social transnationalism'. This collectively links cross-border networks, focusing them in a transnational civil society that cuts across international borders. It serves to link together individuals and groups from various different national societies by developing and then institutionalizing linkages between geographically separate *but like-minded persons and groups* (Attina, 1989: 344).

In sum, transnational civil society

- is an expression of soft power;

- focuses attention on development of regularized, often expanding, interactions that occur between individuals and groups across national boundaries;

- involves a situation where at least one participant actor in such interactions is a *non-state actor*;

- unlike domestic civil society, is not *territorially* fixed;

- has a field of action that is fluid – implying that geographical boundaries can change as a result of the influence of new or newly relevant issues and changing circumstances;

- does not operate on *behalf of* a national government – such as that of the USA, India or Iran – nor seek to advance the corporate interests of an intergovernmental organization, for example, the European Union or the United Nations;

- represents and focuses specific norms, values and objectives shared by numerous people, including *national liberation* (for example, the Palestine Liberation Organization), *environmental protection* (Greenpeace; Friends of the Earth) and *better human rights* (Amnesty International; the International Committee of the Red Cross; Human Rights Watch).

Religious actors and transnational soft power

Transnational actors hardly ever control territory – although the Taliban government in Afghanistan did allow Osama bin Laden and al-Qaeda considerable freedom of movement in the country until prevented by the US invasion in 2001. More generally, 'failed' states may allow terrorist groups, including religious terrorist groups, greater freedom of action than when there is a functioning central government (Thürer, 1999). But to undermine or enhance international order, any transnational actor, including religious ones, would necessarily have an impact upon state sovereignty. What is state sovereignty? For Bealey, it is 'a claim to authority, originally by sovereign monarchs, but by states since the Treaty of Westphalia in 1648. A state becomes sovereign when other states recognise it as such' (Bealey, 1999: 306). Thus state sovereignty refers to a state's independence from overt interference by another state or states. Bealey's definition makes no mention of non-state actors, whether secular or religious.

Absence of focus on religious bodies when discussing sovereignty in international relations is not entirely surprising: it reflects key presumptions encouraged by 400 years of international history and the impact over time of a comprehensive secularization process (Philpott, 2002). It is important to note, however, that before the development of the modern international system, both Islam and Christianity involved geographically extensive transnational religious communities, carriers of both religious soft and hard power. This underlines that modern religious transnational movements are not *de novo* but have important historical foundations.

Islam expanded from its Arabian heartland in westerly, easterly, southerly and northerly directions from the seventh century and as a result created the *ummah*, that is, the global community of Muslims. Vast territories in Africa and Asia and smaller areas of Europe (parts of the Balkans and much of the Iberian peninsular) came under Muslim control. However, Islam was unable to deal with the emergence of centralized European polities: the Muslims' European empire fell, a consequence of the rise of centralized European states with their superior firepower and organizational skills. In sum, Islam, a religious, social and cultural system, grew to become a global religion via the growth of a transnational religious community but was increasingly challenged by non-Muslim polities in Europe.

Christendom is another historic example of a transnational religious society that, unlike the *ummah*, no longer exists (Lewis, 1990). During medieval times 'Christendom' referred to a generalized conception among Christians of being subject to universal norms and laws derived from the word of God; these ideas informed international conceptions of order, reflected in such concerns as the religious basis of 'just war' theories (Dolan, 2005). Later, contemporaneous with the demise of Islam as a major cultural force in Europe, European expansion to non-European areas in what we now know as the 'developing world' facilitated the growth of various transnational Christian communities. From the early sixteenth century, the transnational spread of Christianity was facilitated by the search for gold in South America by Spanish and Portuguese 'explorers'. This eventually led to the establishment in the 'New World' of various European-administered colonies; contemporaneously, Christian Europeans also grabbed territory in the Caribbean and in Asia. Overall, the geographical spread of Christianity was inextricably linked to European expansion, a major component of a web of global interactions with significant impacts on international order via the establishment of European colonies. Later, however, the public role of religion became increasingly marginal to political outcomes as secular states rose to prominence in Europe and elsewhere. During the nineteenth and twentieth centuries, international relations developed in the context of an international order both moulded and challenged by various often clashing secular ideologies – nationalism, communism, and liberal democracy.

In sum, prior to the seventeenth century, religious interactions were pivotal to the emergence of an embryonic international system, employing both soft and hard power, before significantly declining in importance until recently. Christian and Muslim transnational religious communities significantly pre-dated the emergence of centralized secular states and the current international order regime. Over time, as a result of transnational expansion, both Christianity and Islam grew to become numerically the largest world religions, conveying their associated civilizations around the world.

Seyom Brown and the concept of ideational power

Transnational interactions between religious actors can involve various expressions of soft power, built on interactions of ideas and personnel that link together people in different countries in pursuit of shared goals. But the outcomes in this regard are controversial. We have already noted the work of Samuel Huntington and his concept of the 'clash of civilizations'. Now, it is time to examine the work of Seyom Brown and his concept of ideational power.

Brown's concept of 'ideational power' focuses on religion and culture as a transnational idea in international relations which both informs the development of transnational civil society and is a source of soft power. For Brown (1995: 157)

> formation and disintegration of the world's empires, the establishment and demise of hegemonic spheres of influence, and the maintenance by ordinary countries of their independence and way of life are functions not simply of the distribution of military and economic power. The only durable cement of nations and empires cannot be coerced or purchased. Over the long haul, it is ideas that bind more than chains or bank accounts . . . .

Brown contends that a state's ability to 'prevail in conflicts' with its opponents depends 'on the attractive power of ideas that bind people to one another in communities and impel them to sacrifice personal possessions and security, even their lives' for the state. Implicitly, Brown is referring here to the power of soft power: when people are encouraged to act as a result of ideas to which they are attracted, they are demonstrating the attractive soft power of such ideas. For Brown, the side of a discussion, disagreement, competition or conflict that one feels compelled to adhere to, depends significantly on the ideational community that one feels most connected to in relation to a specific issue (ibid.). Brown identifies several ideational communities:

- *Muslims.* More than one-eighth of the world's population – nearly one billion people – are followers of Islam; together they comprise the *ummah* (global Muslim community).

- *Arabs.* This is an ethno-cultural, not a religious, bond that unites people whose sense of identity derives from their 'Arab-ness' (less than 40 per cent of the world's Muslims are Arabs).

- *Roman Catholics.* Followers of the world's biggest Christian religion amount to more than one billion, around 15 per cent of the overall global population.

- *Other Christians.* Among the biggest Christian groups in this category are the various Protestant and Orthodox churches, comprising together around 400 million people worldwide.

- *Jews.* The total number of Jews around the world amount to more than 15 million people. A total of 75 per cent live outside Israel, with around 6 million (40 per cent) living in the USA.

- *Pan-Africanism and the Black diaspora.* This is a uniting idea centring on a shared sense of 'African' identity.

- *'Eastern' religions.* Among them Brown includes Hinduism, Buddhism, and Shintoism in Japan.

- *'Others'.* This category includes: Hispanics, environmentalists (for example, Greenpeace International, Friends of the Earth), human rights activists (Amnesty International, Human Rights Watch), and peace activists (in the UK, the Campaign for Nuclear Disarmament).

From this list, we can see that Brown's notion of ideational communities focuses on both religious/cultural and secular groups and organizations. It also raises a question of importance for international relations: To what extent, if at all, do such transnational entities, especially religious ones, threaten state sovereignty and hence international order? The issue gains added piquancy by the fact that most theories of international relations have not devoted much sustained attention to religious and cultural phenomena. This may be because various (primarily secular) transnational linkages and penetration have usually been examined in international relations literature primarily to assess their significance for traditional questions of (secular) political and economic security. In other words, a conventional security bias in most of the literature on transnational actors in international relations explains a corresponding lack of focus on religious and cultural actors (Baylis, 2005).

Until recently, with the rise of Islamic and other forms of religious fundamentalisms, such actors were judged to be remote from central questions affecting states' and human kind's security. The explanation for this neglect lies in a key assumption embedded in the social sciences. One presupposition, especially evident in theories of modernization and political development, was that the future of the integrated nation-state lay in secular participatory politics. The assumption was that nation-building would be ill-served by perceived 'obscurantist' beliefs such as religion; nearly everywhere it seemed, secular political leaders dominated, displacing once-powerful religious figures. The implication was that, in order successfully to build nation-states, political leaders would have to remain as neutral as possible from the entanglements of particularist claims, especially those derived from religious beliefs, norms and values. Politics must be separated from religious and cultural concerns to avoid dogmatism and encourage tolerance among citizens, as a crucial prelude to building viable nation-states. Decades of apparently unstoppable movement towards increasingly secular societies in Western and other 'modernized' parts of the world reinforced the assumption that religion and piety would everywhere inevitably become private matters. Consequently, in international relations analysis, religion was regarded as an increasingly minor problem of little or no significance in the search for national unity and political stability.

Such a view, we have already noted, is problematic. If it was correct, how could we explain and account for the significance of religion for current international relations, not least significant religious transnational actors with various political, social and developmental goals that in some cases form transnational civil societies (Florini, 2000: 8–9; Rudolph and Piscatori, 1997; Thomas, 2005)? To examine this issue further in the next sections of the chapter we focus upon three examples of transnational religious actors: American evangelical Protestants, the Roman Catholic Church, and the Organization of the Islamic Conference.

American evangelical Protestants

The old religious right led by Jerry Falwell and Pat Robertson, trying to battle Satan with school prayers and right-to-life amendments, is on the ropes. It is being succeeded by evangelicals who are using their growing clout to skewer China and North Korea, to support Israel, to fight sexual trafficking in Eastern Europe and slavery in Sudan, and, increasingly, to battle AIDS in Africa (Kristoff, 2002: A21).

In the United States, American evangelical Protestants were often linked with various figures, including Jerry Falwell and Pat Roberston, whose focus was, as the quotation from Kristoff suggests, concerned with bringing religion back into the public realm. Internationally, their concern was also 'trying to battle Satan'; in this context, international Communism represented the Devil. D'Antonio argues that right-wing American evangelical Protestants aided and abetted 'anti-Communist' forces in both Latin America and Africa in the 1980s, during the closing years of the Cold War (d'Antonio, 1990). Such right-wing evangelical Protestants not only had their 'eyes set on heaven' but were also concerned with 'earthly' political matters. They were often stridently anti-Communist, with a vision of the world rooted in a literal interpretation of the Bible that encouraged them to move in right-wing circles (Martin, 1990; Freston, 2001). The obvious inference is that they were likely to become strategic allies of military and civilian dictators. For example, during the 1980s and 1990s, American-style evangelical Protestantism made considerable advances in Guatemala at the expense of the Roman Catholic Church. During this time, American Protestants built alliances with assorted conservative politicians, such as the former president Rios Mott (Martin, 1990). The transnational alliance between American and local right-wing Protestant evangelicals was based on shared religious and political convictions. Both parties had a common goal: to undermine or destroy the socially progressive policies that liberation theology activists within the Roman Catholic Church in Guatemala had sought to develop (Haynes, 1998: 56–9).

Another example of American evangelical Protestants' transnational political involvement comes from Southern Africa, also during the 1980s and 1990s. Like their counterparts in Guatemala, right-wing American evangelical Protestants also worked to aid anti-Communist political forces, in this case anti-government rebel movements, RENAMO (Mozambique) and UNITA (Angola). Both RENAMO and UNITA were involved in long-running civil wars against their 'Communist' governments in a conflict which was portrayed to the outside world as a battle of 'pro-religion freedom fighters' versus 'godless communist' regimes (Pieterse, 1992). The wider context was that during the Cold War successive governments in the USA were particularly concerned at what they perceived as a concerted attempt by the Soviet Union to expand its influence not in only Latin America – via the baleful influence of Cuba – and sub-Saharan Africa. In this context, right-wing American evangelical Protestants were concerned both to confront Satan (that is, Communism) and to 'win souls for Christ' (that is, attract converts from Roman Catholicism) (d'Antonio, 1990; Martin, 1990; Freston, 2001).

It is by no means clear, however, that their efforts were coordinated or funded by the US government or one of its agencies. Nevertheless, one of the clearest examples of the dual religious and political role of American evangelical Protestants during the 1980s comes from Zimbabwe. In 1988, Robert Mugabe's government curtailed proselytizing among Mozambican refugees in Zimbabwe by American evangelical Protestant organizations, including Jimmy Swaggart Ministries, World Vision International and Compassion Ministries. All were accused of close links with RENAMO. Suspicions appeared to be confirmed when a South African, Peter Hammond, of Front Line Fellowship, and six American missionaries of the Christian Emergency Relief Teams (CERT) were captured in Tete province by Mozambique government soldiers in late 1989 (Southscan, 1989). The overall point is that various politically conservative, mostly American, evangelical Protestant individuals and groups worked to aid anti-Communist allies in Mozambique and Angola during their civil wars. However, this does not seem to have been a campaign involving either the hierarchies of the churches themselves or the government of the USA.

Evangelical Protestantism in Southern Africa in the 1980s

Front Line Fellowship was founded on a South African military base in Namibia, allegedly by soldiers who wanted to take Bibles into Angola on their raids; in other words, they were soldier-missionaries, virulently anti-Communist, mostly drawn from the (former Rhodesian) Selous Scouts and Five Recce, the South African Special Forces unit which ran RENAMO. A local Zimbabwean church, Shekinah Ministries, associated with an American Protestant evangelist, Gordon Lindsay, was discovered aiding the RENAMO (Mozambique National Resistance) bandits in Mozambique in 1987. In neighbouring Angola the counter-productive nature of the MPLA government's anti-religion policy was evidenced in the Ovimbundu highlands and to the south-east, where 'a resistant Church of Christ in the Bush developed in tandem with UNITA (National Union for the Total Independence of Angola)' (Haynes, 1996: 223).

After the Cold War, the transnational focus of American evangelical Protestantism shifted away from a concern with confronting and defeating Communism. Kristoff (2002) argues that the shift in focus is represented by a 'new internationalist' agenda. This refers to the fact that after the Cold

War their focus has moved away from anti-Communism to a concern with international development and human rights issues. Such concerns include: religious freedom (especially in relation to the twin *bête noires*, China and North Korea), supporting Israel, fighting sexual trafficking in Eastern Europe and slavery in Sudan and battling AIDS in Africa (Mitchell, 2003).

This agenda also implies that there will be a pronounced focus on political concerns. What happens when right-wing evangelical Protestantism, based on scriptural orthodoxy, participates in the often-volatile politics of Latin America and sub-Saharan Africa? Freston (2006) poses two specific questions in relation to this issue:

- What is the likely outcome: democratic politics of the ballot box or an authoritarian politics of command from on high?

- Does the evangelical faith of the Bible hinder or promote a politics of the ballot box?

Freston offers a useful comparative perspective on this important issue. The context is that in many parts of Latin America and some African countries, right-wing evangelical Protestantism with roots in the USA is challenging historical regional Catholic religious dominance. According to Freston, in Latin America Protestant identity is being forged in relation to the dominant Catholicism, producing an adversarial style of Protestantism that significantly informs the role of associated evangelicalism in Latin American civil society (Freston, 2004: 102–8).

Freston on American Protestant evangelicals

Freston (2001) has examined the role of American Protestant evangelicals in three regions of the developing world: Asia, Africa and Latin America. He explains that a useful working definition of the term 'evangelical' would stress four main characteristics:

- *conversionism* (emphasis on the need to change one's life);

- *activism* (particularly missionary efforts);

- *biblicism* (the special importance of the Bible, though not necessarily fundamentalist 'inerrancy'); and

- *crucicentrism* (stressing the centrality of Christ's sacrifice on the cross).

Freston makes it clear that while many Protestants are *evangelical*, this does not mean that all are right-wing fundamentalists, believing in the inerrancy of the Bible. This also suggests that it is a mistake to differentiate between established 'main-line' Protestant churches and evangelical ones. In fact, many among the former are also strongly evangelical. For example, evangelicals are prominent (indeed growing) in the Church of England as well as in the Anglican Church of Kenya, whose archbishop in the 1990s, David Gitari, was also a prominent critic of the then governing regime of President Daniel arap Moi (Haynes, 1998: 116–17).

Freston (2001) draws several conclusions on the characteristics of Protestant evangelical politics. First, politically they span the spectrum from far left to extreme right. Secondly, evangelical conservatism in personal morals and social matters does not automatically translate into endorsement of right-wing parties and dictatorship. For example, a number of churches and pastors heartily endorsed the socialist Sandinista government of Nicaragua from 1979 to 1990, while others were fiercely critical of the regime. Similarly, evangelical parliamentarians of varying ideological hues can be found in Brazil, while at the grassroots many pastors and believers are also strong supporters of the Brazilian labour movement (Haynes, 1998: 51–7).

Thirdly, it is an overstatement to link Protestant evangelicals in the developing world with United States-backed right-wing politics. For example, while some evangelical churches are conservative, there may well be a clear division between the leadership of a church and its rank-and-file members, who will have a variety of political views (Haynes, 1998; Freston, 2001, 2004, 2006). Fourthly, conclusive evidence of direct CIA or State Department influence on such evangelicals is also very hard to substantiate.

Finally, there is an important cultural factor to note. In many Latin American countries, such as Chile, where Catholicism is either predominant or the established church, evangelicals find themselves adopting a more defensive posture (Fleet and Smith, 2000). In others, including Mexico, where anticlericalism was linked to national independence, evangelicals have historically been part of the political establishment (Freston, 2004: 102–8).

The Roman Catholic Church

We can draw a parallel between how the right-wing American Protestant evangelical focus has shifted in recent years from a singular 'anti-Communism' to a wider focus on development and human rights with the changing concerns of the Roman Catholic Church over the same period. During the 1980s and 1990s, the Church's transnational focus was squarely anti-Communism and against authoritarian governments then common in Latin America, Eastern Europe, and sub-Saharan Africa. A Roman Catholic civil society headed by the Pope offered support and encouragement to pro-democratization initiatives (Philpott, 2004). It played an important role in bringing about the 'third wave of democracy', between the mid-1970s and the mid-1990s (Huntington, 1991; Haynes, 2001a).

This development was the outcome of a lengthy historical process whereby both the Church and, increasingly, democratic states, especially in Europe, came to tolerate each other. During the third wave of democracy, the Church exercised a direct influence upon democratization in several countries – strongly in Poland, Lithuania, Spain, the Philippines, Brazil, and various African countries, but weakly elsewhere, for example Argentina. Philpott concludes that the Church was most likely to be influential in this regard when the popular perception was to see it as quite distinct from the state in various ways: in its governance, transnational links, domestic alliances and in its identification with national identity (Philpott, 2004: 42).

The overall context is that of the debate about the nature of 'Catholic modernism', a movement in the nineteenth and twentieth centuries among Catholics that sought to reconcile Christianity with modern views of the world. During the nineteenth century, the Roman Catholic Church was against both liberalism and democracy, a stance which carried on after the First World War when the Church was widely seen as their 'uncompromising opponent' (Rueschemeyer et al., 1992: 281) In the 1920s and 1930s, the Church tried to deal with the rise of Fascism in Italy and Spain by giving it at least tacit support. After the Second World War the Church enjoyed a close relationship with avowedly conservative Christian Democratic parties in Italy and (West) Germany, because they emphasized a political programme opposed to secular socialism and social democracy. It was not until the Second Vatican Council of 1962–65 (known as Vatican II) that the Pope and other senior figures in the Church began publicly to express concern with normatively 'progressive' issues, including human rights and democracy (Hastings, 1979: 173).

The Roman Catholic Church and social justice

Both the papacy and the Church took an increased interest in social justice issues, especially development and human rights, from the 1960s following the end of the Second Vatican Council in 1965. This was in the midst of a momentous period for international relations, with major potential and actual significance for international order concerns. First, there was the transition from

(Continued)

colonial to post-colonial rule in Africa and the aftermath of decolonization in Asia. Secondly, it was also the period of the rise of radical liberation theology primarily in Latin America and also in several other developing countries, including the Philippines and South Africa (where it was known as Black Theology [Haynes, 1996: 69–70, 150–1]). However, it was not the case that Roman Catholic officials from such developing regions and countries were necessarily championing liberation theology against the wishes of the Church's senior figures: in fact, it was often the case that Roman Catholic officials in Latin America, Africa and East Asia were strongly opposed to the socially progressive articulations emanating from Vatican II, and, at least initially, did little or nothing concrete to further their progress (Vaillancourt, 1980).

Articulation of an institutional Roman Catholic concern with social justice issues from the 1960s was followed, in the 1980s and 1990s, by a period of momentous change at the global level, a shift from the 'old' order to a new global one – and the Church was important in these changes. In particular, the Church was heavily involved in the breakdown of Communism in Eastern Europe, especially in the emblematic case of Poland (Philpott, 2004). The Church was a key player in encouraging Poland's fundamental political reforms in the late 1980s and early 1990s (Haynes, 1998: 93–4). In this regard, policies had an important transnational element, especially in relation to the institutional role of the Vatican and the personal leadership of the then Pope, John Paul II who was Polish. Especially encouraged by John Paul II's expressions of support, Polish Catholics increasingly represented both a counter-culture and alternative social space to the official Communist ideology and channels (Casanova, 1994). This led, in 1980, to the creation of the Solidarity movement that both articulated and expressed Catholic social ethics as a counter-statement to those of Communism. This reflected not only a significant convergence between national and religious identity in Poland, but also, just as importantly, it symbolized the failure of Communist (secular) identity fundamentally to implant itself in the hearts and minds of most Poles, a people whose cultural heritage was firmly based in their Catholic traditions and history. In sum, the Catholic heritage and traditions were a vital resource in helping create and then sustain resistance to Communism not only in Poland but also more widely in Eastern Europe. Note, however, that the key role of the Church in Poland's democratization is but one example of a much wider trend observable during the 1980s and 1990s. Witte observed that 'twenty-four of the thirty-two new democracies born since 1973 are predominantly Roman Catholic in confession', including those in: Brazil, Chile, the Philippines, South Korea, Poland, Hungary, Lithuania and various Latin countries, including Nicaragua and Guatemala (Witte, 1993: 11).

Prominent examples of the Church's transnational political involvement also come from various African countries. The Roman Catholic Church is by far the largest in Africa, with more than 140 million baptized followers. This means that about one in four Africans are Roman Catholics, roughly 13 per cent of the global total.[3] The Church's well-developed institutional structure under the Pope's leadership facilitates its ability to act transnationally – albeit with strong centralized control from the Vatican, a factor that encouraged its recent involvement in some of Africa's democratic changes. The involvement of the Church in Africa's democratic transitions followed the Pope's encyclical of January 1991 (*Redemptoris Missio*), centrally concerned with the Church's duty to help 'relieve poverty, counter political oppression and defend human rights'. Senior Roman Catholic figures – in, *inter alia*, Benin, Congo-Brazzaville, Togo, Gabon, and Zaire (now the Democratic Republic of the Congo) – were centrally involved in processes of democratic reform in each country. In each case they were selected by popular acclaim to chair their country's national democracy conferences (Gifford, 1994). Their aim was to attempt to reach consensus and develop a collective strategy involving both government and opposition over the democratic way forward. Why were Roman Catholic leaders chosen by popular acclaim to chair national democratization conferences? As Philpott notes, the answer is that, despite the often close personal relations with their countries' authoritarian governments, in popular perceptions such figures were representatives of an important, transnational organization *that was not perceived as being in thrall to the various authoritarian governments* (Philpott, 2004: 43). This was in part because of the churches' independent financial positions that enabled them to provide various manifestations of much-needed societal welfare – including, educational, health and developmental programmes – to the obvious satisfaction of numerous ordinary people.

It might seem, on the face of it, that the Roman Catholic Church's involvement in both the anti-Communist revolution in Poland and the contemporaneous process of Africa's democratization was a clear example of a transnational religious organization that worked to undermine state sovereignty. However, in both cases, the Church's role should be seen *not* as symptomatic of a desire to undermine state sovereignty, but rather primarily to reflect significant processes of both deepening globalization and nationalization which increasingly affected the Church at this time. The background was that to validate its claims to *catholicity* (that is, universality) the institutional Roman Catholic Church and its leader, the Pope, had to try to resolve two sets of tensions: the first was related to its role as a religious establishment that potentially involved conflict between the Vatican, national churches, and the increasingly global character and outlook of the transnational body of believers.

Looking at Catholicism globally throughout the twentieth century and particularly since the 1960s, three interrelated processes in dynamic tension with one another are apparent. Their interaction led to international outcomes with ramifications for international order. First, over time, as a consequence of its transnational growth there was both a global strengthening of papal supremacy and of the Vatican's administrative centralization. But this was also a period of evolving ideas within the Church in the context of a major debate over the issue of 'Catholic modernism'. One of the most important indications of this process was Vatican II (1962–65) and its result: an ensuing, general *aggiornamento* ('liberalization') that produced not only a pronounced trend towards administrative and doctrinal centralization but also a homogenization and globalization of Catholic culture at the elite level throughout the Catholic world. John Paul II, the Polish pope who died in 2005, was a key figure in carrying through this process (Philpott, 2004). In terms of international order, however, the centralizing and globalizing trend was important in facilitating the later ability of the Church to be a significant actor in many domestic and international fora in relation to a wider number of political, social, developmental and human rights concerns (Casanova, 1994).

Secondly, and occurring simultaneously with the process of Vatican and papal centralization was a parallel process: internationalization of the Church's administrative structures and globalization of *Catholicism* as a set of religious norms and practices. This reflected a trend emphasized in the twentieth century and beyond: by the 1960s, the Roman Catholic Church was no longer principally either a *Roman* or even a *European* institution. The global number of Roman Catholics nearly doubled in the 45 years after 1960, increasing from around 600 million in 1960, to nearly 1 billion in the mid-1990s, to 1.1 billion in 2005 (http://news.bbc.co.uk/1/hi/world/4243727.stm). Growth was especially focused on Africa and Asia – emphasizing a shift in the Roman Catholic population from Europe and North America to Latin America, Africa and Asia. As a consequence, the nature of the episcopal and administrative cadres of the Church underwent modification. The First Vatican Council (1869–70) was mainly a European event – albeit with 49 prelates from the USA, comprising one-tenth of the assembled bishops;

by Vatican II, a century later, Europeans no longer formed a majority of the 2,500 bishops in attendance. Instead, they came from most parts of the world: around 10 per cent – that is, 228 individual bishops – came Asia and Africa. This was the consequence of three connected developments: decolonization, growth in numbers of African and Asian Catholics and the indigenization of national churches. The overall result of the Church's extra-European geographical emphasis became clear: *internationalization of Catholicism from the middle of the twentieth century.* This meant that the Church was no longer inevitably centred on Rome and the Vatican. Instead, numerous, geographically dispersed, centres of Catholicism emerged, and this development helped to facilitate growth of transnational Catholic networks and exchanges of all kinds. Criss-crossing nations and world regions, they often bypassed Rome. In sum, in the decades after Vatican II, Catholicism became less centred on Rome although under John Paul II in particular the institution of the papacy became more prominent in international affairs. This was an important development, as it helped provide a focus on certain global values and norms – especially democracy, human rights and development – providing causes célèbres for the burgeoning Catholic transnational networks (Haynes, 1998, 2001b; Philpott, 2004).

Thirdly, there was a contemporaneous process at the national level of 'nationalization' and centralization of 'national' Catholic churches. After Vatican II, national conferences of bishops were institutionalized in many countries, an evolution which reinforced the dynamics of a process of nationalization that earlier had been carried out primarily by different forms of Catholic Action. These were lay groups – that is, not *religiously* associated with the Church – that sought to mobilize ordinary Catholics to defend and promote the interests of the Church after the Second World War era. This was a time, it is important to note, that was widely perceived by many Catholics as characterized by an increasingly hostile, modernized, above all *secular* environment (Vaillancourt, 1980; Casanova, 1994). As a consequence, Catholic political mobilization was principally orientated towards putting pressure on governments, either to resist disestablishment of the Church or to counteract secularist movements and parties, especially and most obviously socialist and Communist ones. However, Catholic recognition of the principle of religious freedom, together with the Church's gradual change of attitude toward the modern secular environment – increasingly, it came to accept developments linked to modernization, including a trend, in many countries, towards societal secularization – served to facilitate significant fundamental transformation of national Catholic churches. They ceased being or aspiring to be state compulsory institutions and instead evolved into free religious institutions linked to civil societies. One consequence was that Catholic churches came to dissociate themselves from authoritarian regime and some entered into overt conflict with them, for example, in Poland, in various African and Latin American countries (Philpott, 2004: 32).

In conclusion, the traditional position and attitude of the Catholic Church towards political regimes was that of neutrality towards all forms of government. That is, government was seen as 'legitimate' as long as its policies did not systematically infringe the corporate rights of the Church – to religious freedom and to the exercise of its functions. Under these circumstances, the Church would not question the general legitimacy of governing regimes. However, as the examples of the Church's recent political involvement in, *inter alia*, Poland and Africa suggest, the Church's view of what comprised a 'legitimate' government underwent significant change over time. Increasingly, its view was grounded in recognition that a 'legitimate' government had responsibilities to its citizens: to afford them a clear measure of democracy and a satisfactory array of human rights. In other words, modern forms of democracy were now the *only* acceptable form of polity, based normatively on universalist principles of individual political freedoms and civil rights.

We can conclude our discussion of the development of the Roman Catholic Church's transnational relations by noting the following points:

- A combination of factors – globalization, nationalization, secular involvement, and voluntary disestablishment – ultimately led the Roman Catholic Church to adopt a significant change of orientation, both within and between countries.

- National churches ceased viewing themselves as 'integrative community cults' of the nation-state.

- Instead, they adopted new transnational global identities that in certain circumstances – especially those provided by the existence of authoritarian governments – encouraged them to confront the state over a lack of democracy, human rights and development. Among the most significant developments involving the Church in the decades after Vatican II ended in 1965 were global dynamics favouring democracy and human rights and an associated international order which became a key focus of Catholic transnationalism.

- These developments became especially prominent in international relations in the 1980s and 1990s. This was a notable period in international history that was characterized by: collapse of the network of socialist states, (temporary) global defeat of national security doctrines, crisis of the established principle of non-interference in the internal affairs of states, general disavowal of state-led models of economic development and modernization, and a greater focus on civil society as an alternative source of soft power both within countries and transnationally.

The Organization of the Islamic Conference

We saw that the Roman Catholic Church's transnational activities focused broadly on human rights issues in the decades following the end of Vatican II in 1965. We also noted that this period was more generally characterized by increased activity of religious transnational actors; in the examples examined so far in this chapter the focus has been on Christian – Catholic and Protestant – examples. In order to provide a more balanced view, our final example comes from the Muslim world, and focuses upon the Organization of the Islamic Conference (OIC).

For some, the end of the Cold War and the unfolding of unprecedented acts of transnational terror on September 11, represented new civilizational cleavages, with Islam attaining renewed prominence in Western political concerns (Sheikh, 2002). Often perceived from ethnocentric or sensationalist viewpoints, how best can we understand Islam, as a strategic entity, in contemporary international relations? One important focus in this regard is the OIC, an entity sometimes referred to as the 'Muslim United Nations' (Kalin, 2006). This is because of the OIC's widespread international involvement in attempts to settle various post-Cold War conflicts, including: the first Gulf War (1990–91), the Palestine problem, the Balkan wars, the Chechnya campaign, and the nuclear competition in South Asia between Pakistan and India. The OIC also has an agenda that is concerned with striving for unity and solidarity among Muslim peoples, fighting against terror and extremism of all kinds, and recovering the middle path of moderation (http://www.oic oci.org).

The OIC is a 'moderate' Islamic intergovernmental organization whose aim is to increase cooperation, decrease conflict, build the international standing of Muslims and develop good and stable relations between the *ummah* and the West (Sheikh, 2002; Ahsan, 1988). Our focus here is not only to examine the OIC's general influence on international relations but also to both make and illustrate the point that, contrary to much popular belief, not all transnational Islamic organizations want to overthrow the established international order and institute a global Islamic state (*khalifa*). Instead, since its establishment in 1969, the OIC has been a forum for senior Muslim figures to discuss both religious and political issues and to find the path of moderation in international relations (Ahsan, 1988). Its overall role, however, has not been much debated in the literature, although there is agreement that its role in international relations is relatively insignificant (Esposito, 2002; Sheikh, 2002; Azbarzadeh and Connor, 2004; Kepel, 2004; Roy, 2004). We will see that one key reason for this is that whereas the OIC professes to be the primary voice of the *ummah*, to extend the global growth and influence of Islam (Sardar, 1985), it has been dogged for decades by competition between leading members, including Saudi Arabia, Iran, Pakistan, and Egypt (Haynes, 2001b). Overall, Dogan (2005) avers the OIC has played a marginal role in the foreign policies of the member states. However, at this juncture of international relations, it is suggested that the organization can and should assume a more active role (Ghorbani, 2005). The OIC is believed capable of helping Muslims and Islamic states to pull together for 'a unified ethical approach to such issues as international terrorism, international development, and democracy. This role of the organization is critical for both ending "clashes" between "civilizations" and bringing peace to the "Greater Middle East"' (Dogan, 2005: 1).

The Organization of the Islamic Conference: structures and processes

The OIC is an intergovernmental organization with a Permanent Delegation to the United Nations. In 2006, it comprised 57 mostly Muslim countries focused in the Middle East, North and West Africa, Central Asia, South-East Asia, and the Indian subcontinent. Three countries are not full members but enjoy 'observer status': Thailand, Bosnia-Herzegovina, and the Central African Republic. The OIC proclaims its purpose is to serve the interests of the world's 1.3 billion Muslims (http://www.oic-oci.org/).

The OIC was initiated by Saudi Arabia. It was a project that sought to outflank and undermine the contemporaneous attempt to project secular pan-Arabism led by Egypt's then ruler President Nasser (Kepel, 1994). The OIC was established by the agreement of the participants of Muslim Heads of State at Rabat, Morocco, in 1969. Its first conference was convened at Jeddah, Saudi Arabia, in 1970.

The OIC is a relatively unstructured organization. Its main institution is the Conference of Foreign Ministers, although a conference of members' heads of state is also held every three years. In addition, there is a Committee for

(Continued)

Economic and Trade Cooperation (COMEC), as well as a Secretariat with Political, Cultural, Administrative, and Financial divisions each headed by a deputy secretary-general. Various other bodies have also been established within the OIC, including the International Islamic Press Agency (1972), the Islamic Development Bank (1974), the Islamic Broadcasting Organization (1975), and the Islamic Solidarity Fund (1977). Finally, over the years the OIC has also established various ad hoc bodies with the aim of trying to help resolve specific international conflicts involving Muslims in various parts of the world. There is an OIC 'contact group' on the Kashmir question, as well as 'an assistance mobilization group' charged with generating aid for Bosnia-Herzegovina (http://www.oic-oci.org/).

What does the OIC aim to achieve in international relations? For Sardar (1985: 51–2), the OIC has the

ability to bring all the nations of the Muslim world, even those who have openly declared war on each other, under one roof, and to promote cooperation and communication between Muslim people that has not been possible in recent history. Moreover, it has the potential of becoming a powerful institution capable of articulating Muslim anger and aspiration with clarity and force. . . . The creation of the OIC . . . indicates that the movement of a return to Islamic roots is a transnational phenomenon . . . .

Sardar is claiming that the main purpose of the OIC *should* be to promote Islamic solidarity and strengthen cooperation among member states in the social, cultural, scientific, political and economic fields. The OIC, an organization of nearly 60 Muslim countries, sees itself as a supporter of the established international order. The organization sees threats to international order as a threat to the international society of states and, as a result, it seeks to develop and sustain good relations with all states, including non-Muslim ones.

Although the idea of an organization for coordinating and consolidating the interests of both Muslims and Islamic states originated in 1969 and meetings of the Conference have regularly been held since the 1970s, the OIC only began to attract Western attention from the early 1980s, following the Islamic revolution in Iran. From that time the OIC has often been a battleground, a place to play out the rivalries of leading Muslim countries, including Saudi Arabia, Iran, Pakistan, and Egypt. From the perspective of some Western observers, the OIC encourages a transnational 'Islamic fundamentalism' and, as a result, is a serious threat to Western security.

Huntington claimed that after the Cold War, potentially coordinated by the OIC, radical Muslim-majority countries dissatisfied with the existing international order were poised en masse to enter into a period of conflict with the West. From that time, successive United States governments – led by George H. W. Bush (1989–93), Bill Clinton (1993–2001) and George W. Bush (2001–9) – collectively put much effort into combating Islamic fundamentalist groups and movements around the world, as their main goal was to undermine the stability of friendly regional governments; successive US presidents were also energized by a desire to minimize the perceived threat from 'rogue states' – including the Islamic Republic of Iran – judged to be a key threat to international order. Iran's government, successive US administrations have claimed, is a sponsor of transnational religious terrorism (Hauser, 2006) and might seek to use its leading position in the OIC as a vehicle for its aspirations.

There is, however, a fundamental flaw in the perception that the OIC is an important *collective* sponsor of transnational religious terrorism: the leading members of the OIC are frequently at each other's throats and thus find it difficult to agree on what the organization should do. Over the last 20 years, much attention has been focused in the OIC on wars involving its members, including the Iran–Iraq War (1980–88), Iraq's invasion of Kuwait (1990–01), civil war in former Yugoslavia in the 1990s, and US invasions of Afghanistan (from 2001) and Iraq (from 2003). Yet such was the lack of concord between leading OIC members that the organization's sixth summit – held in Dakar, Senegal, in December 1991 – was attended *by less than half of the members' heads of state*. This not only reflected the OIC's long-standing international ineffectiveness but also highlighted serious cleavages within the global Islamic community more generally. Discord between OIC members led to fears that the organization would fade from the international political scene because of its failure to generate or focus real Islamic solidarity.

By the mid-1990s the OIC was concerned about the global image of Islam. The 1994 summit sought to create a code of conduct regarding terrorism and religious extremism in order to try to deal with the 'misconceptions' that associated Islam with violence – especially among some Western governments and populations. As a result, in an attempt to bolster the OIC's credentials as an organization committed to strengthening international order, members formally agreed not to allow their territories to be used for any terrorist activities. In addition, none would 'morally or financially' support Muslim 'terrorists' opposed to member governments. However, with states such as Iran and Sudan (both charged with supporting extremist Islamic groups in other nations) signing the OIC statement, it was possible to see the agreement as little more than a face-saving measure that sought to mask continuing deep divisions in the OIC on the issue. The overall point is that the OIC has never managed to function as an organization capable of achieving its goals of enhancing the global position of Muslims, largely because of divisions between its members. Some have sought to cultivate transnational links with radical Islamic groups primarily as a means to further their own influence, but this is individualistic *realpolitik* not an institutional campaign coordinated by the OIC per se.

We illustrate this contention by a focus upon the chief rivals for power in the OIC: Iran and Saudi Arabia. Over time, these states have used some of their oil wealth to try aggressively to expand their international influence. Post-revolutionary Iran developed two linked foreign policy objectives: first, to proselytize its Shi'ite version of Islam and, second, to increase its influence in what its government perceives as Western-dominated international order. Iran's government has been linked with radical Shi'ite groups in various countries, including Lebanon, Bahrain, and Iraq, while also seeking to develop links with radical Sunni Muslims in Nigeria and elsewhere in Africa. Iran's influence was especially notable in the 1980s, a time of burgeoning oil revenues and revolutionary fervour. Iran's diplomatic representatives in Lagos, the capital of Nigeria, were accused of distributing radical Islamic literature and posters of Iraq's leader, the late Ayatollah Khomeini. The moderate chief Imam of Lagos Central mosque, Ibrahim Laidi, criticized these activities as perilous for the religious peace of his country. Nigeria's government was critical of the activities of some Iranian embassy staff who, it claimed, tried to introduce what it saw as fundamentalist and revolutionary doctrines to 'corrupt' Nigerian Islamic culture and worship (Haynes, 1998: 221).

Iran's attempt to target Nigeria in order to help it achieve its foreign policy objectives should be seen in the context of its rivalry with Saudi Arabia in the OIC. Iran's government wished to create pockets of influence in Africa as the first step of a campaign to achieve a much higher profile in the region. In February 1986, Iran's spiritual leader, Sayyid Ali Khameini, stated that Iran 'will survive, defend and protect our revolution and help others in the same cause of Islam to establish the rule of God wherever they are in the world' (*Sunday Triumph* [Lagos], 23 February 1986). A symptom of Iran's growing influence in Africa was exemplified by its close alliance with the Islamic rulers of Sudan. Saudi Arabia, on the other hand, until the 1990–91 Gulf War Sudan's main ally, lost much of its influence as a result of its friendship with the USA.

Saudi Arabia, like Iran, utilized Islam as a foreign policy tool, when it suited the country's revolutionary government. For example, during Ethiopia's civil war (1974–91), Saudi Arabia's support for the Eritreans remained constant, despite their leadership passing from Muslims to Marxist–Leninists and Christians in the mid-1980s. Overall, what this brief discussion of the foreign policies of Iran and Saudi Arabia in Africa in the context of OIC disharmony has sought to show is that both governments sought to use Islam to help them to pursue their individual goals, targeting putative allies among local Muslims to help them.

In conclusion, both Iran and Saudi Arabia have pursued Islam-orientated foreign policies with religious objectives that underpinned and reinforced their more conventional – that is, secular – national interest goals. However, their role as agents provocateurs in the context of Islamically inspired political protest is a complex one. On the one hand, there are often localized reasons behind the outbreak of Islamic opposition, perhaps economic or ethnicity-linked while, on the other hand, there are often foreign interests at work among the already disaffected. Two decades of strong oil revenues gave both Iran and Saudi Arabia the financial ability to prosecute aggressive foreign policies in which a separation of political, diplomatic and religious goals was very difficult to make. Iran's biggest drawback – that it is predominantly a Shi'ite country when most African Muslims are Sunni – was partially offset for some African Muslim radicals – for example, in Nigeria – by Iran's bona fide revolutionary credentials. Some ambitious African Muslim radicals allowed themselves to be seduced by Iran's revolutionary message for two reasons: it gave them an immediately recognizable radical programme for their own societies' politically marginalized and alienated; and, secondly, it offered such Muslim radicals a political platform from which to launch attacks on incumbent Muslim elites associated with the championing of an often welcome religious orthodoxy and social conservatism. Saudi Arabia's concerns, on the other hand, were less revolutionary in orientation: to aid alternative groups of Muslims to build a Saudi-style Islamic state by stages over time (*Sunday Triumph* [Lagos], 23 February 1986).

This suggests that the rise of radical Islam was not in response to encouragement from the OIC, or from individual countries such as Iran. Instead, it came in the context of decades of perceived Western hegemony and accompanying secular modernization, encouraged by a numerically small Westernized elite in many Muslims countries in the Middle East and elsewhere. From the 1960s, throughout the Muslim world, secular-orientated governments sought to impose what were widely seen as Western not Islamic values. As a result of rulers' secularism, socialism and nationalism made inroads, and traditional Muslim forms of community and civility were undermined. But by the early 1970s secular modernization was in crisis, leading to social and cultural dysfunctions and declining state legitimacy. The official response to growing popular discontent was slow to emerge and, when it did, it primarily took the form of attempted economic rather than political reforms. In many countries, popular demands for change stemmed from a rapidly growing recourse to Islamic values and teachings that sought to fill the vacuum left by vacuous attempts to modernize using the Western template. And, as the state's ability to deliver development faded as a result of economic contractions, popular Islamic organizations stepped in, providing welfare, education and health care that the state could or would no longer provide.

The issue of Iran–Saudi Arabia rivalry in the context of the OIC was a key issue for the organization in the 1980s and 1990s. In addition, especially since September 11, 2001, the OIC has been greatly affected by several interrelated issues: the US-directed 'war on terror', the global role of the USA more generally, and the Muslim world's responses to these developments. These concerns were a focus of the December 2005 OIC summit, which declared its condemnation of all terrorism, while stressing the need to criminalize all its aspects, including financing. The OIC also took the opportunity to reject, in line with Islamic tenets, *any* claimed justification – for example from al-Qaeda – for the deliberate killing of innocent civilians. In addition, the OIC also condemned 'extremism', while calling for developing educational curricula in schools that 'strengthen the values of understanding, tolerance, dialogue and pluralism'. Finally, the OIC also took the opportunity to offer its encouragement to Iraq to complete its transitional political process and elect a full-term government under its new democratic constitution (http://www.whitehouse.gov/news/releases/2005/12/20051212.html).

Khan (2001) has studied the international role of the OIC and its attempt to represent Islam globally and transnationally and the implications for international relations. He avers that the OIC is an important organization in the Muslim world. Although it is not always considered to be very successful owing to a lack of coordination, the OIC has been attempting to institutionalize and represent Islam at a global level and is a major interlocutor with the European Union (Silvestri, 2005). It is clear that the OIC can have a cooperative role in contemporary world politics. To achieve this objective, the OIC must attempt to improve its strategy of intra-organizational cooperation. As Ghorbani notes, 'It is the responsibility of the OIC to show Islam is a religion protecting the interdependence image in world politics not a religion for hegemonic purposes' (Ghorbani, 2005: 9). In the post-9/11 era, Muslim countries are heavily concerned with various security issues, and the OIC has sought to focus attention on the principles of building a global cooperative policy in this regard. Achieving this goal, however, will depend on the ability of the OIC to endorse rules and laws pertaining to both social life and international security and strive to present a 'realistic' nature of Islam that reflects its core concerns as a religion of moderation and empathy.

Conclusion

The global Muslim community, the *ummah*, is a good example of a transnational civil society (the Roman Catholic Church is another), which has responded to globalization in various ways. Shared beliefs, relating especially to culture, sentiments and identity, link all Muslims, yet at the same time Islam is significantly divided by various doctrinal issues especially the schism between Sunni and Shia interpretations of the faith, an issue which has been played out in the OIC in relation to the rivalry between Iran and Saudi Arabia. The post-9/11 focus on transnational religious extremism has tested the ability of the OIC to provide leadership to the *ummah* and the signs are that the organization lacks the skill and political will to translate its frequent condemnations of terrorism and extremism into practical policies and programmes (Cherry, 2002).

Like Islam, the Roman Catholic Church has developed extensive transnational links with important ramifications for the development of local and inter-state religious–political cultures and international order. This example emphasizes that global networks of religious activists exist who communicate with each other, feed off each other's ideas, collectively develop religious ideologies with political significance, perhaps aid each other with funds, and, in effect, form transnational groups whose main intellectual referent derives from religious dogma which is of much greater relevance to them than secular ideologies, such as nationalism, Communism, Fascism and liberal democracy. The goal is the creation of communities of believers where religious norms and values are highlighted. Over the last few decades, interpersonal communications have been greatly facilitated by the mass use of the telegraph, telephone, personal computer, email, and fax machine. This communications revolution helped stimulate a globalization of ideas that governments could not control, such as the importance of human rights and democracy. The Roman Catholic Church was influential in some national contexts in helping undermine the hegemony of authoritarian governments but this should not be seen as a more general threat to state sovereignty or international order.

Finally, American evangelical Christians sought to aid and abet 'anti-Communists' in Latin America and Africa in the 1980s and early 1990s, achieving religious and political influence in Guatemala and various African countries, including Angola, Mozambique and Zimbabwe. After the Cold War, however, the transnational focus of American evangelical Protestantism shifted away from a concern with confronting and defeating Communism towards a varied agenda, characterized by Kristoff (2002) as featuring a focus on 'internationalism'. Moving away from a singular concern with anti-Communism, this was a concern with international development and human rights issues.

Notes

1   Zionism is primarily a *political* project which seeks to create a national home for the Jews. It emerged during the second half of the nine-teenth century in Western Europe, before spreading in addition to Eastern Europe. Zionism's ideas extended quickly, and soon tens of thousands of Jews believed in its goals and as a result emigrated to Israel/Palestine in their thousands in the early years of the twentieth century. During the 1920s and 1930s, Jews established farms (mostly communal farms called *kibbutzim*), built homes and businesses in the cities, and overall established an important and growing new Jewish presence in Palestine. Twenty years later, in 1948, Zionists living in Palestine declared the new, independent nation of Israel. Although there were some religious Zionists, Zionism was largely a secular movement. However, even secular Zionists referred to the Hebrew Bible (the Jewish term for what Protestant Christians call the Old Testament) as the root of a new post-diaspora Jewish culture in Israel, what they considered to be 'their Land'. Overall, recognition of the national identity of the Jews is fundamental to Zionism, as is rejection of their exile and a belief in the impossibility of assimilation into non-Jewish cultures.

2   I prefer the use of the term 'transnational civil society', as the alterna-tive – 'global civil society' – seems to suggest that what is in focus is

literally a global network of transnational groups; however, in nearly all cases this is not so. The great majority are regionally-orientated (Florini, 2000).

3   The Americas have nearly half of the world's baptized Catholics, with 49.8 per cent (approx 541 million); Europe accounts for 25.8 per cent (approx 282 million); Africa has 13.2 per cent of the total (approx 143 million); Asia – 10.4 per cent (approx 113 million); Oceania – 0.8 per cent (approx 9 million) (http://news.bbc.co.uk/1/hi/world/4243727.stm).

Questions

1   Define the term 'religious transnational actor' and explain how such entities impact upon international relations. Illustrate your answer with two examples of such actors.

2   To what extent are transnational religious actors able to extend their networks as a result of globalization and the associated communications revolution?

3   How does the international resurgence of religion affect the ability of the Roman Catholic Church to influence social and political developments within countries?

4   Do you agree with Kristoff that American evangelical Protestants are the 'new internationalists'?

5   Why does the Organization of the Islamic Conference find it so difficult to act collectively in international relations?

Bibliography

Ahsan, A. (1988) *The Organization of the Islamic Conference: An Introduction to an Islamic Political Institution*, Herndon, VA: International Institute of Islamic Thought.

d'Antonio, M. (1990) *Fall From Grace: The Failed Crusade of the Christian Right*, London: Deutsch.

Attina, A. (1989) 'The study of international relations in Italy', in H. Dyer and L. Mangasarian (eds), *The Study of International Relations: The State of the Art*, Basingstoke: Macmillan, pp. 344–57.

Azbarzadeh, S. and Connor, K. (2004) 'The Organization of the Islamic Conference: sharing an illusion', *Middle East Policy*, 12(2), pp. 72–80.

Baylis, J. (2005) 'International and global security in the post-cold war era', in J. Baylis and S. Smith (eds), *The Globalization of World Politics: An*

Introduction to International Relations, 3rd edn, Oxford: Oxford University Press, pp. 297–324.

Bealey, F. (1999) *The Blackwell Dictionary of Political Science*, Oxford: Blackwell.

Beck, U. (2005) *Power in the Global Age*, Cambridge: Polity Press.

Bouta, T., Kadayifci-Orellana, S. Ayse and Abu-Nimer, M. (2005) *Faith-Based Peace-Building: Mapping and Analysis of Christian, Muslim and Multi-faith Actors*, The Hague: Netherlands Institute of International Relations.

Brown, S. (1995) *New Forces, Old Forces and the Future of World Politics*, London: Harper/Collins.

Burchill, S. (2005) 'Liberalism', in S. Burchill, A. Linklater, R. Devetak, J. Donnelly, M. Paterson, C. Reus-Smit and J. True, *Theories of International Relations*, 3rd edn, Basingstoke and New York: Palgrave, pp. 55–82.

Buzan, B. (2004) *From International to World Society? English School Theory and the Social Structure of Globalisation*, Cambridge: Cambridge University Press.

Carlson, J. and Owens, E. (eds) (2003) *The Sacred and the Sovereign*, Washington, DC: Georgetown University Press.

Casanova, J. (1994) *Public Religions in the Modern World*, Chicago and London: University of Chicago Press.

Cherry, K. (2002) 'Defining terrorism down: What Muslim nations really think', *National Review Online*, 4 April. Available at: http://www.nationalreview.com/comment/comment-cherry040402.asp

Dogan, N. (2005) 'The Organization of the Islamic Conference: an assessment of the role of the OIC in international relations'. Paper prepared for the Third ECPR General Conference, Budapest, September 2005.

Dolan, C. (2005) *In War We Trust: The Bush Doctrine and the Pursuit of Just War*, Aldershot: Ashgate.

Esposito, J. (2002) *Unholy War*, New York: Oxford University Press.

Fleet, M. and Smith, B. (2000) *The Catholic Church and Democracy in Chile and Peru*, Notre Dame, IA: University of Notre Dame Press.

Florini, A. (2000) *The Third Force: The Rise of International Civil Society*, Tokyo and Washington, DC: Japan Center for International Exchange/Carnegie Endowment for International Peace.

Freston, P. (2001) *Evangelicals and Politics in Asia, Africa and Latin America*, Cambridge: Cambridge University Press.

Freston, P. (2004) *Protestant Political Parties: A Global Survey*, Aldershot: Ashgate.

Freston, P. (ed.) (2006) *Evangelical Christianity and Democracy in Latin America*, Oxford: Oxford University Press.

Ghorbani, A. (2005) 'The Organization of Islamic Conference and its contribution to world politics'. Paper prepared for the Third ECPR General Conference, Budapest, September 2005.

Gifford, P. (1994) 'Some recent developments in African Christianity', *African Affairs*, 93, (373), pp. 513–34.

Hastings, A. (1979) *A History of African Christianity, 1950–75*, Cambridge: Cambridge University Press.

Hauser, C. (2006) 'Bush says Iran leader's letter fails to address nuclear issue', *The New York Times*, 11 May. Available at: http://select.nytimes.com/gst/abstract.html?res=F00717FC3C5A0C728DDDAC0894DE404482&n=Top%2fNews%2fWorld%2fCountries%20and%20Territories%2fIran

Haynes, J. (1996) *Religion and Politics in Africa*, London: Zed.

Haynes, J. (1998) *Religion in Global Politics*, Harlow: Longman.

Haynes, J. (2001a) *Democracy in the Developing World: Africa, Asia, Latin America and the Middle East*, Cambridge: Polity.

Haynes (2001b) 'Transnational religious actors and international politics', *Third World Quarterly*, 22(2), pp. 143–58.

Held, D. (2003) 'Cosmopolitanism: taming globalization', in D. Held and A. McGrew (eds), *The Global Transformations Reader*, 2nd edn, Cambridge: Polity Press, pp. 514–29.

Huntington, S. (1991) *The Third Wave: Democratization in the Late Twentieth Century*, Norman: University of Oklahoma Press.

Jackson, R. and Owens, P. (2005) 'The evolution of international society', in J. Baylis and S. Smith (eds), *The Globalization of World Politics: An Introduction to International Relations*, 3rd edn, Oxford: Oxford University Press, pp. 45–62.

Juergensmeyer, M. (2005) 'Religion in the new global order'. Available at: http://www.maxwell.syr.edu/moynihan/programs/sac/paper%20pdfs/marks%20paper.pdf Accessed 18 April 2006.

Kalin, I. (2006) 'OIC: voice for the Muslim world?', *ISIM Review*, 17, Spring, pp. 36–7.

Keck, M. and Sikkink, K. (1998). *Activists Beyond Borders: Advocacy Networks in International Politics*, Ithaca, NY: Cornell University Press.

Kepel, G. (1994) *The Revenge of God*, Cambridge: Polity.

Kepel, G. (2004) *The War for Muslim Minds: Islam and the West*, London: Harvard University Press.

Khan, Saad S. (2001) *Reasserting International Islam: A Focus on the Organization of the Islamic Conference and Other Islamic Institutions*, Oxford: Oxford University Press.

Kristoff, N. (2002) 'Following God abroad', *New York Times*, 21 May, p. A21.

Lewis, B. (1990) 'The roots of Muslim rage', *The Atlantic Monthly*, September, pp. 52–60.

Lipschutz, R. (1992) 'Reconstructing world politics: the emergence of global civil society', *Millennium*, 21(3), pp. 389–420.

Martin, D. (1990) *Tongues of Fire: The Explosion of Protestantism in Latin America*, Oxford: Basil Blackwell.

Mitchell, M. (2003) 'A theology of engagement for the "newest internationalists"', *The Brandywine Review of International Affairs*, Spring, pp. 11–19.

Nye, J. (2004) *Soft Power: The Means to Success in World Politics*, New York: Public Affairs.

Petito, F. and Hatzopoulos, P. (2003) *Religion in International Relations: The Return from Exile*, Basingstoke and New York: Palgrave Macmillan.

Philpott, D. (2002) "The challenge of September 11 to secularism in international relations', *World Politics* 55 (October 2002), 66–95.

Philpott, D. (2004) 'The Catholic wave', *The Journal of Democracy*, 15(2), pp. 32–46.

Pieterse, J. (1992) 'Christianity, politics and Gramscism of the right', in J. Pieterse (ed.), *Christianity and Hegemony*, Oxford: Berg, pp. 1–31.

Roy, O. (2004) *Globalised Islam: The Search for a New Ummah*, London: Hurst.

Rudolph, S. and Piscatori, J. (eds) (1997) *Transnational Religion and Fading States*, Boulder, CO: Westview.

Rueschemeyer, D., Stephens, E. and Stephens, J. (1992) *Capitalist Development and Democracy*, Cambridge: Polity.

Sardar, Z. (1985) *Islamic Futures: The Shape of Ideas to Come*, London and New York: Mansell Publishing.

Shani, G. (2002) 'A revolt against the West': politicized religion and the international order. A comparison of the Islamic *Umma* and the Sikh *Qaum*', *Ritsumeikan Annual Review of International Studies*, Volume 1, pp. 15–31.

Sheikh, N. (2002) *The New Politics of Islam: Pan-Islamic Foreign Policy in a World of States*, London: Routledge Curzon.

Silvestri, S. (2005) 'Towards a European policy for Islam?' Paper prepared for the Third ECPR General Conference, Budapest, 8–10 September 2005.

Southscan (1989) 'Far-right military church group captured – and released – by Frelimo', 4, 41, 3 November, p. 317.

Spickard, J. (2003) 'What is happening to religion? Six sociological narratives'. Unpublished manuscript, available at: http://www.ku.dk/Satsning/Religion/indhold/publikationer/working_papers/what_is_happened.PDF Accessed 14 April 2006

Stepan, A. (1988) *Rethinking Military Politics: Brazil and the Southern Cone*, Princeton, NJ: Princeton University Press.

Sullivan, M. (2002) *Theories of International Relations: Transition vs. Persistence*, Basingstoke and New York: Palgrave.

Thomas, S. (1999) 'Religion and international society', in J. Haynes (ed.), *Religion, Globalization and Political Culture in the Third World*, Basingstoke and New York: Macmillan, pp. 28–44.

Thomas, S. (2005) *The Global Resurgence of Religion and the Transformation of International Relations: The Struggle for the Soul of the Twenty-First Century*, New York and Basingstoke: Palgrave Macmillan.

Thürer, D. (1999) 'The "failed State" and international law', *International Review of the Red Cross*, no. 836, pp. 731–61.

Vaillancourt, J.-G. (1980) *Papal Power: A Study of Vatican Control over Lay Catholic Elites*, Berkeley: University of California Press.

Willetts, P. (2005) 'Transnational actors and international organizations in global politics', in J. Baylis and S. Smith (eds), *The Globalization of World Politics: An Introduction to International Relations*, 3rd edn, Oxford: Oxford University Press, pp. 425–47.

Witte, J., Jr (1993) 'Introduction' in Witte, J., Jr (ed.), *Christianity and Democracy in Global Context*, Boulder CO: Westview, pp. 1–21.

Further reading

M. Fleet and B. Smith, *The Catholic Church and Democracy in Chile and Peru*, University of Notre Dame Press, 2000. This volume analyses the social and political impact of Catholicism in Latin America, with particular emphasis on Chile and Peru. Fleet and Smith describe how the Catholic Church, at various levels, continues to influence the political and social structure of both countries. They also examine how the Church was, and still is involved in contemporary politics. The overall conclusion is that the Roman Catholic Church remains a vital force in Latin America.

A. Florini, *The Third Force: The Rise of International Civil Society*, Japan Center for International Exchange/Carnegie Endowment for International Peace, 2000. This book poses and answers three important questions related to 'international civil society': (1) how influential is it? (2) how sustainable is that influence? and (3) how desirable is it?

P. Freston, *Evangelicals and Politics in Asia, Africa and Latin America*, Cambridge University Press, 2001. Freston's book is a pioneering comparative study of the political aspects of the new mass evangelical Protestantism of sub-Saharan Africa, Latin America and parts of Asia. He examines 27 countries from these three continents, unearthing both specificities and generalities. His conclusion focuses especially on the implications of evangelical politics for democracy, nationalism and globalization in many different parts of the world.

S. Khan, *Reasserting International Islam: A Focus on the Organization of the Islamic Conference and Other Islamic Institutions*, Oxford University Press, 2001. Khan provides a very useful reference work on the general topic of intergovernmental Islamic organizations, with a special focus on the Organization of the Islamic Conference. He offers both objectivity and a balanced approach to a subject that is often discussed rather subjectively.

S. Rudolph and J. Piscatori (eds) *Transnational Religion and Fading States*, Westview, 1997. The editors' focus is on what they see as a clear and significant dilution of state sovereignty in international relations. The book's contributors examine how the crossing of state boundaries by religious movements leads to the formation of various transnational civil societies. They seek to challenge the notion of a 'clash of civilizations', by looking at the origins of conflicts and the dual potential of religious movements as sources of conflict resolution and peacebuilding as well as often violent conflict. Contributors draw examples from a variety of regions and world religions.

P. Willetts, 'Transnational actors and international organizations in global politics' in J. Baylis and S. Smith (eds), *The Globalization of World Politics: An Introduction to International Relations*, 3rd edn, Oxford University Press, 2005. Willetts offers detailed coverage of the development of international relations theory in relation to transnational and intergovernmental relations.

CHAPTER 6

Religion, conflict, conflict resolution and peacebuilding

I n this chapter we examine how religion impacts on outcomes in international relations related to conflict, conflict resolution and peacebuilding. After introducing the topic, we focus, first, on how religious issues are often implicated in what is known as the 'international politics of identity', with variable outcomes. Following that, we examine two significant contemporary phenomena with integral roles in recent and current international conflicts: (1) al-Qaeda, an example of an international religious terrorist organization; and (2) 'failed states', often noted as 'safe havens' for such groups. Finally, we examine examples of religious initiatives in relation to international conflict resolution and peacebuilding, with examples drawn from Africa (Mozambique) and Europe (Bosnia-Herzegovina). The overall conclusion is that religious actors, because of associated values, beliefs and norms, can be an important contributor both to conflicts and their resolution.

By now, it should be clear that the main task addressed in this book – to explain and account for involvement of religious actors in international relations, especially since the Cold War ended in 1989 – is not straightforward. In part, this is because there is no single, elegant theoretical model that would enable us to deal adequately with all relevant cases of religious involvement in contemporary international relations. On the other hand, we have noted that the influence of religion in contemporary international relations is often related to its ability to exercise soft power. In addition, globalization – that is, the historically unprecedented current global changes characterized by swift urbanization, industrialization, environmental damage, and significant technological, economic and political changes – has impacted upon religion everywhere, by undermining traditional value systems, including in many cases those linked to religious beliefs. A consequence is that, around the globe, especially in parts of the developing world that have missed out on many of the benefits of globalization, many people are said to feel both disorientated and troubled, and some (re)turn to religion as a way of dealing with associated existential angst (Norris and Inglehart, 2004). Many find in religion a source of comfort, serenity, stability and spiritual uplifting. At the same time, however, some also experience new or renewed feelings of identity that not only help provide believers' lives with meaning and purpose but can also in some cases contribute to inter-religious competition, conflict, or war (Carlson and Owens, 2003). In terms of international conflicts, three aspects stand out in the literature: the impact of some religious fundamentalisms; international religious terrorism and how it thrives in 'failed' states; and the controversy surrounding 'the clash of civilizations' (Gopin, 2000; Appleby, 2000; Juergensmeyer, 2000).

First, many observers associate various manifestations of religious 'fundamentalism' with inter- or intra-religion conflicts, in both domestic and international contexts (Marty and Appleby, 1991–95). While varying in many ways, many religious fundamentalisms share a common world-view, leading them to adopt a 'set of strategies, by which [these] beleaguered believers attempt to preserve their distinctive identity as a people or group' in response to real or imagined attacks from non-believers who, they believe, are trying to draw them into a 'syncretistic, areligious, or irreligious cultural milieu' (Marty and Appleby, 1993: 3). In such a context, fundamentalists' 'defence of religion' can develop into social or political offensives with domestic and/or international ramifications.

Secondly, 'failed' states may provide the circumstances that encourage conflicts linked to religious terrorism (Juergensmeyer, 2005). Examples of recent and current failed states include Yugoslavia, Iraq, Somalia, and Afghanistan. Such states are unstable environments that invite external military involvement from powerful international actors, such as the USA, the EU or NATO. Internationally powerful actors may get involved in an attempt to try to prevent or curtail local political violence – often contoured by religious and/or ethnic factors – so that it does not spill over into neighbouring countries and regions. The circumstances prevailing in failed states may encourage people to turn to religion as a result of a feeling that their existential security is threatened (Thomas, 2005). In addition, the absence of effective central government provides circumstances conducive for international religious terrorist groups, such as al-Qaeda, to thrive; in some cases, failed states – including Afghanistan, Iraq, and Somalia – have all become 'safe havens' in recent years for al-Qaeda, and launching pads for their attacks (Burke, 2004). For example, Gunaratna avers that al-Qaeda has cells in up to 60 countries worldwide, dispensing money and logistical support and training to radical Islamist groups in numerous countries, many of which are geographically distant from the failed state, including the Philippines and Indonesia (Gunaratna, 2004; Haynes, 2005a: 224–43; Howard and Sawyer, 2004).

Thirdly, the 9/11 attacks on the USA were a key event in the debate about the role of religion in international conflict, especially in the way that they focused attention on al-Qaeda's international religious terrorism and led to the 'war on terror' (Kepel, 2004; Roy, 2004; Juergensmeyer, 2005). For some scholars, analysts and policy makers – especially but not exclusively in the USA – 9/11 marked the practical onset of Samuel Huntington's 'clash of civilizations' between the 'Christian' West and the Islamic world (Huntington's response to his critics can be seen in Ethics and Public Policy Center, 2002). Others have contended, however, that 9/11 was not the start of the clash of civilizations but rather the last gasp of Islamic radicalism (Kepel, 2004; Roy, 2004). All would agree, however, that as Reus-Smit underlines, 'the events of September 11 thrust culture on to the international agenda', providing Huntington's 'clash of civilizations' thesis with 'a new lease of life'. Henceforward, many commentators were 'no longer inhibited in attributing essentialist characteristics to "The West" and "Islam"'. Instead, there was an 'overwhelming tendency . . . to naturalize and reify culture, carving ethically and racially defined lines across the globe' (Reus-Smit, 2005: 211).

Duffield on global governance and the new wars

As Duffield explains, war is now an important aspect of the development discourse. As a result, aid agencies are now heavily involved in humanitarian assistance, conflict resolution and the social reconstruction of war-torn societies. In the post-Cold War era, what he calls 'new wars' – for example, in Africa and the Balkans – led to a response from the international community, suggesting that new systems of global governance may be emerging. Duffield also focuses upon a 'neo-medieval' situation whereby fragmented sovereignties – especially in 'failed states', examined below – confront weakened or absent central authority (Duffield, 2001).

When it comes to religion in international relations, conflict is not the only focus worthy of our attention; there are also numerous and growing numbers of attempts by religious actors to help resolve conflicts and build peace. Appleby (2006) points out, more than a decade after the publication of a seminal text, Douglas Johnston and Cynthia Sampson's *Religion, the Missing Dimension of Statecraft* (1994), there have been numerous subsequent books and journal articles exploring how religious actors can help resolve conflicts and build peace. Appleby (2006: 1) summarizes an initial set of findings regarding religious peacebuilding and faith-based diplomacy, as follows:

- Religious leaders are uniquely positioned to foster non-violent conflict transformation through the building of constructive, collaborative relationships within and across ethnic and religious groups for the common good of the entire population of a country or region.

- In many conflict settings around the world, the social location and cultural power of religious leaders make them potentially critical players in any effort to build a sustainable peace.

- The multigenerational local or regional communities they oversee are repositories of local knowledge and wisdom, custodians of culture, and privileged sites of moral, psychological and spiritual formation.

- Symbolically charged sources of personal as well as collective identity, these communities typically establish and maintain essential educational and welfare institutions, some of which serve people who are not members of the religious community.

We briefly examined the role of religious actors in conflict resolution in the context of globalization in Chapter 3. The material on this topic in this chapter is devoted mainly to two empirical examples of such activity, in Mozambique and Bosnia-Herzegovina. Before turning to the issue of religious attempts to resolve conflicts and build peace, we start with the topic of religion in international conflict.

Religion and international conflict

What is international conflict?

The term 'international conflict' can refer to three kinds of conflict: between: (1) different nation-states, (2) people and organizations in different nation-states and (3) inter-group conflicts *within* a single country – especially when one group is fighting central government for independence or increased social, political, or economic power (ter Haar, 2005).

Recent examples of international conflict involving religion include Muslims in Chechnya and Kosovo against, respectively, the governments of Russia and Serbia, as well as Christians in Sudan contesting the rule of the central government in Khartoum (Malek, 2004). However, such conflicts are actually widely distributed in various world regions. For example, in many Middle Eastern countries Islamist groups – perhaps drawing inspiration from Iran's Islamic revolution of 1979, the continuing Palestinian *intifadah* against Israel and/or al-Qaeda's anti-Western exploits – are engaged in often violent anti-state campaigns (Milton-Edwards, 2006). In neighbouring Israel, Jewish fundamentalist groups, some of which, such as, Kach and Kahane Lives have employed sometimes extremist tactics in recent years in their conflicts with the government, for example in relation to the handing over of the Gaza strip to the Palestinians in August 2005 (Ehteshami, 2002).

In South Asia, Sri Lanka has experienced a lengthy civil war between Buddhist Sinhalese and Hindu Tamils that has not only cost thousands of lives but has also drawn in India, the regional giant. In India itself, the then prime minister Indira Gandhi was killed by her Sikh bodyguard in 1984, while in 1992 an explosion of militant Hinduism transformed India's political landscape, catalysed by the Babri Masjid mosque incident at Ayodhya. On this occasion, militant Hindus pulled down a mosque on a site that they claimed was originally the location of a Hindu temple. Following this, Hindu nationalists, focused politically in the Bharatiya Janata Party (BJP), achieved significant political gains and for a decade until May 2004, when the BJP lost power to a resurgent Congress Party, it was the dominant party in government. During this time, India's international relations with neighbouring Pakistan were affected by the politicization of Hindu–Muslim relations, especially in relation to the status of Kashmir, a region claimed by both countries (Kumaraswamy, 1999).

Turning to East and South-East Asia, Christian-majority Philippines has restive Muslim minority groups engaged in long-running conflicts with the state. In neighbouring Indonesia, popular resistance to Indonesian rule in East Timor – which gained independence from Indonesia in 1999 – was reflected in a religious statistic: hundreds of thousands of ethnic Timorese converted to Catholicism following Indonesia's takeover in 1974. For many Timorese, religious conversion was necessary in order clearly to differentiate themselves from *Muslim* Indonesia (more than 90 per cent of Indonesians are Muslims). A Catholic bishop, Bishop Belo, was awarded the Nobel Peace Prize in 1996 for his efforts to try to reconcile the two sides (Kohen, 1999).

Many African countries have also been afflicted by religious and/or ethnic conflicts. For example, Nigeria has experienced many clashes in recent years between Muslim and Christians; hundreds of people have been killed and injured (Isaacs, 2003). In addition, Sudan has endured three decades of religious and ethnic conflict – between Muslims, Christians and followers of traditional African religions – before a peace settlement was reached in 2005. Elsewhere in Africa, various countries – including Burundi, Democratic Republic of Congo, Liberia, Rwanda, Sierra Leone, and Uganda – have also experienced civil wars in recent years, conflicts characterized by religious and/or ethnic clashes.

Finally, even the conventionally 'modernized' and 'developed' countries and regions – such as, the USA and Europe – have not been immune to political conflicts informed by religious concerns. In America, the 9/11 attacks on New York and the Pentagon led directly to the Bush administration's 'War on Terror', widely seen by Muslims around the world as an 'anti-Islam' campaign (Shlapentokh et al., 2005). In Europe, recent and continuing conflicts in both former Yugoslavia (between Muslims in Bosnia and Kosovo and mostly Orthodox Christian Serbs) and Russia (Chechnya/Dagestan) also have religious dimensions. The Yugoslav conflicts appeared to have a determining influence, first, on our thinking about conflict in the post-Cold War era and, secondly, about how to deal with those conflicts. For example, the European Union used the Yugoslav conflict as a way more generally of seeking to reform and adjust its own practices in relation to regional conflicts. In addition, other international institutions, including the US military, the North Atlantic Treaty Organization, the United Nations and the World Bank were all greatly affected by the Yugoslav conflict and were as a result transformed by it (Johnson, n.d.)

Three conclusions emerge from our brief summary of the involvement of religious actors in contemporary international conflicts:

- Threats to international peace and security derive from a number of religious (ethnic, national, and racial) conflicts.

- These 'identity conflicts' highlight societal cleavages and pose potentially serious threats to national integration, as well as hampering chances of national political and economic progress in many, mainly developing, countries (http://www.cossa.org/ethnicity.htm).

- Many such conflicts have their roots in historically-based hatreds, many of which were suppressed during the Cold War, a time when international conflicts tended to be seen through the lens of secular ideological competition

Religion and the international politics of identity

The notion of 'identity' is normally applied to individuals, but it can also be collective, extending to countries and their various ethnic and religious communities. Individuals may feel personally injured when they perceive that others – who they believe share identity – are being ill-treated. Religious conflicts are typically based on identity clashes between self-identified, often polarized, groups, within or between countries. Malek notes that 'for an "identity" or inter-group conflict to occur, the opponents must assign an identity to themselves and their adversaries, each side believing the fight is between "us" and "them."' Conflicts where the antagonists seem to be fighting about their identities are called 'identity-based conflicts' or 'inter-group conflicts' (Malek, 2004).

What are key sources of identity? Many identities are based on shared values, beliefs, or concerns that include not only religion but also political ideologies, nationality, or culture (Gopin, 2000, 2005). But this does not imply that people's identities are necessarily monolithic entities: in fact, everyone's self-conception is a unique combination of many identities (religion, nationalism/ethnicity, gender, class, community, family, gender, and so on) and their relative importance and compatibility differs at various times and circumstances. This implies that identities are constructed from various traits and experiences, many of which are subject to interpretation. For example, race and religion are especially important identities in some societies, but not others. Some analysts speak of religion or ethnicity as ancient, unchanging phenomena, while others stress that such sources of identity are actually socially constructed: that is, people choose their history and ancestry and, as a result, may *create*, as much as *discover*, differences from others (Gopin, 2000; Malek, 2004).

In itself, a sense of identity is not a bad thing. But when a sense of identity helps to create or encourage intense, destructive conflicts, then analysts refer to what they call 'destructive' identities (Rosen, 2005). That is, if an identity is heavily reinforced or underpinned *and* is highly significant to someone, such as religion, ethnicity or nationality, then (real or imagined) threats to that sense of identity can be difficult to ignore. In a group, cultural patterns can create conflict as they may inherently include a tendency to mistrust other groups or to belittle them. Of course, when ideologies polarize, the result can be conflict. For example, a group with a racist identity, or one based on a belief that their religion is *inherently* superior to any other, would likely regard others with different religious beliefs as essentially inferior. If such a group believed that it was going to be the victim of attack from another group, they would likely seek to defend themselves. Fearing physical attack, the group may act pre-emptively to prevent the feared attack, thus threatening the other side. The consequence of threat and counter-threat is often a self-perpetuating destructive struggle, for example between Israel and the Palestinians (Rosen, 2005). Such a situation can be exacerbated by the actions of political leaders – individuals who may seek to benefit personally from construction of exclusive identities – who may gain power as a result of arousing the emotions and enmity of members of their group against others. Identity is often created by past interactions. In short, as Kamrava avers, 'it is their sense of identity which largely determines how people behave politically and in turn view their own political environment' (Kamrava, 1993: 164).

Identity and international relations

In international relations, identity can be source of competition and conflict. The problem, however, as Horowitz notes, is that 'attempting to isolate the use of identity in international relations is incredibly difficult. Most generically, identity is the subtext of almost any argument in international relations' (Horowitz, 2002: 1). On the other hand, according to Pevehouse and Goldstein (2005), the use of identity as a variable in studies of international relations is likely to increase in coming years. For various reasons, many identities once assumed by international relations scholars to be stable are likely to be questioned. It is possible that already well-developed theories of identity from other fields, such as social identity theory, will expand into international relations. One context where this is likely to be important for international relations is the issue of identity crises, often said to be linked to the impact of 'failed' modernization and attempts at national integration, especially in the developing world. In some contexts, such circumstances may give rise to international religious terrorism (Gopin, 2000; Appleby, 2000; Juergensmeyer, 2000)

International religious terrorism

The word 'terrorism' comes from the Latin *terrere*, 'to cause to tremble'. Juergensmeyer explains that it is not the *motive* but the *interpretation* of the act that makes and defines it as terrorism. He makes the point that 'we', the public, witness terrorism and 'our' government 'affix[es] the label on acts of violence that makes them terrorism' (Juergensmeyer,

2000: 5). Juergensmeyer makes it plain that terrorism is both a controversial and subjective issue, not least because it is difficult objectively to differentiate between tactics and goals of 'terrorists' ('violence-loving fanatics') and 'freedom fighters' ('romantic idealists'). To try to overcome the inherently subjective connotation of the term, Keohane suggests a more neutral one: 'informal violence'. This is 'violence committed by nonstate actors who capitalize on secrecy and surprise to inflict great harm with small material capabilities', and can be contrasted with state sponsored or directed, 'formal violence' (Keohane, 2002: 1). For those employing terrorism, the threat or use of violence 'from below' serves to emphasize specific issues, grievances, or demands. The aim is to gain concessions from the authorities on certain political issues, such as minority rights and regional autonomy. Both secular and religious groups are routinely labelled as terrorists by human rights organizations, including Amnesty International and Human Rights Watch. They have condemned terrorism in countries around the world, including suicide bombings employed by Palestinians in their conflict with Israel, by the Basque separatists of ETA in Spain, by Kashmiri extremists in Kashmir, Chechen rebels taking hostages in a Moscow theatre, killings by Maoist groups in Nepal and Peru, and kidnappings by various armed groups in Colombia (Weimann, 2006).

International religious terrorist groups

In recent years, a number of groups and organizations have been labelled as 'religious terrorists' by various governments, including those of the USA and Britain. Examples are found among all the world religions. Among Muslim groups, we can note: Abu Sayyaf, Moro Islamic Liberation Front (both Philippines), al-Qaeda (worldwide), Armed Islamic Group (Algeria), Egyptian Islamic Jihad and Gamat al-Islamiya (Egypt), Great Eastern Islamic Raiders' Front (Turkey), Hamas, Palestinian Islamic Jihad (both West Bank and Gaza Strip), Hizbullah (Lebanon), Islamic Movement of Central Asia (Central Asia), Islamic Movement of Uzbekistan (Uzbekistan), Jemaah Islamila (Indonesia), Lashkar-e-Toiba (Pakistan), Students Islamic Movement of India (India). Jewish religious terrorist groups are: Jewish Defence League (USA), Kach and Kahane Chai (both Israel). Finally, there is one Buddhist group (Aum Shrinrikyo, Japan), one Sikh organization (Babbar Khalsa, India) and one Christian group, American Christian Patriot movement (USA), that are classified as religious terrorist entities (the US Office of Counterterrorism supplies a list of 'foreign terrorist groups' at: http://www.state.gov/s/ct/rls/fs/37191.htm).

Certain things are clear about terrorism whoever perpetrates it for whatever purposes. First, terrorists are nearly always few in number, yet quite capable of spreading fear and insecurity widely among populations. Secondly, those who employ terrorism use such violence in pursuit of tactical political ends and, thirdly, they have a variety of political goals. What, if anything, distinguishes terrorism from other types of political violence? For political violence to qualify for the epithet, terrorism, it must feature particular use of 'techniques, targets, and goals . . . To be effective, [it] must be well-planned and directed – in other words, it must embody political skill. Such acts are intended to coerce a wider target into submitting to its aims by creating an overall climate of fear' (Hague and Harrop, 2001: 120). Norris, Kern and Just define 'terrorism' as 'the *systematic* use of coercive intimidation against civilians for political goals'. The reference to 'systematic coercion' differentiates terrorism from more random forms of political violence (Norris et al., 2003: 3).

Terrorism can be confined within a country's borders, or it may be internationally focused. Terrorism is domestic when both victims and perpetrators are confined within the borders of a single nation-state. In some cases, widespread domestic group terrorism can develop into civil war, with the objective of undermining and ultimately overturning incumbent political authorities. But where such violence is successfully contained, it may be that group dissent can be focused via more conventional channels, for example, the Irish peace process that while by no means unproblematic did lead both formerly violent republicans and nationalists to contest democratic elections in Northern Ireland. On the other hand, the existence of peace negotiations is not necessarily enough to quell political violence, for example, in relation to the Israel–Palestine issue.

Terrorism is international when it involves victims or perpetrators from more than one nation-state. International religious terrorism

- significantly undercuts the state's monopoly of violence;
- exploits the privatization of violence and the instruments of violence;
- flourishes in failed states, that is, in countries where state control is weak or non-existent;
- moves and manoeuvres within the many spaces created or aided by technological globalization.

Since 9/11, much evidence has emerged to indicate that some terrorist groups now operate internationally. The short-term goal of such groups – notably al-Qaeda and its allies – is almost always to try to damage the morale of civilian populations, to destabilize the governments of countries they oppose, and to seek to encourage such governments to meet their demands (Burke, 2004).

But this is not to claim that there was no religious terrorism before 9/11. As Hoffman points out, in fact religion was 'the major driving force behind international terrorism during the 1990s'. Table 6.1 illustrates that there were many serious terrorist acts in the 1990s that 'in terms of the number of people killed or the political implications – all have had a significant religious dimension' (Hoffman, 1998–99).

While for many people it was 9/11 that introduced Osama bin Laden's organization to their attention, Hoffman's data shows that it was nearly a decade earlier – in February 1993 – that al-Qaeda first attacked the World Trade Center, New York City. In addition, since Hoffman compiled his data, there have been numerous further successful attacks perpetrated by al-Qaeda or those affiliated to it against various – Western and non-Western – targets, including bomb attacks in Bali, Casablanca, Istanbul, Madrid, Nairobi and London. To explain the involvement of al-Qaeda in religious terrorism, we examine its genesis and concerns in the next section.

Al-Qaeda and international religious terrorism

On September 11, 2001 Americans were confronted by an enigma similar to that presented to the Aztecs – an enigma so baffling that even elementary questions of nomenclature posed a problem: What words or phrase should we use merely to *refer* to the events of that day? Was it a disaster? Or perhaps a tragedy? Was it a criminal act, or was it an act of war? Indeed, one awkward tv anchorman, in groping for the proper handle, fecklessly called it an accident. But eventually the collective and unconscious wisdom that governs such matters prevailed. Words failed, then fell away completely, and all that was left behind was the bleak but monumentally poignant set of numbers, 9–11 (Harris, 2002)

America's new enemies seem to have no demands. They can't be bought, bribed, or even blackmailed. They only want to strike a blow at any cost. And if a suicide hijacker or bomber really believes that by dying in his jihad he'll go straight to heaven and Allah's loving embrace, what earthly reward could the US or anybody else possibly offer as a substitute? (Sacks, 2001)

TABLE 6.1 International religious terrorism in the 1990s

1992–c.2002	Algeria	Bloodletting by Islamic extremists claimed an estimated 120,000 lives.
February 1993	India	Thirteen car and truck bombings shake Bombay, killing 400 and injuring more than 1,000, in revenge for the destruction of an Islamic shrine.
February 1993	USA	Al-Qaeda radicals bomb New York City's World Trade Center, attempting to topple one of the twin towers onto the other, reportedly while releasing a deadly cloud of poisonous gas.
December 1994	France	Air France passenger jet is hijacked by terrorists belonging to the Algerian Armed Islamic Group (GIA), who plotted unsuccessfully to blow up themselves, the aircraft, and the 283 passengers on board precisely when the plane was over Paris, which would have caused the flaming wreckage to plunge into the crowded city below.
March 1995	Japan	Apocalyptic Buddhist religious cult, Aum Shrinrikyo, releases sarin nerve gas in Tokyo subway system, killing a dozen people and wounding 3,796 others. Reports suggest that the group also planned to carry out identical attacks in the USA.
April 1995	USA	Members of the American Christian Patriot movement, seeking to foment a nationwide revolution, bomb the Alfred P. Murrah Federal Office Building in Oklahoma City, killing 168 people.
July–October 1995	France	GIA unleashes a wave of bombings in Paris Metro trains, outdoor markets, cafes, schools, and popular tourist spots, killing 8 and wounding more than 180.
November 1995	Israel	Jewish religious extremist assassinates Israeli premier Yitzhak Rabin, viewing it as the first step in a mass murder campaign designed to disrupt the peace process.
February–March 1996	Israel	String of attacks by Hamas suicide bombers kills 60 people and turns the tide of Israel's national elections.
April 1996	Egypt	Machine-gun and hand-grenade attack by Egyptian Islamic Jihad on a group of Western tourists kills 18 outside their Cairo hotel.
June 1996	Saudi Arabia	Religious militants, linked to al-Qaeda, and opposed to the reigning al-Saud regime in Saudi Arabia, perpetrate truck bombing of US Air Force barracks in Dhahran, killing 19 people.
November 1997	Egypt	Terrorists belonging to the Gamat al-Islamiya (Islamic Group) massacre 58 foreign tourists and 4 Egyptians at the Temple of Queen Hatshepsut in Luxor, Egypt.
August 1998	Kenya and Tanzania	Attackers believed to have been financed by al-Qaeda leader, Osama bin Laden, bomb US embassies in Mombasa and Dar-es-Salam, killing 257 people, including 12 Americans, and injuring more than 5,000 in Kenya, and killing 10 people and injuring dozens in Tanzania.

Source: Hoffman, 1998-99

It is likely that, without the 9/11 attacks on New York and the Pentagon, this chapter would have had quite a different focus. This is because the attacks themselves, as well as linked bombings that followed, led to a significant change in perceptions of the role of religious actors in international conflict. Now it was no longer sufficient to see states as the only actors capable of inflicting large-scale, international political violence: 9/11 led to the deaths of nearly 3,000 people, while subsequent bombs killed hundreds more. Above all, the 9/11 attacks emphasized that international religious terrorism was now an important factor in international conflict. It called for: (1) a new comparative focus on the many themes of conflict and violence traditionally covered in the international relations literature, and (2) examination of links between failed states and international religious terrorism. We shall turn to the latter issue in the next section of the current chapter.

Table 6.1 indicates that there were numerous examples of religious terrorism in the 1990s. Yet it was almost singlehandedly the tragic events of 9/11 that raised the issue to the top of the international agenda – and kept it there. Henceforward national territories of many states were regarded as potential subjects of murderous violence from international religious terrorists; and such people might be physically located almost anywhere. In other words, 9/11 made it crystal clear that geographical space was no longer a fundamental barrier to external attacks against states, a concept that was already anachronistic with respect to thermonuclear war, but now seemingly obsolete. The 9/11 al-Qaeda attacks on the Twin Towers and the Pentagon made the job of those seeking to understand international conflicts more difficult than before. There was now a pressing new challenge: to understand the nature of interconnections between international conflicts and domestic politics in a newly emphasized context, one where the 'hard shell' of the state appeared irreversibly crushed. Smith also notes that the 9/11 attacks emphasized that states are 'no longer, if they ever were, the key actors in major international arenas' (Smith, 2002: 177). In addition, the kind of international religious terrorism exemplified by 9/11 underlines that religious terrorist groups, such as al-Qaeda, are particularly hard to deal with as they do not 'map onto state structures', but 'work in the spaces between them'. That is, the *raison d'être* of international religious terrorist groups such as al-Qaeda is not defined by territory but by their commitments and beliefs. This means that al-Qaeda is a very different type of organization compared to the state, both in terms of its members and followers' commitment to a transnational identity – Islam – and its nebulous structure. Al-Qaeda is the reverse of the modern state: a group of interlocking institutions with hierarchies of power and authority, whose identity is focused on the nation.

September 11 and international conflict

What was the impact of 9/11, both on the USA and international relations more widely? There were two key ramifications for the USA. First, the 9/11 attacks were a profound challenge to the US government. While international political violence and terrorism issues were already important areas of concern prior to September 11, the attacks were the first on such a scale perpetrated by a non-state actor. Secondly, there was a profound impact on ordinary Americans' sense of security, as the quotations at the start of this section from Harris and Sacks – both Americans and journalists – make plain. Americans' sense of safety was shattered by 9/11. The last time that the continental United States suffered anything at all comparable to the 9/11 attacks was nearly 200 years ago, when the British burned down the White House in 1814. Since then, Americans had lived in an atmosphere of invulnerability from foreign attack for nearly two centuries – until September 11.

The significance of 9/11 for international conflict is also clear in relation to the unequal global distribution of power, a state of affairs that globalization (the focus of Chapter 5) is often said to make worse. This is because, as Hurrell notes, globalization is believed to emphasize 'many kinds of negative externalities, including the reaction of many marginalized groups, the creation of new channels for protest, and, in particular, the facilitation of new patterns of terrorist and other kinds' of political violence (Hurrell, 2002: 189). In addition, as Keohane contends, 'effective wielding of large-scale violence by nonstate actors reflects new patterns of asymmetrical interdependence and calls into question some of our assumptions about geographical space as a barrier' (Keohane, 2002: 30). In other words, the unequal global distribution of power is said to encourage the religion-inspired political violence of 9/11 and subsequent al-Qaeda bomb outrages around the world (Haynes, 2005b).

Societies around the world responded to 9/11 in broadly cultural terms. Some Western governments, including those of Britain, Italy, Japan, and Spain, strongly supported the American people and their government, in relation both to 9/11 and to subsequent wars in Afghanistan and Iraq (Shlapentokh et al., 2005). Some ordinary Muslims, on the other hand, are said to have seen 9/11 differently: it represented an attempt by Islam to 'fight back' against the USA (in particular) and the West (in general) (Hammond, 2003: 83; Milton-Edwards, 2006: 175–6). It seems obvious that 9/11 was calculated not simply to wreak terrible destruction but also to create a global media spectacle. For some among the mass of 'downtrodden ordinary Muslims', bin Laden was already a hero prior to 9/11. This constituency was an important target audience for the highly visual spectacle of the destruction of the Twin Towers and the attack on the Pentagon. Thus for al-Qaeda a key goal of 9/11 was to grab the attention of ordinary (Sunni) Muslims, and to encourage them to make connections between the attacks and the multiple resentments already felt against the USA in many parts of the Islamic world as a result of US support for unrepresentative rulers in the Arab world, American invasions of Iraq (1990–91, 2003) and Afghanistan (2001–02) and the treatment of the Palestinians by America's ally, Israel (Dolan, 2005). Together, these issues reflect a depth of hatred in many parts of the Muslim world, a level of concern that is not restricted to small numbers of religious or political radicals. Exacerbated by years of US refusal to censure Israeli actions in relation to the Palestinians, Muslim resentment is also a result of failure to deal with the privations and humiliations inflicted on Iraq following the downfall of Saddam Hussein in March 2003 and his subsequent arrest nine months later. On the other hand, it is plausible to suggest that the resentment of at least some Muslims actually goes wider than these specific issues. If this is the case, then even if solutions for the Afghanistan, Iraq and Palestine issues were found, it might not be enough to undercut the potential for terrorist attacks on the USA and its allies. This is because, as Hurrell notes, it is 'plausible that much [Muslim] resentment has to do with the far-reaching and corrosive encroachments of modernization, westernization and globalization' (Hurrell, 2002: 197).

Was 9/11 the start of the clash of civilizations or the last gasp of Islamic radicalism?

The events of September 11, 2001, as well as many subsequent terrorist outrages, were perpetrated by al-Qaeda or its followers; all involved extremist Muslims that wanted to cause destruction and loss of life against 'Western' targets that nevertheless often led to considerable loss of life, for example in Istanbul and Casablanca, among Muslims (Milton-Edwards, 2006). The US response – the Bush administration's 'war on terror' – targeted Muslims, some believe rather indiscriminately, in Afghanistan, Iraq and elsewhere (Dolan, 2005). Some have claimed that these events marked the start of Huntington's (1993, 1996) 'clash of civilizations' between Islam and the West. In such views, the 9/11 attacks and the US response suggested that Huntington's prophecy about clashing civilizations was now less abstract and more plausible than when first articulated in the early 1990s. Others contend, however, that 9/11 was not the start of the clash of civilizations, but the last gasp of Islamic radicalism that had seen significant setbacks in Algeria and Egypt in the mid-1990s (Kepel, 2004; Roy, 2004; Milton-Edwards, 2006: 104). We can also note, however, that 9/11 not only had major effects on both the USA and international relations but also contributed to a surge of Islamic radicalism in Saudi Arabia. This was a result not only of the presence of US troops in the kingdom, as highlighted by bin Laden, but also of a growing realization that 'the function of the *ulema* is . . . to establish the hegemony of the ruling Amir [king] and his family' (Fandy, 1999: 25)

It is, however, difficult or impossible to be sure regarding the actual level of support for bin Laden and al-Qaeda in the Muslim world, although there *is* a high degree of anti-US resentment and a widespread belief among many Muslims that the West is anti-Islam (Shlapentokh et al., 2005; Norris and Ingelhart, 2004). Such a perception was fuelled by what is seen throughout much of the Muslim world as often uncritical American and European support for the government of Israel, the US-led invasions of Afghanistan and Iraq, and the subsequent slow speed of rebuilding viable and legitimate administrations in both countries. At the same time, there are important voices in the USA appearing to play up the notion of civilizational conflict. For example, a Democratic Congressman, Tom Lantos, stated in November 2001 that: 'unfortunately we have no option but to take on barbarism which is hell bent on destroying civilization . . . You don't compromise with these people. This is not a bridge game. International terrorists have put themselves outside the bonds of protocols' (Interview with Tom Lantos, BBC Radio 4, *Today* programme, 20 November 2001, quoted in Hurrell, 2002: 195.)

Hurrell believes that such remarks reflect a deep-rooted tradition in Western international thought that believes it is appropriate to set aside normal rules of international relations in certain circumstances, for example, 'certain kinds of conflict or in struggles with certain kinds of states or groups' (Hurrell, 2002: 195). During the centuries of Western imperialism, there were frequent debates about what rights non-Christian and non-European peoples should enjoy. In the centuries of competition and sometimes conflict between Christianity and Islam, there arose the notion of holy war – that is, a special kind of conflict undertaken outside 'any framework of shared rules and norms' – as well as that of 'just war' waged for 'the vindication of rights' within a shared framework of values (Dolan, 2005; Berman, 2005: 25–6). In addition, there is a further strand of conservative Western thought that 'asserts that certain kinds of states and systems cannot be dealt with on normal terms, that the normal rules that govern international relations have to be set aside'. For example, during the 1980s, the Reagan government in the USA averred that there was a basic lack of give-and-take available when dealing with Communist governments, which meant that it was appropriate that some basic notions of international law could be set aside in such contexts. This conservative tradition is also manifested in the remarks of Congressman Lantos noted above,[1] and suggests that available options are restricted to the choice of to 'contain or to crusade'. It also indicates that 'such positions clearly continue to resonate within and around the current US administration' (Hurrell, 2002: 193–5)

'Failed' states, religion and international conflict

> One of the principal lessons of the events of September 11 is that failed states matter – for national security as well as for humanitarian reasons. If left to their own devices, such states can become sanctuaries not only for terrorist networks, organized crime and drug traffickers as well as posing grave humanitarian challenges and threats to regional stability (Commission on Post-Conflict Reconstruction, 2003: 4)

> On traditional grounds of national interest, Afghanistan should be one of the least important places in the world for U.S. foreign policy – and until the Soviet invasion of 1979, and again after the collapse of the Soviet Union in 1991 until September 11, the United States all but ignored it. Yet in October 2001 it became the theater of war (Keohane, 2002: 35).

The US government responded to the 9/11 attacks with an assault in 2001–02 on both the Islamist Taliban regime and al-Qaeda bases in Afghanistan. At that time, the theocratic Taliban government controlled much of Afghanistan, a 'failed state' with a shattered social and political structure. Following more than two decades of constant warfare, the country was a nation in ruins, with numerous towns and cities reduced to rubble, and with its social and political structure destroyed by years of unremitting conflict. These circumstances allowed al-Qaeda to set up bases, with the explicit or implicit agreement of the Taliban regime. According to Thürer, failed states like that of Afghanistan, 'are invariably the product of a collapse of the power structures providing political support for law and order, a process generally triggered and accompanied by anarchic forms of internal violence' (Thürer, 1999: 731). In short, failed states (French, '*états sans gouvernement*') are characterized by total or at least substantial collapse of both institutions and law and order, the consequence of serious and prolonged conflict. Robert Rotberg notes that 'nation-states fail when they are consumed by internal violence and cease delivering positive political goods to their inhabitants. Their governments lose credibility, and the continuing nature of the particular nation-state itself becomes questionable and illegitimate in the hearts and minds of its citizens' (Rotberg, 2003: 1). Former UN Secretary-General, Boutros Boutro-Ghali (1995: 9) described the situation as follows:

> A feature of such conflicts is the collapse of state institutions, especially the police and judiciary, with resulting paralysis of governance, a breakdown of law and order, and general banditry and chaos. Not only are the functions of government suspended, but its assets are destroyed or looted and experienced officials are killed or flee the country. This is rarely the case in inter-state wars. It means that international intervention must extend beyond military and humanitarian tasks and must include the promotion of international reconciliation and the re-establishment of effective government.

Failed states and underdevelopment

Currently existing 'failed states' are invariably former Communist or developing countries, affected by three main geopolitical factors:

- *End of the Cold War.* During the Cold War (late 1940s–late 1980s), the two superpowers – the USA and the Soviet Union – often helped to maintain illegitimate or unrepresentative governments in power. The purpose was to preserve them as potential or actual allies. The superpowers often supplied such governments with military equipment and sometimes personnel. The demise of the Cold War meant that such support was, often summarily, withdrawn, putting sometimes intolerable pressure on unpopular regimes that had relied on external support for their survival. In the absence of a sufficiently developed and cohesive political opposition, there was no trouble-free move to democracy but instead in some cases – for example, Somalia and the Democratic Republic of Congo – there was a total breakdown of the authority of central government.

- *Heritage of colonial regimes.* Typically, colonial administrations were in power for sufficient time to destroy or seriously undermine traditional social structures, without in most cases replacing them with working constitutional structures and/or an effective sense of national identity. Often, competing perceptions of identity focused on religion and/or ethnicity and helped to exacerbate societal divisions and encourage state breakdown. Examples include Liberia, Sierra Leone and Côte d'Ivoire.

(Continued)

> ■ *Incomplete processes of modernization.* Often serving to encourage both social and geographical mobility, modernization processes were rarely matched by nation-building processes that would lead to the placing of the post-colonial state on firm political, economic and social foundations. Examples include Iraq and Afghanistan.[2]

From the political and legal point of view, the phenomenon of the 'failed state' is characterized by geographical and territorial, political, and functional factors:

■ *Geographical and territorial.* Failed states are normally characterized by an *implosion* rather than an *explosion* of the structures of power and authority, with a wholesale disintegration and destructuring of the institutions of political authority. But although they are associated with internal and endogenous problems, failed states always have significant – and unwelcome – political ramifications for neighbouring countries and regions, making conflicts much more likely.

■ *Political.* This refers to internal collapse of law and order and the state structures – government, police, armed forces – that normally guarantee it. Such a collapse can lead to such a serious fragmentation of state authority that the result is civil war. Often, such conflicts will be focused on religious and/or ethnic divisions. In such circumstances, rebels fight for one of two reasons: to strengthen their own position within the existing state or to start a new one.

■ *Functional.* This state of affairs is associated with the 'absence of bodies capable, on the one hand, of representing the State at the international level and, on the other, of being influenced by the outside world' (Thürer, 1999: 731). Note, however, that this does not imply that external actors will not be very interested in resolving the problems reflected in the failed state; they will do this because they are aware that failed states are likely to be significant sources of international conflict.

In sum, failed states: (1) are invariably non-democracies, (2) contain an absence of workable political structures that facilitate state breakdown, (3) feature serious political, economic and social instability, (4) may degenerate into civil war and (5) often encourage the establishment or embedding of religious terrorist organizations.

The US-led 'war on terror' targeted a failed state in 2001–02 – Afghanistan. The conflict was later extended to another 'failed state', Iraq, under the leadership of Saddam Hussein.[3] Alleged links between Saddam's regime and al-Qaeda was a stated reason for the US-led invasion of Iraq in March 2003 and of Saddam's subsequent arrest in December 2003. However, in both Iraq and Afghanistan, following the US-led invasions, there were inconclusive attempts to rebuild both countries.

In conclusion, the claim is not that all failed states feature intra- or inter-religion competition and conflict, although circumstances linked to state failure may be especially conducive to their development, including creation and development of bases for religious terrorist groups; certainly this was the case in both Afghanistan and Iraq, and to some extent also in Bosnia and Chechnya. The overall point, however, is that when states fail they encourage a reversion of popular loyalties that in the absence of a state may well find a focus in religious and/or ethnic solidarity. It also underlines that in failed states people may be more likely to turn to religion in circumstances where in many cases their existential security is under serious threat. Tisdall notes these factors in relation to the development of a serious Islamist threat in Somalia, another failed state. The US government was 'pursuing a proxy war against al-Qaida backed jihadis that analysts say is turning Somalia into a new front in the "war on terror"' (Tisdall, 2006). But according to the UK-based, independent non-governmental organization, the International Crisis Group (ICG), the USA has got it wrong and spreading Islamist ideas are not Somalia's main problem: 'Somalis in general show little interest in jihadi Islamism; most are deeply opposed'. The main problem, the ICG averred, was that the USA, singularly focused on the admittedly serious threat of al-Qaeda, would by its efforts make worse existing divisions and undermine Somalia's attempts to build a transitional government (International Crisis Group, 2005).

The role of religious actors in conflict resolution and peacebuilding

Religious actors of various kinds that attempt to resolve conflicts between conflicting groups and build peace are often referred to in the literature as 'religious peacemakers' or as 'faith-based organizations' (Appleby, 2000, 2006; Gopin, 2000, 2005; ter Haar, 2005).[4] Such groups are most likely to be most successful when (1) they have an international or transnational reach, (2) they consistently emphasize peace and avoidance of the use of force in resolving conflict, and (3) when there are good relations between different religions in a conflict situation, as this will be the key to a positive input from them (Appleby, 2006: 1–2). In addition, as we saw in Chapter 1, as the world religions theoretically share a broad theological and spiritual set of values then, theoretically, this should facilitate their ability to work together to resolve conflicts and build peace. The overall question is: How can the world religions help to build and then sustain peaceful coexistence in multi-faith societies, while advocating reconciliation and fairness in a world which often seems characterized by social and political strife and economic disparity? Appleby notes that while there is much promise in this regard, two major problems remain: (1) 'there is often a failure of religious leaders to understand and/or enact their potential peace-building roles within the local community', and (2) many religious leaders lack the ability to 'exploit their strategic capacity as transnational actors' (Appleby, 2006: 2)

On the other hand, according to David Smock in a report produced for the United States Institute for Peace, many faith-based organizations' international-conflict resolution focus is increasing and in some cases becoming more effective. According to Smock:

- Faith-based non-governmental organizations are increasingly active and increasingly effective in international peacebuilding.

- Faith-based organizations have a special role to play in zones of religious conflict, but their peacebuilding programmes do not need to be confined to addressing religious conflict.

- Although in some cases peacebuilding projects of faith-based organizations resemble very closely peacebuilding by secular NGOs, in most instances the various religious orientations of these faith-based organizations shape the peacebuilding they undertake.

- The peacebuilding agendas of these organizations are diverse and range from high-level mediation to training and peacebuilding-through-development at grassroots levels.

- Very often peace can be promoted most efficiently by introducing peacebuilding components into more traditional relief and development activities (Smock, 2001:1)

Bouta, Kadayifci-Orellana and Abu-Nimer conclude that faith-based peacebuilding initiatives 'have contributed positively' to peacebuilding in four main ways, by providing: (1) 'emotional and spiritual support to war-affected communities', (2) effective mobilization for 'their communities and others for peace', (3) mediation 'between conflicting parties', and (4) a conduit in pursuit of 'reconciliation, dialogue, and disarmament, demobilization and reintegration' (Bouta et al., 2005: ix)

Overall, what is clear is that there are many faith-based organizations engaged in peacemaking activities in relation to specific contexts and conflicts, in various parts of the world including Africa, Asia and Europe (notably former Yugoslavia) (Bouta et al., 2005; Appleby, 2006; Smock, 2004). In the next section we examine two specific initiatives in this regard: the work of the Catholic lay organization Sant'Egidio in Mozambique and the efforts of faith-based organizations to help resolve the conflict in Bosnia-Herzegovina.

In both Mozambique and Bosnia-Herzegovina, faith-based organizations have been successful in helping to rebuild good community relations and develop peace between previously warring communities. Left to their own devices, it is very likely that conflicting groups in both areas would have failed to reach a modus vivendi and perhaps lapse back into conflict – with potentially destabilizing effects on regional and international stability and peace. As Mozambique's president Joaquim Chissano said in the context of peacebuilding efforts in his own country following the end of his country's civil war in 1992: 'Conflicts, particularly violent conflicts between and within states in other parts of Africa, and in the world in general, are also a danger to our peace and tranquillity. Helping other peoples keep and maintain peace is also a way of defending our own peace' (Harsch, 2003: 16).

Conflict resolution and peacemaking in Mozambique and Bosnia-Herzegovina

In this section we examine several examples of the activities of faith-based organizations involved in conflict resolution and peacebuilding activities in two regions of the world: Africa and the Balkans.

Sant'Egidio, conflict resolution and peacemaking in Mozambique

Large-scale violence in many African countries is associated with social conflicts. Numerous regional countries – including, Liberia, Sierra Leone, the Democratic Republic of Congo, Côte d'Ivoire, Liberia, Nigeria, Sierra Leone, Burundi, Rwanda, Angola, Sudan and Mozambique – have been beset by serious political violence, with a proliferation of armed conflicts and numerous deaths of local people, most of whom were civilian non-combatants. In addition, as Harsch notes, millions more 'succumbed to war-related epidemics and starvation' (Harsch, 2003: 1). In all such cases, conflicts were informed by a variety of issues, including religious and/or ethnicity factors.

Many traditional – that is, non-religious – conflict resolution and peace-building missions were established to monitor peace agreements between established armies holding separate territories. But they discovered success hard to find, not least because they were not necessarily well suited to deal with such conflicts. Many recent conflicts in Africa have been civil wars or insurgencies, with multiple armed factions and with grievances rooted in various factors, including: poverty, inequality and other development issues. Moreover, even when peace accords were successfully negotiated, it was not always the case that all political and military leaders were able or willing fully to control their followers. In some countries, such as Sierra Leone and Liberia, local fighters, who profited from the chaos of war, saw more advantage in continuing to fight than to lay down their arms (Harsch, 2003: 14).

Would faith-based organizations have more success than non-religious entities in helping to resolve conflicts and put peace back on the agenda? While the evidence is mixed in this regard (Appleby, 2006), it is the case that in some African conflicts faith-based organizations have met with success. Perhaps the most illustrative case of this type of peacemaking was the mediation by the Catholic organization Sant'Egidio, credited with playing a key role in ending the civil war in Mozambique in 1992.

Sant'Egidio is an international Catholic non-governmental organization (NGO) that takes part in attempts at peacemaking in various conflicts in many parts of the world. Originally, its principal focus was to serve the needs of the urban poor in Italy (Bouta et al., 2005: 71). Founded in 1968 in Italy, Sant'Egidio has grown and now has approximately 50,000 members in 70 countries. Sant'Egidio is a Church public lay association, formally recognized by the Catholic Church but with an autonomous statute. This means that its membership is 'lay' – that is, not professionally religious – although its adherents have a clear religious motivation, an important part of its negotiation activities. Appleby explains that Sant'Egidio began its activities with charity, humanitarian action and development cooperation uppermost in its thinking, concerns moulded by spirituality and shared principles, including prayer, communicating the gospel, solidarity with the poor and dialogue with other religions (Appleby, 2006: 10). However, despite its avowedly religious orientation, Sant'Egidio's conflict resolution and peacebuilding activities have focused more on 'non-religious' conflicts than on 'religious' conflicts, and more on the international level than on the national or local level.

During the early 1980s, Sant'Egidio became engaged in various international dialogues. The aim was to try to prevent or reduce tension between conflicting groups and to seek to mediate between them. Since then Sant'Egidio has played an active peacebuilding role in several African countries beset by civil war, including: Algeria, Burundi, Democratic Republic of Congo, Côte d'Ivoire, Mozambique and Sierra Leone. It has also been active elsewhere, including: Colombia, Guatemala, and Kosovo. In each case, the country was beset by serious conflict between polarized groups; in some cases, conditions were exacerbated by the fact that the effectiveness of central government to administer had diminished significantly (Smock, 2004).

One of the clearest success stories of Sant'Egidio's peacemaking efforts occurred between 1989 and 1992 when the organization was extremely influential in resolving the civil war that had ravaged Mozambique since the mid-1970s. The Catholic Archbishop of Beira, Don Jaime Goncalves, was familiar with Sant'Egidio and its work from the years he had spent in Rome. In the wake of well-intentioned but eventually unsuccessful efforts to end the war emanating from the international community, Archbishop Goncalves thought Sant'Egidio might succeed in bringing the government together to talk peace with the rebels of the Mozambican National Resistance (RENAMO) insurgents. He was right: the effort took months but eventually Sant'Egidio not only contacted the RENAMO leadership but also encouraged Mozambican government officials to agree to meet with them (Bouta et al., 2005: 71–2).

Sant'Egidio was successful in its efforts because both RENAMO and the government perceived Sant'Egidio as an organization characterized both by a welcome neutrality and a compassionate outlook, with but one interest in Mozambique: to end the civil war and promote peace. That is, Sant'Egidio was understood to have no political or economic agenda; throughout the negotiations this perception was bolstered as the organization demonstrated a position of both even-handedness and neutrality (Smock, 2004). As far as the Mozambique government was concerned, as an NGO Sant'Egidio could set up a meeting between RENAMO and the government without it meaning that the RENAMO rebels would be regarded as an entity with the same status as the ruling regime. But Sant'Egidio also had a second important asset: 'humble awareness of its own shortcomings in orchestrating international diplomacy, which caused it to seek out the special expertise of governments and international organizations' (Smock, 2004: 1). The nucleus of Sant'Egidio's mediation team was the Archbishop of Beira, Don Jaime Goncalves, an Italian socialist parliamentarian and former diplomat, and two key leaders of Sant'Egidio. These efforts were complemented not only by the United Nations but also by ten national governments, including those of the USA, Italy, Zimbabwe and Kenya. Once peace negotiations were successfully completed in 1992, the United Nations assumed responsibility for the implementation of the peace agreement. Over the last fifteen years, Mozambique has been peaceful. There have been several national-level elections, won by the ruling FRELIMO (Frente de Libertação de Mozambique) party. RENAMO has served as the main political opposition to the government (Appleby, 2006).

In conclusion, the mediation work of Sant'Egidio in Mozambique illustrates how faith-based organizations with relevant skills can offer a unique ability to mediate between previously warring factions. They do this by building on a reputation for neutrality and compassion and by utilizing not only their own skills but also those of other – not necessarily – institutions, in an initiative which, in the case of Mozambique, brought the battling parties together and brought the civil war to a close (Bouta et al., 2005: 72–3).

Conflict resolution and peacebuilding in Bosnia-Herzegovina

States consumed by civil war are not confined to Africa or elsewhere in the developing world. During the 1990s, former Yugoslavia was consumed by various conflicts, including a serious imbroglio in Bosnia-Herzegovina. There, the conflict drew the attention of the international community and efforts from various faith-based organizations, both Christian and Muslim, to try to resolve the civil war, end conflict and build peace. Following these efforts, the US Institute of Peace (USIP) commissioned a study to measure the success of these efforts. The guiding research questions were:

- How effectively can faith-based NGOs advance reconciliation in Bosnia-Herzegovina?

- Can faith-based NGOs be effective agents of inter-faith reconciliation, particularly when they share a religious identity with one party involved in the conflict?

■ Are these NGOs more likely to be agents of reconciliation or contributors to additional division?

Research into the issue for the USIP was primarily undertaken over a fifteen-month period by Branka Peuraca. She was at the time, the early 2000s, a graduate student at Tufts University's Fletcher School of Law and Diplomacy. During her research, Peuraca studied the work of Christian (Protestant, Catholic, Orthodox), Muslim and Jewish organizations (including Catholic Relief Services, World Vision, United Methodist Committee on Relief, Islamic Relief Worldwide, and local NGOs such as Abraham/Ibrahim [Mozjes, 2002]). The findings were reported in a Special Report published in 2003 (United States Institute of Peace, 2003).

Peuraca found an impressive number of international and local faith-based organizations operating in Bosnia, with many contributing to ethno-religious reconciliation. She also found, however, that some early efforts at reconciliation between often-polarized communities had been ineffective, even counter-productive, a judgement endorsed by other research findings (Bouta et al., 2005; Mozjes, 2002). Reconciliation was not helped by the fact that some Muslim organizations – such as the 'Advisory and Reformation Committee', said to be a front organization for al-Qaeda – were suspected of having ties to Islamist terrorist groups in Algeria, Saudi Arabia, and Afghanistan (Kurop, 2001; Bodansky, 2001). Yet despite these concerns, Peuraca's overall assessment of the conflict resolution and peacebuilding initiatives of the faith-based NGOs was that many – Christian, Muslim, and Jewish – had made significant contributions to ethno-religious reconciliation in Bosnia-Herzegovina. Concrete successes included the formation in 1997 of Bosnia's Inter-Religious Council, composed of leaders from the four religious communities (Muslim, Orthodox Christian, Roman Catholic, and Jewish), and various NGOs (including Catholic Relief Services, World Vision, the United Methodist Committee on Relief, Islamic Community of Bosnia-Herzegovina, and Women to Women) (Smock, 2004; Bouta et al., 2005). Together these initiatives encouraged inter-faith collaboration both generally and in regard to specific local educational, and infrastructural projects. Such cooperation had a functional effect: in 'planning and implementing local development projects, ethno-religious enemies end[ed] up cooperating with each other' (Smock, 2004: 1).

The inter-faith dialogue work in Bosnia organized by Reverend David Steele of the Center for Strategic and International Studies (CSIS) is also worthy of mention. CSIS is not a faith-based organization, although it has effectively facilitated not only inter-faith dialogues but has also been instrumental in founding a local Bosnian Centre for Religious Dialogue that, it is hoped, will continue with this work. In addition, Dr Steele has developed an approach to organizing inter-faith dialogues that has proved to be effective not only in Bosnia-Herzegovina, but also in Serbia, Kosovo, and Macedonia (Smock, 2004: 1; Bouta et al., 2005: 85–7). Overall, CSIS activities in Bosnia and elsewhere in former Yugoslavia underline that appropriate and enlightened activities undertaken by various kinds of NGOs can help bring together groups and communities that had previously been torn apart by inter-religious and cultural conflict, contributing significantly in the case of Bosnia-Herzegovina to inter-religious and community reconciliation. In sum, the example of Bosnia-Herzegovina provides evidence that faith-based organizations and other NGOs can also help bridge religious divisions, decrease the degree of inter-group hostility, and focus attention on a collective responsibility to rebuild society after debilitating conflict.

In summary, we have discovered the following characteristics of faith-based and other organizations in Mozambique and Bosnia-Herzegovina, whose focus is on conflict resolution and peacebuilding:

- In both countries, faith-based NGOs were both active and effective in conflict resolution and peacebuilding efforts. In both cases, their efforts seemed to have greater impact because of the involvement of other, non-religious, organizations. It is important to underline, however, that faith-based organizations do have a special role to play in zones of inter-community conflict, yet their efforts to build peace do not necessarily have to be applied *only* in relation to religious or ethnic conflict.

- Such organizations' peacebuilding agendas were varied, including high-level mediation, and at the grassroots, training and peace-through-development initiatives. While direct approaches to peace-making were sometimes effective, such efforts were likely to be successful when complemented by the introduction of aspects of peacebuilding into both relief and development activities.

- In both contexts, Mozambique and Bosnia-Herzegovina, peacebuilding programmes were mostly new and to some degree experimental. As a result, given the novelty of such programmes, it is unsurprising that there is more to learn in relation to such initiatives. Consequently, various organizations – including the United States Institute for Peace (http://www.usip.org/) and the Netherlands Institute of International Relations (www.clingendael.nl/) – have recently conducted useful

evaluations of faith-based organizations' contributions to conflict resolution and peacebuilding and their research is likely to be valuable in
giving guidance for the future.

Conclusion

In this chapter we have examined the role of religion in conflicts, conflict
resolution and peacebuilding. Regarding conflict, we saw that inter-religion
tensions and competition are often implicated in the 'international politics
of identity', an issue that is frequently associated with various post-Cold
War conflicts. We focused upon two phenomena which play important roles
in contemporary international conflicts: (1) al-Qaeda, a key example of an
international religious terrorist organization; and (2) 'failed states' in various
parts of the world that function as 'safe havens' for international religious
terrorists and where existential circumstances, as in Somalia, Iraq and
Afghanistan, encourage various forms of conflict.

In the second half of the chapter we turned to the role of faith-based organizations in conflict resolution and peacebuilding. Aware that this is a
complex and multifaceted issue, we focused on two specific examples of
such initiatives, in Mozambique and Bosnia-Herzegovina. The context is
that while the religious causes of conflict receive plenty of public attention,
religious peacemakers' efforts in conflict resolution and peacebuilding tends
to get much less attention and publicity (Smock, 2004; Appleby, 2006). Research indicates, however, that most religious faiths encourage their members to work towards conflict resolution and peacemaking (Bouta et al.,
2005). This is reflected in the fact that growing numbers of religious organizations seem to be looking for opportunities to promote peace, including in
circumstances where religion itself is seen to contribute to conflict, such as
in Bosnia-Herzegovina (United States Institute for Peace, 2003). Overall, the
hope is that, as a result of increased public recognition and support, and development of more effective peacemaking strategies, the international conflict resolution and peacemaking skills of faith-based organizations will be
able to develop their full potential.

Notes

1   Such remarks did not seem to affect Congressman Lantos's electoral
    popularity. In the March 2004 Democratic primary in California's 12th
    Congressional District he gained 71.6 per cent of the votes cast. His
    nearest challenger acquired 19.8 per cent (http://www.lantos.org/).

2   Afghanistan was never formally colonized – although current state and society characteristics are not noticeably different from many contemporary states in the developing world that were controlled by colonial powers.

3   Note that this implies another meaning of the term 'failed state': 'aggressive, arbitrary, tyrannical or totalitarian' governing regime, which has *failed* according to norms and standards of current international law (Thürer, 1999: 731).

4   A general definition of a faith-based organization is: an 'organization, group, program or project that provides human services, and has a faith element integrated into their organization' (http://www.raconline.org/info_guides/faith/faithfaq.php#faith).

Questions

1   Giving two examples, explain why religious actors are involved in recent attempts at conflict resolution and peacebuilding.

2   Why is the notion of identity often implicated in religious competition and conflict?

3   What are the key factors necessary to end conflicts and build peace?

4   Focusing on the civil war in Mozambique, how was Sant'Egidio able to bring both factions to the negotiating table?

5   Why is it said that many religions have key principles in common that enables them to find agreed ways to peace in some conflict situations?

Bibliography

Appleby, R. Scott (2000) *The Ambivalence of the Sacred: Religion, Violence and Reconciliation*, Lanham, MD: Rowman and Littlefield.

Appleby, R. Scott (2006) 'Building sustainable peace: the roles of local and transnational religious actors'. Conference paper prepared for the Conference on New Religious Pluralism in World Politics, Georgetown University, 17 March.

Berman, R. (2005) 'The German perception of the United States since September 11', in V. Shlapentokh, J. Woods and E. Shiraev (eds), *America: Sovereign Defender or Cowboy Nation?*, Aldershot, and Burlington, VT: Ashgate, pp. 15–28.

Bodansky, Y. (2001) *Bin Laden: The Man who Declared War on America*, Rochlin, CA: Form: Prime Lifestyles.

Bouta, T., Kadayifci-Orellana, S. Ayse and Abu-Nimer, M. (2005) *Faith-Based Peace-Building: Mapping and Analysis of Christian, Muslim and Multi-faith Actors*, The Hague: Netherlands Institute of International Relations.

Boutros-Ghali, B. (1995) 'Concluding statement by the United Nations Secretary-General Boutros Boutros-Ghali of the United Nations Congress on Public International Law: Towards the twenty-first century: international law as a language for international relations', 13–17 March, New York.

Burke, J. (2004) *Al-Qaeda: The True Story of Radical Islam*, Harmondsworth: Penguin.

Carlson, J. and Owens, E. (eds) (2003) *The Sacred and the Sovereign*, Washington, DC: Georgetown University Press.

Commission on Post-Conflict Reconstruction (2003) 'Play to win'. Final report of the bi-partisan Commission on Post-Conflict Reconstruction, Washington, DC/Arlington, VA: Center for Strategic and International Studies (CSIS) and the Association of the U.S. Army (AUSA). Available at: http://www.csis.org/isp/pcr/playtowin.pdf Accessed 5 November 2003.

Dolan, C. (2005) *In War We Trust: The Bush Doctrine and the Pursuit of Just War*, Aldershot: Ashgate.

Duffield, M. (2001) *Global Governance and the New Wars: The Merging of Development and Security*, London: Zed Books.

Ehteshami, A. (2002) 'The Middle East: Iran and Israel', in M. Webber and M. Smith, *Foreign Policy in a Transformed World*, Harlow: Pearson Education.

Ethics and Public Policy Center (2002) 'Religion, culture, and international conflict after September 11. A conversation with Samuel P. Huntington', Washington DC: Ethics and Public Policy Center. Available at: http://www.eppc.org/programs/religionandmedia/publications/pubID.1537,programID.37/pub_detail.asp Accessed 16 March 2004.

Fandy, M. (1999) *Saudi Arabia and the Politics of Dissent*, Basingshoke: Palgrave.

Gopin, M. (2000) *Between Eden and Armageddon: The Future of World Religions, Violence and Peacemaking*, New York and London: Oxford University Press.

Gopin, M. (2005) 'World religions, violence, and myths of peace in international relations', in G. ter Haar and J. Busutill (eds), *Bridge or Barrier: Religion, Violence and Visions for Peace*, Leiden: Brill, pp. 35–56.

Gunaratna, R. (2004) *Combating Terrorism*, Singapore: Times Academic Press.

ter Haar, G. (2005) 'Religion: source of conflict or resource for peace?', in G. ter Haar and J. Busutill (eds), *Bridge or Barrier: Religion, Violence and Visions for Peace*, Leiden: Brill, pp. 3–34.

Hague, R. and Harrop, M. (2001) *Comparative Government and Politics: An Introduction*, 5th edn, Basingstoke: Palgrave.

Hammond, P. (2003) 'Review article: Making war and peace', *Contemporary Politics*, 9, 1, pp. 83–90.

Harris, L. (2002) 'Al Qaeda's fantasy ideology', *Policy Review Online*, August–September, no. 114. Available at: http://www.policyreview.org/AUG02/harris.html Accessed 10 March 2004.

Harsch, E. (2003), 'Africa builds its own peace forces', *Africa Recovery*, 17(3), pp.1, 14–16, 18–20.

Haynes, J. (2005a) *Comparative Politics in A Globalizing World*, Cambridge: Polity.

Haynes, J. (2005b) 'Al-Qaeda: ideology and action', *Critical Review of International Social and Political Philosophy*, 8(2), pp. 177–91.

Hoffman, B. (1998–99) 'Old madness: new methods. Revival of religious terrorism begs for broader U.S. policy', *Rand Review*, 2(22): 11–17.

Horowitz, M. (2002) 'Research report on the use of identity concepts in international relations'. Available at: http://www.wcfia.harvard.edu/misc/initiative/identity/publications/horowitz1.pdf Accessed 25 May 2006.

Howard, R. and Sawyer, R. (eds) (2004) *Defeating Terrorism: Shaping the New Security Environment*, Guilford, CT: McGraw-Hill/Dushkin.

Huntington, S. (1993) 'The clash of civilisations?', *Foreign Affairs*, 72(3), pp. 22–49.

Huntington, S. (1996) *The Clash of Civilizations*, New York: Simon and Schuster.

Hurrell, A. (2002) '"There are no rules" (George W. Bush): International order after September 11', *International Relations*, 16, 2, pp. 185–204.

International Crisis Group (2005) *Somalia's Islamists*, Africa Report No. 100, December, London: International Crisis Group.

Isaacs, D. (2003) 'Islam in Nigeria: Simmering tensions', BBC News online, 23 September. Available at: http://news.bbc.co.uk/1/hi/world/africa/3155279.stm. Accessed 1 December 2005.

Johnson , R. (n/d; probably 2002) 'Reconstructing the Balkans: The effects of a global governance approach'. Unpublished manuscript. The Brookings Institution, Washington, DC, USA. Available at: www.cpogg.org/paper%20amerang/Rebecca%20Johnson.pdf Accessed 1 October 2003.

Johnston, D. and Sampson, C. (eds) (1994) *Religion, the Missing Dimension of Statecraft*, Oxford: Oxford University Press.

Juergensmeyer, M. (2000) *Terror in the Mind of God: The Global Rise of Religious Violence*, Berkeley, CA: University of California Press.

Juergensmeyer, M. (2005) 'Religion in the new global order'. Available at: http://www.maxwell.syr.edu/moynihan/programs/sac/paper%20pdfs/marks%20paper.pdf Accessed 18 April 2006.

Kamrava, M. (1993) *Politics and Society in the Third World*, London: Routledge.

Keohane, R. (2002) 'The globalization of informal violence, theories of world politics, and the "liberalism of fear"', *Dialog-IO*, Spring 2002, pp. 29–43.

Kepel, G. (2004) *The War for Muslim Minds: Islam and the West*, London: Harvard University Press.

Kohen, A. (1999) *From the Place of the Dead: The Epic Struggles of Bishop Belo of East Timor*, New York: St Martin's Press.

Kumaraswamy, P. R. (1999) 'South Asia after the Cold War', in L. Fawcett and Y. Sayigh (eds), *The Third World Beyond the Cold War*, Oxford: Oxford University Press, pp. 170–99.

Kurop, M. Christoff (2001) 'Al Qaeda's Balkan Links', *The Wall Street Journal Europe*, November 1. Available at: http://www.balkanpeace.org/hed/archive/nov01/hed4304.shtml Accessed 10 March 2004.

Malek, C. (2004) 'Identity (Inter-Group) conflicts'. Available at: The Conflict Resolution Information Source, University of Colorado, website: http://v4.crinfo.org/CK_Essays/ck_identity_issues.jsp Accessed 25 October 2005.

Marty, M. and Appleby, R. Scott (1993) 'Introduction' in M. Marty and R. Scott Appleby (eds), *Fundamentalism and the State: Remaking Polities, Economies, and Militance*, Chicago: University of Chicago Press, pp. 1–9.

Milton-Edwards, B. (2006) *Islam and Violence in the Modern Era*, Basingstoke and New York: Palgrave Macmillan.

Mozjes, P. (2002) 'Report on the international conference on reconciliation in Bosnia, Dubrovnik, Croatia, 12–14 September, 2002'. Available at: http://www.georgefox.edu/academics/undergrad/departments/socswk/ree/mojzes_rot.doc Accessed 25 May 2006.

Norris, P. and Inglehart, I. (2004) *Sacred and Secular: Religion and Politics Worldwide*, Cambridge: Cambridge University Press.

Norris, P., Kern, M., and Just, M. (2003) 'Framing Terrorism', in P. Norris (ed.) *Framing Terrorism: The News Media, the Government and the Public*, New York: Routledge, pp. 3–27.

Pevehouse, J. and Goldstein, J. (2005) *International Relations*, London: Harlow.

Reus-Smit, C. (2005) 'Constructivism', in S. Burchill, A. Linklater, R. Devetak, J. Donnelly, M. Paterson, C. Reus-Smit and J. True, *Theories of International Relations*, 3rd edn, Basingstoke and New York: Palgrave Macmillan, pp. 161–87.

Rosen, D. (2005) 'Religion, Identity and Mideast Peace'. The 10th Annual Templeton Lecture on Religion and World Affairs. Available at: http://www.fpri.org/enotes/20050923.religion.rosen.religionidentitymideastpeace.html Accessed 25 May 2006.

Rotberg, R. (2003) 'The failure and collapse of nation-states: breakdown, prevention and fear', in R. Rotberg (ed.), *When States Fail: Causes and Consequences*, Princeton, NJ: Princeton University Press, pp. 1–49.

Roy, O. (2004) *Globalised Islam: The Search for a New Ummah*, London: Hurst.

Sacks, G. (2001) 'Why I miss the Cold War', *Los Angeles Daily Journal* and the *San Francisco Daily Journal*, 2 October. Available at: www.glennsacks. com.

Shlapentokh, V., Woods, J. and Shiraev, E. (eds) (2005) *America: Sovereign Defender or Cowboy Nation?*, Aldershot, and Burlington, VT: Ashgate.

Smith, S. (2002) 'The end of the unipolar moment? September 11 and the future of world order', *International Relations*, 16(2), pp. 171–183.

Smock, D. (2001) 'Faith-based NGOs and international peacebuilding'. Special report no. 76, United States Institute of Peace, October. Available at: http://www.usip.org/pubs/specialreports/sr76.html Accessed 4 February 2006.

Smock, D. (2004) 'Divine intervention: regional reconciliation through faith', *Religion*, 25(4). Available at: http://hir.harvard.edu/articles/1190/3/ Accessed 1 September 2005.

Thomas, S. (2005) *The Global Resurgence of Religion and the Transformation of International Relations: The Struggle for the Soul of the Twenty-First Century*, Basingstoke and New York: Palgrave Macmillan.

Thürer, D. (1999) 'The "failed state" and international law', *International Review of the Red Cross*, no. 836, pp. 731–61.

Tisdall, S. (2006) 'The land the world forgot', *The Guardian*, 23 May.

United States Institute of Peace (2003) 'Special report: Can faith-based NGOs advance interfaith reconciliation? The case of Bosnia and Herzegovina'. Available at: http://www.usip.org/pubs/specialreports/sr103.pdf Accessed 1 February 2006.

Weimann, G. (2006) *Terror on the Internet: The New Arena, the New Challenges*, Washington, DC: The United States Institute of Peace Press.

Further reading

R. Scott Appleby, *The Ambivalence of the Sacred: Religion, Violence and Reconciliation*, Rowman and Littlefield, 2000. Appleby describes how both terrorists and peacemakers can emerge from the same community and be followers of the same religion. One kills while the other strives for reconciliation. Appleby explains what religious terrorists and religious peacemakers share in common, what causes them to take different paths in fighting injustice and how a deeper understanding of religious extremism can and must be integrated more effectively into our thinking about tribal, regional, and international conflict.

M. Duffield, *Global Governance and the New Wars: The Merging of Development and Security*, Zed Books, 2001. As Duffield explains, war is now an important part of development discourse. In recent years, numerous aid agencies have become involved in humanitarian assistance, conflict resolution and the social reconstruction of war-torn societies. Focusing on the nature of the new – post-Cold War – wars, in Africa, the Balkans, Central Asia, as well as the international community's response, or lack of it, Duffield examines the novel systems of global governance emerging at the current time.

M. Gopin, *Between Eden and Armageddon: The Future of World Religions, Violence and Peacemaking*, Oxford University Press, 2000. It is now widely accepted that there has been a widespread resurgence of religion in recent years. Recent years have seen a meteoric rise in the power and importance of organized religion in many parts of the world. While there has been much attention on the relationship between violence and religious militancy, Gopin explains that both historically and at the present time, many religious people have also played a critical role in peacemaking within numerous cultures. He poses two key questions: In the twenty-first century, will religion bring upon further catastrophes? Or will it provide human civilization with methods of care, healing, and the creation of peaceful and just societies?

G. ter Haar G. and J. Busutill (eds), *Bridge or Barrier: Religion, Violence and Visions for Peace*, Brill, 2005. This book discusses the transformative role of religion in situations of violent conflict. It considers both the constructive sides of religious belief and particularly explores ways in which religion(s) may contribute to transforming conflict into peace.

D. Johnston and C. Sampson (eds), *Religion, the Missing Dimension of Statecraft*, Oxford University Press, 1994. As the Cold War era became history, Johnston and Sampson claim that humanity was entering an era when international conflict would be increasingly based on racial, ethnic, national, and religious clashes – the most intractable sources of conflict, and those with which conventional diplomacy is least suited to deal. They claim that religion plays a crucial role in many international conflicts, yet state diplomacy often ignores or misunderstands its role. This collection of case studies and theoretical pieces aims to restore this 'missing dimension' to its rightful place in the conduct of international diplomacy.

M. Juergensmeyer, *Terror in the Mind of God: The Global Rise of Religious Violence*, University of California Press, 2000. Juergensmeyer documents the global rise of religious terrorism while seeking to comprehend the 'odd attraction of religion and violence'. Basing his study on scholarly sources, media accounts and personal interviews with convicted terrorists, Juergensmeyer exercises caution with the term 'terrorist'. He prefers to emphasize the large religious community of supporters who make violent acts possible rather than the relatively small number who carry them out. Juergensmeyer identifies certain 'cultures of violence' in many religious (Christianity, Judaism, Islam, Hinduism, Sikhism and Buddhism).

CHAPTER 7

Religious 'fundamentalisms' and international relations

Anybody who had prophesied 30 years ago that the 20th century would end with a resurgence of religion, with great new cathedrals, mosques, and temples rising up, with the symbols and songs of faith everywhere apparent, would, in most circles, have been derided. (Woollacott, 1995)

The quote from Woollacott suggests that the current widespread resurgence of religion is a highly unexpected development. It is important to make it clear, however, that the various examples of 'religious fundamentalisms' and the current resurgence of religion in many parts of the world are not the same thing (Berger, 1999; Thomas, 2005).[1] In other words, contemporary manifestations of religious fundamentalism are an aspect of a more general religious resurgence in most but not all parts of the world, although Western Europe appears to be an exception to the general trend (Hadden, 1987; Shupe, 1990; Bruce, 2003; Norris and Inglehart, 2004). It also implies that it is not the case that any religious activity or conception of religion that refuses to accept that religion should be 'privatized' necessarily becomes a form of fundamentalism. For example, both Tony Blair and George W. Bush might be described as 'Christian statesmen', that is, they appear to believe strongly in the public role of religion, yet neither of them could credibly be described as religious fundamentalists (Ahmed, 2003; Jervis, 2005).

It is useful to think of the various manifestations of contemporary religious fundamentalism as a counter-movement often militantly opposed to what followers perceive as the inexorable onwards march of secularization, leading to political and public marginalization and privatization of religion.

To many observers and 'ordinary' people, a further defining characteristic of any form of religious fundamentalism is its social and political conservatism. Socially, religious fundamentalism is regarded as backward looking, anti-modern, inherently opposed to change. Note, however, that if this was actually the case it would be very difficult satisfactorily to explain the sometimes revolutionary political demands and programmes of some religious fundamentalist thinkers and activists. Some, particularly Islamists in the Middle East and elsewhere in the Muslim world, aim to overthrow regimes that they regard as un- or anti-Islamic and replace them with more authentically Islamic governments. On the other hand, some Christian fundamentalists in the USA – people who believe in the inerrancy of the Bible and subscribe to a modern form of millenarianism (that is, the teaching in Christianity that Jesus will rule for 1,000 years on earth) – may seem to fit more closely conventional wisdom. This is because they are often linked to conservative political forces, for example in the USA, whose aim is to seek to undo what they judge to be symptoms of unwelcome liberalization and the relaxation of traditional social and moral mores characteristic, they believe, of secularization (Religion and Ethics Newsweekly, 2004).

Religious fundamentalisms and 'deprivatization'

Religious fundamentalist movements are often linked to the impact of separate but closely linked developments: modernization and secularization. Together they served to undermine the political and social importance of religion in many countries. As a result, there was widespread religious 'deprivatization' – that is, collective attempts to engage or re-engage with public social and political issues – of previously privatized religions in many parts of the world, including the West (the USA, Israel and Western Europe). What such Western areas were long thought to have in common was a more or less clear tripartite division of democratic polities into state, political society and civil society. According to much conventional social science wisdom such an arrangement should, inevitably, lead to religious 'privatization' – that is, its public marginalization – and corresponding decline in social and political importance (Bruce, 2003). As we shall see, however, the assumption turned out to be wrong in both the USA and Israel.

But where the process of religious privatization is not so far advanced – that is, in most 'developing' countries – *fear* of imminent or creeping privatization can provide a stimulus for religious actors, including religious fundamentalists, to act in the political sphere in order to try to *prevent* religious privatization. In many cases, various secular political ideologies – including liberal democracy, social democracy or socialism – have been tried by ruling governments over the years and, in many cases, were seen to fail to deliver their promises of societal progress and improvement (Haynes, 2002). A consequence is that, in many countries, religious fundamentalism, sometimes allied with nationalism, ethnicity, or communalism (as in India), has served as a mobilizing ideology to focus opposition to the status quo (Juergensmeyer, 1993). Note that the suggestion is *not* that such movements were necessarily unimportant in the past: growth and eventual politicization of Christian conservatism in the USA over the last three decades, as well as successive waves of Islamic reform over the last two centuries in West Africa and elsewhere, would belie that argument (Haynes, 1993). The point is that the overtly political goals of many contemporary religious fundamentalist movements are best understood as a response to the existential insecurities associated with modernization, secularization and globalization, where a (re)turn to 'religious fundamentals' is seen as the best prescription for desirable changes.

Religious fundamentalism and international relations

In international relations, religious fundamentalism is often associated with conflict, not least because religious fundamentalists are often seen to be intolerant and unable to reach compromise solutions to shared problems with those who do not share their views (Juergensmeyer, 2000; Appleby, 2000). Examining this issue, in this chapter we examine several manifestations of contemporary religious fundamentalism to see how they affect international relations, with examples drawn from Christianity, Hinduism, Islam and Judaism. We examine how best to understand these phenomena, before explicating and assessing the main socio-political and religious characteristics of each.

Accounting for religious fundamentalism

According to Woodhead and Heelas, religious fundamentalism is a 'distinctively modern twentieth-century movement' albeit with 'historical antecedents' (Woodhead and Heelas, 2000: 32). Conceptually, the term has been widely employed since the 1970s to describe numerous, apparently diverse, religious and political developments around the globe (Caplan, 1987). However, the term was first used a century ago by conservative Christians in the USA to describe themselves: they claimed they wanted to get back to what they saw as the 'fundamentals' of their religion, as depicted in the Bible. Such people typically came from 'main-line' – that is, established – Protestant denominations, not usually the Roman Catholic Church. Now, however, the label 'religious fundamentalism' has become a generic term, widely applied to a multitude of groups from various religious traditions, comprising people who share a decidedly conservative religious outlook (Simpson, 1992).

Generally speaking, both the character and impact of fundamentalist doctrines are located within a nexus of moral and social concerns centring on state–society interactions. In some cases, the initial defensiveness of 'religious fundamentalists' came from a belief that they were under attack from modernization and secularization and/or the intrusion of alien ethnic, cultural or religious groups. Sometimes this developed into a broad socio-political offensive to try to redress the situation, in particular targeting political rulers and lax co-religionists for their perceived inadequacies and weaknesses. Informing their religious and political outlooks, religious fundamentalists turn to core religious texts – such as the Christian Bible or the Quran – to find out God's 'opinion' on various social and political topics, often through the use of selected readings which may form the basis of programmes of reform (Marty and Appleby, 1991).

Religious fundamentalism and 'failed modernity'

Contemporary religious fundamentalisms are often said to be rooted in the failed promise of modernity, reactive against perceived unwelcome manifestations of modernization, especially declining moral values or perceived undermining of the family as a social institution (Haynes, 2003). To many religious fundamentalists God was in danger of being superseded by a gospel of technical progress accompanying sweeping socio-economic changes. Around the world, the pace of socio-economic change, especially since the Second World War, everywhere strongly challenged traditional habits, beliefs and cultures, and societies were under considerable and constant pressure to adapt to modernization. Not least, in an increasingly materialist world one's individual worth was increasingly measured according to secular standards of wealth and status; religion seemed ignored, belittled or threatened. Thus to many religious fundamentalists unwelcome social, cultural and economic changes were the root cause of what they saw as a toxic cocktail of religious, moral and social decline.

Religious fundamentalisms: definitional issues

It is time to confront a significant analytical problem. It is sometimes suggested that 'religious fundamentalism' is an empty and therefore meaningless term. It is said to be erroneously and casually employed, primarily 'by Western liberals' in relation 'to a broad spectrum of religious phenomena which have little in common except for the fact that they are alarming to liberals!' (Woodhead and Heelas, 2000: 32). This view contends that the range of people and groups casually labelled 'fundamentalist' is so wide – from the revolutionary political Islamism of the Iranian ideologue, Ali Shariati, the Egyptian Sayyid Qutb, the Pakistani Maulana Maududi, and the Saudi Arabian, Osama bin Laden, through socially conservative Christians in the USA, such as Pat Robertson and Jerry Falwell, to Bal Thackeray, leader of India's Shiv Sena party – that the term lacks clarity, precision and meaning. As a consequence, Hallencreutz and Westerlund (1996: 4) aver, the broad use of the term 'religious fundamentalism'

> has become increasingly irrelevant. In sum, viewed as a derogatory concept, tied to Western stereotypes and Christian presuppositions, the casual use of the term easily causes misunderstandings and prevents the understanding of the dynamics and characteristics of different religious groups with explicit political objectives.

We shall turn later to the various political objectives of religious fundamentalists. For now, we can note that, despite such criticisms, the term 'religious fundamentalism' is commonly found in both academic and popular discourse. Numerous journal articles and books on the topic have appeared, including important volumes in the 1990s by Marty and Appleby (1991–95) and Lawrence (1995), which used the term analytically. Thus by no means all analysts and observers reject use of the term. Those accepting its analytical and explanatory relevance do so because they perceive contemporary religious fundamentalist thinkers and movements around the world – albeit encompassing very different religious traditions – as having some important features in common, including: core beliefs, norms and values. These include:

- 'a desire to return to the fundamentals of a religious tradition and strip away unnecessary accretions
- an aggressive rejection of western secular modernity
- an oppositional minority group-identity maintained in an exclusivist and militant manner

- attempts to reclaim the public sphere as a space of religious and moral purity
- a patriarchial and hierarchical ordering of relations between the sexes' (Woodhead and Heelas, 2000: 32).

Marty and Appleby on religious fundamentalism

Drawing on data compiled from studies of numerous religious fundamentalist groups from several religious traditions in different parts of the world, Marty and Appleby arrive at the following definition of religious fundamentalists. They are people who hold a 'set of strategies, by which beleaguered believers attempt to preserve their distinctive identity as a people or group'. They see themselves acting in response to a real or imagined attack from those who, they believe, want to draw them into a 'syncretistic, areligious, or irreligious cultural milieu' (Marty and Appleby, 1993a: 3). Following an initial sense of defensiveness as a result of perception of attack from unwelcome, alien forces, fundamentalists may well go on to develop an offensive strategy aimed at altering radically prevailing socio-political realities in order to 'bring back' religious concerns into public centrality.

In sum, it can be stated that religious fundamentalists have the following in common:

- They fear that their preferred religiously-orientated way of life is under attack from unwelcome secular influences or alien groups.
- Their aim is to create traditionally orientated, less modern(ized) societies.
- As a result, many pursue campaigns in accordance with what they believe are suitable religious tenets in order to change laws, morality, social norms and, in some cases, domestic and/or international political configurations.
- Many are willing to contest politically with ruling regimes in various ways if the latter's jurisdiction appears to be encroaching into areas of life – including, education, gender relations and employment policy – that religious fundamentalists believe are integral to their vision of a religiously appropriate society, one characterized by a certain kind of 'pure' moral climate.

- They may also actively oppose co-religionists who they believe are excessively lax in upholding their religious duties – as well as followers of rival or opposing religions whom they may regard as misguided, evil, even satanic.

Even those rejecting the general use of the term 'religious fundamentalism' might accept that it has relevance in one specific context: self-designated Christian fundamentalists in the USA. Emerging over a century ago, such people – believing implicitly in the inerrancy of the Bible – sought to resist what they saw as the unacceptable inroads of secular modernity. Until the 1970s, US Christian fundamentalists were often apolitical, even in some cases excluding themselves from the public realm. Over time, however, many began to realize that retreating from the world was actually self-defeating, because as a result they could not hope to alter what they saw as catastrophically unwelcome developments intrinsically linked to modernization and secularization. In recent years, Christian fundamentalists in the USA have become increasingly vociferous, an influential political constituency. Leaders of the movement have included Jerry Falwell, founding leader of the organization Moral Majority (formed in 1979, dissolved in 1989), as well as two recent but unsuccessful presidential candidates: Pat Robertson and Pat Buchanan. However, usage of the term has been rather flexible, sometimes used in reference to the broad community of religious, mostly Christian, conservatives and at other times to denote a small subset of institutionalized organizations pursuing explicit goals of cultural and economic conservatism. Many Christian fundamentalists in the USA coalesce in a movement known initially when it was founded in the 1970s as the 'New Christian Right'; now it is referred to as either 'the Christian Right' or 'the Religious Right', with the latter term implying that other religious traditions are also present. In short, the Religious Right is an important religious/social/political movement in the USA, not exclusive to but generally linking conservative American Christians (Bruce, 2003; Dolan, 2005).

The Religious Right in the USA

The Religious Right first came to public prominence following the decision of the US Supreme Court in 1972 in the famous 'Roe versus Wade' court case over abortion rights. Since then it has been consistently – and in recent years increasingly politically – active. The Religious Right has extensive media interests, sponsoring a network of Christian bookshops, radio stations, and television

(Continued)

evangelists. In relation to social issues, it advocates severely limiting or banning abortion, is against legal recognition of homosexual marriage and pornography, and advocates the use of prayer in schools. All these concerns stem from the fact that it believes that religion is increasingly marginalized in American public life (Dolan, 2005).

Prior to the 1970s, the Religious Right had been a subculture, keeping distance from electoral politics. But with a new focus on social conservatism, around the time of the presidency of Ronald Reagan (1981–89), Republican Party strategists – together with neo-conservatives and right-wing ideologues – encouraged its politicization as part of the New Right fusionism that ushered Ronald Reagan into the presidency in 1981. In recent years, the Religious Right has been increasingly concerned with foreign policy issues, making common cause with secular neo-conservatives in focusing US foreign policy on various issues, especially 'religious freedom' – particularly among minority Christian and Jewish populations in Muslim and Communist nations (Hacker and Pierson, 2005: 127–9). In the late 1990s and early 2000s the Religious Right gave strong electoral support to George W. Bush, who became president for the first time in 2001, before re-election in 2005 (Halper and Clarke, 2004).

In sum, despite ideological and political differences among the different organizations that make up the movement, members of the Religious Right share in common a belief that excessive secularism poses a degree of threat to liberty, democracy and pluralism. The Religious Right is 'radical' in that its members advocate often extreme and dramatic changes in society. It is 'religious' in that its intellectual and religious position draws to some degree from religious doctrines and texts in the Bible.

The use of the Bible by the Christian conservatives in the USA draws attention to the fact that religious fundamentalists generally use holy books as a key source for their ideas. However, drawing on the example of American Christian conservatives, many analysts who employ the terms 'religious fundamentalism' suggest that it is only properly applicable to Christianity and the other 'Abrahamic' religions of the 'book': Islam and Judaism. This is because Christian, Islamic and Jewish fundamentalists all take their defining dogma from what they believe to be the inerrancy of God's own words set out in their holy books. In other words, singular scriptural revelations are central to each set of fundamentalist dogma in these three religions. The inference is that, because Hinduism does not have its own central tenets of political, social and moral import conveniently accessible in a holy book or books, then it is not logically possible for there to be Hindu fundamentalists. However, somewhat confusingly, as we shall see later, in recent years 'religious fundamentalist' movements have emerged from within Hinduism with demonstrably political goals and electoral successes. As we shall see, such groups are not defined by their absolutist insistence upon the veracity of God's revealed will, but instead by a desire to recapture elements of national identity perceived by Hindu fundamentalists as being lost through perceived cultural dilution or mixing or because of perceived deviations from accepted religious philosophy and/or teachings (Ram-Prasad, 1993: 288). On the other hand, some sources suggest that radical Hindu activists are now attempting to create something resembling an Abrahamic religion with at least a hierarchy of gods, a superior one (implying the development of monotheism, that is, belief in one god alone) and a composite, authoritative scripture (Roy, 2002).

'Islamic fundamentalism'/Islamism

Bealey (1999: 140, my emphasis) defines religious fundamentalism in terms of a

> religious position claiming strict adherence to basic beliefs. This frequently results in intolerance towards other beliefs and believers in one's own creed who do not strictly observe and who do not profess to hold an extreme position. Thus Protestant fundamentalists scorn Protestants who fail to perceive a danger from Catholicism; Jewish fundamentalists attack Jews with secularist leanings; and Muslim fundamentalists believe that they have a duty to purge Islam of any concessions to cultural modernisation. *A political implication is the tendency of fundamentalists to turn to terrorism.*

While the Muslim world, like the Christian universe, is divided by religious disputes, it is also the case that many Muslims would accept that they are linked by belief, culture, sentiments and identity, collectively focused in the global Muslim community, the *ummah*. It is also the case that there were clear international manifestations of what we might call 'Islamic resurgence', especially after the humbling defeat of the Arabs by Israel in the Six-Day War of June 1967 and the Iranian revolution a dozen years later.

Like their Jewish and Christian counterparts, Islamic fundamentalists (or Islamists, the term many analysts prefer), take as their defining dogma what are believed to be God's words written in their holy book, the Quran. In other words, singular scriptural revelations are central to Islamic fundamentalist dogma. We have also noted that a defining character of all religious fundamentalisms is social conservatism. As already noted, however, this does not imply a corresponding political conservatism, characterized by an unwillingness to countenance significant political changes. But what of Bealey's most contentious claim, that religious fundamentalists, including Islamic fundamentalists, are noted for a political 'tendency' to 'turn to terrorism'?

Let's start by noting that Islamist groups work to change the current social and political order by the use of various political means. These include incremental reform of existing political regimes by various means, including, if allowed, taking part in and winning elections through the auspices of a political party, as well as the use of political violence or terrorism *in some circumstances*. But what might these circumstances be? And is this course of action linked to the very nature of their fundamentalist beliefs? As a way of answering these questions, it is useful to refer to some of the ideas expressed by several noteworthy twentieth-century Islamist thinkers: Maulana Maududi, Sayyid Qutb, Ayatollah Khomeini and Ali Shariati.

Born in India, Maulana Maududi (1903–79) was one of the most influential Muslim theologians of the twentieth cenury. His philosophy, literary productivity and tireless activism contributed immensely to the development of Islamic political and social movements around the world. Maulana Maududi's ideas profoundly influenced Sayyid Qutb of Egypt's *Jamiat al-Ikhwan al-Muslimun* (the Muslim Brotherhood), another leading Muslim philosopher of the twentieth century. Together, Maududi and Qutb are considered the founding fathers of the global Islamist movement. Maududi's ideas about the Islamic state are widely regarded as the basic foundation for the political, economical, social, and religious system of any Islamic country that wishes to live under Islamic law (*sharia*). This is an ideological system that, while intentionally discriminating between people according to their religious affiliations, in no way prescribes the acceptability of political violence, much less terrorism.

Sayyid Qutb (1906–66) was an Egyptian, a prominent Islamist and member of the Muslim Brotherhood, the Arab world's oldest Islamist group, which advocates an Islamic state in Egypt. Qutb's political thinking was deeply influenced by the revolutionary radicalism of a contemporaneous Islamist, Maulana Maududi. Qutb's ideological development fell into two distinct periods: before 1954, and following a sojourn in the USA; from 1954 until his execution by the Egyptian government in 1966, following imprisonment and torture by the secularist government of Gamal Abdel Nasser. Following an attempt on Nasser's life in October 1954, the government imprisoned thousands of members of the Muslim Brotherhood, including Qutb, and officially banned the organization. During his second, more radical phase, Qutb declared 'Western civilization' the enemy of Islam, denounced leaders of Muslim nations for not following Islam closely enough, and sought to spread the belief among Sunni Muslims that it was their duty to undertake *jihad* to defend and purify Islam. Note, however, that in this conception *jihad* does not necessarily imply anti-Western conflict; instead, it refers to an individual Muslim's striving for spiritual self-perfection.

Ayatollah Ruhollah Khomeini (1900–89) was Iranian Shi'ite leader and Head of State in Iran from 1979 until his death in 1989. He was arrested (1963) and exiled (1964) for his opposition to Shah Muhammad Reza Pahlavi's regime. He returned to Iran on the Shah's downfall (1979) and established a new constitution that gave him supreme powers. His reign was marked by a return to strict observance of the Islamic code. Iran's revolution was divided into two stages: the first saw an alliance of liberal, leftist, and Islamic groups oust the Shah; the second stage, often named the 'Islamic Revolution', saw the ayatollahs come to power. During the second stage Khomeini achieved the status of a revered spiritual leader among many Shia Muslims. In Iran he was officially addressed as Imam[2] rather than as Ayatollah. Khomeini was also a highly influential and innovative Islamic political theorist, most noted for his development of the theory, the 'guardianship of the jurisconsult'.

The Iranian, Dr Ali Shariati (1933–77), was another influential Islamist. Shariati was a sociologist, well known and respected for his works in the field of the sociology of religion, including *Mission of a Free Thinker* and *Where Shall We Begin* (http://www.shariati.com/). He was strongly influenced by the work of the West Indian author and revolutionary, Franz Fanon (1925–61). Shariati urged Muslims to 'abandon Europe' and 'end the impossible task of acting as intermediaries between them and the forces at work in the colonisation project'. In this respect Shariati's ideas reflect similar concerns in Asia, the Middle East and Africa, that echoe and reflect what might be called a shared 'Third World consciousness' and a growing resentment at the outcomes of current and historical episodes of Western involvement and interaction (Milton-Edwards, 2006: 81).

In sum, the various concerns expressed by Maududi, Qutb, Khomeini and Shariati reflect in somewhat different ways a shared focus on Islamist 'growth, exploration and generation of discourse of protest against the West' (Milton-Edwards, 2006: 81). What they have in common, in other words, is a shared sense that the West – because of its expansionism and perceived disdain for religion in general and Islam in particular – is a key problem for Muslims around the world.

This concern with inequality and injustice, with its perceived roots in a historical Western hegemony manifested in an earlier period by colonialism and imperialism and now via global capitalist economic control, is said to be a key factor encouraging the growth of Islamism throughout the Muslim world (Akbar, 2002). The end of the First World War in 1918 coincided both with the demise of the Turkish Ottoman empire and the onset of Arab nationalism. Throughout the Middle East, nations began to demand political freedom from de facto British or French colonial rule that, as a result of League of Nations mandates, replaced Ottoman power. The nationalist struggle was also informed by the extent to which emerging, predominantly Muslim, states in the Middle East should seek to employ the tenets of Islamic law (*sharia*) in their legal and political systems. The issue of the Islamicization of polities in the Middle East had a precedent in some parts of the Muslim world in the form of anti-imperialist and anti-pagan 'holy wars' (*jihads*) which had periodically erupted from the late nineteenth century, especially in parts of West Africa and East Asia (Akbar, 2002). These were regions where conflicts between tradition and modernization, and between Islam and Christianity, were often especially acute, frequently fuelled by European colonialism and imperialism.

Going further back, to the emergence of Islam 1,400 years ago, Muslim religious critics of the status quo have periodically emerged, opposed to what they perceive as unjust, unacceptable forms of rule. Contemporary Islamists can be seen as the most recent examples of this trend. This is because they characterize themselves as the 'just' involved in a *jihad* ('holy war') against the 'unjust', primarily but not exclusively their own domestic political rulers. Sometimes, as with the current al-Qaeda campaign, a key enemy is located internationally (Haynes, 2005a, 2005b). Overall, there is a dichotomy between the 'just' and the 'unjust' in the promotion of social change throughout Islamic history that parallels the tension in the West between 'state' and 'civil society'. In other words, 'just' and 'unjust', like 'state' and 'civil society', are mutually exclusive concepts where a strengthening of one necessarily implies a weakening of the other. The implication is that the 'unjust' inhabit the state while the 'just' look in from the outside, seeking to reform political and social systems and mores that they regard as both corrupt and insufficiently Islamic. Contemporary Islamic fundamentalists regard themselves as the Islamic 'just', striving to achieve their goal of a form of direct democracy under the auspices of Allah and *sharia* law. In some conceptions of Islamic rule, a religious and political ruler, the *caliph*, would emerge, a figure who would use his wisdom to settle disputes brought to him by his loyal subjects and rule the polity on Allah's behalf (Fuller, 2003: 13–46).

Islamism and democracy

For some Islamic thinkers, like the Syrian intellectual Dr Muhammad Shahrur, 'democracy, as a mechanism, is the best achievement of humanity for practicing consultation (*Shura*)' (quoted in Fuller, 2003: 61). Note, however, that his view does not necessarily imply Western liberal democratic notions centring on popular sovereignty. This is because Islamists see sovereignty as being exclusively in Allah's hands, and implying 'a means of obtaining unanimity from the community of believers, which allows for no legitimate minority position' (Dorr, 1993: 151–2). For Islamists the goal is to achieve unanimity about the desirability of an authentically Islamic polity. In many Muslim countries in the 1980s, especially among the Arab nations of the Middle East, various Islamist movements and political parties emerged, using various means – including the ballot box – to try to win, usually unsuccessfully, political power (Nasr, 2001). What such Islamist entities often have in common is a deep suspicion or disdain for liberal democracy, seen as an irredeemable Western concept, fatally flawed and compromised, of irrelevance to Muslims because it leads inexorably to morally deficient, secular, Westernized societies. As a young Algerian graduate of the Islamic Science Institute of Algiers noted: 'The modern world is going through a major moral crisis which can be very confusing to young people. Just look at what is happening in Russia. Personally I have found many of the answers and solutions in Islam' (Quoted in Ibrahim, 1992).

Shared beliefs, relating to culture, sentiments and identity, link Muslims in the global *ummah*. As a result, it is unsurprising that certain international events appear to influence the contemporary Islamic resurgence, of which Islamism is an important although not the only aspect (Milton-Edwards, 2006). Among them, we can note two: the humbling defeat of Arab armies by Israel in the calamitous Six-Day War of June 1967 and the Iranian revolution (1979). The sense of inferiority and defeat that the Six-Day War engendered was to some extent lightened by the Iranian revolution a dozen years later (Saikal, 2003). Since then, a lethal combination of often poor government, high unemployment and apparently generalized social crisis in many Muslim countries has interacted with growing inequalities and injustices at the global level to encourage Islamist movements throughout much of the Muslim world (Akbar, 2002). This development can also be associated more generally with widespread, failed attempts at modernization and the impact of globalization, Western hegemony and American domination (Milton-Edwards, 2006).

Islamists are of course also concerned about domestic political, social and economic issues. Throughout the Middle East many rulers appear content to receive large personal incomes from the sale of their countries' oil for US dollars, with little in the way of beneficial development effects for the majority of their citizens. In addition, many such leaders do little to develop more representative polities, plan successfully for the future, or seek means to reduce un- and underemployment. In short, there has been a skewed modernization process featuring, on the one hand, urbanization and limited industrialization and, on the other, growing numbers of dissatisfied citizens, some of whom turn to Islamist vehicles of political change to reflect their strong opposition to incumbent rulers and their developmental failures (Nasr, 2001; Esposito, 2002).

The contemporary Islamic revival, of which Islamism is a key aspect, is generated primarily in urban settings (Esposito, 2002; Juergensmeyer, 2000). The key issue is what can Islam do for Muslims in the contemporary world? Can the faith rescue communities and societies from decline, purify them and help combat both internal and external forces of corruption and secularization? For many Islamic radicals the Iranian revolution of 1979 was a particularly emblematic event in this regard (Saikal, 2003: 69–88). This is because the revolution enabled Ayatollah Khomeini – after the revolution, the supreme political, religious and spiritual authority – to put into place and enforce *sharia* law as the law of the land, to pursue a proclaimed commitment to social justice, and to try to roll back Western hegemony at the international level with its economic, political and cultural influences. Over time, however, despite Western fears, while the revolution undoubtedly energized Islamic radicals throughout the world, it was not followed by a consequential revolutionary wave affecting the Muslim world. Instead, governments in many Muslim-majority countries – such as Algeria, Egypt and Libya – responded to real or perceived Islamist threats with a variable mixture of state-controlled re-Islamicization, reform and coercion (Husain, 1995). In response, many grassroots Islamist movements turned attention to local social and political struggles, with the overall aim of a re-Islamicization of society 'from below', focusing on the requirement for personal and social behaviour necessary to be Islamically 'authentic', in line with religious tradition. Political violence was not rare, although not eschewed, for example in Algeria and Egypt, if judged necessary by the radicals for their community's 'purification'. In addition, from the 1980s and 1990s onwards, movements within countries sought to develop transnational networks that were often difficult for states to control, contributing to conditions of social, political and economic instability in many Muslim societies (Voll, 2006; Casanova, 2005).

An interesting example comes from Algeria. There was much Western concern in the early 1990s as it appeared that Algeria was about to be taken over by Islamic fundamentalists who, it was believed, were about to win parliamentary elections. This fear led the governments of France and the USA to support a successful military *coup d'état* in early 1992 to prevent this feared outcome. The assumption was that if the radical Muslims achieved power they would summarily close down Algeria's newly refreshed democratic institutions and political system as they had earlier done in Iran. Following the coup, the main Islamist organizations were banned, and thousands of their leaders and supporters incarcerated. A civil war followed which finally fizzled out in the early 2000s; over its course an estimated 120,000 Algerians died (Volpi, 2003).

While the political rise of radical Islam in Algeria had domestic roots, it was undoubtedly strengthened by financial support from patrons such as the government of Saudi Arabia. In addition, there were the mobilizing experiences of Algerian *mujahideen* ('holy warriors'), who served in Afghanistan during the anti-Soviet war in the 1980s. On returning home, many such people were no longer content to put up with what was regarded as an un-Islamic government. There was also a large cadre of (mostly secondary) school teachers from Egypt working in Algeria at this time. Many were influenced by the ideas of the Egyptian Muslim Brotherhood or its radical offshoots, and they were believed to have introduced similar radical ideas to Algerian youth (Volpi, 2003; Tahi, 1992).

The overall point is that the emergence and consolidation of Islamism over the last three decades has had both domestic and international causes. On the one hand, in many countries its domestic appearance was often linked to failures of modernization to deliver political and developmental promises. As a result, Etienne and Tozy argue, the Islamic resurgence of the 1980s and 1990s carried within it Muslim 'disillusionment with progress and the disenchantments of the first 20 years of independence' (Etienne and Tozy, 1981: 251). Faced with a state power that sought to destroy or control formerly dominant Muslim communitarian structures and replace them with values, norms, beliefs and institutions focusing on the concept of a *national citizenry* – based on the link between the state and the individual – popular (as opposed to state-controlled) Islamist movements emerged in many Muslim countries. In short, the Muslim political 'reawakening' expressed in various expressions of Islamism can usefully be seen primarily in relation to its *domestic* capacity to oppose the state: 'It is primarily in civil society that one sees Islam at work' (Coulon, 1983: 49). In addition, there are significant international issues that have also encouraged Islamist world-views, notably the perceived unjust impact of globalization and Western economic and cultural power.

Christian fundamentalism

We have seen that for some Muslims, poverty and declining faith in the developmental and political abilities of their governments led to their being receptive to Islamist arguments. In such circumstances, poverty and feelings of hopelessness may be exacerbated by withering of community ties, especially when people move from the countryside to the town in a search for paid employment. When traditional communal and familial ties are seriously stretched or sundered, religion-orientated ones may replace them, often appealing to the poor and dispossessed. In the USA, on the other hand, Christian fundamentalists are found among all strata of society, including affluent, successful people (Wald, 1991: 271). Clearly, it would be absurd to argue that poverty and alienation explain the widespread existence of Christian fundamentalists in the USA. In fact, as we noted earlier, Christian fundamentalism in the USA is quintessentially modern, offering a response to contemporary conditions and events.

It is not, however, only in the USA that one finds significant groups of people that are classified as 'Christian fundamentalists'. Africa has millions of such people who, like their Muslim counterparts, see a religious fundamentalist world-view as a necessary corrective to failed modernization. In regard to Africa, some scholars link the failed developmental promises of independence in the 1960s to the rise of Christian fundamentalism several decades later (Gifford, 2004; Haynes, 1996) In such views, Christian fundamentalism is reactive against unwelcome manifestations of modernization – such as, poverty, marginalization and insecurity. In addition, in some cases, such as Nigeria, a turn to Christian fundamentalist world-views has coincided with a perception that many local Muslims are increasingly belligerent and assertive (Isaacs, 2003).

The recent growth of Christian fundamentalism in various parts of the developing world, notably Latin America and Africa, is said to be the result of a merging of two existing strands of Christian belief – Pentecostalism and conservative Protestantism (Gifford, 1990). American television evangelists, such as Pat Robertson, Jim and Tammy Bakker, Jimmy Swaggart and Oral Roberts, were instrumental in bringing together the two strands in the 1970s and 1980s. Such people often call themselves 'born-again' Christians. They may either remain in the main-line Protestant denominations (for example,

Episcopalian, Presbyterian, Methodist, Baptist and Lutheran) or in the Catholic Church (where they are known as 'charismatics'), or worship in their own denominational churches (Gifford, 1991).

'Born-again' Christians

'Born-again' Christians are Christians who have experienced a distinct, dramatic conversion to faith in Jesus; most are members of certain Protestant churches that stress this experience. The term is expressed in the following words attributed to Jesus in the Gospels: 'Except a man be born again, he cannot see the kingdom of God.' The aim of becoming 'born again' is to make beneficial changes to one's life spiritually, through communion and other interaction with like-minded individuals. To this end, groups may come together to pray and to work for both spiritual redemption and material prosperity, sometimes perceived as inseparable from each other. When the latter goal – that of material prosperity – is viewed as paramount, this may lead to charges that the theological appeal is in fact little more than a mindless and self-centred one to personal well-being.

Often, 'born-again' Christians stress religious elements associated with Pentecostalism: that is, experiential faith, the centrality of the Holy Spirit, and the spiritual gifts of glossolalia ('speaking in tongues'), faith healing, and miracles. Such people are sometimes described as 'fundamentalist' in the sense of wishing to get back to the fundamentals of the faith as they see them. The 'born-again' world-view is embedded in certain dogmatic fundamentals of Christianity, with emphasis placed on the authority of the Bible in all matters of faith and practice; on personal conversion as a distinct experience of faith in Christ as Lord and Saviour (being 'born-again' in the sense of having received a new spiritual life); and, evangelically, in helping others have a similar conversion experience.

To this end, some churches sponsor missionaries who are required to look to 'God alone' (by way of followers' contributions) for their financial support. They may believe that their church is a lone force for good on earth, locked in battle with the forces of evil; the latter may even manifest itself in the form of Christians who do not adhere to the 'born-again' world-view. Unsurprisingly, such 'born-again' conservatives are often strongly opposed to the ecumenical movement – because of its more liberal theological views, which may include a concern for social action in pursuit of developmental goals, in tandem with spiritual concerns.

'Born-again' Christians typically seek God through personal searching rather than through the mediation of a hierarchical institution. In sum, 'born-again' Christians may see themselves as offering converts two main benefits: worldly self-improvement and ultimate salvation, within a context of what are perceived as Christian 'fundamentals', including a strong belief in the perceived inerrancy of the Bible.

Some accounts suggest that members of such 'born-again' groups are politically more conservative than those in the mainstream churches and that such people are willing to submit, rather unquestioningly, to those in authority (Moran and Schlemmer, 1984; Roberts, 1968). In addition, they are said to assimilate easily to the norms of consumer capitalism which helps further to defuse any challenges to the extant political order (Martin, 1990: 160). In addition, in theological and academic debates they are often judged in relation to two other issues: their contribution to personal, social and political 'liberation', and their potential or actual role as purveyors of American or other foreign cultural dogma in non-Western parts of the world. It is also claimed that the 'born-again' doctrine may offer converts hope, but it is a hope without practical manifestation in the world of here and now; it does not help with people's concrete problems nor in the creation of group and class solidarities essential to tackle socio-political concerns (Martin, 1990: 233). The reason for this political conservatism, it is alleged, is that conservative evangelical churches collectively form an American movement of sinister intent (Gifford, 1991).

Cognisant of such concerns, the spread of conservative American-style 'born-again' churches in Africa, Latin America, and elsewhere was greeted with concern by leaders of the established Protestant and Catholic churches, who saw their followers leaving for the new churches in large numbers. Often sponsored by American television evangelists and local churches, thousands of born-again foreign crusaders were seen to promote American-style religion and, in some cases, conservative politics from the 1980s. Ardently anti-Communist, they worked to convert as many ordinary people as possible to a conservative Christian faith and in the process, it is argued, to promote America's political goals (d'Antonio, 1990).

It was also alleged that a new religio-political hegemony emerged as a result of the impact of American fundamentalist evangelicals. Pieterse asserts, for example, that the so-called 'faith' movement gained the cultural leadership of Christianity in many parts of the 'developing' world, largely because of its social prestige and ideological persuasiveness (Pieterse, 1992: 10–11). It was said that norms, beliefs, and values favourable to the interests of the USA were disseminated among the believers as a fundamental part of religious messages. What this amounts to is that individuals who converted to the American-style evangelical churches were, it was claimed, victims of manipulation by this latest manifestation of neo-colonialism; the objective was not, as in the past, to spirit away material resources from colonial areas, but rather to deflect popular efforts away from seeking necessary political and economic structural changes, in order to serve American strategic interests and those of American transnational corporations.

Jewish fundamentalism

Since the establishment of the state of Israel as a homeland for the Jews in 1948, there has been intense controversy in the country over whether the state should be a modern, Western-style country – that is, where normally religion would be privatized – or a *Jewish* state with Judaist law and customs taking precedent over secular ones. Luckmann noted nearly four decades ago that the state of Israel was characterized by a process of bureaucratization along rational business lines, reflecting for many Jewish Israelis, he argued, accommodation to an increasingly 'secular' way of life (Luckmann, 1969: 147). According to Weber's well-known classificatory schema, Israel would be judged a 'modern' state, that is, with a powerful legislative body (the Knesset) enacting the law; an executive authority – the government – conducting the affairs of the state; a disinterested judiciary enforcing the law and protecting the rights of individuals; an extensive bureaucracy regulating and organizing educational, social and cultural matters; and with security services – notably the police and the armed forces – protecting the state from internal and external attack (Weber, 1978: 56).

Yet, to many people, Israel is not 'just' another Western state. This is largely because in recent years religion seems to have gained an increasingly central public role. Religious Jews warn of the social catastrophes that they believe will inevitably occur in their increasingly secular, progressively more 'godless', society, while many non-religious Jews see such people as intolerant religious fanatics – Jewish fundamentalists. Such matters came to a head in November 1995. The then Prime Minister, Yitzhak Rabin, was assassinated by Yigal Amir, a 25-year old Jewish fundamentalist, because of Rabin's willingness to negotiate with the Palestine Liberation Organization (PLO) to end its conflict with the state of Israel. Rabin's murder led some Israelis to fear that violence would increasingly characterize the already tense relationship between religious and secular Jews. Yet what appeared initially to some observers to be the onset of a religious war among the Jews eventually only had a limited impact in Israel, a setting where, despite much intense political and social conflict, religious interests were not consistently powerful enough to determine major issues of public policy (Sandler, 2006: 46–7).

On the other hand, the murder of Rabin by a Jewish fundamentalist appeared to be a clear manifestation of the willingness of 'Jewish fundamentalists [to] attack Jews with secularist leanings' in pursuit of their religious and political agendas (Bealey, 1999: 140). The killing of Rabin also served to focus attention on the growing polarization in Israel between, on the one hand, non-religious or secular Jews, and, on the other, highly religious or 'fundamentalist' Jews. The latter are characterized by a determination personally to follow the 'fundamentals' of Judaism as they see them, and work towards getting them observed in both public and private life (Silberstein, 1993; Ravitzky, 1993). Contemporary Jewish fundamentalism – manifested by organizations such as Gush Emunim – is believed, in part, to be a result of the impact of Israel's victory over the Arabs in the 1967 war (Sprinzak, 1993). For many religious Jews this was a particular triumph as it led to the regaining of the holiest sites in Judaism from Arab control, including Jerusalem, the Temple Mount, the Western Wall and Hebron. This was taken as a sign of divine deliverance, an indication of impending redemption. Even some secular Jews spoke of the war's outcome in theological terms.

Gush Emunim and Jewish fundamentalism in Israel

Gush Emunim was founded after the 1978 Camp David agreement between Israel and Egypt, which resulted in the handing back of the Sinai desert to the latter. Other fundamentalist groups, such as the late Rabbi Meir Kahane's banned organization, Kach, fulminated against the return of territory to Muslim Egypt or any other non-Jews. The biblical entity, Eretz Israel, they argued, was significantly larger than the contemporary state of Israel. To hand back any territory to Arabs is tantamount, they maintained, to going against God's will as revealed in the Old Testament of the Christian Bible. Simmering religious opposition to the peace plan with the PLO, involving giving autonomy to the Gaza Strip and to an area around Jericho, reached tragic levels in February 1994 when a religious zealot, Baruch Goldstein, linked with militants of two extremist groups – Kach (Thus) and Kahane Chai (Kahane Lives) – murdered 29 Muslims during a dawn attack on a mosque in the occupied West Bank town of Hebron. After the massacre Israel's government banned both Kach and Kahane

(Continued)

Chai, a sign of its commitment to crush religious extremist groups that systematically used violence to try to achieve their goals. However, their banning apparently did not eliminate the political influence of Jewish fundamentalist groups
in Israel (Sandler, 2006: 45–7).

Jewish identity has long been understood as an overlapping combination of religion and nation. Put another way, the Jews of Israel tend to think
of themselves as a nation inhabiting a *Jewish* state created by their covenant
with God (Ravitzky, 1993). The interpretation of the covenant and its implications gave rise to the characteristic beliefs and practices of the Jewish people. Vital to this covenant was the promise of the land of Israel. Following
their historical dispersions under, first, the Babylonians and then Romans,
Jews had prayed for centuries for the end of their exile and a return to Israel.
However, except for small numbers, Jews lived for centuries in exile, often in
separate communities. During the diaspora, while awaiting divine redemption to return them to their homeland, many Jews' lives were defined by
halacha (religious law), which served as a national component of Jewish
identity. The Jews' historical suffering during the diaspora was understood
as a necessary continuation of the special dedication of the community to
God. In sum, Jewish fundamentalist groups in Israel are characterized by an
utter unwillingness to negotiate with Palestinians over what they see as land
given by God to the Jews for their use in perpetuity. In addition, especially
since the Israeli government cleared the Gaza Strip of Jewish settlements in
August 2005, there has been another issue of massive importance to many
Jewish fundamentalists. Sandler puts it like this: 'Who or what prevails? Is it
the law of God or the law of the State?' (Sandler, 2006: 47). For Jewish fundamentalists, the issue is especially significant and difficult to resolve as
both the contemporary State of Israel and the biblical 'Land of Israel' have
important religious associations.

Hindu fundamentalism

Since the 1970s, Christian, Muslim and Jewish fundamentalists have all ex-
hibited 'a refusal to be restricted to the private sphere of religious traditions'
(Casanova, 1994: 6). Until the 1990s it was less remarked upon that there
was also a contemporaneous resurgence of Hindu beliefs in India, variously
labelled Hindu fundamentalism or Hindu nationalism, a development that
reflected the influence of the ideology of Hindutva. Hindutva is a Hindi

word (meaning 'Hindu-ness' in English), a neologism thought up by Vinayak Damodar Savarkar in his 1923 pamphlet *Hindutva: Who is a Hindu?* Today the term refers to movements, primarily in India, that advocate Hindu nationalist/fundamentalist ideas and objectives. The Bharatiya Janata Party (BJP: Indian People's Party), India's ruling political party between 1996 and 2004, is closely linked with a variety of organizations and movements that collectively promote *Hindutva*. Their joint name is the Sangh Parivar, meaning 'family of associations'. Its leading organizations are the Rashtriya Swayamsevak, Bajrang Dal and the Vishwa Hindu Parishad.

Hindutva

Hindutva is a right-wing Hindu religious ideology that grew to prominence during the twentieth century (Chiriyankandath, 2006: 52). However, it did not play an important role in Indian politics until the late 1980s. From that time, following two events, it attracted many formerly moderate Hindus. The first was Rajiv Gandhi's government's use of a large parliamentary majority to overturn a Supreme Court verdict with which many conservative Hindus disagreed (the Shah Bano case). The second was the infamous quarrel between Hindus and Muslims over ownership of a 16th-century Mughal Babri mosque in Ayodhya. Some Hindus maintained that it was both birthplace and site of the original temple of Rama, a figure that Hindus believe was anavatar of God. Following growing frictions between Muslims and Hindus, the mosque was destroyed by a Hindu mob in 1992, leading to riots across India (Juergensmeyer, 1993).

Juergensmeyer notes that 'one of the reasons why India has been vulnerable to the influence of Hindu nationalists is that Hinduism can mean so many things' (Juergensmeyer, 1993: 81). On the whole, Hindu fundamentalists, like their counterparts in other religious traditions looked at in this chapter, react intensely against secular visions of modern nationalism. They employ a number of strategies for change, including targeting: the traditional secular parties, such as the once dominant Congress Party, India's Muslim minority, the political process itself, and the country's secular political culture that since independence has underpinned it. What is striking about the Indian case is how consistently Hindu fundamentalists aim at *political* targets in order to solve what they see as *religious* problems, including consolidation of religious identities and values. The level of violence associated with the Hindu fundamentalist movement became intense in the 1990s, with frequent political assassinations. The Indian case is also useful for understanding the variety of ways in which religious militants seek to achieve their objectives, from political violence to electoral politics. Both strategies have at their heart a total rejection of India's secular state, a notion at the heart of the country's political culture since independence (Adeney and Saez, 2005).

India's secular state emerged out of the trauma of a communal holocaust, leading, in 1947, to partition along communal lines, with (East and West) Pakistan as the designated homeland for Muslims. Since then, it has been impossible in India to replicate a Western version of secularism through a strict institutional separation between church and state. This is partly because Hinduism, the religion of more than 80 per cent of the over one billion Indians, does not have an institutionalized hierarchy – hence, no 'church' – and partly because of the historically short time since the founding of India, not much more than half a century ago. Comparable attempts at building secular states in Western Europe, it should be remembered, took at least several centuries.

The rise of the politics of religious identity in India underlines a central problem: how can religiously plural India survive the creation of a powerful sense of Hindu identity focused in political vehicles, movements and parties? A total of 82 per cent of the more than one billion Indians are Hindus, 11 per cent are Muslims, 2.5 per cent are Christians, and 1.6 per cent are Sikhs. There are also small numbers of Buddhists, Parsis, Jains, as well as followers of various traditional religions. Because of such diversity it was central to the concept of the Indian state at independence that its leaders would pursue a development path firmly located within a secular socio-political and cultural milieu. The core of this Indian secularism was tolerance towards religious plurality – denoted in the Sanskrit phrase *sarva dharma sambhava* ('equal treatment for all religions').

Initially a party with most support in the north of India, especially in Hindi-speaking areas and among urban middle-class traders, the BJP built up electoral support over time. In 1989 it won 85 seats in parliament. This was the launching point for the BJP to become a key aspect of mainstream Indian political life. Later, it achieved major electoral successes, winning more parliamentary seats in 1996 than any other party (161 of 545), yet still falling well short of an overall majority. Soon after, the BJP was, however, able to form a government. Its supreme leader, Atal Bihari Vajpayee, became Prime Minister, although the government soon fell to a confidence vote. In the elections of 1998 and 1999, the BJP again gained the largest number of parliamentary seats and as a result successfully formed governments; again Vajpayee became Prime Minister. Confounding some critics, when in power the BJP ruled with relative moderation, seeking to avoid many contentious Hindu nationalist issues that were seen as core to its ideology. For example, it

promoted economic reforms and development, encouraging foreign investment. In addition, the BJP sought to some degree to move away from the
Hindu fundamentalism of the Rashtriya Swayamsevak in a bid to appeal to
Muslim voters. Nonetheless, BJP party members were accused of complicity
in the violence that killed perhaps as many as 2,000 in Gujarat in Febru-
ary/March 2002. In elections held in 2004 the BJP was defeated by a Congress
Party-led coalition.

Perhaps the most significant implication of the recent electoral successes
of the BJP was not the likelihood of the formal founding of a 'Hinduized'
state, which may never come about, but the general stimulation it provided for extremists from other cultural groups. It appears to many observers
that secular features of the Indian state are weakening, helping to
fuel political campaigns, not only by Hindu extremists, but also from
Muslim, Christian and Sikh groups. However, this is not necessarily Hindu
fundamentalism – which would for many observers be rooted in a common
understanding linked to the revealed words of God in a holy book as a set
of socio-political aspirations and goals – but rather a *nationalist* project
with the goal of the projection of a wider Hindu *identity* at its core
(Chiriyankandath, 2006: 53–8).

Various theories have been offered to explain the resurgence of political religion – especially Hindu fundamentalism – in India in recent years; many see
the 1980s as a crucial period (Adeney and Saez, 2005). But why the 1980s? It
was not a decade when India's government overtly sought to privatize religion,
but it was a period of pronounced economic instability as well as 'new distor-
tions of the homogenised Western menu of modernity and its consumerist culture peddled through its multinationals' (Ray, 1996: 10). This coincided with
the re-emergence of the question of both Hindu and Sikh national identity, issues which quickly became central to India's political scene.

Explanations for the religio-political resurgence of Hindu nationalism can
be roughly divided into political, psychological, socio-economic, cultural and
'the impact of modernization' theories. However, it is important to note that
they are not mutually exclusive – none can claim exclusively to be 'correct' –
but that taken together they may explain reasonably well the rather unexpected recent resurgence of political Hinduism in India.

Arguing for a *political* explanation, Juergensmeyer asserts that the secular
Congress Party government, which ruled from independence until the mid-
1970s, became a target for the wrath of Hindu nationalists because it was
perceived to be favouring Muslims, Sikhs, Christians and other religious minorities (Juergensmeyer, 1989: 100). While 'the rise of Sikh fundamentalism

in the Punjab especially played on Hindu nerves' (Copley, 1993: 57), increased Muslim assertiveness, following the Iranian revolution, seemed to many Hindus also to threaten them.

Secondly, *psychological* theories stress high-caste alarm at the conversion to Islam of *Dalits* (erstwhile 'untouchables') in various parts of India, especially the well-publicized case in 1984 of the Tamil Nadu village of Meenakshipuram (Copley, 1993: 57). This incident is thought to have led many Hindus to vote for the leading Hindu nationalist party, the BJP, in following elections. More generally, Chiriyankandath (1996) notes that many conservative Hindus were incensed over the government's protection of mosques built over Hindu sacred sites during the Mughal period. In 1984 the Vishwa Hindu Parishad (VHP), a Hindu fundamentalist movement linked to the BJP, called for a reassertion of Hindu control over a dozen such sites. Observers point out that many Muslims would have consequently seen themselves as the main focus of Hindu attacks, perhaps in turn encouraging Islamic radicalism (Sisson, 1993: 58–9; Talbot, 1991: 149–51).

Also encouraging communal friction was political instability caused by *economic uncertainty*, the third factor. In the 1980s, Callaghy notes, the Indian economy was suffering serious problems: 'the balance of payments and inflation moved beyond control; foreign exchange reserves dropped; a debt crisis loomed; and pervasive statism and bureaucratic controls were having increasingly negative consequences' (Callaghy, 1993: 194–5). The government attempted (initially, timidly) to liberalize the economy; the main impact, however, was probably unintended: the creation of a tiny group of super rich and a growing stratum of extremely poor people. Many urban middle-class Hindus were unsettled by the economic reforms and, like many poor Hindus, looked to a party, notably the BJP, promising that Hindus would be privileged over other groups. In sum, economic changes were, it is suggested, an important factor in the growing appeal of Hindu nationalism among both the poor and the rapidly expanding sector of urban middle-class producers and consumers.

Fourthly, Hindu nationalism received *a cultural boost* when the immensely popular Hindi serializations of the *Ramayana* and *Mahabharatha* appeared on state television in the early 1990s. Observers assert that these television programmes helped to foster an all-India Hindu self-consciousness.

Finally, it is in the wider context of cultural change where the final set of theories – those linked to the impact of modernization – are located. As Chiriyankandath notes, 'much of the recent electoral success of the neo-religious parties can be ascribed to their endeavour to provide those uprooted from their traditional environment with a bridging ideology' (Chiriyankan-dath, 1994: 36–7). What he is referring to is the Hindu nationalist appeal that not only offered to many an intensely needed emotional tie with the past, but also claimed to provide a 'philosophical and practical framework for coping with, and regulating change'. The BJP aim, according to K. R. Malkani, a vice-president of the party and its chief theoretician, was to 're-main anchored to our roots as we modernise so we don't lose ourselves in a tidal wave of modernisation' (quoted in ibid.). From the mid-1990s to the mid-2000s, the BJP-led central government appointed Hindu nationalists to leading roles in many educational establishments, giving them the opportu-nity to revise school textbooks, especially in history and the social sciences, so that they would better correspond to the Hindu fundamentalist interpre-tation of the world (Lall, 2005). In sum, the BJP and other Hindu funda-mentalists expressed their ideology in political programmes that focused on reinterpreting responses to the impact of Western expansion and accompa-nying technological modernization within the historically well-established Hindu religious traditions.

These five factors collectively helped to facilitate the rise of Hindu funda-mentalism from the 1980s, while at the same time leading to an increase in religious minorities' self-awareness, including among Muslims, Sikhs and Christians. Over time, various Hindu fundamentalist movements, including the Vishwa Hindu Parishad, attempted to develop a 'semetized', 'fundamen-talist' version of Hinduism, while Hindu nationalist political parties, notably the BJP, fought for political power, often successfully. Unlike Sikh nationalists who, because of their small numbers and intra-group schisms, cannot plaus-ibly achieve their objective – an independent homeland for Sikhs, Khalistan – through the electoral process, Hindu nationalists progressed electorally in the 1990s, until thrown out of power in May 2004, when the Congress Party re-gained its leading place in government. Prior to that, for the preceding two decades, the BJP had made considerable electoral advances, in a context identified by the party's leader, Lal Krishna Advani, as characterized by 'pseu-dosecularism' that, he believed, favoured India's religious minorities (Juer-gensmeyer, 1993: 81). For many years, this approach was regarded favourably by tens of millions of voters in India.

Conclusion

The concept of popular religious interpretations, including religious funda-mentalist ones, is not new; there have always been opponents of main-stream religious interpretations. What is novel, however, is that in the past manifestations of popular religion were normally bundled up within strong frameworks that held them together, serving to police the most extreme tendencies, as in the Christian churches, or were at least nominally under the control of the main-line religion, as with popular sects in Islam. In the contemporary era, however, it is no longer possible to keep all religious tendencies within traditional organizing frameworks. This is primarily a consequence of two developments: (1) widespread, destabilizing change after the Second World War, summarized here as modernization and secularization; and (2) religious privatization, in both the developed and developing worlds.

Religious fundamentalism can be divided into two categories: the 'religions of the book' (Islam, Christianity and Judaism) and nationalist-orientated Hinduism. Scriptural revelations relating to political, moral and social issues form the corpus of fundamentalist demands. Sometimes these are markedly conservative (most US or African Christian fundamentalists), sometimes they are politically reformist or even revolutionary (some Islamist groups), and sometimes they are xenophobic, racist and reactionary (some Jewish fundamentalist groups, such as Gush Emunim, Kach and Kahane Chai, and various Islamist groups). Hindu 'fundamentalism', on the other hand, assumed a nationalist dimension when it sought a rebirth of national identity and vigour denied in the past, zealots considered, by unwelcome cultural dilution and inadequate government.

The various fundamentalist groups examined in this chapter tend to share: a disaffection and dissatisfaction with established, hierarchical, institutionalized religious bodies; a desire to find God through personal searching rather than through the mediation of institutions; and a belief in communities' ability to make beneficial changes to their lives through the application of group effort. This desire to 'go it alone', not to be beholden to 'superior' bodies, tends to characterize any of the groups we have examined. For some, religion offers a rational alternative to those for whom modernization has either failed or is in some way unattractive. Its interaction with political issues over the medium term is likely to be of especial importance, carrying a serious and seminal message of societal resurgence and regeneration in relation to both political leaders and economic elites.

Notes

1   The claim that there is a *global* resurgence of religion' is contested. Critics point especially to Western European countries where, apparently without exception, secularization appears to be continuing (Wallis and

Bruce, 1992; Wilson, 1992; Bruce, 2003). Elsewhere, the apparent resurgence of religion is often linked to questions of existential security (Norris and Inglehart, 2004).

2   The term Imam means a male spiritual and temporal leader regarded by Shi'ites as a descendant of Muhammad, divinely appointed to guide humans.

Questions
Religious 'fundamentalisms' and international relations

1   Why is 'religious fundamentalism' often regarded as 'anti-modern'?

2   Can religious fundamentalism be politically reformist? Illustrate your answer by reference to *two* named countries.

3   What is religious 'fundamentalism'? Why is it important in some contexts for political outcomes?

4   What do the religious fundamentalisms associated with Christianity, Islam, Judaism and Hinduism have in common, and how do they differ?

5   What is the impact of religious fundamentalism on international relations?

Bibliography

Adeney, K. and Saez, L. (eds) (2005) *Coalition Politics and Hindu Nationalism*, London: Routledge.

Ahmed, K. (2003) 'And on the seventh day Tony Blair created . . .', *The Observer*, 3 August. Available at: http://observer.guardian.co.uk/politics/story/0,6903,1011460,00.html Accessed 26 May 2006.

Akbar, M. J. (2002) *The Shade of Swords: Jihad and the Conflict Between Islam and Christianity*, London: Routledge.

d'Antonio, M. (1990) *Fall From Grace: The Failed Crusade of the Christian Right*, London: Deutsch.

Appleby, R. Scott (2000) *The Ambivalence of the Sacred: Religion, Violence and Reconciliation*, Lanham, MD: Rowman and Littlefield.

Bealey, F. (1999) *The Blackwell Dictionary of Political Science*, Oxford: Blackwell.

Berger, P. (1999) (ed.) *The Desecularization of the World: Resurgent Religion and World Politics*, Grand Rapids/Washington, DC: William B. Eerdmans/Ethics and Public Policy Center.

Bruce, S. (2003) *God Is Dead: Secularization in the West*, Oxford: Blackwell.

Callaghy, T. (1993) 'Vision and politics in the transformation of the global political economy lessons from the Second and Third Worlds', in R. Slater, B. Schutz and S. Dorr (eds), *Global Transformation and the Third World*, Boulder, CO: Lynne Rienner, pp. 161–258.

Caplan, L. (ed.) (1987) *Studies in Religious Fundamentalism*, Albany, NY: State University of New York.

Casanova, J. (1994) *Public Religions in the Modern World*, Chicago and London: University of Chicago Press.

Casanova, J. (2005) 'Catholic and Muslim politics in comparative perspective', *Taiwan Journal of Democracy*, 1 (2), pp. 89–108.

Chiriyankandath, J. (1994) 'The politics of religious identity: a comparison of Hindu nationalism and Sudanese Islamism', *Journal of Commonwealth and Comparative Politics*, 32 (1), pp. 31–53.

Chiriyankandath, J. (1996) 'Hindu nationalism and regional political culture in India: a study of Kerala', *Nationalism and Ethnic Politics*, 2 (1), pp. 44–66.

Chiriyankandath, J. (2006) 'Hinduism and politics', in J. Haynes (ed.), *The Politics of Religion: A Survey*, London: Routledge, pp. 48–58.

Copley, A. 1993. 'Indian secularism reconsidered from Gandhi to Ayodhya', *Contemporary South Asia*, 2 (1), pp. 47–65.

Coulon, C. (1983) *Les Musulmans et le Pouvoir en Afrique Noire*, Paris: Karthala.

Deiros, P. (1991) 'Protestant fundamentalism in Latin America', in M. Marty and R. Scott Appleby (eds) *Fundamentalisms Observed*, Chicago: University of Chicago Press, pp. 142–96.

Dolan, C. (2005) *In War We Trust: The Bush Doctrine and the Pursuit of Just War*, Aldershot: Ashgate.

Dorr, S. (1993) 'Democratization in the Middle East', in R. Slater, B. Schutz, and S. Dorr (eds), *Global Transformation and the Third World*, Boulder, CO: Lynne Rienner, pp. 131–57.

Esposito, J. (2002) *Unholy War*, Oxford and New York: Oxford University Press.

Etienne, B. and Tozy, M. (1981) 'Le glissement des obligations islamiques vers le phenomene associatif à Casablanca', in Centre de Recherches et d'Études sur les Sociétés Méditerranénnes, *Le Maghreb Musulman en 1979*, Paris, pp. 235–51.

Fuller, G. (2003) *The Future of Political Islam*, New York and Basingstoke: Palgrave Macmillan.

Gifford, P. (1990) 'Prosperity: a new and foreign element in African Christianity', *Religion*, 20 (3), pp. 373–88.

Gifford, P. (1991) *The New Crusaders: Christianity and the New Right in Southern Africa*, London: Pluto Press.

Gifford, P. (1994) 'Some recent developments in African Christianity', *African Affairs*, 93 (373), pp. 513–34.

Gifford, P. (2004) *Ghana's New Christianity: Pentecostalism in a Globalising African Economy* London: C. Hurst and Co.

Hacker, J. and Pierson, P. (2005) *Off Center: The Republican Revolution and the Erosion of American Democracy*, New Haven, CT and London: Yale University Press.

Hadden, J. (1987) 'Towards desacralizing secularization theory', *Social Forces*, No. 65, pp. 587–611.

Hallencreutz, C and Westerlund, D. (1996) 'Anti-secularist policies of religion', in D. Westerlund (ed.), *Questioning the Secular State: The Worldwide Resurgence of Religion in Politics*, London: Hurst, pp. 1–23.

Halper, S. and Clarke, J. (2004) *America Alone: The Neo-Conservatives and the Global Order*, Cambridge: Cambridge University Press.

Haynes, J. (1993) *Religion in Third World Politics*, Milton Keynes: Open University Press.

Haynes, J. (1996) *Religion and Politics in Africa*, London: Zed.

Haynes, J. (2002) *Politics in the Developing World*, Oxford: Blackwell.

Haynes, J. (2003) 'Religious fundamentalism and politics', in L. Ridgeon (ed.), *Major World Religions: From their Origins to the Present*, London: RoutledgeCurzon, pp. 324–75.

Haynes, J. (2005a) 'Al-Qaeda: ideology and action', *Critical Review of International Social and Political Philosophy*, 8 (2), pp. 177–91.

Haynes, J. (2005b) 'Islamic militancy in East Africa', *Third World Quarterly*, 26 (8), pp. 1321–39.

Husain, M. Zohair (1995) *Global Islamic Politics*, New York: HarperCollins.

Ibrahim, Y. (1992) 'Islamic plan for Algeria is on display', *The New York Times*, 7 January.

Isaacs, D. (2003) 'Islam in Nigeria: simmering tensions', BBC News online, 23 September. Available at: http://news.bbc.co.uk/1/hi/world/africa/3155279.stm Accessed 1 December 2005.

Jervis, R. (2005) 'Why the Bush doctrine cannot be sustained, *Political Science Quarterly*, 120 (3), pp. 351–77.

Juergensmeyer, M. (1989) 'India', in S. Mews (ed.), *Religion in Politics: A World Guide*, Longman: Harlow, pp. 98–107.

Juergensmeyer, M. (1993) *The New Cold War? Religious Nationalism Confronts the Secular State*, Berkeley and London: University of California Press.

Juergensmeyer, M. (2000) *Terror in the Mind of God: The Global Rise of Religious Violence*, Berkeley: University of California Press.

Lall, M. (2005) 'Indian education policy under the NDA government', in K. Adeney and L. Saez (eds), *Coalition Politics and Hindu Nationalism*, London: Routledge, pp. 153–70.

Lawrence, B. (1995) *Defenders of the Faith: The International Revolt Against the Modern Age*, Columbia: University of South Carolina Press.

Luckmann, T. (1969) 'The decline of church-oriented religion', in R. Robertson (ed.), *The Sociology of Religion*, Baltimore, MD: Penguin, pp. 141–51.

Martin, D. (1990) *Tongues of Fire: The Explosion of Protestantism in Latin America*, Oxford: Basil Blackwell.

Marty, M. E. and Appleby, R. Scott (eds) (1991) *Fundamentalisms Observed*, Chicago: The University of Chicago Press.

Marty, M. E. and Appleby, R. Scott (eds) (1993a) *Fundamentalisms and Society*, Chicago: The University of Chicago Press.

Marty, M. E. and Appleby, R. Scott (eds) (1993b) *Fundamentalisms and the State*, Chicago: The University of Chicago Press.

Marty, M. E. and Appleby, R. Scott (eds) (1994) *Accounting for Fundamentalisms*, Chicago: The University of Chicago Press.

Marty, M. E. and Appleby, R. Scott (eds) (1995) *Fundamentalisms Comprehended*, Chicago: The University of Chicago Press.

Milton-Edwards, B. (2006) *Islam and Violence in the Modern Era*, Basingstoke and New York: Palgrave Macmillan.

Moran, E. and Schlemmer, L. (1984) *Faith for the Fearful?*, Durban: Centre for Applied Social Studies.

Nasr, S. Vali Reza (2001) *Islamic Leviathan: Islam and the Making of State Power*, Oxford: Oxford University Press.

Norris, P. and Inglehart, I. (2004) *Sacred and Secular: Religion and Politics Worldwide*, Cambridge: Cambridge University Press.

Pieterse, J. (1992) 'Christianity, politics and Gramscism of the right: introduction' in J. Pieterse (ed.), *Christianity and Hegemony: Religion and Politics on the Frontiers of Social Change*, Oxford: Berg, pp. 1–31.

Ram-Prasad, C. (1993) 'Hindutva ideology: extracting the fundamentals', *Contemporary South Asia*, 2 (3), pp. 285–309.

Ravitzky, A. (1993) *Messianism, Zionism and Jewish Religious Radicalism*, Tel Aviv: Am Oved.

Ray, A. (1996) 'Religion and politics in South Asia', *Asian Affairs*, 1 (1), pp. 9–12.

Religion and Ethics Newsweekly (2004) 'Interview: Leo Ribuffo' [Ribuffo is a historian of conservative Christianity in the USA], April 23. Available at: http://www.pbs.org/wnet/religionandethics/ week734/interview3.html Accessed 17 March 2005.

Roberts, B. (1968) 'Protestant groups and coping with urban life in Guatemala City', *American Journal of Sociology*, 73, pp. 753–67.

Roy, A. (2002) 'Fascism's firm footprint in India', *The Nation*, 30 September. Available at: http://www.ratical.org/co-globalize/AR093002.pdf Accessed 26 May 2006.

Saikal, A. (2003) *Islam and the West: Conflict or Cooperation?*, New York and Basingstoke: Palgrave Macmillan.

Sandler, S. (2006) 'Judaism and politics', in J. Haynes (ed.), *The Politics of Religion: A Survey*, London: Routledge, pp. 37–47.

Shupe, A. (1990) 'The stubborn persistence of religion in the global arena', in E. Sahliyeh (ed.), *Religious Resurgence and Politics in the Contemporary World*, Albany, NY: State University of New York Press, pp. 17–26.

Silberstein, L. (1993) 'Religion, ideology, modernity: theoretical issues in the study of Jewish fundamentalism', in L. Silberstein (ed.), *Jewish Fundamentalism in Comparative Perspective: Religion, Ideology, and the Crisis of Modernity*, New York and London: New York University Press, pp. 3–26.

Simpson, J. (1992) 'Fundamentalism in America revisited: the fading of modernity as a source of symbolic capital', in B. Misztal and A. Shupe (eds), *Religion and Politics in Comparative Perspective: Revival of Religious Fundamentalism in East and West*, Westport, CT and London: Praeger, pp. 10–27.

Sisson, R. (1993) 'Culture and democratization in India', in L. Diamond (ed.), *Political Culture and Democracy in Developing Countries*, Boulder, CO: Lynne Rienner, pp. 37–66.

Sprinzak, E. (1993) 'Fundamentalism, ultranationalism, and political culture: the case of the Israeli radical right', in L. Diamond (ed.), *Political Culture and Democracy in Developing Countries*, Boulder, CO and London: Lynne Rienner, pp. 247–78.

Tahi, M. S. (1992) 'The arduous democratisation process in Algeria', *The Journal of Modern African Studies*, 30 (3), pp. 400–20.

Talbot, I. (1991) 'Politics and religion in contemporary India', in G. Moyser (ed.), *Politics and Religion in the Modern World*, London: Routledge, pp. 135–61.

Thomas, S. (2005) *The Global Resurgence of Religion and the Transformation of International Relations: The Struggle for the Soul of the Twenty-First Century*, New York and Basingstoke: Palgrave Macmillan.

Voll, J. (2006) 'Trans-state Muslim movements in an era of soft power'. Paper prepared for the Conference on New Religious Pluralism in World Politics, Georgetown University, 17 March.

Volpi, F. (2003) *Islam and Democracy: The Failure of Dialogue in Algeria*, London: Pluto.

Wald, K. (1991) 'Social change and political response: the silent religious cleavage in North America', in G. Moyser (ed.), *Religion and Politics in the Modern World*, London: Routledge, pp. 239–84.

Wallis, R. and Bruce, S. (1992) 'Secularization: the orthodox model' in S. Bruce (ed.), *Religion and Modernization*, Oxford: Clarendon Press, pp. 8–30.

Weber, M. (1978) *Economy and Society*, Berkeley: University of California Press.

Wilson, B. (1992) 'Reflections on a many sided controversy', in S. Bruce (ed.), *Religion and Modernization*, Oxford: Clarendon Press, pp. 195–210.

Woodhead, L. and Heelas, P. (eds) (2000) 'Introduction to Chapter Two: Religions of difference', *Religion in Modern Times*, Oxford: Blackwell, pp. 27–33.

Woollacott, M. (1995) 'Keeping our faith in belief', *The Guardian*, 23 December.

Further reading

K. Adeney and L. Saez (eds) *Coalition Politics and Hindu Nationalism*, Rout-
    ledge, 2005. This book traces the emergence of the Bharatiya Janata
    Party (BJP) in India and the ways in which its Hindu nationalist
    agenda has been affected by the constraints of being a dominant
    member of a coalition government. The authors take stock of the
    party's first full term in power in the late 1990s and the 2004 elec-
    tions. They assess the BJP's performance in relation to its stated
    goals, and more specifically how it has fared in a range of policy
    fields – centre–state relations, foreign policy, defence policies, the
    'second generation' of economic reforms, initiatives to curb corrup-
    tion and the fate of minorities.

B. Brasher (ed.) *Encyclopaedia of Fundamentalism*, Routledge, 2001. This very
    useful A–Z resource focuses on the major religious, political and social
    forces in the contemporary world. Featuring over 200 entries, with ex-
    tensive illustrations and excerpts from primary source materials, the
    volume explores fundamentalism in religions around the globe, provid-
    ing valuable insights into associated movements and their sometimes
    profound impact on the religious, social and political worlds.

J. Esposito, *Unholy War*, Oxford University Press, 2002. Introducing the
    topic of Islamism via the September 11 attacks on the World Trade
    Center and the Pentagon, Esposito examines the teachings of Islam:
    the Quran, the example of the Prophet, Islamic law, *jihad* (holy war),
    the use of violence, and terrorism. In his analysis, he demonstrates
    that anti-Americanism (and anti-Europeanism) are not the sole pre-
    serves of Islamists but instead cut across many Arab and Muslim soci-
    eties, a response to US foreign policy, for example, the bombing and
    invasion of Afghanistan. On the other hand, he explains, most Mus-
    lims are appalled by the acts of violence committed in the name of
    their faith.

B. Lawrence, *Defenders of the Faith: The International Revolt Against the Mod-
    ern Age*, University of South Carolina Press, 1995. According to
    Lawrence, religious fundamentalists are 'the righteous remnant turned
    vanguard', last-ditch defenders of God. They regard themselves as
    fighting what they perceive to be dangerous modernist values of per-
    sonal autonomy and relativism. Lawrence argues that fundamentalism
    is a form of ideology not theology, informing outlooks common to
    certain American Protestants, Muslims and right-wing, 'quasi-Hasidic'

Israeli parties such as Gush Emunim. The first half of the book discusses Eurocentrism, nationalism and the marginalization of religion in Western Europe. The second half consists of case studies drawn from the three major monotheistic religions. He predicts that, in the long run, fundamentalism will not be able to control public discourse or activity in any major nation-state.

M. E. Marty and R. Scott Appleby (eds) *Fundamentalisms Comprehended*, The University of Chicago Press, 1995. This book is the final volume in the 'Fundamentalism Project', a series of books edited by Marty and Appleby that brought together prominent scholars from around the world. Their brief was to explore the nature and impact of fundamentalist movements in the twentieth century. Drawing on an interdisciplinary programme conducted by the American Academy of Arts and Sciences, the series of books is dedicated to promoting an understanding of fundamentalism at a time – the 1990s – when misinformation and misperceptions had exacerbated national and international conflicts. The four previous volumes are also well worthy of investigation, as they provide much information on social, political, cultural and religious contexts of fundamentalism in the major religious traditions.

In the final volume of the series, *Fundamentalisms Comprehended*, the contributors return to, and test, the project's opening principle: fundamentalisms in all faiths share certain 'family resemblances'. Several of the essays reconsider the project's original definition of fundamentalism ('a reactive, absolutist and comprehensive mode of anti-secular religious activism'), while others challenge the notion that fundamentalism is a 'distinctively modern phenomenon', while still others question whether the term 'fundamentalist' can accurately be applied to movements outside Christianity, Judaism and Islam, that is, non-Abrahamic religions.

PART THREE

Religion and international relations: country and regional focus

CHAPTER 8

The United States

The Constitution of the United States makes it clear that there should be no institutionalized links between religion and politics. This is explicitly stated in the first amendment of the Constitution – 'Congress shall make no law respecting an establishment of religion or prohibiting the free exercise thereof' – and restricts politics and religion to separate realms. In addition, unlike several European countries – including, Germany, Italy and Sweden, where Christian Democratic parties have been influential for decades – the USA does not have a tradition of political parties with a religious focus. On the other hand, as Reichley, notes, 'religion has always played an important part in American politics' (Reichley, 1986: 23). The republic's founders drew on religious values and rhetoric in forming the new nation, and churches were involved in the controversy about slavery and the resulting civil war in the middle of the nineteenth century. During the twentieth century, religious groups were participants in various campaigns, including: prohibition of the sale of alcohol, enactment of women's right to vote, New Deal measures to increase social welfare in the 1930s, and the passage of laws covering civil rights in the 1960s (Wald, 2003).

Separation of church and state as specified in the US Constitution guarantees freedom of religion. As already noted, the USA is among the most religious of Western countries, especially when measured by the proportion of Americans who regularly attend religious services (Green, 2000). Yet, in contrast to many Western European countries, such as Britain or Sweden, there are no universally accepted symbols of the polity in the USA, such as monarchy (for example, Britain) or state church (for example, Sweden: the Church of Sweden, or *Svenska kyrkan*). Instead, as discussed below, the values and rituals of *civil religion* traditionally provided an unofficial means of articulating national identity in the USA.

Religious voices from various denominations are currently politically significant in the USA. Some groups of religious actors, notably conservative

Christians gathered together under the rubric of the Christian or Religious Right, have been particularly important – not least because they significantly influenced the outcomes of the 2000 and 2004 presidential elections, contests that led to the election and re-election of a born-again Christian, George W. Bush. In recent years, in addition, the Religious Right has also been an important foreign policy voice, influencing US policy in various ways (Taylor, 2005; Hehir et al., 2004). Other religious groups are also noted for their political significance, including Catholics and the Nation of Islam (Green, 2000). In order to explain and account for the political significance of these religious actors, in both domestic and international contexts, this chapter has the following structure. We start by looking at the general issue of religion and politics in the USA in order to understand why religious actors have become important in recent years. After that, we examine three key groups: the Religious Right, US Catholics and the Nation of Islam, especially Louis Farrakhan's radical strand. Finally, we look at the influence of these religious organizations in relation to two specific areas of US international concern: (1) the conflict in Iraq and the 'war on terror', and (2) the emergence of an 'evangelized foreign policy', involving an inter-religion coalition focusing on human rights and social welfare issues in various global 'black spots', including North Korea and Sudan.

Religion and politics in the USA

In the USA, the allowable limit of 'religious expression by public authority' generates a lively and continuing debate among Americans (Wald, 1991: 238). The controversy is not new: the US political system has long presented a fertile environment for the expression of religious differences in the public realm, despite the official predominance of a secular political environment (Wald, 2003). Prospects for a religious presence in public life in America are, however, high owing to several factors: first, unlike most Western Europeans, a large proportion of Americans – said variously to be between 40 and 70 per cent, astonishingly high by Western standards (Norris and Inglehart, 2004) – regularly attend religious services, attesting to the high popular regard that many Americans have for their religious beliefs.[1] Secondly, there have long been strong ties between religious affiliation and ethnic identity in the USA. Thirdly, there is a remarkable diversity of religious opinion in the country. Because of these factors, religion is an important feature in defining terms of political competition in America (Wald, 2003).

According to Wald, religion in America retains political significance 'through such diverse paths as the impact of sacred values on political perceptions, the growing interaction between complex religious organizations and State regulatory agencies, the role of congregational involvement in political mobilization and the functionality of Churches as a political resource for disadvantaged groups' (Wald, 1991: 241). This is not to imply that things have remained static: America's progress towards modernity has greatly affected its people's patterns of religious commitment. This is because modernity – the USA is said to be the most modern country in the world (Thomas, 2005: 143) – has long encouraged tendencies towards both religious *differentiation* – that is, there are a great many extant religions *and* divisions within religions – and religious *voluntarism*, that is, people increasingly feel that their religious choices are less an ascriptive trait, conferred by birth, and more a matter of choice and discretionary involvement (Wald, 2003).

To examine these issues, in this chapter we focus upon three significant religious organizations in the USA: the Religious (or Christian) Right, the Catholic Church, and the Nation of Islam,[2] examining their domestic and international political influence. We focus on three main questions:

- *To what extent are religious actors politically important in the USA?*

- *Has religion recently gained increased political and social prominence?* For four decades, from the 1930s to the 1960s, there was little consistent engagement in US politics from religious organizations. At this time, the country was characterized by high levels of piety, yet religion was effectively 'privatized' and, as a result, without sustained political influence. Some groups managed intermittent influence, for example, in the 1960s the Nation of Islam achieved some public and political visibility under the leadership of Malcolm X (born Malcolm Little in 1925 in Omaha, Nebraska). In addition, during the same decade, some Christian churches played a significant part in the Civil Rights movement. Here we can note the particular prominence of a Christian leader, Dr Martin Luther King, who was assassinated in 1968. King was both a Baptist minister and a figurehead of the Southern Christian Leadership Conference. In addition, at the time of the Vietnam War in the 1960s and early 1970s, various Christian leaders, especially from the Catholic Church, were prominent in anti-war peace protests. Now, however, various religious actors, notably but not exclusively from among the Religious Right, are *consistently* involved in an array of socio-political issues.

- *What happens when there is religious involvement in America's foreign policy?*

Civil religion and church–state relations

We start with an examination of the concept of *civil religion* and outline the main features of church–state relations in the USA.

Civil religion

Robbins and Anthony define civil religion as the 'complex of shared religio-political meanings that articulate a sense of common national purpose and that rationalize the needs and purposes of the broader community' (Robbins and Anthony, 1982: 10). According to Coleman, 'American civil religion has a complex relationship with the polity – a relationship that reflects the history of the United States' (Coleman, 1996: 27). Traditionally, religious belief was not associated with any single political position in America; instead, the language of *civil religion* was intended to be used by all. From the 1970s, however, the contribution of religion to political culture and the judicial sphere underwent significant change. Not least, certain religious groups, notably the Religious Right, developed comprehensive political agendas consistently couched in religious terms (Reichley, 2002). In addition, over time religious cleavages did not disappear as America modernized. Instead, religious alignments were redefined, with group differences extending to new social and political issues.

Rousseau and Bellah on civil religion

The American state historically attempted to create the concept of civil religion as a unifying ideology. The Swiss philosopher, Jean-Jacques Rousseau (1712–78), first used the term, *civil religion* in *The Social Contract*, originally published in 1762 (Rousseau, 2004). For Rousseau, civil religion referred to the religious dimension of a polity; over time, the term became an important concept in the sociology of religion, largely through the work of an American, Robert Bellah. In an influential article published in 1967, 'Civil religion in America', Bellah attempted to define the notion of a civic faith and assess its significance in the history of post-colonial America. To Bellah, civil religion is the *generalized* religion of the 'American way of life', existing with its own integrity alongside the more particularistic faiths of Judaism and the various Christian denominations. The concept of civil religion in America underpins the idea that a democratic United States is the prime agent of God in history, implying a collective faith that the American nation serves a transcendent purpose in history. While, as already noted, the political and religious spheres are differentiated structurally in America, civil religion nonetheless theoretically furnishes a symbolic way to unite the two.

Like Alexis de Tocqueville (2003 [1835]), who visited America in 1831, the contemporary American political scientist, Robert Bellah, saw civil religion in the USA as essential to restrain the self-interested elements of American liberalism, turning them instead towards public-spirited forms of citizenship that allow republican institutions both to survive and thrive. Bellah argued that civil religion was a fundamental requisite for stable democracy in America, given the United States' highly pluralistic and individualistic culture. He also contended that civil religion made a positive contribution to societal integration by binding a fractious people around a common goal, imparting a sacred character to civic obligation. For Bellah, the generic concept of civil religion also provided an important public manifestation of religion, as opposed to the more privatized orientations of particular faiths. For him, of specific interest was the problem posed both by the increasing structural differentiation of private from public sectors and by growing religious diversity, which together made general acceptance of a shared conception of moral order and cosmos increasingly implausible. Bellah also claimed that civil religion in America was the medium through which people perceived common values in a society built, on the one hand, on ideals of mutual tolerance and unity and, on the other, on cultural and religious pluralism. Ironically, however, just as Bellah was relaying his views about civil religion in the late 1960s, things were beginning to change.

Bellah's *The Broken Covenant*

In *The Broken Covenant* (1975; second, revised edition, 1992) Bellah's ideas about the unifying power of civil religion were undermined by the social changes that served to erode public confidence in the US 'project', significantly represented by the concept of civil religion and helping to weaken the shared religious tradition that traditionally had sustained faith in the republic. Various national reverses and scandals had shattered the social consensus so central to civil religion. These included the Vietnam War (1954–75; USA involved, 1961–75) and the political scandal called 'Watergate' that led to the resignation of President Richard Nixon in August 1974. In addition, societal unity was undermined by societal fragmentation over a number of moral and ethical issues, including: the issue of decriminalization of 'soft' drugs, such as cannabis, gender- and race-based discrimination, abortion rights, increased rates of cohabitation, permissiveness towards sexual expression in art and literature, reduced sanctions against homosexuality and the Supreme Court decision prohibiting prayers in school. For some, especially within the burgeoning Religious Right, these changes collectively reflected an abhorrent, yet fundamental, shift away from traditional Judaeo-Christian morality that, as a result, fatally undermined civil religion as a unifying concept.

In sum, whereas civil religion was once widely viewed as a crucial component in an understanding of the USA as a unified society, held together by shared religious agreement about morality and ethics and considered of central importance to the health of American public life, over time things fragmented (Green, 2000). The civil religion ideal was seriously eroded by various national political setbacks and scandals from the 1970s, some of which had their roots in foreign policy reverses, such as Vietnam. Today, it is sometimes argued that the concept of civil religion in the USA is dead. Others maintain, however, that it is still a force with which to be reckoned. For Wald, 'if the core of the concept [is] the tendency to hold the nation accountable to divine standards, then the case can be made that US political culture has actually been revitalized by the rise of the "New Christian Right" (NCR)' (Wald, 1991: 256). We turn to this point shortly.

Religious fragmentation and politics

During the decade of the 1970s, the USA was greatly affected by both internal and external factors that significantly undermined the sense of national identity. Later, in the 1990s and early 2000s, many Americans were seriously afflicted by interlinked economic, political and cultural insecurities. Many angry white people blamed African-Americans and immigrants for taking their jobs, while unemployed African-Americans looked to blame the Hispanics. Out of a population of 300 million, 40 million Americans – more than one-eighth – had no health insurance, while blue-collar wages had fallen by nearly 20 per cent in real terms since the 1970s. In the context of globalization, middle management was being regularly 'downsized', and manufacturing jobs were being relocated to low-wage countries in Asia, especially China, and to South America, notably Mexico, the USA's southern neighbour. Meanwhile, the richest 2 per cent of the population controlled the majority of the wealth (Abramsky, 1996: 18). A single company, communications giant AT & T shed 40,000 jobs, while its chief executive enjoyed a $5 million (£3.2 million) rise in the value of his share options. In short, the USA was racked by scapegoating and chronic insecurity in the 1990s. And then 9/11 occurred (Hassner, 2002).

In the 1990s, what had once been an ideological left–right *vertical* split in American politics had become a *horizontal* split. On the one hand, there were the elites and the educated, who for the most part believed in the benefits of globalization. On the other hand, there were many further down the socio-economic scale who feared globalization for its apparently deleterious effects on jobs and security (Hacker and Pierson, 2005). What was the impact of globalization on religion in politics in the USA? Once a speechwriter for Richard Nixon, the discredited president forced to resign in 1974 as a result of the Watergate scandal, Pat Buchanan was able to gain some credible early victories in Republican caucuses and primaries in the presidential election campaign of 1996. He managed this by stressing not only his conservative religious views but also his economic nationalism: he claimed that, if elected, he would pull America back from the North American Free Trade Association and the World Trade Organization. Given the manifest insecurities affecting many millions of Americans, it was unsurprising that such populism was widely appealing. Buchanan's economic guru was Ludwig Erhard, the architect of Germany's post-war economic reconstruction, who devised the thesis that economics is not simply a series of equations but a philosophy which takes note of the human soul, an idea enshrined in Buchanan's notion of 'conservatism of the heart'. In the 1996 presidential race, Buchanan was initially able to attract many of the so-called 'Reagan Democrats', disaffected blue-collar workers who feared the loss of their jobs as a result of globalization. Buchanan achieved his best results in areas of the country where politically and socially conservative Christian evangelicals were most numerous, notably the South.

Buchanan's short-lived electoral successes, especially among Christian conservatives, is not evidence that growing material insecurity persuaded Americans to *return* to religion, because they never left it. Rooted in a unique historical legacy, there is both religious pluralism and vibrancy in the USA. As Bruce notes, this is contrary to what the secularization thesis proposes: religious pluralism is associated in the USA with increased, rather than diminished, religious adherence (Bruce, 1992: 5). To understand why this is the case, we need to bear in mind that, to a considerable degree, religious dissenters from Europe forged the American nation. Such people understood that elimination of state-established churches and a guarantee of religious freedom were the price of a reasonable degree of civil cordiality in a pluralistic society. Ironically, Christian churches thrived when cut loose from the paternalistic hand of government; evangelical activism became, and continues to be, a phenomenon of and force in society, now boosted significantly by the activities of numerous 'televangelists' ('television evangelists'), including Pat Robertson, Oral Roberts and Kenneth Copeland.[3] Statistics measuring religiosity in the USA confirm the deep-rootedness and longevity of religious adherence, *not* its revival (Norris and Ingelhart, 2004). As a result, we can note that, like their parents and grandparents, most Americans are people who have religious beliefs, especially a belief in God: nearly three-quarters of Americans claim membership of a church, and more than 90 per cent express belief in God (Hertzke, 1989: 298).

Pollsters and scholars often focus on the politically salient religious cleavages in American society, in part because they seem to be changing fast. There is a traditional tripartite split among Christians. A 1978 poll indicated that Catholics comprised approximately 30 per cent of the population; 'main-line', that is, moderate or liberal, Protestant churches – the Episcopalian (the US equivalent of the Church of England), the Lutheran and the Methodist – encompassed 35 per cent; and 22 per cent identified themselves as evangelical Christians. Jews accounted for about 5 per cent, and Muslims, Hindus, and Sikhs numbered about 3 per cent each, around 9 per cent in total. A total of 9 per cent of Americans regard themselves as 'secularists' (Kepel, 1994: 104).

The 1978 poll was conducted in the middle of a twenty-five-year decline in membership of the main-line Protestant denominations, which eventually led to a loss of one-third of members, that did not level off until the late 1980s. Theologically conservative evangelical Churches, on the other hand, saw dramatic growth in the same period, reflecting a major restructuring of religious alignments. The evangelical Southern Baptist Convention, for example, is now by far the largest Protestant denomination in America with around 16 million members. Other fast-growing churches include the Assemblies of God, Nazarenes, Seventh Day Adventists and the Mormons, while the fastest-growing church in the South is the New Covenant Fellowship, an evangelical interdenominational group. Sociologist Dean Kelley explains the trend towards such churches in the following way: 'While the mainline Churches have tried to support the political and economic claims of [US] society's minorities and outcasts, it is the sectarian groups that have had most success in attracting new members from these very sectors of society' (Kelley, 1986: xxv).

There are four distinct religious groupings in the USA, roughly comparable in terms of the numbers of those adhering to them: (a) main-line Protestants; (b) conservative, often evangelical, Christians; (c) Roman Catholics and (d) 'others' (including, Jews, Muslims, Sikhs, Hindus, atheists and agnostics) (Kohut and Rogers, 2002). Note, however, that patterns of religious adherence are not static. The proportion of both main-line Protestants and Catholics is declining, while that of conservative evangelical Christians and 'others' is increasing (Bates, 2006).

What does this imply for the relationship between religion and politics in the USA, both domestically and in relation to the country's international relations? We can note the following in relation to domestic factors. First,

traditional, politically salient Protestant–Catholic divisions that once virtually defined US society were replaced by a split between, on the one hand,
mainly conservative evangelical Christians and, on the other, theological
liberals (Hertzke, 1989: 298). Until the 1940s, the politically salient division
between early and later immigrants had principally hinged on the fact that
the former were solidly Protestant and the latter firmly Catholic (Casanova,
1994: 168). Yet division was not expressed in religious terms per se; rather it
focused largely on questions about social welfare and labour policy: that is,
the chief electoral issue was the clash between the 'haves' – mostly main-
line Protestants – and the 'have nots' – often recent Catholic immigrants.
After the Second World War, the Democratic Party bound together most
Catholics, Jews and evangelical Protestants, white and black alike, largely
because they were outsiders, prompting them to form a de facto coalition to
contest the electoral ground with their rivals: 'main-line' Protestant Republicans. Until about 1960 this electoral equation held; afterwards it was increasingly likely that Catholics, Protestants, and to a certain degree
African-Americans and Jews, engaged politically under the banner of either
party (Wald, 1991: 265; Wald, 2003).

In 1992, main-line Protestants voted narrowly for the Democratic challenger Bill Clinton against the incumbent Republican president, George H.
W. Bush (42/37 per cent). A total of 20 per cent voted for the 'third force'
maverick, Ross Perot. This closely reflected the overall national vote. Conservative born-again Christians provided core support for Jimmy Carter's
presidential campaign in 1976, Ronald Reagan's in 1980 and 1984, that of
the 'televangelist' Baptist preacher, Pat Robertson in 1988, the conservative
Catholic Pat Buchanan's in 1992 and 1996, and the campaigns of George W.
Bush in 2000 and 2004. The psephological point is that even though numbers of mostly conservative evangelical Christians increased over time, until
recently they did not exhibit high levels of electoral solidarity. Consequently, what might be called 'the right-wing Christian vote' was unable decisively to determine the outcome of presidential elections in the 1990s. But in
both 2000 and 2004, conservative evangelical Christians were pivotal in
George Bush's electoral triumphs (Green et al., 2005).

'Moderate' Catholics, on the other hand, were by no means uniform politically; for example, such people were not monolithically anti-abortion. For
forty years, following the Second Vatican Council ('Vatican II') in 1965, US
Catholics have been divided between: (1) devout and regular worshippers
who largely accept the teachings of the Church on birth control and abortion, and (2) people whose church attendance is more casual and who live
with little apparent regard to papal encyclicals. In 1992 and 1996 Catholics

voted for Clinton over his Republican challengers, slightly more pro-Clinton than the national average. In the 2000 and 2004 elections, on the other hand, Catholics switched to George Bush in significant numbers (Duin, 2004). In the latter year, it is estimated that the President increased his vote by nine million, of which seven million were Catholics, even though his challenger, John Kerry, was himself a Catholic (Green et al., 2005).

The 'others' are a motley group: Hindus, Jews, Muslims, Sikhs and secularists, collectively the most loyal Democratic base. In 1992 they went for Clinton over Bush by a heavy margin of 63 to 26 per cent, with an additional 10 per cent voting for Perot (Walker, 1996). Whereas the Jews have traditionally been of political importance, 'exercis[ing] impressive influence through robust organizations, eminent leadership, and focused political agendas', they have recently been out of the political spotlight; instead, Muslims, have 'emerged as a visible political force', the result both of immigration and conversions of inner-city African-Americans (Hertzke, 1989: 299). With an important political vehicle in the controversial Nation of Islam (discussed below), African-American Muslim converts began to exercise some political clout in such strategic cities as Detroit, Washington and Chicago. In the 2000 and 2004 elections, despite the hopes of the Bush campaign, only about a quarter of American Jews voted for George Bush (Besser, 2004; Taylor, 2005).

In conclusion, over time the traditional Protestant–Catholic division was replaced by a fragmentation of religious-political alignments: new patterns of group affiliation focusing primarily on moral and social issues, including, *inter alia*, recreational drug use, pornography, homosexuality, abortion and marital fidelity. The result was 'a pronounced attitudinal gap between practising Christians and non-believers', revealing distinctive religious preferences which do not conform to the historical dimension previously defining religious conflict on public issues (Wald, 1991: 265–6).

In the next section we examine three influential religious constituencies: (1) the Religious Right, (2) US Catholics, and (3) the Nation of Islam, before turning to the issue of their significance for America's international relations.

Politically significant religious groups in the USA

The Religious Right

It used to be said that every four years, at the time of the US presidential elections, American and foreign journalists rediscovered religion. This was the periodic occasion when the media scented the electoral possibilities of the influence on electoral outcomes of the Religious Right, the politically influential corpus of millions of mostly 'born-again', socially and politically conservative Christians. This interest reflected the fact that the Religious Right has become a significant domestic political lobby group. An early classification, the 'New Christian Right', was used in the 1970s to refer to a surge in political activity among Protestant fundamentalists and conservative evangelicals. Over time, however, its usage has become more flexible, sometimes referring to a broad community of generic religious conservatives and at other times referring to a small subset of institutionalized organizations pursuing goals characterized by cultural, social and political conservatism. Prior to the 1970s, the US conservative evangelical movement was a subculture, largely keeping its distance from electoral politics. But with a new focus on social conservatism, around the time of the presidency of Ronald Reagan (1981–89), Republican Party strategists – together with neo-conservatives and other right-wing ideologues – encouraged the politicization of conservative evangelicals as part of the New Right fusionism that ushered Ronald Reagan into the presidency in 1981 and returned him to power in 1985 (Taylor, 2005).

What the Religious Right believes

Despite ideological and political differences among the different organizations that make up the movement, most members of the Religious Right would believe that at home secularism poses a serious threat to liberty, democracy and pluralism. The Religious Right is 'radical' in that it advocates dramatic changes in society. It is 'religious' in that its members and leaders tend to base their ideologies upon religious doctrines drawn from the Bible. In 2004, it was estimated that those claiming identification with the ideas of the Religious Right in the USA comprised around 20 per cent (some 60 million people) of the adult population of some 300 million (Green et al., 2005; Bates, 2006). At home, the Religious Right seeks to uphold and perpetuate 'Christian values', regarding as anathema manifestations of what are regarded as 'excessive liberalism', including: legal abortion, absence or downgrading of prayers in state-run schools, and science teaching that adopts a rationalist, rather than a 'Creationist', perspective (Halper and Clarke, 2004).

From the 1980s, the Religious Right began to make common cause on many foreign policy issues with secular neo-conservatives, serving to focus concerns more widely on countries where basic religious freedoms were suppressed, notably minority Christian and Jewish populations in some Muslim and Communist nations. Overall, the key foreign policy goal was a generalized one – 'the spread of freedom', often directed against shadowy adversaries: 'international terrorism' and 'radical Islam'. Groups within the Religious Right especially concerned with foreign policy include: the National Association of Evangelicals, Empower America, and the Foundation for the Defense of Democracy. As we shall see later, the Religious Right interpreted 9/11 as 'an apocalyptic contest between good and evil', and a leader of the Religious Right, Pat Robertson, claimed that Islam 'is not a peaceful religion' (Halper and Clarke, 2004: 196; Taylor, 2005).

US Catholics

America's largest church is the Catholic Church. It has an estimated 61 million members, 26 per cent of all Christians in the USA (http:// www. adherents.com/largecom/com_romcath.html). Like the mainly Protestant Religious Right, the Catholic Church has also sought actively to influence policy via dialogue with political leaders, including the president and his close advisers. Over the years, Catholic religious leaders have sought to influence federal policies and programmes in a number of areas, including: the legal right of women to have abortions, government policies for social justice concerns both at home and abroad, the nuclear arms race and deterrence, especially during the Cold War, and, most recently, the ethics of the 'War on Terror' and the US invasions of Iraq (http://www.usccb.org/index.shtml). As far as the abortion issue is concerned, some Catholics have allied themselves with the Religious Right, because its recent presidential candidates (Gary Bauer, Pat Buchanan and Pat Robertson) consistently stated their opposition to abortion under any circumstances. Yet, that issue apart, most Catholic opinion has traditionally been more liberal, to the political left of the Religious Right. For example, in 1992 Catholics voted for Bill Clinton over George Bush, Snr, by 44 to 36 per cent, slightly more pro-Clinton than the national average. They maintained a similar margin in favour of Clinton in 1996 (Walker, 1996; Reichley, 2002). In 2000, George W. Bush had narrowly lost among Catholics (Associated Press, 2004). However, Bush increased his vote by nine million in 2004, of which seven million were Catholics, even though his challenger John Kerry was a Catholic. Bush won 52 per cent of the Roman Catholic vote, with the support of 56 per cent of white Catholics, defeating the first Catholic presidential candidate from a major party since John F. Kennedy.

Because main-line Protestant denominations now claim only a quarter of the US population, almost on a par with their fast-growing conservative evangelical competitors who make up 23 per cent of the overall electorate

(Bates, 2006), Catholics, comprising about a quarter of Americans, hold a significant position in a keen cultural and political struggle with the Religious Right. Although once aliens in a Protestant land, the vast majority of Catholics now feel comfortable in American society. However, there are political divisions between ordinary Catholics, reflected in their leaders' political pronouncements. On the one hand, bishops' pastoral letters on nuclear arms and the economy have given ammunition to social gospel liberals, while, on the other, anti-abortion pronouncements and support for public accommodation of faith buoy some cultural conservatives. Overall, the pluralism of American Catholicism helps both to shape and to constrain the Church's political influence.

US Catholics: both American *and* 'Roman'

American Catholicism has been shaped by consecutive waves of immigration – Irish, Italians, Central and Latin Americans – to become a multi-ethnic, territorially organized national Church. The Catholic Church underwent swift Americanization after the First World War; within 50 years, that is, by the 1960s, assimilation of most American Catholics of Irish and Italian origin into the mainstream of US life was complete. However, the American Catholic Church has had to live with two specific sources of tension, the result of being a member of the universal Roman Catholic Church, that is, it is *both* Roman and American. As a result, it is caught between the traditional Church principle of prescribed membership and the voluntary denominational principle dominant in the American religious environment. The result is conflict between the traditional episcopal, clerical and authoritarian governance structures of the Church and the democratic, lay and participatory principles permeating America's polity (Casanova, 1994: 176).

In terms of church–state relations, American Catholicism has stood to the left and the right of government at different times. It has demanded more from a 'right wing' position than any administration in the 1980s, 1990s or early 2000s was able or willing to offer – that is, a constitutional amendment equating abortion with murder – while, from the left, it has been open in its opposition to US support for Latin American dictators in the 1980s, the continuing nuclear arms race, and, most recently, the war in Iraq and the War on Terror.

During the first half of the twentieth century, Catholic devotion became less communitarian and more privatized, moving towards progressively higher levels of generality: from the village to the ethnic neighbourhood to American Catholic community to American national community to world community. US Catholics learnt to compartmentalize rigidly two spheres of life, the religious and the secular. According to Casanova, Catholicism became 'restricted to the religious sphere, while Americanism was restricted to the secular sphere' (Casanova, 1994: 181). However, in the 1950s as the Cold War with the Soviet Union deepened, the associated anti-Communist crusade served to end the tension of being both Catholic and American. Casanova explains that 'this was a crusade all freedom-loving people could join, those fighting for republican freedom and those fighting for the freedom of the Church. Rome and the republic could at last be allies' (Casanova, 1994: 183). By the late 1960s, however, many lay Catholics had become increasingly more dovish than many of their religious leaders, Protestants and the general population in relation to the Vietnam War. Only in 1971, long after many other religious leaders and ordinary Americans had unequivocally condemned the war, did the US Catholic bishops admit that it was no longer a 'just war' (Wald, 1991: 264).

Liberalizing Catholic attitudes on a range of social issues stemmed to a large degree from the Second Vatican Council ('Vatican II') which ended in 1965. Vatican II led to a radical transformation of American Catholicism, a radical reform from *above* coming from *abroad,* albeit moulded by the specific American political context. The consequence was that a new and activist intellectual stratum emerged within American Catholicism, manifested among bishops, priests, nuns and laity alike, and focused on greater concern for social justice, and in 'offer[ing] broader, more universalistic perspectives which challenged the nationalist particularism of the American civil religion' (Casanova, 1994: 178). Three discrete issues – abortion, nuclear weapons, and economic and social justice – exemplified the new type of public Catholicism that emerged after Vatican II.

President Bush's controversial meeting with Vatican official Cardinal Angelo Sodano in 2004, when he reportedly asked for American Catholic bishops to become more politically aggressive on cultural, family and life issues, specifically gay marriage, is said to be evidence that Bush 'hoped the Vatican would nudge [US Catholics] toward more explicit activism' (Joyce, 2004). On the other hand, the US Catholic Church was one of the institutions that Bush is said to have 'thumbed his nose at in invading Iraq' (Jackson, 2004). Shortly before his death on 2 April 2005, the late Pope John Paul II asked rhetorically in his World Day of Peace Message ('Do not be overcome by evil but overcome evil with good'): 'How can we not think with profound regret of the drama unfolding in Iraq, which has given rise to tragic situations of uncertainty and insecurity for all?' (http://www.vatican.va/holy_father/john_paul_ii/messages/peace/documents/hf_jp-ii_mes_20041216_xxxviii-world-day-for-peace_en.html).

In addition, Pax Christi, the US Catholic Peace Movement, strongly criticized the invasion of Iraq. It noted in late 2005 that nearly three years of occupation had left more than 2,000 US soldiers dead and more than 10,000 seriously wounded. Tens of thousands of Iraqis had died as a result of the conflict and countless numbers were wounded. Iraqi resistance to the occupation had grown both in numbers and sophistication, waging daily attacks on both US forces and the Iraqi government (http://www.paxchristiusa.org/news_events_more.asp?id=641).

The overall point is that while increased numbers of US Catholics voted for George W. Bush in 2004 compared to 2000, there were significant manifestations of Catholic institutional opinion expressed both in the USA and internationally that expressed significant reservations in relation to US foreign policy in Iraq after 9/11.

The Nation of Islam

The Nation of Islam (NOI) is the subject of this section of the chapter. Its most important strand is led by the controversial Louis Farrakhan. The NOI is similar to the Religious Right and US Catholics in two important ways: (1) it has become politically more vocal in recent years, following decades of relative non-involvement in politics; and (2) current political activism is primarily a reaction to governmental policies and programmes judged detrimental to members' interests, including the war in Iraq.

Islam and the Nation of Islam in the USA

Islam is said to be the swiftest growing religion in the United States. It passed Judaism as the second largest in the mid-1990s, totalling over five million adherents (Nyang, 1988: 520; Gardell, 1996: 48). Growth is mainly due to conversions from other religions, especially Christianity. Most American Muslims maintain a low political profile, for example, very few openly express sympathies with Islamic radicals in Iran, Iraq, Afghanistan or elsewhere. However, outspoken exceptions do exist – mainly in the African-American community, especially in the Nation of Islam where Islam has also made significant inroads via conversions (Harris, 1999).

W. D. Fard, also known as Farad Muhammad, an itinerant salesman and religious teacher, founded the Nation of Islam in Detroit in 1930. Fard, who seems to have regarded himself as God, met one Elijah Poole, a Southern man with a rural background, whom he 'anointed' as his divine messenger, dubbing him Elijah Muhammad. Fard died in 1933, leaving his people in Elijah Muhammad's care. Under Muhammad's stewardship, the NOI prospered, forging its way as a variant under the general umbrella of Islam. Although the NOI's early efforts in the name of Islam were both denied and rejected by most mainstream Muslims, the organization was able to gain members both during the 1930s – a period of economic arid social instability characterized by the Great Depression – and after the Second World War. During the 1950s and early 1960s it gained notoriety under the inspirational leadership of Malcolm X, an advocate of black separatism, black nationalism and black pride (Harris, 1999: 43–4). During the 1970s, the NOI went through a thorough-going theological transformation: under the leadership of Elijah Muhammad's son, Imam Warith Deen Muhammad, it moved swiftly towards mainstream Sunni Islam (Gardell, 1996: 54), becoming the 'largest body of Sunni Muslims in the United States' (Nyang, 1988: 526). Imam Muhammad strove to hasten the assimilation of the members of the NOI into the mainstream of American society, to try to realize, like other American citizens, the fruits and benefits of the American Dream. Under his leadership, the NOI tried to achieve for its predominantly African-American followers what many Protestants, Catholics and Jewish Americans had already achieved: increased prosperity and status. Assimilation into mainstream USA society was to be achieved through 'emphasis on self-pride and on the dignity of self-help and self-development within the framework of their community' (Nyang, 1988: 526). By starting small businesses, NOI members were to become increasingly self-confident, propelling them towards greater involvement in the 'American Dream'.

The assimilationist agenda of Imam Muhammad met opposition from a strand of opinion in the NOI. In 1977, Louis Farrakhan started a politically militant counter-movement within the NOI, which later developed into a separate group; I shall refer to it here as 'radical NOI'. Farrakhan's group differs in two key ways from the NOI mainstream: (1) it does not believe in the 'American Dream', and (2) 'Elijah Muhammad never intended for us to follow completely what is called orthodox Islam' (Farrakhan quoted in Gardell, 1996: 55). The theology of Farrakhan's group is rather different from mainstream Islam, with roots in the tradition of African-American religious nationalism. Nonetheless, during the 1990s Farrakhan developed working relations with foreign radical Muslim organizations and states, including

Libya. In effect, Farrakhan's faction sought 'outward accommodation to Islamic orthopraxy while refining the reasons for rejecting Islamic orthodoxy' (Gardell, 1996: 57).

Preaching a virulent mixture of anti-Semitism, anti-corruption, pro-community, self-help and African-American separatism, Farrakhan sought to focus alienated African-Americans' frustrations for political purposes. Estimates of the numbers of members of Farrakhan's radical NOI range between 10,000 and 30,000, with up to 500,000 additional 'sympathizers' (Fletcher, 1994). Farrakhan's main idea is for African-Americans to work together in common pursuit of group self-interest and solidarity, but not to seek assimilation within the mainstream of American society. The Nation's ideologists 'focus on the prime symbols of American civil religion, which are given a revised and reversed meaning in order to expose the diabolical nature of American society' (Gardell, 1996: 63). Like born-again Christian evangelicals, members of Farrakhan's faction of the NOI believe that America is on the road to self-destruction, a declining civilization where the social fabric is falling apart. Drugs, criminality, unemployment, poverty and pornography are all regarded as signs of the Final Days. While awaiting Armageddon, NOI radicals demand a separate black state 'in an area fertile and rich in minerals, as compensation for all the centuries of unpaid slave labour' (Gardell, 1996: 63).

Besides stressing the desirability of autonomous development in separate enclaves, the radical NOI strives to promote the building of a separate African-American infrastructure. Until the 1970s, that is, during the leadership of Elijah Muhammad, the Nation prospered economically, establishing hundreds of business enterprises, becoming, according to one source, 'the most potent organized economic force in the black community' (Lincoln, 1973: 97). In the late 1970s, the NOI's assets were estimated at $60–80 million (Mamiya, 1982:144). When Imam Muhammad took over the organization's leadership from his father, he dismantled the financial empire in order to facilitate the transition into the Muslim mainstream. The consequence of declining economic power is that Farrakhan sought to rebuild his organization's financial base, primarily via the People Organized and Working for Economic Rebirth (POWER) programme. As a result, from the mid-1980s radical NOI developed various business enterprises, including 'shampoo and skin care ranges, publishing firms, restaurants, hotels, agribusinesses, food importers and banking' (Gardell, 1996: 64–5), while also organizing its own welfare agencies (Smart, 1989: 374).

Under Farrakhan's leadership radical NOI has been a vocal critic of President Bush, especially in relation to the conflict in Iraq. In October 2002, six months before the US-led invasion, Farrakhan claimed that Bush, not Iraq, was a 'world menace'. Farrakhan was also sharply critical of Israel and said a thirst for Iraqi oil and pressure from Israel were the real motives behind President George W. Bush's push towards war with Iraq. Going to war for Israel's benefit would be like 'the tail wagging the dog', Farrakhan said. After stating, as it turned out, correctly, that Iraq had no weapons of mass destruction, Farrakhan claimed that Bush's real reason for invading Iraq was to prevent it from developing a military machine on a par with that of Israel (Crumm and Lords, 2002).

Following the invasion of Iraq in March 2003 and the contemporaneous 'War on Terror', Farrakhan said in May 2004 that the USA 'faced ruin' unless it changed course in the Middle East. He also spoke of the USA's place in biblical prophecy and of what he called misuse of US military power in the world. Farrakhan, who wrote several letters to President George W. Bush from 2001, also claimed that the US government had been 'hijacked' by a small group of neo-conservatives who believed that around the world, especially in the Middle East, Islam must be cowed to ensure the survival of Israel. He named various neo-conservatives – including Chairman of the Defense Policy Board Richard Perle, Assistant Secretary of Defense Paul Wolfowitz and writers Bill Kristol and William Bennett – who he said worked towards the overthrow of Saddam Hussein before 9/11.[4] 'Had he (President Bush) not been so preoccupied with the neo-conservatives' idea of Iraq, he might have been able to connect the dots of the many warnings that were coming to America from her friends around the world and avoided the tragedy of 9/11', Farrakhan said. He added, 'Iraq is to the Arab world as Germany is to Europe . . . Her science and technology far exceeds the rest of the Arab world'. Finally, Farrakhan claimed that Muslims in Africa, the Middle East and Asia perceive the war in Iraq as a war on Islam, placing the safety of US citizens overseas at risk (Swanson, 2004). In sum, in relation to the US invasion of Iraq and the War on Terror, Farrakhan has acted as a gadfly, consistently accusing the Bush administration of malevolence towards Muslims, especially in Iraq, under the pretext of making America safer.

In conclusion, our discussion of three important religious constituencies in the USA – the Religious Right, US Catholics and the Nation of Islam – underlines the following:

■ Each has become increasingly politicized from the 1970s, although their core concerns have differed over time.

■ Both domestic and foreign policy issues have been a focus.

- In recent years, various foreign policy concerns – including those stimulated by 9/11 and including subsequent US-led wars in Iraq and against 'Terror', as well as others, including religious freedom and social justice issues – have become key issues of US foreign policy in which religious actors have an input.

US foreign policy and religion: the conflict in Iraq, the 'war on terror', and an 'evangelized foreign policy'

The events of September 11, 2001 ('9/11') and the subsequent 'War on Terror' were of pivotal importance for subsequent direction and focus of American foreign policy. September 11 led to a new, fearful, foreign policy climate for the USA, providing a tragic opportunity for George W. Bush and key neo-conservative advisers and policy makers to attempt to redraw the political map of the Middle East towards democracy and 'freedom'. This in turn had a profound impact upon the USA's international relations more generally. Post-9/11 foreign policy was put into effect via the US-led invasions of Afghanistan and Iraq. In the former country, the goal was not merely to oust the Islamist government, the Taliban, from power and to kill or capture local al-Qaeda leaders and personnel, or, in the latter, to eliminate Saddam Hussein and his regime and their alleged Weapons of Mass Destruction (Seipel and Hoover, 2004). Both policies were ideologically informed by the fusion of two mutually reinforcing sets of ideas: religious ones emanating from the Religious Right, dovetailing with influential neo-conservatives' secular security concerns.

The then National Security Advisor Condoleezza Rice stated in April 2002 that 9/11 was an 'earthquake' that 'started shifting the tectonic plates in international politics' (Rice, 2002). Deputy Secretary of Defense Paul Wolfowitz opined in *Vanity Fair* magazine a year later on 9 May 2003 that:

> The most significant thing that has produced what is admittedly a fairly significant change in American policy is the events of September 11th . . . If you had to pick the ten most important foreign policy things for the United States over the past 100 years [9/11] would surely rank in the top ten if not number one. It's the reason why so much has changed.

Two months after that, on 9 July 2003, in an address to the Armed Services Committee, Defense Secretary Donald Rumsfeld averred that Washington now viewed the world 'through the prism of 9/11' (Dinan, 2003). Collective-ly, these remarks from Rice, Wolfowitz, and Rumsfeld underline the impor-tance of 9/11 for subsequent US foreign policy.

We noted in Chapter 1 that to date there has been relatively little sys-tematic, comparative research on the impact of religious actors on foreign policy formation and execution. We saw in Chapter 2 that to wield influ-ence, religious actors must be able to exercise what Joseph Nye calls soft power. How and under what circumstances might religious actors influence a state's foreign policy in the direction they would like? A starting point is to note that as 'religion plays an important role in politics in certain parts of the world', then it is likely that there will be 'greater prominence of religious organizations in society and politics' in some countries but not others (Tel-hami, 2004: 71). On the other hand, the ability of a religious actor to trans-late *potential* ability into *actual* influence on foreign policy depends on several factors. First, can it access and thus potentially influence foreign pol-icy decision-making processes? This ability should not be understood only in terms of formal institutional access, important though this is; it also de-pends on another, equally important factor: the ability to influence policy via other means, for example, the media. The USA has a democratic political system that offers accessible decision-making structures and processes. This potentially offers many sorts of actors, both religious and secular, opportu-nities to influence policy formation and execution, both domestic and for-eign (Hudson, 2005: 295–7). However, the idea that religious actors must 'get the ear of government' by 'lobby[ing] elected representatives and members of the executive branch' directly is a very limited and tradition-al understanding of influence. In addition, 'interest groups can make cam-paign contributions, vote in elections, try to mould public opinion, etc' (Mearsheimer and Walt, 2006: 6).

Yet religions are not just run-of-the-mill lobby groups. In addition, they may have a form of influence that while indirect is nevertheless instrumental in helping construct the mindset of those that have responsibility for making policy in relation to the issue in question. But what questions are raised? What issues are of concern? What terms are used? How are they thought about? And even if a religious actor gets access to formal decision-making structures and processes it does not *guarantee* their ability significantly to influ-ence either policy formation or execution. To have a profound policy impact, it is often necessary to build and consolidate close relations with key players in both society and politics, as well as to foster good relations with influen-tial print and electronic media. Overall, religious actors' ability to influence the foreign policies of states is likely to be greatest when, as in the USA after

9/11, there is ideological empathy between key religious and secular leaders and power holders – that is, when religious actors can employ soft power to try to achieve their objectives. We can note the influence of the Religious Right in relation to US foreign policy in the Middle East, especially after 9/11. Leading figures included Gary Bauer, head of an advocacy group, American Values, and Republican presidential contender in 2000; Jerry Falwell, prominent Southern Baptist and televangelist; Ralph Reed, former executive director of the Christian Coalition and candidate-to-be Lieutenant Governor of Georgia in 2006; Pat Robertson, former Republican presidential candidate and televangelist; Dick Armey, former Republican congressman and co-chair of Freedom Works,[5] and Tom DeLay, a prominent member of the Republican Party. These men enjoyed close personal relationships with President George W. Bush and his key confidantes, including John Bolton, Robert Bartley, William Bennett, Jeane Kirkpatrick and George Will (Mearsheimer and Walt, 2006: 6; Mazarr, 2003; Bacevich and Prodromou, 2004). Some individuals, such as Michael Gerson, a Bush policy adviser, speechwriter (and a man who helped coin the phrase, 'axis of evil') and former journalist, has links to both groups: Gerson is not only 'a member of an evangelical Episcopal church in suburban Virginia' but is also a driving force behind President Bush's 'emphasis on a global spread of what the president sees as God-given rights' (LaFranchi, 2006).

As Table 8.1 indicates, the current influence of religion on US foreign policy is not unique, as historically there has often been a link between US foreign policy goals and religious concerns.

To account for the current influence of the Religious Right on US foreign policy, we need to take into account the general importance of norms, values and ideology in the making of foreign policy. As Finnemore and Sikkink note, 'the ways in which norms themselves change and the ways in which they change other features of the political landscape . . . [make] static approaches to International Relations . . . particularly unsatisfying during the current era of global transformation when questions about change motivate much of the empirical research we do' (Finnemore and Sikkink, 1998: 888). This highlights the importance of paying analytical attention to the relationship between *ideational* and *material* issues to account for changes in US foreign policy after 9/11. It reflects a shift from the predominance of secular foreign policy goals during the Cold War to a shift in emphasis in the 1990s whereby religious concerns became more significant. During the Clinton era (1993–2001), 'left-leaning [religious] activists' had access 'to top administration officials. After [George W.] Bush took office, evangelical Christian leaders were the ones able to arrange sessions with senior White House aides' (Page, 2005).

TABLE 8.1 US foreign policy and religion

Period	Mission	Adversary	Means
Pre-revolutionary colonial America (1600–1776)	Millennium	Papal antichrist	Example as 'city on the hill'
Revolutionary and founding era (1776–1815)	Empire of liberty	Old world tyranny, 'hellish fiends' (Native Americans)	Example, continental expansion, without entangling alliances
Manifest Destiny (1815–1848)	Christian civilization	Savages or 'children' (Native Americans)	Examples, continental expansion, without entangling alliances
Imperial America (1898–1913)	Christian civilization	Barbarians and savages (Filipinos)	Overseas expansion, without entangling alliances
Wilsonian Internationalism (1914–1919)	Global democracy	Autocracy and imperialism	International organizations and alliances
Cold War liberalism (1946–89)	Free world	Communism	International organizations and alliances
Bush and neo-conservatism (2001–)	Spread of freedom	International terrorism, radical Islam	Unilateral action with ad hoc alliances

Source: Judis, 2005

In this regard, the influence of the Religious Right was pivotal, but not entirely novel. In the 1980s, during the presidency of Ronald Reagan, a man who shared many of their ideals and goals, the Religious Right began to consolidate itself as a significant lobby group (Haynes, 1998: 28–33; Halper and Clarke, 2004: 182–200; Judis, 2005). The second key component in the shift in US foreign policy after 9/11 was the influence of a group known as neo-conservatives ('neo-cons'); their rise to political dominance coincided with the rise in the Religious Right's influence. Both groups shared common ground and beliefs and the alliance between them deepened following 9/11 (Oldfield, 2004). Lieven (2004) notes five key developments in the 1990s that led to their deepening association: (1) narrowing of Christian beliefs, (2) sense of being under threat from globalization, (3) growing desire to resist external influences, (4) harking back to a golden age, and (5) readiness to use all available means to achieve successful policy outcomes in crucially important areas. Influential groups that can be located ideologically within the corpus of the Religious Right include the National Association of Evangelicals,[6] Empower America and the Foundation for the Defense of Democracy. According to Halper and Clarke, such organizations interpreted 9/11 as 'an apocalyptic contest between good and evil', an interpretation shared by at least some neo-conservatives (Halper and Clarke, 2004: 196). In addition, a leading member of the Religious Right, Pat Robertson, claimed after 9/11 that Islam 'is not a peaceful religion' (Halper and Clarke, 2004: 196). This concern dovetailed with a key foreign policy goal of the Religious Right: to spread religious freedom to parts of the world that were said to lack it, notably many Communist and Muslim countries, including Sudan (Seipel and Hoover, 2004).

Over time, however, there has developed what LaFranchi calls an 'evangelized foreign policy' (LaFranchi, 2006). This policy is represented not only by a continuing focus upon Iraq but also incorporates other concerns represented in the following laws that have reshaped US foreign policy, including diplomacy towards key countries including China and Saudi Arabia:

- The International Religious Freedom Act (1998). This makes freedom of religion and conscience a 'core objective' of US foreign policy. It also established an office and an annual international religious freedom report that grades countries on rights. The measure was lobbied for by 'a coalition of conservative Christians, Jews, Catholics, mainline Protestants, Tibetan Buddhists and others' (Page, 2005)

- The Trafficking Victims Protection Act (2000). This law seeks to do away with the international crime syndicates that dispatch children and women from the developing world into prostitution and sweatshops.

- The Sudan Peace Act (2002). Conservative evangelicals promoted this law, along with others outraged by the Khartoum government's attacks on southern Christians and animists. The law and its accompanying sanctions are credited with helping create the road map for the 2003 ceasefire and the peace treaty the following year.

- The North Korea Human Rights Act (2004). Korean Americans and conservative Christians lobbied for this bill. It aimed not only to focus US attempts to help defectors from North Korea but also to focus attention on the country's egregious human rights violations and its nuclear weapons programme.

- Conservative evangelical Christians' influence is also seen in the Bush administration's focus both on AIDS in Africa and in attacks on international family-planning activities (MacAskill, 2006).

The overall result, according to Alan Hertzke, author of *Freeing God's Children: The Unlikely Alliance for Global Human Rights* (2004), is that, since the mid-1990s, conservative evangelicals provided the most important influence in a new, highly significant, human rights movement emanating from the USA. In doing so, they helped create 'a new architecture for human rights in American foreign policy'. Hertzke also contends that '[w]ithout a determined constituency pressuring for engagement in international affairs, it would be likely that – given the difficulties in Iraq – you would have had the administration hunkering down a bit, and the American people with them . . . But instead, you have these substantial forces pushing on human rights causes and demanding intervention' (Page, 2005). The overall result is that American conservative evangelicals have broadened their perspective and widened their agenda, focusing on a number of international human rights issues. This is not to imply that domestic social issues have lost significance, but it does indicate that a concern with social welfare issues both at home and abroad have encouraged them to develop broader alliances in often unexpected ways, including with the Jewish community and main-line Christian organizations, as well as on college campuses and in traditional religious and secular human rights organizations, which have long been interested in such foreign causes (Green et al., 2003). According to LaFranchi, 'In just a few years, conservative Christian churches and organizations have broadened their political activism from a near-exclusive domestic focus to an emphasis on foreign issues . . . Even as many in Washington trumpet the return of realism to US foreign policy and the decline of the neoconservative hawks, the staying power of the evangelicals is likely to blunt what might otherwise have been a steep decline in Wilsonian ideals' (LaFranchi, 2006).

In sum, we have noted that the recent roles of religious ideas in foreign policy formation and execution can be seen during the later stages of the Cold War in the 1980s, the Clinton era of the 1990s and the Bush administrations in the early 2000s. In each phase, various religious constituencies, especially the Religious Right, saw the USA to be involved in an international struggle between 'good' and 'evil'. During the 1980s this was a 'secular' evil (the USSR), while in the 1990s and early 2000s 'evil' was Janus-faced: Islamist terrorism and human rights denials; both in their different ways were opposed to core US values: democracy and individualistic human rights. Consequently, US political leaders were encouraged to exhibit a high level of moral courage and character, attributes said to be rooted in a range of 'American values', necessary requirements in order to speak out and act in defence of the claims of 'good' over 'evil'. For example, when President George W. Bush talked of how the Cold War was 'won' and how the 'War on Terror' would be won in the future, he focused upon a twin necessity: for America to show both moral courage and character. He linked such virtues, both implicitly and explicitly, to values derived from his religious beliefs. For example, in May 2001, Bush spoke in Warsaw of how, he claimed, Communism had been humbled by 'the iron purpose and moral vision of a single man: Pope John Paul II' ('Remarks by the President in address to faculty and students of Warsaw University', 2002). A year later, in Prague, he returned to this theme, stating that: 'in Central and Eastern Europe the courage and moral vision of prisoners and exiles and priests and playwrights caused tyrants to fall' ('President Bush previews historic NATO Summit in Prague', 2002).

Such concerns contextualize President Bush's claims not only to want to help establish 'freedom and democracy' in the Middle East region but also to improve human rights in a number of contexts around the world, including North Korea and Sudan. Such a virtue was also characteristic of President Reagan's concerns nearly two decades before about the moral imperative of overturning Communism, and like President Bush, Reagan drew his inspiration in this respect from religious values and beliefs. This is not to claim, however, that either Bush or Reagan always privileged religious over secular values. Indeed, Hurd labels President George W. Bush a 'Christian secularist' (Hurd, 2004). The justification for this seemingly contradictory, even oxymoronic, juxtaposition of terms is to be found in the fact that in the USA secularism is a deep-rooted political tradition that, like in some Western European countries, notably France, developed over a long period. In the USA, however, secularism is also linked in important ways to various religious traditions, notably Judaeo-Christianity focused in the concept of civil religion, a fusing of ideas and values that provides US secularism with identifiably 'religious' values.

For example, President Bush calls for 'secular democracy' in both Afghanistan and Iraq. Note, however, that this is the same form of secularism that appears in the constitution of India: that is, no one religion is favoured over others, yet religion is theoretically and officially privatized, removed from the public domain. This situation is conventionally accepted – *theoretically and officially* – in many Western, especially Western European countries, not only the USA: separation of religion and politics is believed a necessary prerequisite for successful democracy. Yet, as we have seen in the case of the USA in this chapter, the official view does not accord with reality. As a result, when President Bush expresses evidence of a world-view strongly informed by conservative Christian values and norms, this is not necessarily deemed to be unacceptable by the great majority of Americans. When Bush claims, as he did in a 2003 speech, that 'liberty is both the plan of Heaven for humanity, and the best hope for progress here on earth' ('President Bush discusses freedom in Iraq and Middle East', 2003), there is no reason to believe that most Americans disagree with him. Yet, this duality of religious and secular ideas appears on the surface contradictory: Bush appears to be *simultaneously* both secular *and* religious in his public statements. One way of dealing with the conundrum is to note that secularism can come in different forms, with potentially inconsistent effects. Nicholas Wolterstorff of Yale Divinity School suggests that Bush relies on what he (Wolterstorff) calls a 'theistic account of political authority' ('Pew Forum on Religion and Public Life', 2003). According to Wolterstorff, 'among the ways a theistic account of political authority is distinct from all others is that it regards the authority of the State to do certain things as transmitted to it from someone or something which already has that very same authority' (ibid.). Thus God is believed to be transmitting directly to the political power holder, in this case Bush. Through Bush's articulation of what he believes are God's imperatives, the state gains the theistically-derived power and right to provide judgement in legislative and/or judicial forms. These concerns were also apparent when Bush mused in November 2002 that: 'Dwight Eisenhower said this of Radio Free Europe and Radio Liberty – "The simplest and clearest charter in the world is what you have, which is to tell the truth." And for more than 50 years, the charter has been faithfully executed, and it's the truth that sets this continent free' ('What World Leaders Say About RFE/RL', 2002). It seems highly unlikely that Bush's choice of words *unwittingly* plagiarized those of the evangelist John. Instead, it is much more likely that they were a *deliberate* restatement of words that clearly link what are to him two sets of 'truths': the 'truth' of liberal democracy and divinely-revealed 'truth'. And, from what we have seen in this chapter, it is by no means certain that most Americans would disagree with him.

Conclusion

At the start of the chapter, I posed three questions:

- *Is religion an important political actor in America?*
- *Has religion recently gained increased political and social prominence?*
- *What happens when there is religious involvement in America's foreign policy?*

We are now in a position to provide some answers. First, evidence suggests that religion is an intermittently important political actor: recently the Religious Right was able to enlist support from secular neo-conservatives in relation to post-9/11 foreign policy towards Iraq and Afghanistan. In addition, since the 1990s a broad coalition of religious organizations, featuring but not always led by conservative evangelicals, has helped to focus US foreign policy under both Clinton and Bush on human rights and social welfare issues.

Secondly, the Nation of Islam (NOI) is also an example of a politically active, religiously defined community. Farrakhan's NOI achieved some support, especially among African-Americans, but was unable to have much policy influence, including in relation to foreign policy. Like the Religious Right and some Catholics and their leaders, the NOI deems it necessary to pursue its aspirations through political involvement. The NOI is like the Religious Right in at least two respects: (1) it has put forward its candidates for political office, and (2) it has had some electoral impact (Harris, 1999: 182–3). Although differing greatly in terms of their political aspirations, what these groups also have in common is that they sought to become more political for similar reasons: they believed that successive governments led the USA in unacceptably anti-religious, anti-social and amoral directions. They also thought that it was necessary to seek change through theologically appropriate programmes and policies. Overall, the combined political impact of the Religious Right, NOI and Catholics falsifies the secularization thesis: in contemporary America the drive towards modernity has not marginalized religion in the public realm; instead, modernization stimulated various religious actors into greater political involvement, including in some cases in relation to foreign policy. Overall, while the religious actors examined in this chapter were not able consistently to dominate the political agenda to the extent they might have liked, collectively their political influence was considerable in both domestic and foreign policy.

Thirdly, nearly two decades after the end of the Cold War and the collapse of the Soviet Union, the USA now pursues a range of foreign policies that significantly draw on often mutually reinforcing religious and secular ideas, norms and values, including the championing of human rights which includes religious freedom, democracy, and social welfare.

Notes

1   In February and March 2002 the Washington-based, Pew Research Council conducted a survey of 2,002 adults in the USA. Questions about religious preference were included. The results were as follows: Christian 84 per cent, Jewish 1 per cent, Muslims <1 per cent, 'Other non-Christian' 1 per cent, No religious belief 13 per cent, Don't know 1 per cent (Kohut and Rogers, 2002).

2   I am not including America's five to seven million Jews in this survey,
     even though it is widely agreed that Jews have exercised considerable
     influence through the strength of their organizations and leadership,
     with an international political focus that concentrates primarily on pro-
     tection of Israel against its enemies. However, there is not a clear-cut
     American Jewish position in relation to either US domestic or foreign
     policy, primarily because America's Jews are now firmly established
     throughout political circles in the country (Reichley, 1986).

3   A list of more than 80 prominent US televangelists is available at:
     http://en.wikipedia.org/wiki/List_of_U.S._televangelists

4   Bob Woodward of *The Washington Post* said in his book *Plan of Attack*
     (2004) that planning for an invasion of Iraq began in late November
     and December 2001.

5   Freedom Works was founded in 2004, following merger between Citi-
     zens for a Sound Economy and Empower America.

6   Led by Pastor Tom Haggard, and representing 45,000 churches and 30
     million members across the USA, 'sixty member denominations cur-
     rently serve as the foundation for the NAE' (http://
     www.nae.net/index.cfm?FUSEACTION-nae.benefits).

Questions

1   Examine and assess the political impact of the Religious Right on US
     politics under the presidencies of George W. Bush.

2   What are the implications for international relations of US Catholics
     being part of a transnational religious movement concerned with social
     justice and welfare issues?

3   Assess the influence of the Nation of Islam on contemporary US politics.

4   What is an 'evangelized foreign policy' and how does it relate to the
     involvement of religious organizations in current US foreign policy?

5   Do religious norms and values affect how the US government has
     fought the 'War on Terror'?

Bibliography

Abramsky, S. (1996) 'Vote redneck', *The Observer, Life Magazine*, 27 October,
     pp. 16–19.

Associated Press (2004) 'Election reinforces USA's religious schism', *USA
     Today*, 4 November. Available at: http://www.usatoday.com/news/
     politicselections/2004-11-04-religion_x.htm Accessed 11 November
     2005.

Bacevich, A. and Prodromou, E. (2004) 'God is not neutral: religion and U.S. foreign policy after 9/11', *Orbis*, Winter, pp. 43–54.

Bates, S. (2006) 'Wing and a prayer: Religious right got Bush elected – now they are fighting each other', *The Guardian*, May 31.

Bellah, R. (1967) 'Civil religion in America', *Dædalus, Journal of the American Academy of Arts and Sciences*, Winter, 96(1), pp. 1–21.

Bellah, R. (1975; revised edn. 1992) *The Broken Covenant*, Chicago: Uiversity of Chicago Press.

Besser, J. (2004) 'Bush gets 24 percent of Jewish vote – less than GOP hoped for', *The Jewish News* Weekly, 5 November. Available at: http://www. jewishsf.com/content/2-0-/module/displaystory/story_id/24038/format/html/displaystory.html Accessed 11 November 2005.

Bruce, S. (1992) 'Introduction', in S. Bruce (ed.), *Religion and Modernization*, Oxford: Clarendon Press, pp. 1–7.

Casanova, J. (1994) *Public Religions in the Modern World*, Chicago and London: University of Chicago Press.

Coleman, S. (1996) 'Conservative Protestantism, politics and civil religion in the United States', in D. Westerlund (ed.) *Questioning the Secular State: The Worldwide Resurgence of Religion in Politics*, London: Hurst, pp. 24–47.

Crumm, D. and Lords, E. (2002) 'Farrakhan says Bush, not Iraq, is world menace', *Detroit Free Press*, 10 October. Available at: http://www.freep.com/news/locway/farr9_20021009.htm Accessed 17 August 2005.

Dinan, S. (2003) '9/11 spurred war, Rumsfeld says', *Washington Times*, 9 July. Available at: http://washingtontimes.com/national/20030709-114950-9370r.htm Accessed 11 November 2005.

Duin, J. (2004) 'Bush makes significant gains in two polls of Catholic voters', *The Washington Times*, 4 October. Available at: http://www.washingtontimes.com/national/20041004-123844-3867r.htm Accessed 11 November 2005.

Finnemore, M. and Sikkink, K. (1998) 'Norms and international relations theory', *International Organization* 52(4), pp. 887–917.

Fletcher, M. (1994) 'Mullah of Chicago's mean streets', *The Guardian*, 17 February.

Gardell, M. (1996) 'Behold I make all things new! Black militant Islam and the American apocalypse', in D. Westerlund (ed.) *Questioning the Secular State: The Worldwide Resurgence of Religion in Politics*, London: Hurst, pp. 48–74.

Green, J. (2000) *The Diminishing Divide: Religion's Changing Role in American Politics*, Washington, DC: Brookings Institution Press.

Green, J., Rozell, M. and Wilcox, W. (eds) (2003) *The Christian Right in American Politics: Marching to the Millennium*, Washington, DC: Georgetown University Press.

Green, J., Smidt, C., Guth, J. and Kellstedt, L. (2005) 'The American religious landscape and the 2004 presidential vote: increased polarization', Washington, DC: The Pew Forum on Religion and Public Life.

Hacker, J. and Pierson, P. (2005) *Off Center: The Republican Revolution and the Erosion of American Democracy*, New Haven, CI and London: Yale University Press.

Halper, S. and Clarke, J. (2004) *America Alone: The Neo-Conservatives and the Global Order*, Cambridge: Cambridge University Press.

Harris, F. (1999) *Something Within: Religion in African–American Political Activism*, Oxford: Oxford University Press.

Hassner, P. (2002) 'The United States: the empire of force or the force of empire?', Chaillot Paper 54, September, Paris: European Union Institute for Security Studies.

Haynes, J. (1998) *Religion in Global Politics*, Harlow: Longman.

Hehir, J. Bryan., Walzer, M., Richardson, L., Telhami, S., Krauthammer, C. and Lindsay, J. (2004) *Liberty and Power: A Dialogue on Religion and US Foreign Policy in an Unjust World*, Washington, DC: Brookings Institution Press.

Hertzke, A. (1989) 'United States of America', in S. Mews (ed.), *Religion in Politics: A World Guide*, Harlow: Longman, pp. 298–317.

Hertzke, A. (2004) *Freeing God's Children: The Unlikely Alliance for Global Human Rights*, Lanham, MD: Rowman and Littlefield Publishers.

Hudson, M. (2005) 'The United States in the Middle East', in L. Fawcett (ed.), *International Relations of the Middle East*, Oxford: Oxford University Press, pp. 283–305.

Hurd, E. S. (2004) 'The political authority of secularism in international relations', *European Journal of International Relations*, 10(2), June, pp. 235–62.

Jackson, D. (2004) 'Bush's Vatican strategy', *The Boston Globe*, June 15. Available at: http://www.boston.com/news/globe/editorial_opinion/oped/articles/2004/06/15/bushs_vatican_strategy/ Accessed 11 November 2005.

Joyce, K. (2004) 'The Catholic Divide? Culture warriors try again with the "Catholic Divide"', *The Revealer*, 15 June. Available at: http://www. therevealer.org/archives/timely_000426.php Accessed 11 November 2005.

Judis, J. (2005) 'The chosen nation: the influence of religion on US foreign policy', *Policy Brief*, no. 37, March 2005.

Kelley, D. (1986) *Why Conservative Churches are Growing: A Study in Sociology of Religion*, New York: Harper and Row.

Kepel, G. (1994) *The Revenge of God*, Cambridge: Polity.

Kohut, A. and Rogers, M. (2002) 'Americans struggle with religion's role at home and abroad', March 20, Washington, DC: Pew Research Council.

LaFranchi, H. (2006) 'Evangelized foreign policy?', *The Christian Science Monitor*, 2 March. Available at: http://csmonitor.com/2006/0302/p01s01-usfp.htm Accessed 2 June 2006.

Lieven, A. (2004) *America, Right or Wrong: An Anatomy of American Nationalism*, Oxford and New York: Oxford University Press.

Lincoln, C. E. (1973) *The Black Muslims in America*, Boston: Beacon Press.

MacAskill, E. (2006) 'US blocking international deal on fighting Aids', *The Guardian*, 2 June.

Mamiya, L. (1982) 'From Black Muslim to Bilalian: the evolution of a movement', *Journal of the Scientific Study of Religion*, 2(6), pp. 138–51.

Mazarr, M. (2003) 'George W. Bush, idealist', *International Affairs*, 79(3), pp. 503–22.

Mearsheimer, J. and Walt, S. (2006) 'The Israeli lobby and U.S. foreign policy', *The London Review of Books*, 28(6), 23 March. Available at: www.lrb.co.uk Accessed 6 April 2006.

Norris, P. and Inglehart, I. (2004) *Sacred and Secular: Religion and Politics Worldwide*, Cambridge: Cambridge University Press.

Nyang, S. (1988) 'Islam in North America', in S. Sutherland, L. Houlden, P. Clarke and F. Hardy (eds), *The World's Religions*, London: Routledge, pp. 520–9.

Oldfield, D. (2004) 'The evangelical roots of American unilateralism: the Christian Right's influence and how to counter it', *Foreign Policy in Focus*. Available at: http://www.fpif.org/papers/2004evangelical.html Accessed 8 April 2005.

Page, S. (2005) 'Christian Rights' alliances bend political spectrum', *USA Today*, 14 June. Available at: http://www.usatoday.com/news/

washington/2005-06-14-christian-right-cover_x.htm Accessed 2 June 2006.

'Pew Forum on Religion and Public Life' (2003) Conference on 'Theology, morality, and public life', The University of Chicago Divinity School, 26 February. Event transcript available at: http://pewforum.org/events/index.php?EventID=39 Accessed 5 October 2005.

'President Bush discusses freedom in Iraq and Middle East' (2003) 'Remarks by the President at the 20th Anniversary of the National Endowment for Democracy, United States Chamber of Commerce, Washington, D.C.'. Available at: http://www.whitehouse.gov/news/releases/2003/11/20031106-2.html Accessed 5 October 2005.

'President Bush previews historic NATO Summit in Prague' (2002) 'Remarks by the President to Prague Atlantic Student Summit Prague, Czech Republic 22 November, 2002'. Available at: http://usa.usembassy.de/etexts/docs/bush201102.htm Accessed 4 October 2005.

Reichley, A. James. (1986) 'Religion and the future of American politics', *Political Science Quarterly*, 101(1), pp. 23–47.

Reichley, J. (2002) *Faith in Politics*, Washington, DC: Brookings Institution Press.

'Remarks by the President in address to faculty and students of Warsaw University (2002) at Warsaw University, Warsaw, Poland'. Available at: http://www.whitehouse.gov/news/releases/2001/06/20010615-1.html Accessed 4 October 2005.

Rice, C. (2002) 'Remarks by National Security Advisor Condoleezza Rice on Terrorism and Foreign Policy', Paul H. Nitze School of Advanced International Studies, Johns Hopkins University, Kenney Auditorium Washington, DC Text available at: http://www.whitehouse.gov/news/releases/2002/04/20020429-9.html Accessed 11 November 2005.

Robbins, T. and Anthony, D. (1982) *In God We Trust: New Patterns of Religious Pluralism in America*, New Brunswick: Transaction.

Rousseau, J.-J. (2004 [1762]) *The Social Contract*, Harmondsworth: Penguin.

Seipel, R. and Hoover, D. (2004) *Religion and Security: The New Nexus in International Relations*, Lanham, MD: Rowman and Littlefield Publishers.

Smart, N. (1989) *The World's Religions*, Cambridge: Cambridge University Press.

Swanson, A. (2004) 'Analysis: Iraq occupation endangers U.S.', *Washington Times*, 6 May. Available at: http://www.washingtontimes.com/upi-breaking/20040506-042407-9978r.htm Accessed 17 August 2005.

Taylor, M. Lewis (2005) *Religion, Politics, and the Christian Right: Post-9/11 Powers in American Empire*, Minneapolis, MN: Augsburg Fortress Publishers.

Telhami, S. (2004) 'Between faith and ethics', in J. B. Hehir, M. Walzer, L. Richardson, S. Telhami, C. Krauthammer and J. Lindsay, *Liberty and Power. A Dialogue on Religion and U.S. Foreign Policy in an Unjust World*, Washington, DC: Brookings Institution Press, pp. 71–84.

Thomas, S. (2005) *The Global Resurgence of Religion and the Transformation of International Relations: The Struggle for the Soul of the Twenty-First Century*, New York and Basingstoke: Palgrave Macmillan.

de Tocqueville, A. (2003 [1835]) *Democracy in America: And Two Essays on America*, Harmondsworth: Penguin.

Wald, K. (1991) 'Social change and political response to the silent religious cleavage in North America', in G. Moyser (ed.), *Religion and Politics in the Modern World*, London: Routledge, pp. 239–84.

Wald, K. (2003) *Religion and Politics in the United States*, 4th edn, Lanham, MD: Rowman and Littlefield.

Walker, M. (1996) 'Praying for a God-fearing president', *The Guardian*, 7 February.

'What World Leaders Say About RFE/RL [Radio Free Europe/ Radio Liberty]' (2002) Available at: http://www.rferl.org/about/impact/bush.asp Accessed 2 August 2005.

Further reading

J. Green, *The Diminishing Divide: Religion's Changing Role in American Politics*, Brookings Institution Press, 2000. Green focuses on religion's influence on American political attitudes and behaviour. The USA, a profoundly religious nation that nonetheless sought to build an impenetrable wall between church and state, is a country where religion and politics are tightly interwoven. Religion has been a powerful moral and cultural force since the nation's founding, but its influence on politics was more subtle in the past, when most presidents and other political leaders considered their religious beliefs to be private. Since the 1980s, however, presidents and presidential candidates have all been quick to express their faith in God. In addition, many citizens – both on left and right – readily acknowledge the importance of religion in guiding their political beliefs and participation. The author argues that religion will continue to alter the political landscape in the current century, perhaps in unexpected ways.

J. Bryan Hehir, M. Walzer, L. Richardson, S. Telhami, C. Krauthammer, and
J. Lindsay, *Liberty and Power: A Dialogue on Religion and US Foreign Policy
in an Unjust World*, Brookings Institution Press, 2004. What role should
religion play in shaping and implementing US foreign policy? Over the
last 50 years, the dominant attitude in the USA on this topic was expressed well by Dean Acheson, Harry Truman's Secretary of State: 'Moral
talk was fine preaching for the Final Day of Judgment, but it was not a
view I would entertain as a public servant'. Now, however, things are
changing. A key question is: How does the USA 'commit itself to freedom' in relation to foreign aid, economic sanctions and military intervention? Moral and faith traditions have much to say about what is
required to achieve this end. And after 9/11, few can seriously doubt the
importance of religious beliefs in influencing relations among peoples
and nations. The contributors to this volume come at the issue from
very different perspectives and offer exceptional and unexpected insights on a question now at the forefront of American foreign policy.

J. Reichley, *Faith in Politics*, Brookings Institution Press, 2002. In this book,
Reichley explores the history of religion in American public life. He
considers several questions that will likely affect future participation
by religious groups in the formation of public policy. The context is
that active participation in electoral politics by some religious groups
has fuelled apprehensions that the traditional separation of church
and state may be threatened.

R. Seipel and D. Hoover, *Religion and Security: The New Nexus in International
Relations*, Rowman and Littlefield Publishers, 2004. Many would agree
that in the context of global security today, religion is not only part of
the problem but also part of the solution. This book explores issues
where religion and security interact, paying particular attention to the
resources within the Abrahamic faith traditions of Judaism, Christianity and Islam that foster sustainable peace. It also seeks to place the
role of the USA in this regard in a wider international context.

M. Lewis Taylor, *Religion, Politics, and the Christian Right: Post-9/11 Powers in
American Empire*, Augsburg Fortress Publishers, 2005. Taylor analyses
right-wing Christian movements in post-9/11 USA. He argues that militant Christian faith must be viewed against a backdrop of American
political romanticism as well as corporatist liberalism in the USA, both
historically and at the present time. He presents an innovative framework for interpreting how Christian nationalists, Pentagon war plan-
ners and corporate institutions today are forging alliances in the USA
that have significant impacts both at home and abroad.

CHAPTER 9

Europe

There is broad agreement that in Europe,[1] especially the Continent's western portion, religion has changed significantly over time, largely owing to the compartmentalization of societies and the reduced power of churches. While one school of thought believes that this is a continuous trend (Gauchet, 1985; Luhmann, 1989; Bruce, 2002; Wilson, 2003; Hirst, 2003), other theorists focus on the regional picture outlook, arguing that religion is still institutionally and politically powerful in many European societies (Casanova, 1994, 2005; Berger, 1999; Davie, 2000, 2002). In addition, many Europeans still perceive themselves to be differentiated or affected by religious and/or cultural criteria; some are of relevance to political outcomes, manifested in various ways (Davie, 2000, 2002). They include:

■ *Catholic/Protestant divisions, especially in Northern Ireland and to an extent in Germany.* In the former, religious–cultural divisions are the main social basis of competing political parties, such as the nationalist Sinn Fein and the loyalist Democratic Unionist Party and Ulster Unionist Party.

■ *Religious differences, roughly along right–left political lines, internal to the main confessional traditions.* In Britain, for example, there is the cross-party, socially conservative Movement for Christian Democracy, while both France and Italy also have Christian political movements.

■ *A variety of church–state relationships.*

However, while such concerns are intermittently important in some domestic European political contexts, they do not usually form part of the region's international relations. In this chapter we examine a key issue in relation to Europe's current domestic and international concerns: Islam, with a focus on the following issues:

- *The impact of globalization on the religious, political and social position of Europe's Muslim minorities.* For most European Muslims, Islam is an important basis of identity which can impact upon various social and political concerns.

- *European fears of Islamic extremism.* This issue came to the fore largely as a result of the September 11, 2001, New York and Pentagon attacks, and the Madrid and London bombings in March 2004 and July 2005 respectively.

- *Muslim Turkey's bid to join the European Union.* Fears of Islamic extremism encourage some Europeans to oppose Turkey's bid to join the European Union. Would Europe's 'Christian cultural identity' be diluted by the admission of Turkey, with its 70 million, mostly Muslim, people?

This chapter is divided into three sections. The first examines the social and political position of Muslims in Europe, focusing on the recent impact of globalization. The second section looks at the impact of transnational Islamic ideas in relation to Britain and France, where two recent issues have highlighted the position of Muslims in both countries. In Britain, the issue was the July 7, 2005, London bombings. In France, a focus on Islam was provided by the Paris riots of October–November 2005. Some commentators claimed that the riots were indicative of a new trend in France: alienated youths from Muslim backgrounds did not see themselves primarily as French but as Muslims, part of the global Islamic *ummah*, empowered and radicalized by extremist ideas.

In the third section, we examine Turkey's controversial application to join the European Union (EU). We discuss the opposition of some EU member states, political leaders and populations to countenance the entry of Turkey to the EU, primarily because it would mean that a large Muslim country – Turkey has a population of more than 70 million people, of whom 99 per cent are Muslims – would join the Union. The fear is that this would not only result in an 'unacceptable dilution' of the EU's claimed 'Christian' cultural characteristics but also further open up Europe to infiltration from Muslim extremism. The chapter's main conclusion is that in Europe, the religious, social and political importance of Islam is consequential in various ways for the region's internal and international relations.

Globalization and Islam in Europe

The extent to which globalization weakens the power of national govern-ments is a matter of debate. Many would, however, agree that despite sig-nificant changes in recent decades, in international relations the nation-state remains the chief wielder of power. Hirst and Thompson (1999) define the legitimacy of the democratic nation-state as its ability to represent the people inhabiting its territory. The more ethnically diverse the people, the more potentially complicated this becomes. However, through a sufficient degree of cultural homogenization, various peoples living together in a national territory can identify both with the state and each other. Rosenau's (1997) concept of 'the Frontier' highlights a factor that poten-tially complicates homogenization. This refers to a new or newly relevant divide emerging from the fact that many nations, including in Europe, now consist of citizens related to countries with which the nation has 'foreign affairs'. And, since domestic and foreign politics increasingly engage with the same issues, the result is that traditional distinction between the two previously autonomous spheres dissolves (Haynes, 2005), in some cases replaced by a new dividing line between citizens.

In Europe, the concept of 'the Frontier' is said to be relevant to the rela-tions between the Muslim minority and host populations. The issue came into sharp focus following the US/British punitive actions in Afghanistan (2001) and Iraq (2003), with repercussions for domestic politics – serious reductions in political support among Muslims for both President George W. Bush in the USA and Prime Minister Tony Blair in Britain, with many among Britain's Muslim community regarding the actions as fundamentally 'anti-Muslim' (Pew Global Attitudes Project Report, 2005). Further problems emerged in 2005 following the publication of the infamous Muhammad cartoons in a Danish newspaper, *Jyllands-Posten* (in English, *The Morning Newspaper/The Jutland Post*).[2]

The controversy erupted after twelve cartoons were published in the news-paper on 30 September 2005. Several of the cartoons portrayed the Prophet Muhammad and some seemed to equate him with terrorism. The purpose, the newspaper claimed, was to contribute to a continuing debate regarding criticism of Islam and self-censorship. The effect, however, was almost cer-tainly not what the newspaper intended, as publication of the cartoons was followed by public protests from Danish Muslim organizations,[3] which helped to disseminate knowledge about them around the world. The controversy swiftly grew, with newspapers in over 50 countries reprinting some or all of the cartoons. The result was often violent protests in many countries, especially in the Muslim world. Both *Jyllands-Posten* – whose office received a bomb threat in January 2006 – and Denmark became a focus of Muslim anger. Demonstrators in the Gaza Strip (Palestinian territory) burned Danish flags; Saudi Arabia and Libya withdrew their ambassadors to Denmark; Danish goods were boycotted across the Middle East, and many Middle Eastern and Asian countries saw violent clashes, with demonstrators attacking the Danish and Norwegian Embassies in Tehran and thousands of protesters taking to the streets in Egypt, the West Bank, Jordan and Afghanistan (Bright, 2006). Overall, the main complaints expressed by critics of the cartoons were that they were both Islamophobic and blasphemous. Their purpose was to humiliate a marginalized Danish minority and more generally to insult Islam. In February 2006 Denmark's prime minister Anders Fogh Rasmussen announced that the Prophet Muhammad cartoons controversy was Denmark's worst international crisis since the Second World War ('70,000 gather for violent Pakistan cartoons protest', 2006).

In Egypt, a government-owned newspaper, *Al-Gomhuria*, stated on 2 February 2006: 'It is not a question of freedom of opinion or belief. It is a conspiracy against Islam and Muslims which has been in the works for years. The international community should understand that any attack against our prophet will not go unpunished'. From Jeddah, Saudi Arabia, a journalist, Amr Al-Faisal, writing in the pro-government *Arab News,* commented on 6 February: 'Muslims are not doing enough to stop the aggression of Western countries, shown by the incident of the Muhammad cartoons. This aggression stems from their weakness'. Al-Faisal proposed a gradual boycott of Western economies coupled with increased self-reliance on Muslim manufacturing capacity ('Muslims voice anger over Muhammad cartoons', 2006).

Supporters of the cartoons claim they illustrate an important issue in an age of Islamist religious terrorism: their publication exercises the right of free speech which the extremists abhor. In addition, the furore illustrated the intolerance of Muslims: similar cartoons about other religions are often printed, supporters claimed, illustrating that Muslims were not being targeted in a discriminatory fashion. In Amman, Jordan, a weekly tabloid newspaper, *Al-Shihan* published three of the cartoons on 1 February 2006, accompanied by pleas for Muslims of the world to 'be reasonable'. Jihad Momani, the editor-in-chief, explained his decision to print because 'people are attacking drawings that they have not even seen'. His action was not, however, accepted in the spirit that he claimed it would be: Momani was swiftly removed from his post and the newspapers withdrawn from the newsstands ('Muslims voice anger over Muhammad cartoons', 2006).

There were international attempts to dampen down the furore. The Organization of the Islamic Conference (OIC) joined the United Nations and European Union in appealing for calm over the Prophet Muhammad cartoons. A statement attributed to the OIC secretary-general, Ekmeleddin Ihsanoglu, along with the UN secretary general, Kofi Annan, and EU foreign policy chief, Javier Solana, said: 'We are deeply alarmed at the repercussions of the publication in Denmark several months ago of insulting caricatures of the Prophet Muhammad and their subsequent republication by some other European newspapers, and at the violent acts that have occurred in reaction to them' (statement quoted in Bilefsky, 2006).

However, Iran attempted to take the lead among Muslims in the controversy. European Union officials expressed concern that Iran, increasingly isolated over its nuclear programme in late 2005 and early 2006, was said to be seeking to exploit the crisis to try to unite the Muslim world against the West (Tisdall, 2006). Iran's largest selling newspaper, *Hamshahri*, announced it was sponsoring a contest to draw cartoons caricaturing the Holocaust in response to the publishing in European papers of caricatures of the Prophet Muhammad. It said that 'private individuals' would offer gold coins to the best 12 artists – the same number of cartoons that appeared in *Jyllands-Posten*. The purpose of the competition, according to the newspaper, was to turn the tables on the assertion that newspapers can print offensive material in the name of freedom of expression ('Muslims voice anger over Muhammad cartoons', 2006).

In sum, the Prophet Muhammad cartoons controversy underlines how the issue of Islam and the position of Muslims in European countries generates intense debate both in Europe and around the world.

Islam and identity in Europe

In many European countries, Islam is usually associated with communities of fairly recent immigrant origin. Muslim immigration largely occurred in the 1970s and 1980s, a time of European regional economic recession and an international environment characterized by international friction between Muslims and the West following Iran's revolution (Cesari and McLoughlin, 2005). In recent years, Muslim numbers have continued to increase as a consequence of children born to Muslim immigrants, as well as conversions. Over time, many Muslims, especially among the second generation, have become politicized, in part because of the impact of globalization.

In his study of construction of Hong Kong identity after Hong Kong's incorporation into China in 1997, Mathews (2000) offers a useful methodological approach to globalization and identity that can be applied to Muslims in Europe. Mathews distinguishes between the state as constructor of culture in the nationalistic sense of 'the people's way of life', related to institutionalized practices, and the global 'cultural supermarket' as producer of free-floating culture items, objects of individual choice. Thus an individual constructs their self-identity in relation to both – and can choose between self-identity as an 'authentic national culture', or a 'completely different' culture, or 'something in between', by combining ethnicity and values. In the Hong Kong example, identity is Chinese ethnicity *plus* democracy/rule of law/human rights/freedom/gender equality, 'plus' being values associated with 'international' British-ruled Hong Kong as opposed to authoritarian 'isolationist' China. Simultaneously, mainland Chinese moving to Hong Kong identified themselves with the same values, to the incredulous chagrin of 'authentic' Hong Kong inhabitants (Mathews, 2000). Mobility and global culture-shopping also give rise to transnational communities whose values and identities are constructed in dialectical relation to both new countries and countries of origins, and therefore cannot be explained simply in terms of one over the other (Kennedy and Roudometof, 2002; Roy, 2004) From this viewpoint, it is possible to argue that ethnicity and culture constitute 'forms' of self-identity which can be filled with different 'value-contents'.

Islam and identity in Europe

In the context of Muslims in Europe, the issue of identity is sometimes controversial among 'second' or 'third' generation Muslims, usually offspring of immigrant parents or grandparents. Such people may experiment with ethnic and national identity in ways that differ from their parents' more fixed identities (Cesari and McLoughlin, 2005). This is especially apparent in recent years when the issue of 'European identity' has been widely discussed and debated, including in the context of Islam. It contrasts with the position a few decades ago when Islam was virtually unknown for most non-Muslim Europeans, with the faith physically manifested in only a few mosques in some major European cities. The situation began to change with the expansion of labour migration in the 1970s. Initially, Muslim immigrants were principally defined by the host society vis-à-vis their economic function (for example, in Germany where Turks were referred to as *gastarbeiter*, or 'guest workers'), their skin colour or their nationality, and

(Continued)

only to a lesser extent by culture and/or religion. According to Nonneman, 'this reflected the migrants' own perception of their place in their European surroundings, and their relative lack of concern with opportunities for socio-religious expression within the context of the host society' (Nonneman, 1996: 382).

The religious and cultural dimension of Islam emerged as an important social and political issue from the late 1970s. It was largely 'the unforeseen consequence of the drastic change in European immigration policy at the time of the 1972–4 recession' (Nielsen, 1992: 2). Although most European governments halted further labour immigration, many did allow family unification. The result was that the Muslim presence in Europe changed from one essentially of migrant workers to social communities in a fuller sense. Contacts and interactions between Muslims immigrants and host societies increased. By the late 1980s, there were collectively about five million Muslims in Britain, France and Germany – countries where male Muslim 'guest workers' families were allowed to join them. Many Muslims became increasingly politicized, especially those of the 'second generation', the offspring of migrant workers and their spouses. Born in Europe, they were familiar from the start with Western assumptions about political participation. In some countries – for example, Britain and France – it was relatively easy to acquire citizenship. An effect of the accompanying expectations on the part of these Muslims became apparent in their increased willingness to agitate for what they perceived as their social, political and economic rights.

Islamic 'fundamentalism' and globalization: the impact on Europe

This coincided with the intrusion of various international events and concerns into the domestic scenes of many European countries – including the issue of 'Islamic fundamentalism' following Iran's 1979 revolution. There was also a significant phase in the expansion of globalization from the 1980s, reflected in various media reporting international issues in greater depth than previously. Partly as a result of real or perceived discrimination and insensitivity to cultural differences, some European Muslims – especially among the second generation born in Europe – identified with fellow Muslims' political causes in the Middle East, including the Palestinians' struggle for a homeland and the goals of the Iranian revolution. Sections of public opinion in the host societies reacted by focusing

(Continued)

on the perceived excesses of 'Islamic fundamentalism', for example in Iran or Saudi Arabia, and claimed that European Muslims were a threat to political and social stability because they too were likely to be 'Islamic fundamentalists'. This was also a time of relatively high unemployment in many European countries, a situation encouraging and generating hostility towards Muslims. The overall result was increasing friction between Muslim and host communities in various European countries from the 1980s and 1990s (Amiraux, 2005).

While 'Islamic fundamentalism' (or Islamism) is often perceived as religiosity with an *individualized* focus, it can also be thought of as an *institutional* alternative to Islam's relationship with liberal values in Europe. Islamists typically see 'Western liberalism' as both unauthentic and antipathetic to their culture and religion (Marty and Appleby, 1997; Hirst and Thompson, 1999; Turner, 1994, 2000; Roy, 2004). As a 'cultural authenticity-brand', Islamism is sometimes regarded as comparable to other global religious 'roots-movements', including New Age, Spirituality, Neo-paganism and Occultism (Roy, 2004; Katz, 2005). A focus on Islamism also provides a useful illustration of the relation between research and identity. Although Islamism is a marginal type of religiosity, it now dominates research and public debate to the extent that in both Europe and the USA 'Islam' is often identified unthinkingly with 'Islamic fundamentalism' (Roy, 2004; Sen, 2006).

Olivier Roy on Islamic fundamentalism

The French author and analyst of Islam, Olivier Roy, argues that to counter European fundamentalist constructions of Islam, it is necessary to raise, significantly, public awareness of the majority of Muslims in Europe. According to Roy, many 'do all those things fundamentalists say Muslims should not do', including: selling and drinking alcohol, voting for secular parties, having non-Muslim friends, marrying non-Muslims – yet they still consider themselves to be good Muslims (Roy, 2004).

Roy's comments raise an important question: To what extent, if at all, is there an inevitable and unbridgeable incompatibility between Muslims in Europe, their values, norms and beliefs, and the secular organizing principles of non-Muslim European societies? Esposito (2002), Ayubi (1991) and Piscatori (1986) contend that there is no real incompatibility because Islam is primarily pragmatic, with separation between, on the one hand, religious principles and institutions and, on the other, the temporal ruler and the state. As a result,

(Continued)

Piscatori (1986) contends, there are not only grounds for expectations of compatibility between Islamic precepts and the 'world of nation-states' but also no impracticable obstacles of principle to a reasonable degree of compatibility between 'Islamic' and 'Western' practices regarding citizenship and the nature of socio-political organization. As Nonneman notes, 'European Muslims' reactions (themselves varying strongly) may often be less a matter of "Islamic practice" than of a cultural minority's sense of discrimination leading to a search for rallying points' (Nonneman, 1996: 384).

This is not to suggest that Muslims in Europe are necessarily complaisant about the norms, values and practices they encounter. Muslim leaders often express concern for the development of their faith and its adherents, especially in relation to the moral well-being of the young. For many Muslims, Western society is essentially meaningless, rootless, characterized by crime, juvenile delinquency, riots, collapse of marriages, and sexual promiscuity (Ahmed, 1992). Some Muslims believe that Islam could provide an alternative and appropriate lifestyle satisfactorily contrasting with European secular societies' crass materialism and selfishness. In a bid to achieve this goal, some Muslims in Europe choose to pursue the goal of Islamicization via what Roy (2004) calls 'neo-fundamentalism'. 'Neo-fundamentalism' refers to a transnational Islamic community emerging from Europe and constructed largely through the internet. It identifies Muslim identity as *sharia*, but breaks with traditional Islamic jurisprudence in which Muslim minorities are obliged only to follow *sharia* ritual, not its legislation (Roy, 2004). Within this parameter, the call for *sharia* has widely different implications. The francophone Swiss Muslim intellectual and scholar, Tariq Ramadan, advocates liberal reform of *sharia*, but nevertheless challenges existing European models of citizenship by explicitly making *sharia* the guiding principle for Muslim citizens. Combined with his call for European Muslims to represent the oppressed South against Western neo-liberal imperialism, his message is potentially divisive (Ramadan, 2003: 172ff.)

Ramadan, who was named by *Time* magazine in 2000 as one of the 100 most important innovators of the twenty-first century, argues that Islam can and should feel at home in the West.[4] In *Western Muslims and the Future of Islam* (2003), Ramadan focuses on Islamic law (*sharia*) and tradition in order to analyse whether Islam is in conflict with Western ideals. According to Ramadan, there is no contradiction between them. He also identifies several key areas where Islam's universal principles can be 'engaged' in the West, including education, inter-religious dialogue, economic resistance and spirituality. As the number of Muslims living in the West grows, the question of what it means to be a Western Muslim becomes increasingly important to the futures of both Islam and the West. While the media are focused on radical Islam, Ramadan claims, a silent revolution is sweeping Islamic communities in the West, as Muslims actively seek ways to live in harmony with their faith within a Western context. French, English, German, and American Muslims, both women and men, are reshaping their religion into one that is faithful to the principles of Islam, dressed in European and American cultures, and definitively rooted in Western societies. Let us examine Ramadan's ideas in relation to Muslims living in Britain and France.

Tariq Ramadan on the 'Islamic state'

The goal of the Swiss intellectual, Tariq Ramadan, is to create an independent Western Islam, anchored not in the traditions of Islamic countries but in the cultural reality of the West. He urges a fresh reading of Islamic sources, in order to interpret them for a Western context. This would enable a new understanding of universal Islamic principles that could open the door to integration into Western societies. He then shows how these principles can be put to practical use. Ramadan also contends that Muslims can – indeed *must* – be faithful to their principles while participating fully in the civic life of Western secular societies. In his book, *Western Muslims and the Future of Islam* (2003), Ramadan offers a striking vision of a new Muslim identity, one which rejects once and for all the idea that Islam must be defined in opposition to the West.

Britain

Britain is home to approximately 1.6 million Muslims, comprising people originally from Pakistan, Bangladesh, Africa, Cyprus, Malaysia, the Middle East and, most recently, Eastern Europe (primarily Bosnia-Herzegovina). Until the 1960s, Islam was a relatively obscure religion in Britain; there were only a few mosques in major cities, including Cardiff, Liverpool, Manchester, South Shields and London's East End. The situation changed with the expansion of Muslim labour migration in the 1970s. At this time, as a result of a change in immigration policy, British governments halted further labour immigration, while allowing family unification (Nielsen, 1992: 2). As a result, the Muslim presence in Britain changed from one of primarily migrant workers to social communities in a fuller sense. As a result, contacts significantly increased between Muslim families and the British host society.

During the 1980s, some Muslims – especially among the second generation, offspring of first-generation immigrants and their spouses – became increasingly politicized and in some cases politically active. Such people, with British citizenship and familiar with British assumptions about political participation, began to demand what they saw as their rights. At the same time, a backlash began against some British Muslims from some sections of existing British society. This was in part a consequence of increased fears of 'Islamic fundamentalism', often linked to Iran's 1979 revolution, and more generally with increased Islamic militancy in many parts of the Muslim world. Some sections of British public opinion believed that British Muslim communities were hotbeds of 'Islamic fundamentalism', posing a threat to peace and social stability (McLoughlin, 2005).

Some British Muslims, especially among the young, began increasingly to identify with struggles of fellow Muslims in Israel-controlled Palestinian-majority lands and elsewhere, with some radicals organizing themselves into 'a huge web of Islamic associations of various shades of feeling and opinion' (Kepel, 1994: 37; Ramadan, 2006). Such organizations included: the Young Muslims, Al Muntada al Islami, Muslim Welfare House, Al-Muhajiroun, and Hizb ut-Tahrir; collectively they represented a range of Islamist positions. Hizb ut-Tahrir is often regarded as one of the most radical of such groups. Hizb ut-Tahrir, an Arabic term that translates as the 'party of liberation', is a radical political organization with members throughout the Muslim world and in countries, such as Britain, with significant Muslim populations. An Islamic jurist, Taqiuddin an-Nabhani, formed the organization in Jerusalem in 1953.[5] Hizb ut-Tahrir activists called for Muslim separation from Western society, employing 'anti-Israel, anti-homosexual, anti-liberal rhetoric' (Dodd, 1996).

According to Ansari, some young Muslims in Britain were attracted to Hizb ut-Tahrir and other radical groups because of their deep sense of injustice. He argues that such sentiments increased over time because of 'a huge rise in the number of attacks on Muslims in Britain, increasing threats to civil liberties in the name of security measures, a resurgence in the activities of the far-right in Britain and elsewhere in Europe, and a crackdown on refugees fleeing persecution' (Ansari, 2002: 1). Reflecting such concerns, many British Muslims were said to be concerned primarily about two main issues, one domestic and one external. These were, respectively, defence of their culture and religion, especially in relation to their children's education in Britain. The second was linked to issues of terrorism and international security, especially prominent and focused following the US–British assault on Afghanistan in 2001, the campaign two years later to oust Saddam Hussein in Iraq and the continuing but inconclusive bid to pacify the country's insurgency.

Muslims and education in Britain

The education of their children was a key issue for large numbers of Muslim parents in Britain. In many cases this was linked to a strong desire to safeguard their religion and culture in a strongly secular society. Many British Muslims wanted segregated education – believed necessary in order to prevent young Muslims drifting away from their faith and culture (Travis, 2004). Many Muslim parents wanted their children's school curriculum to include: teachings of Islam, with school prayer facilities; celebrations of the main Muslim festivals, Eid ul Fitr and Eid ul Adha; and exemption from sex education. They also wanted schools to offer halal food and to allow wearing of appropriately 'modest' clothing, especially for girls (Goulborne and Joly, 1989: 92–4). But despite Muslim demands, such conditions were rarely fully met in state schools in Britain. As a result, increasing numbers of Muslim children withdrew from state education, with numbers of Muslim schools in Britain growing more than four times from 24 in the mid-1990s to over 100 in 2002, entrusted with the task of educating over 10,000 Muslim children (Ahmad, 2002). A 2004 opinion survey of 500 British Muslims indicated that, if available, nearly half would send their child to a Muslim school rather than a conventional – that is, secular – state school. Since only a small fraction of Muslim children are already in Muslim schools, this represents a huge latent demand for separate religious schooling. The demand is said to be greatest among men, younger families and the more affluent (Travis, 2004).

Many British Muslims were very concerned about events associated with 9/11, including the wars in Afghanistan and Iraq and their consequences. An opinion survey in March 2004 found that many British Muslims expressed little desire to integrate fully with the host culture and people, a view partly founded in anti-Western resentment at US and UK involvement in Iraq, seen by many simply as a 'war on Islam'. The poll also showed that many British Muslims saw George W. Bush and Tony Blair's continuing 'war against terrorism' as a facet of a more general 'Western' war against both Islam as a faith and Muslims as a group. Finally, nearly two-thirds (64 per cent) believed that Britain's stringent anti-terrorist laws were being used unfairly against Britain's Muslim community (Travis, 2004). While it is not yet clear what their motives were, it seems highly likely that Britain's home-grown Islamist bombers who struck on 7 July 2005 with four bomb attacks in London killing over 50 people were likely motivated at least in part by a deep sense of grievance and injustice at what they perceived as punitive Western policies against Muslims in Afghanistan, Iraq, Israel's occupied territories, and elsewhere.

In sum, the likelihood of the achievement of the kind of aims expressed by Tariq Ramadan for Western Muslims may be seriously undermined by the existence of grievances, both domestic and international. Unless they are resolved, Muslim criticisms of the status quo might significantly undercut chances of the development of a 'Western Islam' advocated by Ramadan and other figures, including Olivier Roy (2004).

France

France is thought to have three times as many Muslims as Britain, around five million people, 7–8 per cent of the population. It is thought that about half have French citizenship, although precise figures are unavailable. This is because the French state is officially secular and officials are forbidden to ask citizens questions about their religion or ethnicity. It is often asserted, however, that while still preponderantly Catholic, France now has more Muslims than Jews or Protestants, historically the country's most significant religious minorities. Overall, Islam is now probably the country's second religion in terms of numbers of followers (Caeiro, 2005: 71).

Growth in the numbers of Muslims in France came, as in Britain, initially by immigration. Most came from France's former North African colonies, including Algeria and Morocco. Although a presence from around the time of the First World War, Muslims arrived in significant numbers in France only in the 1960s. At this time, the government granted asylum to hundreds of thousands of Algerians who had fought on the French side in Algeria's 1954–62 war of independence. During the same decade, France also invited immigrant workers, including many Muslims, to meet the needs of the country's then booming economy. The economic boom soon fizzled out but by the 1970s there were substantial numbers of Muslims in most of France's main towns and cities.

Like Britain, France has had a policy of 'zero immigration' since the 1970s. However, France's Muslim population still increases because of relatively high birth rates, an unknown number of illegal entrants, particularly from Africa, and an exception that allows the reunion of immigrant families. The purpose of the exception makes clear French policy in regard to its Muslims: to legitimize them in French society by integrating them into it. This policy contrasts with that of Britain, where governmental strategy has long been that of 'multiculturalism', that is, encouraging development of separate cultures in an overall context of 'Britishness'.

Successive French governments have claimed to want to integrate the country's Muslims into French society. This implies reducing overt signs of 'Muslim-ness', especially particularistic forms of dress, such as the *hijab* ('Islamic veil'). Reflecting this concern, the so-called 'headscarves of Creil affair' erupted in late 1989, focusing on the desire of several young Muslim women to wear Islamic headscarves at school in the seaside town of Creil. The affair was portrayed in the French media as an attempt to introduce 'communalism' into schools, a traditionally neutral sphere. To explain the passion that this issue raised it is important to note that France is the country where the Enlightenment began, leading to the presumption that the common ground for the French is their 'rationality', implying that religion takes a decidedly secondary position. Now, many French people are highly secular, perceiving visible signs of what they see as religious identity, such as the *hijab*, to be highly disturbing, because they believe it undermines basic French values of secularism (Caeiro, 2005: 78–80).

As in Britain, Islamic networks grew in France during the 1980s and 1990s. Members comprised mainly students and other young people, whose parents were mostly from Algeria or Morocco. Some Islamic activists wanted to stage a trial of strength by confronting the French state on the sensitive ground of *laïcité* (secularism) (Kepel, 1994: 40). The issue seemed to strike a chord with many French Muslims who, it appeared, also wanted 'positive discrimination' in favour of Muslim girls in French state schools. Student militants appointed themselves as the spokesmen of 'Islam', seeking to negotiate 'positive discrimination' for practising Muslims enabling them to withdraw, in some contexts, from French law and replace it with *sharia* law. The Islamic militants found powerful allies in the campaign from other religious entities, including leaders of the French Catholic Church and some Jewish rabbis, who supported them because they too were determined to seek a renewal of their faiths in the face of what they regarded as an increasingly strident *laïcité* (Kepel, 1994: 41). Eventually, despite the protestations of the religious groups, the French national assembly voted overwhelmingly in February 2004 in favour of a ban on the *hijab* and other 'conspicuous' religious symbols in state schools, despite warnings from religious leaders that the law would persecute Muslims and encourage 'Islamic fundamentalism'. The national assembly voted 494–36 in favour of banning 'conspicuous' religious symbols in schools.[6] The law, ratified by the senate in

March 2004, came into effect the following September (Henley, 2004). A total of 78 per cent of French people favoured such a prohibition (as did smaller majorities in Germany (54 per cent) and the Netherlands (51 per cent), Pew Global Attitudes Project Report, 2005).

French Muslims' domestic concerns overlapped with international issues, including the invasions of Afghanistan and Iraq in 2001 and 2003 respectively. Unlike the British government, however, that of France was strongly opposed to the invasion. Did France's large Muslim minority help determine French policy? Such a question is hard to answer, but it does seem clear that President Chirac welcomed (1) the renewed bond between the Muslim community and the rest of the French population that resulted from a common opposition to the war in Iraq, and (2) the boost to his personal popularity that he would no doubt gain from the anti-war stance.

Given this apparent meeting of minds between President Chirac and France's Muslim communities over opposition to the invasions, how can we explain and account for the riots primarily involving youths of Muslim origin that erupted in Paris soon after, in October 2005, and spread to other towns and cities?[7] Two broad arguments have been expressed to explain why they occurred. One was linked to the perceived impact of globalization, the other to domestic factors. According to Watson and Jones (2005),

> The world watches in trepidation as the wildfires of chaos sweep from France across Europe. We are witnessing the fruits of globalization. Rampant unchecked immigration policies and the enforced fusion of multiculturalism form the backbone of the New World Order's systematic purge of the sleeping middle class.

This view expresses what might be called the 'clash of civilizations' argument, whereby the riots were seen in the context of a polarized conflict between 'Western civilization' and 'Islamic fundamentalism'. However, according to de Koning, many of the rioters seemed more in tune with American rappers and spoke in French, not Arabic. Yet this did not prevent a number of prominent French people, including a well-known intellectual and academic, Alain Finkielkraut, and Interior Minister, Nicolas Sarkozy, claiming that the riots were linked to the 'inability' of Muslims to live according to French norms and values. In this view, those who believed that the source of the riots was to be found outside Islam were naive (de Koning, 2006).

Those who claimed that France's riot problem was rooted in domestic factors expressed a second view. Some argued that it was the result of unemployment, a consequence of the country's adhesion to the European Social

Model with attendant high wages, leading to high unemployment, especially among Muslim youths in the *banlieues* of major cities, including Paris (Astier, 2005). Few – certainly not from the peaceful majority in the suburbs whose cars and schools were torched – argued that violence was a legitimate way to express grievances. Yet, what for many was beyond question, the rioting was *not* an affirmation of a distinct religious or ethnic identity, buoyed by a transnational network of Islamists. According to a French sociologist, Laurent Chambon, the riots were not about 'youth gangs inspired by radical Islam'; instead, they were part of a movement against the 'precariousness' of everyday life in the French *banlieues*, that is, the riots were the product of alienation and existential angst (de Koning, 2006: 30).

Overall, few if any French commentators found an ethnic or religious component to the protests. 'Very few in the suburbs are saying: black (or brown) is beautiful. Their message is the exact opposite: neither the colour of our skins nor our names should make us less than fully French' (Astier, 2005). Neither were the riots prompted by religion. On the other hand, many among the urban youths who rioted would define themselves as Muslims, in a way that they would not have done ten or fifteen years ago (de Koning, 2006). In addition, it may well be that the 2004 ban on the wearing of the headscarf in public schools – more accurately, the 'law on religious signs' (the display of Christian as well as Muslim signifiers was prohibited) – was a factor. On the other hand, very few French Muslims challenged the separation of church and state. Mohammed Elhajjioui, a youth in Lille, claimed that the headscarf ban negated the original, tolerant spirit of French-style secularism which guarantees religious freedom (Astier, 2005). Prior to 2004, courts had upheld the right of girls to wear headscarves in schools. Yet a sense of *religious* grievance was not in evidence during the period of unrest, a six-week time when nearly 3,000 rioters were arrested. Certainly, there was no *intifada* called for by Muslim leaders, and virtually all the mosques appealed for calm (Caeiro, 2006). In short, the *banlieues* (suburbs) were seething with anger, but that anger had nothing to do with a desire to be recognized as separate. Separateness appeared to be endured with resentment, certainly not proclaimed with pride. On the other hand, according to de Koning, the riots and accompanying violence did not express a rejection of French ideals as such, rather a deep sense of frustration that those ideals were not being put into practice for such people (de Koning, 2006). What seems clear was the exact opposite of what Alain Finkielkraut claimed: the violence of October and November revealed how *unsuccessful* extremist Muslim groups had been in significantly penetrating the urban youth culture of the *banlieues*. In short, Islam is not the problem; the problem is that the majority of the residents of the *banlieues* are Muslim and/or black and because of this many have been discriminated against for long periods. The youths were rebelling because they still dreamt of being accepted as French, not because they wanted to separate themselves from mainstream French society. In other words, the riots were the result of a refusal to be marginalized, a manifestation of 'a deep acceptance of fundamental French values expressed in the "coupling of liberty and equality". However, if French society supports Sarkozy's push to crush the violence by cleansing the ghettos of their "troublemakers", the next "intifadah of the cities" could well be in honor not of Marianne, France's national emblem and the personification of liberty and reason, but of Musab al-Zarqawi and his successors' (Levine, 2005).

Alain Finkielkraut on the French riots of November 2005

The French philosopher, Alain Finkielkraut, stated in an interview with an Israeli newspaper, *Ha'aretz*, on 18 November 2005 that the riots were 'anti-white, anti-republican pogroms'. They constituted 'a revolt with an ethno-religious character . . . directed against France as a European country. Against France, with its Christian or Judeo-Christian tradition'. While the Interior Minister, Nicolas Sarkozy, supported Finkielkraut, the latter was heavily criticized in France, leading him to apologise a week later in *Ha'aretz* for his outburst (Ben-Simon, 2005). But his analysis was very popular in the USA, Russia and the Netherlands, three countries that were all concerned in different ways with the issue of Islam and the integration of Muslims into society (de Koning, 2006: 30).

In sum, while many but not all rioters were Muslims, with origins in North and sub-Saharan Africa, 'Islamic fundamentalism' was not a driving force, but anger, frustration, alienation and unemployment were.

Conclusion

Our brief surveys of Britain and France indicate that Islamic extremism is a marginal tendency, seemingly of interest only to small groups of Muslim militants without much in the way of popular support. Figures including Tariq Ramadan and Olivier Roy make the point that Islam can be divided into 'good' and 'bad' versions, driving a more general call for an 'Enlightened' Islam. This implies a Muslim *aggiornamento* (liberalization) as a prerequisite to the integration of Muslims into Western societies – setting the necessary conditions not for a privatization of the faith but for a public Islam (Ramadan, 2003; Roy, 2004, 2005; Peter, 2006).

European attitudes to Muslims in Europe and around the world

In 2005, the Pew Global Attitudes Project conducted an extensive survey among more than 17,000 people in 17 countries – including seven European countries. Pew reported that large majorities in various European countries see a perceived rise in Islamic extremism both in their own countries and around the world as worrisome (Pew Global Attitudes Project, 2005: 3). Table 9.1 indicates that in 2005 large majorities of people in various European countries were 'very' or 'somewhat' concerned about 'Islamic extremism' at home and abroad. There were significant concerns about Islamic extremism, both domestically and internationally, in Russia, Spain, Germany, Britain, The Netherlands and France. Before the 7/7 London terrorist attacks, Britons expressed more concern about extremism around the world than they did at home. Perhaps surprisingly, the 7/7 bombings – when over 50 people were killed – and the abortive attempt to replicate them two weeks later, on 21 July 2005, did not trigger significantly a rise in anti-Muslim prejudice in Britain (Pew Global Attitudes Project Report, 2006).

The Pew findings also indicate that for many Europeans, fears of Islamic extremism are closely associated with worries about Muslim minorities who live in their countries. Many non-Muslim Europeans believe that Muslims living in their countries want to remain distinct from society, not consensually adopt European customs, cultures and lifestyles.

TABLE 9.1 European concerns about Islamic extremism

Country	In your country?(%)		In the world?(%)	
	Very	Somewhat	Very	Somewhat
Russia	52	32	51	33
Spain	43	34	45	37
Germany	35	43	48	39
Britain	34	36	43	37
Netherlands	32	44	46	44
France	32	41	46	43
Poland	7	30	23	39

Source: Pew Global Attitudes Project, 2005: 3

TABLE 9.2 Perceptions of Muslims in European countries

Country	'Muslims want to remain distinct' (%)	'Increasing sense of Islamic identity' (%)
Germany	88	66
Russia	72	55
Spain	68	47
Netherlands	65	60
Britain	61	63
France	59	70
Poland	42	20

Source: Pew Global Attitudes Project, 2005

As indicated in Table 9.2, there is also a widespread perception in many European countries – especially those with significant Muslim minorities, such as Britain, Germany and France – that their resident Muslims have a strong and growing sense of Islamic identity.

In the box below we can see some of the replies that the *International Herald Tribune* received in a series of interviews its reporters conducted with a number of Europeans on the issue of Muslims in Europe in the second half of 2005.[8]

European voices and Muslims in Europe

'I'm not surprised at all that so many people are worried about rising extremism. We all saw what happened in London . . . What if Paris is next? Now when I take the metro I am actually a bit worried. I'm afraid, but I'm also annoyed because some of the Muslims in France are becoming very feisty. Like when they whistled and booed during the *Marseillaise* during a football match between France and Algeria last year. They're in our country because they don't want to be in their own, but they criticize France and more and more of the young ones are now parading their Muslim identity.'

- A 23 year-old newspaper vendor in Paris

'Who are the Muslims? In the economic sphere, they are integrated. I think a recognizable part of the Muslim people want to be distinct. The question is wrong because there are many different kinds of Muslims. My friend has married a Muslim from Syria. She can still wear a short skirt. And her mother-in-law does not wear a head scarf . . . As for the immigration issue, it depends who is coming. Many are not qualified. They think there is a better life here. They will be looked after. They have to be fed. The fear is not just that many

(Continued)

Turks will come to Germany if Turkey joins the EU. It's something else as well. The liberals feel that their liberal values will be undermined'.

- A piano teacher in Berlin

'Certainly since Sept. 11 there is a growing emphasis among Muslims on faith, also among young people. There is a growing distance between them and the rest of Dutch society . . . The most orthodox Muslims tell their fellow believers: Either you are a good Muslim and keep your distance from the Dutch ways, or you integrate and corrupt your faith. There is a large group of Muslims that does not agree with this view . . . So people wonder if it is possible to be a Dutch Muslim. The most orthodox preachers and believers want a cohesive Muslim community which they can control'.

- A sociology professor in Amsterdam

'Muslims in France are seen as people who want to impose their religion on others. It's true that their search for an identity seems to have become a lot more pronounced, especially in the younger generations. Sometimes it annoys me, too. When I go to Sri Lanka and visit a temple I have to put on a veil. Why don't they adapt to our culture here?'

- A 34-year-old immigration researcher at a Paris institute

'You cannot separate the issue of Turkey from domestic politics. There is a very important trend emerging and we see this in the Netherlands. The liberal-thinking people . . . have a feeling that the Muslim identity combined with Turkish accession to the EU is putting into danger what the EU has achieved in the societies . . . that the sexual/gender issues, the honor killings, the head scarves, these could become the lifestyles if it continues like this'.

- A European Union parliamentarian born in Germany of Turkish parents

Source: Pew Global Attitudes Project, 2005: 15

Turkey: 'European state' or 'Muslim country'?

The mixed attitudes expressed in both the Pew survey and the *International Herald Tribune* interviews about Islam in Europe find a focus in the issue of Muslim Turkey's proposed entry into the European Union (EU). This question has inspired many comments from politicians and opinion formers to the effect that Turkey's entry into the EU would not only unacceptably dilute 'European identity' but also open up the region to increased threat from transnational Islamist networks (Gul, 2004). In 2005, two-thirds of French (66 per cent) and Germans (65 per cent) opposed Turkey's EU bid, as did a majority of the Dutch (53 per cent). European nations expressing support for Turkey's admittance to the EU included Spain (68 per cent) and Britain (57 per cent) (Pew Global Attitudes Project Report, 2005).

The Republic of Turkey connects Europe and Asia, bridging a divide between (mainly) Muslim Asia and (mainly) Christian Europe. Sharing a border with several Muslim countries – Iraq, Iran and Syria – Turkey is also a member of NATO, an organization dominated by the USA and other Western countries. While the Muslim population of Turkey amounts to 99 per cent of the overall inhabitants,[9] the country emphatically rejected Islamic rule 80 years ago in favour of secular government. Now, however, Turkey's current government – under the control of the moderate Islamic party, the Justice and Development Party – finds itself caught on the horns of a dilemma: on the one hand, Western governments are often suspicious of Islam, a concern exacerbated in recent years by the continuing 'war on terror'; on the other hand, Turkey has an increasingly vocal Islamic constituency at home that dislikes Turkey's growing closeness towards what some see as a 'Christian club', the European Union (Gul, 2004; Walker, 2004).

Stephen Kinzer on Turkey and Europe

Kinzer examines the social and political tensions generated in Turkey by the bid to join the European Union. In his book, *The Crescent and the Star: Turkey Between Two Worlds*, he explores the cult of modern Turkey's founder, Kemal Ataturk, and the country's historical background rooted in Islam. Kinzer also examines Turkish oppression of the Kurds, as well as the long struggle to free Turkey's government from the grip of the military. He also highlights an issue of international significance: can Turkey survive as a secular state in the Islamic world? If not, how would other Muslim countries be able to make the transition to European-style modernity?

According to Kinzer, Turkey reached an important turning point on 17 August 1999. On that day, more than 18,000 Turks were killed in a massive earthquake. The inadequacy of the state's response to the earthquake led millions of Turks to question the entire power structure in Turkey. This was because the authorities had allowed thousands of death-trap buildings to be constructed and then stood by impotently when there was no disaster plan to put into operation when these buildings collapsed (Kinzer, 2001)

In addition, powerful forces of globalization are said to be challenging popular faith even further in the 'powers that be' in Turkey. In 1999, the European Union announced that Turkey was an official candidate for EU membership. According to Kinzer, a wave of ecstatic self-congratulation washed over the country, accompanied by solemn newspaper commentaries declaring it the most important event in the history of the Republic. But the European Union then laid out the conditions under which Turkey could become a member, and the military

(Continued)

and its civilian allies baulked. To repeal limits on free speech, grant every citizen the right to cultural expression, subject the military to civilian control, resolve social conflicts by conciliation, allow citizens to practise their religion as they see fit – suggestions like these froze the generals into immobility (Kinzer, 2006).

Turkey's putative membership of the EU is controversial in Turkey, as it is among current EU member states. Concerns over Islamic extremism are reflected in some European opinions about Turkey's bid to join the EU. However, attitudes towards immigration are even more strongly associated with views about Turkey's admission to the EU. As Table 9.3 indicates, more than two-thirds (68 per cent) of Turks strongly endorse membership of the Union. An equally large majority in Spain (68 per cent) also favours Turkey's admission, as do 57 per cent in Great Britain and 51 per cent in Poland. Elsewhere in Europe, however, majorities oppose allowing Turkey to join the EU: 66 per cent in France, including 30 per cent who strongly oppose; 65 per cent in Germany; and 53 per cent in the Netherlands. The Pew Global Attitudes Survey (2005: 3) adds that

> attitudes toward immigration are associated with these views. Those who consider immigration (from the Middle East and North Africa, or from Eastern Europe) to be a bad thing are more likely to oppose Turkey's membership into the European Union. This pattern is particularly strong in the Netherlands, France and Germany. Similarly, those who are more concerned about Islamic extremism in their homeland are more likely to oppose having Turkey join the E.U., especially in Germany, France, and the Netherlands, but less strongly elsewhere.

TABLE 9.3 Turkey joining the European Union

	In favour (%)	Oppose (%)	Don't know (%)
Turkey	68	27	5
Spain	68	21	11
Britain	57	29	14
Poland	51	22	27
Netherlands	44	53	2
France	33	66	1
Germany	32	65	3

Source: Pew Global Attitudes Survey, 2005: 3

Questions about the political and social role of Islam in Turkey, as well as the impact of globalization, find focus in the long saga of Turkey's bid to join the EU. The advance of European integration implied by the expansion of the EU in recent years is regarded in various ways by academic observers. For some, the EU is an example of 'turbo-charged globalization', while others regard it more as 'a protective shield against the negative "fall-out from" globalization' (Christiansen, 2001: 511–12). Both interpretations can be invoked to explain and account for the EU's recent – and likely future – expansion, not only into southern and eastern Europe but also to the periphery of the region, to include Turkey.

Until 2004, the EU was exclusively a Western European regional grouping of established democracies. However, in May of that year, it expanded both numerically and geographically, to welcome ten new members: Cyprus, Czech Republic, Estonia, Hungary, Latvia, Lithuania, Malta, Poland, Slovakia and Slovenia. In 2007, two further countries, Bulgaria and Romania, are scheduled to join. To some, the new, enlarged EU symbolizes the end to Europe's artificial division at the end of the Second World War. Now, the organization is a pan-European Union. However, the road to EU enlargement was a drawn-out and complex process, dominating the politics of Europe's pan-regional relations for a decade prior to the actual enlargement. The process began with the first manifestations of Euro-enthusiasm from Poland and Hungary in the early 1990s, a time when both countries were emerging from decades of Communist rule. In 1993, the EU officially set out its definition of membership criteria in response to requests to join: aspirant countries must have democratically elected governments, a good human rights regime and liberal economies without 'too much' state control. Shortly after, in early 1994, the first formal EU accession applications were submitted, from Hungary and Poland. Applications then followed from Slovakia, Romania, Bulgaria, Estonia, Latvia, Lithuania, Slovenia, and the Czech Republic (Bardi et al., 2002: 227). Following the EU announcement in 1999 that Turkey was an official candidate for EU membership, at the Helsinki Summit in the following year, Turkey was given the status of being a candidate country for full EU accession.

Political and economic criteria that the EU attaches for aspiring members were important factors in encouraging both democratization (and the consolidation of democracy) and the marketization of their economies. Pridham lists six 'broad types of influence exerted by the EU on democratization in applicant countries' (Pridham, 2000: 299). These amount to a combined 'carrot-and-stick approach'. It features the use of political and economic 'conditionality' in order to encourage aspiring new members to implement satisfactory political economic policies. The chief incentive for applicant members was a 'clear timetable for quick accession to the EU' and 'generous aid, credit and direct investment flows from the member to the candidate countries' (Yilmaz, 2002: 73). However, some observers claim that for the new members the objective of joining the EU goes beyond expected economic benefits; it is also seen as emblematic of a rediscovered, shared 'European-ness'. For Hettne, the 'question "what is Europe?" can only be answered by the political process of self-recognition. It is a social construct, . . . an idea rather than a territory'. It implies that 'the content of "European" can be defined normatively by: a strong role for civil society, various institutionalized forms such as parliamentary decision making, and a democratic culture stressing above all individualism and human rights inherent in the individual human being' (Hettne (2001: 38–9).[10] For our concerns, the issue and application of 'European-ness' is important as it sheds light not only on the question of Turkey's bid for EU membership but also on the larger *problematique* of 'European identity' and where the region's Muslims fit in.

EU membership was the touted reward, *if* Turkey both democratized and made progress towards a human rights regime 'acceptable' to the Union. Turkey's political system is sometimes referred to as a transitional democracy, because the country only relatively recently emerged from decades of strong military political involvement. The EU sought to use both political and economic conditionality[11] to encourage Turkey's government to reform politically and to improve its human rights regime. Turkey's case illustrates, however, that the application of conditionality can lead to a variety of outcomes. While Turkey, on the periphery of Europe, has long aspired to join the EU, for years the country's relatively poor human rights record gave the EU a defensible reason not to progress Turkey's membership application. In recent years, however, Turkey's democratic and human rights record has demonstrably improved, to the extent that EU membership may now be a realizable ambition.[12] There is, however, another important dimension to note. After 9/11, many EU governments seemed to believe that it was better to have Muslim Turkey in the EU rather than, potentially, part of the anti-Western 'axis of evil'. As a consequence, in early 2003, the European Commission recommended that aid to Turkey should be doubled – from €0.5bn to €1.05bn – in 2004–06. This can be seen as a calculated attempt both to encourage Turkey's moderate Islamic government to refrain from military intervention in Iraq as well as concrete encouragement to continue with domestic political and human rights reforms (Osborn, 2003).

Some senior European figures were, however, openly opposed to Turkey's membership bid. For example, in September 2004, Frits Bolkestein, then the EU single market commissioner[13] and former leader of the Dutch Liberal Party, warned that 'Europe's Christian civilization' risked being 'overrun by Islam'. In addition, he claimed, the EU was in danger of 'imploding' in its current form if 70 million Turkish Muslims were allowed to join. Thus, according to Bolkestein, Turkey's entry could undermine Europe's 'fragile' political system, ending all hopes for the Continent's integration. Bolkestein claimed at a speech at Leiden University, the Netherlands, in September 2004 that demography was the 'mother of politics', that is, 'while America had the youth and dynamism to remain the world's only superpower, and China was the rising economic power, Europe's destiny was to be "Islamized"'. Quoting the Orientalist American author Bernard Lewis, Bolkestein warned Europeans that in a few decades Europe could become an 'extension of North Africa and the Middle East'. He also compared the EU to the former Austro–Hungarian empire, which included so many different people from various cultures that it eventually became ungovernable. Bolkestein did, however, imply that a closer relationship between Turkey and 'Europe' would be desirable, under certain conditions:

> Although a secular state, Turkey is still rooted in Islam. As such she could spearhead a cultural continent with its Arab neighbours and thus become the main actor of a culture with its own identity but with whom others can share common humanist values. This idea does not oppose close and friendly association and collaboration with Europe; instead, it could foster a common front against all forms of fundamentalism ('Turkey-European Union', 2004)

Cardinal Joseph Ratzinger (now Pope Benedict XVI) appeared to agree with Bolkestein's views. In an August 2004 interview with the French newspaper *Le Figaro*, Ratzinger commented on Ankara's application to join the EU. He claimed that 'Europe is a cultural and not a geographical continent. Its culture gives it a common identity. In this sense, Turkey always represented another continent throughout history, in permanent contrast with Europe'. It would be wrong, he believed, to equate the two sides for 'mere commercial interests' as it 'would be a loss to subsume culture under the economy'. Like Bolkestein, Ratzinger urged Turkey to assume leadership of the Muslim world, spearheading dialogue with the West (Kay, 2005).

Such controversial interventions encouraged a Turkish response. In December 2004, Turkey's Foreign Minister Abdullah Gul claimed the 'carrot' of EU membership had been a key component of Turkey's 'process of political and economic reform that has been remarkably successful and has received widespread popular support'. Gul also claimed that Turkey was demonstrating strong commitment to internal political, social and economic restructuring that merited recognition by both the European and global community. Moreover, he averred, the numerous requirements for membership had now been addressed and thus fears expressed by figures such as Bolkestein appeared unwarranted. According to Gul, Turkey's Muslim identity would neither be a handicap nor 'political time bomb' Instead, 'positive EU–Turkey relations will show that shared democratic values and political unity prevail, sending the message that a "culture of reconciliation" within Europe is at hand' (Gul, 2004).

The EU Commission was at the time of the interventions of Ratzinger and Bolkestein working on a report on the issue of Turkish accession to the Union. The EU enlargement commissioner, Gunther Verheugen, put forward a broadly positive verdict in numerous interviews. He suggested that Turkey now met various basic tests for EU membership, including a free-market economy and pluralist democracy, conditions that had progressively strengthened since 2002. Moreover, the death penalty has been abolished and the Kurdish language recognized (Walker, 2004). In 2005, EU accession talks finally began with the intention of finding a modus operandi for Turkey to join the Union. But because of the controversy about Turkey's application, the talks were likely to be lengthy, without certainty of success.

Conclusion

In this chapter we examined the following topics:

- *The political and social position of Muslim minorities in Europe*
- *The threat of Islamic extremism in Europe*
- *Muslim Turkey's bid to join the European Union*

In relation to the first issue, we saw that from the 1970s the issue of Muslim assimilation into European societies became a controversial social and political issue, reflecting both domestic and international concerns and issues. From the 1980s, globalization – and its tendency to facilitate transnational networks – suggested to some that the disaffected among Muslim communities in Europe were a Trojan horse for the infiltration of 'Islamic fundamentalism' into Europe. However, evidence emanating from the French riots of 2005 appeared to belie the claim that Islamic extremism would find fertile ground in Europe.

Secondly, the events of 9/11 and subsequent bomb attacks on Madrid (11 March 2004) and London (7 July 2005) helped further to focus popular, governmental and academic concerns on social, religious and political questions in relation to Europe's Muslim communities. The terrorist attacks were widely perceived as a significant turn for the worse in relations between Muslims and non-Muslims in Europe, reinforcing perceptions of the Muslim 'Other' in what for some commentators appeared to be an emerging 'clash of civilizations' between Islam and the West. Others, however, saw the attacks as the acts of international terrorists who unjustifiably used Islam as a bogus vehicle for their murderous escapades.

Our brief surveys of Britain and France indicated that Islamic extremism was in both countries a controversial and marginal tendency, apparently engaging the allegiance of only small groups of Muslim militants with little popular support. We found that Islam can be divided into 'good' and 'bad' versions, a concern driving a more general call for an 'Enlightened' Islam, necessitating, according to some analysts, a general Muslim *aggiornamento* (liberalization) as a prerequisite to the integration of Muslims into Western societies. This would also set the necessary conditions not for a privatization of the faith but for a public Islam (Ramadan, 2003; Roy, 2004, 2005; Peter, 2006).

Thirdly, acceptance in principle of Turkey's application for membership of the EU, announced in 2000, appears to polarize opinion. For some – such as, Frits Bolkestein (former EU commissioner) and Cardinal Ratzinger (now Pope Benedict XVI) – it threatened Europe's sense of cultural identity. For others, however, Turkey's membership of the EU would be useful in helping drive a further wedge between 'Islamic fundamentalists' and moderate Muslims – by showing the latter an important example of what moderation can achieve.

Notes

1   In this chapter we are primarily concerned with Western Europe, but for reasons of brevity will sometimes also use the term 'Europe'.

2   *Jyllands-Posten*, based in a suburb of the city of Aarhus, is Denmark's biggest selling daily newspaper, with a weekday circulation of approximately 150,000 copies.

3   Denmark is home to approximately 150,000 Muslims, amounting to less than 3 per cent of the overall population of 5.4 million. Around a quarter are of Turkish ethnic origin. Earlier migrants came primarily for economic reasons; most later ones, from the 1980s, came as refugees. Currently about 40 per cent of all Muslims in Denmark have a refugee background. Most Muslims live in Denmark's larger cities; most inhabit Copenhagen (http://euro-islam.info/pages/denmark.html).

4   Many of Ramadan's recent articles, in English, can be found at: http://www.tariqramadan.com/rubrique.php3?id_rubrique=43&lang=en

5   In August 2005 the British government considered banning the Islamist group Hizb ut-Tahrir, in a crackdown on terrorism in the wake of the 7/7 London bomb attacks.

6   Banned religious symbols also included the Christian cross.

7   The riots began following the deaths of two boys of Malian origin – Bouna Traore, aged 15 years, and Zyed Benna aged 17. A third boy, Muhittin Altun, also 17, of Turkish Kurdish origin, was severely injured. All three were electrocuted by a transformer in an electric substation, after they ran away thinking that the police, who had demanded their identity documents, were chasing them.

8   Interviews were conducted by Katrin Bennhold in France, Judy Dempsey in Germany, Salman Masood in Pakistan, Evelyn Rusli in Indonesia and Marlise Simons in the Netherlands, all of the *International Herald Tribune*, and Mayssam Zaaroura in Lebanon of *The Daily Star*.

9   Most Turkish Muslims are Sunnis, although a few belong to the Twelver Shia sect. The remaining 1 per cent of the population include Christians, Jews and Bahais.

10 Hettne defines civil society as 'inclusive institutions that facilitate a societal dialogue over various social and cultural borders', while 'identities and loyalties are transferred from civil society to primary groups, competing with each other for territorial control, resources and security' (Hettne, 2001: 40).

11 Yilmaz defines conditionality as the 'effectiveness, visibility and immediacy of external punishments and rewards'. The EU has employed conditionality since the 1980s to achieve certain foreign policy goals – including, good governance, democratization, better human rights, the rule of law, and economic liberalization – in numerous transitional democracies and non-democracies (Yilmaz, 2002: 83).

12 The American non-government organization, Freedom House, reported that 'Turkey [had] registered forward progress as a result of the loosening of restrictions on Kurdish culture. *Legislators made progress on an improved human rights framework, the product of Turkey's effort to integrate into European structures.* At the same time, political rights were enhanced as the country's military showed restraint in the aftermath of a free and fair election that saw the sweeping victory of a moderate Islamist opposition party' (Karatnycky et al., 2003).

13 A spokesperson for the European Commission stressed that the Dutch commissioner 'was speaking in a personal capacity' (http://www.rferl.org/featuresarticle/2004/09/fdc6f2b0-c615-4ee1-a913-ca182c355a43.html).

Questions

1 Why is Western Europe so secular?

2 Examine and assess the comparative political impact of 'moderate' and 'extremist' Islam in *one* European country.

3 To what extent does the post/9/11 'War on Terror' influence Muslim perceptions of Europe?

4 What caused the French riots of November 2005?

5 To what extent is the issue of Turkey's entry to the EU about religion and culture?

Bibliography

'70,000 gather for violent Pakistan cartoons protest' (2006) *Times Online*, 15 February. Available at: http://www.timesonline.co.uk/article/0,,25689-2041723,00.html Accessed 15 May 2006.

Ahmad, I. (2002) 'The needs of Muslim children can be met only through Muslim schools', *The Guardian*, 22 May.

Ahmed, A. (1992) *Postmodernism and Islam: Predicament and Promise*, London: Routledge.

Amiraux, V. (2005) 'Discrimination and claims for equal rights amongst Muslims in Europe', in J. Cesari and S. McLoughlin (eds) (2005) *European Muslims and the Secular State*, Aldershot: Ashgate, pp. 25–38.

Ansari, H. (2002) *Muslims in Britain*, London: Minority Rights Group International.

Astier, H. (2005) 'We want to be French!', 'Open Democracy', 22 November. Available at: http://www.opendemocracy.net/debates/article.jsp?id=6&debateId=28&articleId=3051 Accessed 5 June 2006.

Ayubi, N. (1991) *Political Islam: Religion and Politics in the Arab World*, London: Routledge.

Bardi, L., Rhodes, M. and Nello, S. (2002) 'Enlarging the European Union: challenges to and from Central and Eastern Europe – Introduction', *International Political Science Review*, 23(3), pp. 227–33.

Ben-Simon, D. (2005) 'French philosopher Alain Finkielkraut apologizes after death threats', *Ha'aretz*, 27 November. Available at: http://www.haaretz.com/hasen/pages/ShArt.jhtml?itemNo=650155 Accessed 23 June 2006.

Berger, P. (1999) (ed.) *The Desecularization of the World: Resurgent Religion and World Politics*, Grand Rapids/Washington, DC: William B. Eerdmans/Ethics and Public Policy Center.

Bilefsky, D. (2006) 'Death toll mounts in rioting over cartoons', *International Herald Tribune*, 8 February. Available at: http://www.iht.com/articles/2006/02/07/news/islam.php Accessed 14 May 2006.

Bright, A. (2006) 'Firestorm over Danish Muhammad cartoons continues', *Christian Science Monitor*, 1 February. Available at: http://www.csmonitor.com/2006/0201/dailyUpdate.html Accessed 15 May 2006.

Bruce, S. (2002) *God Is Dead: Secularization in the West*, Oxford: Blackwell.

Caeiro, A. (2005) 'Religious authorities or political actors? The Muslim leaders of the French Representative Body of Islam', in J. Cesari and S. McLoughlin (eds) (2005) *European Muslims and the Secular State*, Aldershot: Ashgate, pp. 71–84.

Caeiro, A. (2006) 'An anti-riot fatwa', *ISIM Review*, 17, Spring, p. 32.

Casanova, J. (1994) *Public Religions in the Modern World*, Chicago and London: University of Chicago Press.

Casanova, J. (2005) 'Catholic and Muslim politics in comparative perspective', *Taiwan Journal of Democracy*, 1(2), pp. 89–108.

Cesari, J. and McLoughlin, S. (eds) (2005) *European Muslims and the Secular State*, Aldershot: Ashgate.

Christiansen, T. (2001) 'European and regional integration', in J. Baylis and S. Smith (eds), *The Globalization of World Politics: An Introduction to International Relations*, Oxford: Oxford University Press, pp. 495–518.

Davie, G. (2000) *Religions in Modern Europe*, Oxford: Oxford University Press.

Davie, G. (2002) *Europe: The Exceptional Case. Parameters of Faith in the Modern World*, London: Darton, Longmann and Todd.

Dodd, V. (1996) 'Jews fear rise of the Muslim "underground"', *The Observer*, 18 February.

Esposito, J. (2002) *Unholy War*, New York: Oxford University Press.

Gauchet, M. (1985) *Le déenchantement du monde*, Paris: Gallimard.

Goulborne, H. and Joly, D. (1989) 'Religion and the Asian and Caribbean minorities in Britain', *Contemporary European Affairs*, 2(4), pp. 77–98.

Gul, A. (2004) 'Turkey's Muslim identity did not prevent Turkey's intense relations with Europe', 16 December, 'Zaman Online. First Turkish paper on the Internet'. Available at: http://yaleglobal.yale.edu/display.article?id=5041 Accessed November 15, 2005.

Haynes, J. (2005) 'Review article: Religion and international relations after "9/11"', *Democratization*, 12, 3 (June), pp. 398–413.

Henley, J. (2004) 'French MPs vote for veil ban in state schools', *The Guardian*, 11 February.

Hettne, B. (2001) 'Europe: paradigm and paradox', in M. Schulz, F. Söderbaum and J. Öjendal, (eds) *'Regionalization in a Globalizing World: A Comparative Perspective on Forms, Actors and Processes*, London: Zed Books, pp. 22–41.

Hirst, R. (2003) 'Social networks and personal beleifs', in G. Davie, P. Heelas, and L. Woodhead (eds), *Predicting Religion*, Aldershot: Ashgate, pp. 86–94.

Hirst, P. and Thompson, G. (1999) *Globalization in Question*, Oxford: Blackwell.

Karatnycky, A., Piano, A. and Puddington, A. (eds) (2003) *Freedom in the World. The Annual Survey of Political Rights and Civil Liberties (2003)*, New York: Freedom House.

Katz, D. (2005) *Occultism: From the Renaissance to the Present Day*, London: Jonathan Cape.

Kay, J. (2005) 'Pope Benedict XVI's political resume: theocracy and social reaction', 22 April. 'World Socialist Web Site'. Available at: http://www.wsws.org/articles/2005/apr2005/pope-a22.shtml Accessed 15 November 2005.

Kennedy, P. and Roudometof, V. (2002) *Communities Across Borders*, London: Routledge.

Kepel, G. (1994) *The Revenge of God*, Cambridge: Polity.

Kinzer, S. (2001) *The Crescent and the Star: Turkey Between Two Worlds*, New York: Farrar Straus Giroux.

Kinzer, S., quoted in 'Turkey, elections, and globalization' (2006). Available at: http://globalization.about.com/library/weekly/aa103102a.htm Accessed 12 May 2006.

de Koning, M. (2006) 'Islamization of the French riots. Interview with Laurent Chambon', *ISIM Review*, 17, Spring, pp. 30–1.

Levine, M. (2005) 'Assimilate or die. Do the French riots portend a coming cultural backlash against globalization?', Mother Jones. Available at http://motherjones.com/commentary/columns/2005/11/assimilate_or_die.html Accessed 5 June 2006.

Luhmann, N. (1989) *Ecological Communication*, London: Polity Press.

Marty, M. and Appleby, R. Scott (eds) (1997) *Religion, Ethnicity and Self-Identity*, London: University Press of New England.

Mathews, G. (2000) *Global Culture/Individual Identity*, London: Routledge.

McLoughlin, S. (2005) 'The state, new Muslim leaderships and Islam as a resource for public engagement in Britain', in J. Cesari and S. McLoughlin (eds) (2005) *European Muslims and the Secular State*, Aldershot: Ashgate, pp. 55–70.

'Muslims voice anger over Muhammad cartoons' (2006), Worldpress.org, 'News and Views From Around the World'. Available at: http://www.worldpress.org/Europe/2261.cfm Accessed 15 May 2006.

Nielsen, J. (1992) 'Muslims, Christians and loyalties in the nation-state', in J. Nielsen (ed.), *Religion and Citizenship in Europe and the Arab World*, London: Grey Seal Books, pp. 1–18.

Nonneman, G. (1996) 'Muslim communities in post-Cold War Europe: themes and puzzles', in I. Hampsher-Monk and J. Stanyer (eds), *Contemporary Political Studies 1996, Volume One*, Proceedings of the annual conference of the Political Studies Association held at Glasgow, 10–12 April, 1996, pp. 381–94.

Osborn, A. (2003) 'EU lifts Turkey's hopes', *The Guardian*, 27 March.

Peter, F. (2006) 'Towards civil Islam? A comparison of Islam policies in Britain and France', *Recht van der Islam*, No. 23.

Pew Global Attitudes Project Report (2005) 'Islamic extremism: common concern for Muslims and Western publics', '17-Nation Pew Global Attitudes Survey', July. Available at: http://pewglobal.org/reports/display.php?ReportID=248 Accessed 12 December 2005.

Pew Global Attitudes Project Report (2006) 'The great divide: how Westerners and Muslims view each other', 22 June. Available at: http://pewresearch.org/reports/?ReportID=28 Accessed 23 June 2006.

Piscatori, J. (1986) *Islam in a World of Nation-States*, Cambridge: Cambridge University Press.

Pridham, G. (2000) *The Dynamics of Democratization: A Comparative Approach*, London and New York: Continuum.

Ramadan, T. (2003) *Western Muslims and the Future of Islam*, Oxford and New York: Oxford University Press.

Ramadan, T. (2006) 'Before the trap springs shut on the Palestinian people, resign!'. Available at: http://www.tariqramadan.com/rubrique.php3?id_rubrique=43&lang=en Accessed 6 June 2006.

Rosenau, J. (1997) *Along the Domestic-Foreign Frontier*, Cambridge: Cambridge University Press.

Roy, O. (2004) *Globalised Islam: The Search for a New Ummah*, London: Hurst.

Roy, O. (2005) *La laicité face à l'islam*, Paris: Stock.

Sen, A. (2006) *Identity and Violence*, New York: Norton.

Tisdall, S. (2006) 'Bush wrongfooted as Iran steps up international charm offensive', *The Guardian*, 20 June.

Travis, A. (2004) 'Desire to integrate on the wane as Muslims resent "war on Islam"', *The Guardian*, 16 March.

'Turkey–European Union' (2004) *AsiaNews.it*, 8 September. Available at: http://www.asianews.it/view.php?l=en&art=1442 Accessed 4 June 2006.

Turner, B. S. (1994) *Orientalism, Postmodernism and Globalism*, London: Routledge.

Turner, B. S. (2000) 'Liberal citizenship and cosmopolitan virtue', in A. Vandenberg (ed.), *Citizenship and Democracy in a Global Era*, Oxford: Polity Press, pp. 18–32.

Walker, M. (2004) 'Walker's world: Turkey's effect on Europe', *The Washington Times*, 6 October. Available at: http://www.washtimes.

com/upi-breaking/20041006-014153-5595r.htm Accessed 17 November 2005.

Watson, P. and Jones, A. (2005) 'The fruits of globalization: rotten to the core. France erupts as rampant immigration reaps its vengeance'. Available at: http://www.prisonplanet.com/articles/november2005/081105rottentothecore.htm Accessed 5 June 2006.

Wilson, B. (2003) 'Prediction and prophecy in the future of religion', in G. Davie, P. Heelas, and L. Woodhead (eds), *Predicting Religion*, Aldershot: Ashgate, pp. 64–73.

Yilmaz, H. (2002) 'External–internal linkages in democratization: developing an open model of democratic change', *Democratization*, 9(2), pp. 67–84.

Further reading

J. Cesari and S. McLoughlin (eds) *European Muslims and the Secular State*, Ashgate, 2005. The starting point for this book is the question of Islam's institutionalization in Europe. The editors argue that secularization represents much more than the legal separation of politics and religion in Europe; for important segments of European societies, it has become the cultural norm. The consequence is that for some, Muslim communities and their claims for the public recognition of Islam are perceived as a threat. The book examines current interactions between Muslims and the more-or-less secularized public spaces of several European states, assessing the challenges such interactions imply for both Muslims and the societies in which they now live. It is divided into three parts: state–church relations, 'Islamophobia', and the 'War on Terrorism'. Overall, it evaluates the engagement of Muslim leaders with the state and civil society and reflects on both individual and collective transformations of Muslim religiosity.

G. Davie, *Religions in Modern Europe: A Memory Mutates*, Oxford University Press, 2000 and *Europe: The Exceptional Case. Parameters of Faith in the Modern World*, London: Darton, Longman and Todd, 2002. These books are concerned with the sociology of religion, with a particular emphasis on (1) currents of religion outside the mainstream churches, (2) the significance of the religious factor in modern European societies and (3) parameters of faith in the modern world. Davie is interested in what she calls 'European exceptionalism', that is, European patterns of religion that are not a prototype of global religiosity, but peculiar to the European continent. It follows that the relatively low levels of religious activity in modern Europe are not simply the result of early modernization; they are part of what it means to be European and need to be understood in these terms. In *Religion in Modern Europe: a Memory Mutates*, she examines this theme from within Europe itself. In *Europe: the Exceptional Case. Parameters of Faith in the Modern World*, she looks at Europe from the outside asking what forms of religion are widespread in the modern world but do not occur in most parts of Europe. Pentecostalism is an obvious example.

T. Ramadan, *Western Muslims and the Future of Islam*, Oxford University Press, 2003. Ramadan argues that Islam can and should feel at home in the West. In this book, he focuses on Islamic law (*Sharia*) and tradition in order to analyse whether Islam is in conflict with Western ideals. According to Ramadan, there is no contradiction between them. He also identifies several key areas where Islam's universal principles can be 'engaged' in the West, including education, inter-religious dialogue, economic resistance and spirituality. As the number of Muslims living in the West grows, the question of what it means to be a Western Muslim becomes increasingly important to the futures of both Islam and the West. While the media are focused on radical Islam, Ramadan claims, a silent revolution is sweeping Islamic communities in the West, as Muslims actively seek ways to live in harmony with their faith within a Western context. French, English, German, and American Muslims, both women and men, are reshaping their religion into one that is faithful to the principles of Islam, dressed in European and American cultures, and definitively rooted in Western societies.

O. Roy, *Globalised Islam: The Search for a New Ummah*, Hurst, 2004. This book is the sequel to Roy's *Failure of Political Islam* (first published in French in 1992 and in English in 1994), in which he argued that the conceptual framework of Islamist parties was unable to provide an effective blueprint for an Islamic state. In *Globalised Islam*, Roy examines the prejudices and simplifications used in much popular culture and media in the West regarding Muslims. He explores how individual Muslims are reacting to (not necessarily against) globalization and westernization. Overall, the book is an extremely useful introduction to the politics of Islam in the Middle East, Europe and the United States.

CHAPTER 10

Africa

The purpose of this chapter is to examine how religion affects the international and transnational relations of Africa.[1] Our focus is Africa south of the Sahara Desert. It is a vast region of 45 states, nearly a quarter of all the world's countries. There is a huge variety of languages, cultures and traditions found throughout the region. On the other hand, almost all African countries share a history both of European colonial control and of concerted proselytization from Christianity and Islam that led to the current situation: hundreds of millions of adherents of both religious traditions are found throughout Africa. However, despite the general societal importance of religion in Africa, very few African countries – Sudan is one example – have state policies closely linked to religion. But what is of widespread significance throughout the region are various transnational networks, both Christian and Islamic. Reflecting this, we focus upon African transnational religious networks: from Christianity, transnational Roman Catholic and Protestant networks, and from Islam, both a moderate transnational organization, Tablighi Jamaat, and 'extremist' Islamist networks, active in Africa. Finally, we examine the impact of the 'evangelization' of US foreign policy in relation to Sudan's recently ended civil war between the Muslim north and the Christian and animist south of the country.

The spread of Islam and Christianity in Africa

During the first half of the twentieth century the pace of growth of Christianity in Africa outstripped that of Islam. Numbers of Christians increased from around 10 million in 1900 to more than 250 million in the early 2000s. Over the same period, the total number of African Muslims grew from about 34 million to nearly 300 million (Barrett et al., 2001). While Christians are spread throughout the entire region, the location of Muslims is more fragmented. Millions of African Muslims live north of the Saharan desert, in the North African countries of Morocco, Algeria, Tunisia, Libya and Egypt. In addition, Africa is predominantly Muslim above the tenth parallel, which cuts through the northern regions of Sierra Leone, Côte d'Ivoire, Ghana, Togo, Benin, Nigeria, Cameroon, Central African Republic, Ethiopia and Somalia. The same line roughly separates Muslim from non-Muslim in Sudan and Chad. Above the tenth parallel, The Gambia, Senegal, Mali and Niger are preponderantly Muslim.

Religious conversions in Africa during the colonial period

During the colonial period in Africa (c.1880–1960), conversion to Christianity and Islam was facilitated among Africans for various reasons. For many Africans, conversion to Islam was a manifestation of antipathy to European colonialism, an alternative modernizing influence opposed to the influence of European Christian missionaries. Islam provided converts with an alternative modernizing world-view, not defined by the colonial order and its foreign norms, but by a perceived 'indigenous' culture that many Africans perceived to be authentically closer to their existing cultures than the 'alien' creed of Christianity. Other Africans, on the other hand, saw conversion to Christianity as a means not only to acquire spiritual benefits but also to gain access to both education and welfare, a key means to acquire 'upward mobility'. During the colonial period, education and welfare provision were under the almost exclusive control of foreign Christian missions.

While various parts of Africa received more proselytization from one faith or the other, Islam and Christianity were only rarely in direct competition. In the Muslim areas, colonial authorities discouraged Christian missionaries from proselytizing. This was because the European-introduced system of rule typically relied on good relations between colonial authorities and local Muslim rulers. The best example of a mutually beneficial relationship in this regard was between Europeans and local Muslim rulers in northern Nigeria. There Lord Lugard's system of indirect rule (actually first developed in Uganda, following Britain's Indian colonial experiences) owed much of its success to the fact that it tampered hardly at all with pre-existing socio-political structures and cultural norms. The local, slave-owning Fulani elite became intermediaries with the colonial administration as a reward for putting down an Islamist revolt in Satiru in 1906. Fulani leaders were able to enlarge their sphere of influence – and to convert more people to Islam – by extending their supremacy over groups of previously autonomous non-Muslims, notably those in what later became Plateau and Borno states.

Until colonial rule was firmly established in Africa, roughly by the time of the First World War, Christian missions often made relatively little headway in their conversion attempts. Nevertheless, the social influence of early missionaries was important. They were aware that teaching a love of Christ was insufficient on its own, realizing that many Africans regarded themselves as in need of material as well as spiritual assistance. It was, therefore, in the missionaries' interest to seek to improve the material knowledge, skills and well-being, via African converts' ability to read, write and have access to Western methods of health protection. In this way, Africans would develop into more useful members of Christian society. Over time, a class of educated Africans emerged, people who owed their upward mobility to the fact that they had converted to Christianity and been able to absorb the benefits of a mission education. By and large, the leaders of post-colonial Africa were drawn from among the ranks of such people.

Islam's spread in Africa

Islam spread from North Africa southwards from the seventh century, pre-dating European colonialism by hundreds of years. Its diffusion was multi-directional. Over time, Islam strongly established itself – reflected in both socio-political organization and religio-cultural developments – among many communities in much of western and, to a lesser yet still significant degree, eastern Africa. Consequently, attempts at mass Christian conversion in those areas in the late nineteenth and early twentieth centuries were, on the whole, singularly unsuccessful. However, Islam made much less progress during the colonial era in central-southern and southern Africa. Its relatively late arrival from the north came up against the rapid spread of European Christianity from the south in the last decades of the nineteenth century; as a result Islam's influence was minimized.

Where they existed, the progress of Islam followed pre-existing trade routes, such as the North African and Indian Ocean ways. Conversions were also made via *jihad* ('holy war') during the nineteenth and early twentieth centuries. In the late nineteenth century, the wider Muslim world experienced the slow demise of the Ottoman empire and the near contemporaneous emergence of Saudi Arabia as champion of Wahhabist reformist ambitions. The growth of the Sufi brotherhoods and their reformist rivals were two developments in African Islam more or less contemporaneous with the consolidation of European rule, while others included: (1) the extension of Muslim networks throughout much of Africa and beyond, and (2) introduction of new, modernizing ideas. Many Muslims joined Sufi brotherhoods to further their own commercial networks, and were often receptive to the reformist ideas of the Wahhabiya and of Pan-Islamic ideals, in the context of urbanization and development of ethnically-orientated Muslim associative groups. Sufi brotherhoods, prospered under colonial rule in, *inter alia*, Senegal, Mauritania, northern Nigeria, Tanganyika, Sudan and Somaliland (Haynes, 1996: 23–50).

The outcome was that various 'versions' of Islam established themselves in Africa, both north and south of the Sahara. In both regions, Africans have long belonged to Sufi brotherhoods. In addition, many ethnic groups, especially in West and East Africa, converted to Islam en masse before and during the colonial era, giving religious belief among such people an ethnic dimension. Some of them would also be members of Sufi brotherhoods, so the latter may also have an ethnic aspect. However, orthodox conceptions of Islam – nearly always Sunni in Africa – are the province of the religious elite, the *ulama* (religious/legal scholars), who look down on the 'uneducated' followers of Sufi Islam who practise 'degenerate' or 'impure' versions of the faith.

Differing manifestations of Islam point to the fact that the faith in Africa covers a variety of interpretations of what it means to be a Muslim. Away from the Arab countries of the north, Islam south of the Sahara can be divided into distinct categories, corresponding to extant social, cultural and historical divisions. The first includes the dominant socio-political and cultural position of Islam in the emirates of northern Nigeria, the lamidates of northern Cameroon and the shiekdoms of northern Chad. In each of these areas, religious and political power is fused in a few individuals; over time a class structure developed based on religious differentiation. Secondly, there are the areas where Sufi brotherhoods predominate, generally in West and East Africa, and especially in Senegal, The Gambia, Niger, Mali, Guinea, Kenya and Tanzania. Thirdly, in a number of African states, Muslims, fragmented by ethnic and regional concerns, are politically marginalized. This is the situation in a number of African countries, including: Ghana, Togo, Benin, and Côte d'Ivoire.

In Sudan, on the other hand, recent rulers sought to utilize Islam as an ideology of conquest and of Arabicization. This policy is primarily directed against the Dinka, the Nuer and other southern Sudanese peoples. Many among the latter took part in a long civil war against the northern Arab-Muslim-dominated state. As we shall see later, this attempt to Islamicize and Arabicize received the attention of US Protestant evangelicals, some of whom encouraged the US government to introduce a law in 2000 that is credited with helping end the civil war in Sudan in 2005 (see Chapter 8 and below).

The campaign of the Sudanese state over the last few years to Islamicize the country is but one manifestation of political Islam, or Islamism in Africa. There are two broad types of Islamist groups found in sub-Saharan Africa. First there are 'moderate' groups, such as Tablighi Jamaat. This transnational Islamic missionary movement, which originated in India, encourages greater religious devotion and observance. Its founder, Mawlana Muhammad Ilyas, strove for a purification of Islam as practised by individual Muslims through following more closely the rules established in the *Sunnah*. Over the years, the Tablighi Jamaat has grown into what Janson describes as probably the largest Islamic movement at the current time (Janson, 2006: 44). Yet, few scholars have paid attention to this fact, preferring in many cases to focus upon radical vehicles of Islam. Yet Tablighi Jamaat is highly significant in many African countries, an expression of moderate Islam that attracts a wide variety of people. As we shall see below, both radical and moderate Islamic groups in Africa seek to attain the same broad goals: improvement in both spiritual and material well-being through closer application of religious tenets. The same point could also be made in relation to many African Christians who, like their Muslim counterparts, often look to transnational religious networks to help them fulfil their goals. In Africa, as in many other regions that we examine in this book, transnational religious actors seek to achieve goals through the inauguration, embedding and development of cross-border associations, building links with like-minded groups via transmission and receipt of interpersonal and inter-group exchanges of information, ideas and/or money. Often encouraged by globalization, such actors inhabit a 'globalizing social reality' where previously significant barriers to communication have considerably diminished. As a result, they can construct national, regional, continental or, in some cases, global networks of like-minded people, a development that may serve to increase their influence.

The Roman Catholic Church: liberation theology in South Africa

We saw in Chapter 5 that the Roman Catholic Church is a highly important transnational actor in contemporary international relations. The Church is important in Africa partly because of the large numbers of Africans who are baptized Catholics – around 120 million people, one-fifth of Africa's population – and partly because it is the only regional religious institution which is also a self-financing transnational organization, a fact that gives the Church considerable societal influence.

Diamond notes the Church's political significance in relation to democratization outcomes in both South Africa and Kenya in the early 1990s. At this time, the Church was at the forefront of societal demands to 'oppose, denounce, frustrate and remove authoritarian regimes' (Diamond, 1993: 49). Leading local Roman Catholics were involved in national conferences in the early 1990s concerned with the post-authoritarian political way forward in various French-speaking African countries, including: Chad, Congo-Brazzaville, Gabon, Mali, Niger, Togo and Zaire (now Democratic Republic of Congo – DRC). Overall, however, outcomes were variable: for example, in Congo-Brazzaville a new government was democratically elected, although the political situation remained tense. In Togo, Chad, Gabon and Zaire, on the other hand, national conferences did not lead, in the short term, either to new constitutions or democratically elected governments. In DRC and Togo, the outcome was initially a stalemate, as opposition forces were initially too weak to unseat these authoritarian leaders. Later, however, both dictators left power under pressure from civil society, including that from the Roman Catholic Church.

In addition to the Church's role in democratization in several African countries, it was also a key actor in the contemporaneous demise of apartheid rule in South Africa and the country's subsequent democratization. Although the Catholic Church is a minority church in South Africa – only 7.1 per cent of South Africans belong to it[2] – it is appropriate to call the Church in South Africa a 'significant player' in relation to the end of apartheid and subsequent democratization because of the Church's ability to apply transnational, institutional and moral pressure against the National Party government of President de Klerk (Haynes, 1996: 96–7, 148–52). During the apartheid era (1948–94), the white-dominated state looked to its main religious ally, a Protestant church, the Dutch Reformed Church (NGK), for religious justification for its policy of 'separate development'. Over time, however, things began to change in response to both internal and external developments, with other non-Afrikaner churches, especially the Roman Catholic Church, becoming increasingly bold in challenging apartheid on both religious and moral grounds. In the mid-1980s, the South African Council of Churches came under black leadership, the ecumenical vanguard for a radical 'Black theology'. Its best-known – and probably most influential – expression was the 'Kairos document', a publication that included both social and contextual analysis to describe the struggle for salvation from public sin. The overall importance of Christian, including Roman Catholic, opposition to white minority rule was clear at the end of the 1980s, when the premises of leading church organizations were fire-bombed by right-wing groups (Harris et al., 1992: 466). In sum, Christian anti-apartheid institutional opposition, especially from the Roman Catholic Church, was influential in encouraging South Africa's government to reform apartheid and begin a process of democratization.

Liberation theology

The impact of transnational ideas linked to Catholicism can be seen in South Africa, where the application of liberation theology and the founding of Latin American-style Basic Christian Communities (BCCs) was a significant event in the 1980s. Both developments significantly informed the advance of 'Black theology'. BCCs first emerged in Latin America in the 1960s, orientated towards community development through the application of group effort. An essentially biblical radicalism, often melded with facets of Marxism–Leninism, the tenets of liberation theology stimulated numerous Roman Catholic priests in Latin America to champion the concerns of the poor. The contemporaneous development of liberation theology focused attention on socio-political divisions and associated political struggles in Latin America. Liberation theology is an intensely political concept, essentially a radical religious response to poor socio-economic conditions. Central to the idea is the notion of dependence and underdevelopment; the use of a class struggle perspective to explain social conflict and justify political action; and the exercise of a political role to achieve both religious and political goals. In the 1960s, the Church in Latin America was radicalized by influential theologians and religious thinkers – such as Gustavo Gutierrez and Paulo Freire – whose ideas were put into effect by mainly younger priests, serving to help develop a socially progressive Catholicism. BCCs were the most concrete sign of the spread of liberation theology concerns in Latin America. The political effects of liberation theology in Latin America are widely believed to have contributed to the democratization of the region from the 1970s (Haynes, 1993: 95–109).

Socially progressive Catholics in South Africa, both black and white, were encouraged by their own ideas of radical Christian theology of liberation to demand fundamental political reforms. Radical Christian theological interpretations gained ground in the 1970s and 1980s, with significant political ramifications. The Institute for Contextual Theology (ICT) declared in 1984 that it wanted to encourage formation of BCCs in South Africa because it saw them as a key vehicle of 'conscientization'.[3] To this goal, the ICT worked to develop 'contextual theology', that is, liberation theology, programmes for study by South Africa's emergent BCCs. Father Albert Nolan, a member of the ICT staff from 1984, published a book with Richard Broderick that quickly became known as *the* 'manual for contextual theology' in South Africa (Nolan and Broderick, 1987). Members of BCCs were encouraged to interpret the Bible for what it says about political oppression and liberation, to seek conscientization through social analysis, and to arrive at an understanding of the need for major structural changes in society. What this amounts to is that Latin American-style liberation theology was being applied to the South African context in order to further the chances of political liberation. In South Africa, liberation theology was known as 'Black' or 'contextual' theology in order to differentiate South Africa's particularistic political environment – with its specific type of race and class exploitation, wide range of Christian, Islamic and traditional religious cultures – from that of Latin America. But the overall aim was the same: political liberation, beginning from an awareness of and a positive approach to what it meant to be a black African Christian during apartheid rule.

Black theology identified 'the concept of salvation with liberation, which leads [it] to justify and support active struggle by [Christian] believers against social exploitation and oppression', involving, when appropriate, class-based political struggle (Schoffeleers, 1988: 186). More generally, the social polarizations which apartheid rule entailed convinced many ordinary Christians in South Africa that the struggle against it was necessarily both theological and political. Ryall (1994) notes that, in effect, the mainstream Christian churches, with the exception of the Roman Catholic Church, had been absorbed into the structures of white dominance during the decades of apartheid rule. None offered a lead to those striving for liberation. Gradually, however, more and more Christian professionals emerged from a condition of conforming to the norms of the apartheid culture, yet for a long time they were 'not so much the servants of God as of temporal power' (Walshe, 1992: 33). Nevertheless, several Anglican priests, including Trevor Huddleston and Michael Scott, campaigned vigorously against apartheid; the former was recalled to England, the latter imprisoned and later expelled from South Africa.

Black theology's development had its origins in the 1960 Cottesloe Conference of the World Council of Churches, which condemned apartheid as an evil system which had led to such atrocities as the Sharpeville massacre.

Over the next 20 years, opposition to the racist government grew steadily worldwide. Within South Africa itself, the focal points of opposition were black township councils, formed explicitly to control and tax urban blacks, and the tricameral, racially-based constitution of 1983 which sought to divide and rule non-whites, to separate 'Indians' and 'coloureds' from blacks by giving the two former groups limited representation, while denying it to the latter. This was the political context that led to the growth of Black theology, which served as an ideology of support for black political struggles that paved the way for the eventual collapse of apartheid and South Africa's democratization process.

US Protestant evangelicals and the growth of African Independent Churches

Africa was on the receiving end of two waves of Protestant evangelization from the USA. The first occurred between the 1920s and the 1950s, and comprised various US churches (Hoekema, 1966: 24-31). The Seventh Day Adventists were especially successful with an estimated 2,000 missionaries in the field by the 1950s, while the American Assemblies of God had about 750 (Wilson, 1985: 309). By the early 1960s, the Full Gospel Businessmen's Fellowship International, founded in 1952 and with headquarters in Los Angeles, had established international chapters in Southern Africa (Hoekema, 1966: 33). It aimed, along with other groups, such as Campus Crusade, Youth With A Mission, and Christ for the Nations, to focus a message of redemption to higher education campuses, particularly West African institutions, where mass conversions took place. A second wave of foreign evangelical penetration of Africa occurred from the 1970s, a result of the success of various American television evangelists, including Pat Robertson, Jim and Tammy Bakker, Jimmy Swaggart and Oral Roberts, who focused upon Africa as a benighted continent crying out to be saved (Gifford, 1994, 2004; Freston, 2001, 2004).

The spread of US Protestant evangelical churches to Africa was greeted with concern by leaders of several of the established churches, who often saw their followers leaving for the foreign churches. Sponsored by American television evangelists and their local allies, thousands of conservative mainly foreign Protestant evangelical crusaders promoted American-style conservative Christianity in the 1980s. Ardently anti-Communist, they worked to convert as many Africans as possible to their type of Christianity and in the process, it is argued, to promote American foreign policy goals of anti-Communism (d'Antonio, 1990).

Pieterse alleges that a new religious and political hegemony developed in Africa as the result of the impact of the US churches. He claims that they were able to gain the cultural leadership of Christianity because of their social prestige and personal persuasiveness. Norms, beliefs and morals favourable to American interests were in turn disseminated as a fundamental aspect of the religious message. What this amounts to, according to Pieterse, was that African converts to the US conservative evangelical churches were victims of manipulation by the latest manifestation of neo-colonialism. The objective was not, however, to spirit away Africa's material resources, but rather to deflect popular political mobilization away from seeking structural change of the society and the economy, in order to serve either American strategic interests and/or financial objectives of US transnational corporations (Pieterse, 1992: 10–11).

Yet, as Mbembe and other have argued, successive waves of foreign Christian proselytization in sub-Saharan Africa resulted not in foreign imposition of an alien doctrine but instead indigenization of Christianity (Mbembe, 1988: 181; Ellis and ter Haar, 2004; Freston, 2004: 1–2). During the colonial era, European-style Christianity tried unsuccessfully to appropriate the richness of the autochthones' imagination and beliefs, in order better to convert and to dominate. But the outcome was different to what was anticipated: African independent churches emerged, while the former mission churches were Africanized. There are now thought to be well over 20,000 African Independent Churches (AICs). Their growth has been swift in a number of countries, including: Nigeria, Kenya, Ghana, Liberia, Malawi, Zimbabwe and South Africa. From small beginnings, some have now reached an impressive size. Among them are: the Church of God Mission in Nigeria (founded by Benson Idahosa) which has more than 2,000 branches. Others, including Andrew Wutawunashe's Family of God Church, Ezekiel Guti's Zimbabwe Assemblies of God Africa (both Zimbabwe), Mensa Otabil's International Central Gospel Church, and Bishop Duncan-William's Action Faith Ministries (both Ghana), have also grown swiftly (Gifford, 2004; Freston, 2001).

African Independent Churches offer a distinctive reinvention of an externally derived innovation, moulded and adapted to offer spiritual rebirth, potentialities for material improvements, and the growth of a new community spirit among followers. Regarding their theology, while adhering to the Bible as an unimpeachable theological source, many such churches also preach the effectiveness of experiential faith, the centrality of the Holy Spirit, the spiritual gifts of glossolalia ('speaking in tongues') and faith healing, and the efficacy of miracles. Their world-view is also often informed by personal conversion as a distinct experience of faith in Christ as Lord and Saviour (being 'born again' in the sense of having received a new spiritual life), and in helping others have a similar conversion experience. Rather than relying on foreign donations, as many of the former mission churches still do to some degree, most African Independent Churches are primarily reliant on members' donations for their upkeep (Gaiya, 2002: 1–7).

Members of AICs often have a strongly moralistic world-view: lying, cheating, stealing, bribing (or being bribed), adultery and fornication are frowned upon. Because members of the churches conceive of a clear division between what is right and what is wrong, they tend to be opposed to public corruption. There is a strong sense that the well-being of society is highly dependent upon good standards of personal morality. The nature of social interactions within some of the AICs also helps to reorientate traditional gender relations and, in the process, transform sexual politics. While some of the churches continue to promote a doctrine of female submissiveness, many do not. This appears to be one of the main attractions of such churches for young, urban women in Lagos, capital of Nigeria. It is particularly in the spheres of marriage, family and sexuality that one finds doctrines and practice in some AICs transforming gender relations quite dramatically.

Millions of Africans have joined AICs in recent years because of the intensity of the prayer experience they offer, the attraction of a simple and comprehensible message that seems to make sense out of the chaos which many perceive all around them, a moral code that offers guidance and the resuscitation of community values, as well as a sense of group solidarity exemplified in the way that individual followers often call each other 'brother' and 'sister'. In addition to spiritual and social objectives, members of AICs often also seek material goals. For some, the hope of prosperity is one of the churches' main attractions, leading to accusations that their message of hope is little more than a mindless and self-centred appeal to personal material well-being.

Although it would be misleading to try to standardize these churches and to assume that they are all the same, some things are clear. First, such churches often function as an alternative for those seeking a religious and social experience that the former mission churches often appear unable to offer. Many AIC members formerly belonged to the Roman Catholic Church and various Protestant denominations. Secondly, many of their followers are young people. Thirdly, regarding their theology, while there is a need for more research, it is clear that the faith gospel of 'health and wealth' is central to many, perhaps most. In Lagos, Nigeria, for example, AIC members run their own catering companies, hospitals, kindergartens and record companies. Employment is offered first to co-religionists because they are considered likely to be honest and to work hard (Corten and Marshall-Fratani, 2001).

The faith gospel was originally an American doctrine devised by the media evangelists in the 1950s and 1960s. Yet much of Africa's traditional religion has always been concerned with fertility, health and plenty. It is by no means clear to what extent such a gospel is still an identifiably American doctrine or whether it has now been thoroughly Africanized. The class make-up of the AICs is diverse: they do not simply minister to the poor or the middle classes or some other identifiable societal group, but find adherents from among all social classes. Another key theological feature is the understanding of spirits in the churches. Like the notion of 'health and wealth', spirits are an essential part of African religious culture. It is by no means clear what the relationship is between this traditional thinking and the demonology of Western Pentecostalism.

Followers of AICs are often concerned with social issues, involving a communal sharing of fears, ills, jobs, hopes and material success. Earthly misfortune is often perceived to be the result of a lack of faith; God will reward true believers. Such believers appear to estimate that people's redemption is in their own hands (or rather in both God's and the individual's hands), and expectations that government could or should supply all or even most of people's needs and deal with their problems is misplaced.

In sum, AICs challenge the Christianity of the former mission churches both intellectually and materially. Such is the concern with the gradual loss of followers, that the main-line Christian churches attack them on two fronts. On the one hand, AICs are accused of being little (if anything) more than Trojan horses of American conservative evangelical churches (Corten and Marshall-Fratani, 2001). However, the fact that some AICs are patronized by wealthy foreign (especially North American) pastors, probably helps confirm to many followers the desirable association between religion and personal prosperity. At the same time many main-line churches have rushed to incorporate glossolalia, faith healing and copious biblical allusions into their services (Haynes, 1996; Gifford, 1994, 2004).

The key point to emerge from our brief survey of attempts by US conservative evangelical churches to spread their influence in Africa was that their significance was overall diminished by the fact that their religious messages were invariably Africanized, often leading to the founding of distinct African churches. Yet this was not a trait of Christianity alone – indigenization also characterized historically how Islam was received in many African countries.

Transnational Islam in Africa

The historical characteristics of the Arab-Islamic–African connection make the relationship between the two regions easy to trace but difficult to assess. Interactions between Islam and Africa began with the intrusion of Arabs and the process of religious conversion. This was a process reflective of the 'dominant Arab/dominated African' relationship which was to become an unhappy component of Africa's historical development, as we shall see below when we examine Arab/non-Arab relations in Sudan. In general, given the historical significance of slavery in Africa, the role of the Arabs in the region was hardly auspicious. This is not to diminish the impact of effects of European colonial rule, for it tended to forge a closer link between the Arabs and the Africans, especially during the post-independence period as both regions fought the struggle against imperialism. Yet the years of colonial rule underlined the fact that divisions widely existed between Muslim Africans, often powerful in their communities, favoured and patronized by some colonialists, and non-Muslim Africans who, often deeply resenting the burden of European colonial control, produced the great majority of African nationalist leaders after the Second World War.

In the post-colonial era, the sometimes uneasy relationship between Muslims and non-Muslims significantly informed political developments not only in Sudan but also in other countries, including: Kenya, Tanzania, Nigeria, Chad and Uganda. Religious rivalry was often informed by two main issues: first, African involvement in the wider Islamic community, including the Organization of the Islamic Conference (OIC) and, second, the role of Arab oil wealth in Africa's economic and social development.

As we saw in Chapter 5, the transnational influence of the OIC has been muted by the inter-organizational rivalry between its leading members. In addition, Africa has been a focus of competition between oil-rich, non-African Muslim countries that have sought to pursue foreign policy goals in Africa, connected to their control of oil wealth and associated attempts to increase regional significance. The governments of Iran, Saudi Arabia and Libya have all been active in Africa since the 1970s, seeking to pursue strategic foreign policy goals that often had the impact, no doubt unintended, of helping to stir up local Muslim discontent. Decades of buoyant oil revenues gave such states the financial ability to prosecute aggressive foreign policies in Africa, where separation of political, diplomatic and religious goals is often difficult to draw. It is clear, however, that Iran's biggest drawback – it is predominantly a Shi'ite country when most African Muslims are Sunni – was partially offset for some African Muslim radicals – for example, in Nigeria during the 1980s – by its obvious revolutionary credentials. Some African Muslim radicals were attracted to Iran's revolutionary message for two main reasons: first, it gave them an immediately recognizable radical programme to try to appeal to politically marginalized and alienated people in their country; and, second, it offered Muslim radicals a political platform from whence to launch attacks on conservative Muslim elites, often close to ruling regimes. Like Iran, Libya also pursued radical goals in Africa, while Saudi Arabia's concerns included trying to counter the influence of Libya and Iran in Africa.

A further focus of the international and transnational impact of Islam in Africa has been the growth of militant Islamic networks in several parts of the region, notably East Africa, close to the Middle East and centres of Islamic radicalism, including Saudi Arabia and Yemen (Overton, 2005). We saw in Chapter 8 that America's post-9/11 'war on terrorism' focused, *inter alia*, on East Africa, although the attacks on the Twin Towers and the Pentagon were not the start of US interest in the region. Earlier, in the early 1990s, a US military mission had failed to pacify insurgents in Somalia. The latter were Islamist organizations, with significant sponsorship and encouragement from Saudi Arabia, which had grown in numbers and influence from the 1980s. They were also conduits of radical Islamist ideologies, a development that led the US and other Western governments to label them 'terrorist' organizations. Such a concern was justified when it became clear that Islamist extremists linked to al-Qaeda were responsible for deadly embassy bombings in 1998 in Kenya and Tanzania, as well as the unsuccessful attack on an Israeli jet in Mombasa (Kenya) in 2002. But before turning to focus on the emergence and development of radical Islamic networks in East Africa, we examine the significance of a 'moderate' transnational Islamic actor, the Tablighi Jamaat, which has its roots in India.

The Tablighi Jamaat: a moderate transnational Islamic network

Tablighi Jamaat is a Pan-Islamic movement that was founded in the late 1920s in the Mewat province of India by Muhammad Ilyas. In Arabic, *tablighi* means 'revitalization' (Rudolph, 1997: 252). The aim of Tablighi Jamaat is 'to deliver (the message)' of Islam, in the belief that this is the first duty of all Muslims. Tablighi activities are normally limited to Muslim communities, as the key aim is their spiritual awakening.

To achieve this goal, the movement encourages Muslims to spend both time and money in pursuit of a spiritual journey (called *gasht*) both to acquire religious knowledge (*taleem*) and in order to promote the faith. During scheduled journeys for the purpose of trying to achieve thee goals, members of each travelling group (called *jama'ats*) exchange information about basic tenets of the faith with each other. In addition, a list of the desired qualities of the *sahabah* (the companions of the Prophet Muhammad) are studied and practised. They are:

- Conviction of faith and belief in the oneness of Allah. This is understood to include the idea that 'the creation cannot do anything without the will of Allah, but Allah can do everything without the creation'. It also includes the belief that complete success in this world and the hereafter is only possible by following as closely as possible the way of life shown by the Prophet Muhammad. Every other course of action is believed to lead inevitably to failure in this world and the hereafter.

- Humility and devotion in *salah*. This refers to the idea of perfection in observance of prayers (*salah*).

- Acquiring knowledge and remembrance of Allah.

- Good behaviour towards both Muslims and non-Muslims. It implies sacrificing one's own needs in order to fulfil another's and also involves respecting one's elders and showing kindness to younger people.

- Purity of intention. This means that all good actions should be solely for the pleasure of Allah.

- Invitation to join Allah. This is concerned with spending both time and money in the 'Path of God, that is, calling people towards God, just as the Prophet Mohammed did' (http://www.tariqjamil.org).

Janson reports on the recent spread of the movement in the West African country, The Gambia. She emphasizes that the Tablighi Jamaat is a transnational missionary movement that encourages greater religious devotion and observance. In The Gambia Tablighi Jamaat missionaries insist that it was the duty of all Muslims, not only the few learned scholars, to carry out Tablighi work. She also emphasizes that Pan-Islamic missionary work has been a characteristic of Tablighi since 1927 when the movement was officially founded in Delhi, India (Janson, 2006: 44).

However, despite the fact that the Tablighi Jamaat is almost certainly the largest contemporary Islamic movement, there has been little scholarly attention paid to it. This is surprising because, as Gaborieau notes, the movement has a worldwide influence on the lives of millions of Muslims. Yet scholars have paid almost no attention to the Tablighi Jamaat. The explanation for this is not only because Africa is often seen, unjustly, as the periphery of the Muslim world but also because by far the greatest attention is paid to radical transnational Islamic movements that often seem to threaten Western security (Gaborieau, 1999: 21).

Some observers contend, however, that the Tablighi Jamaat is actually a radical organization linked to various expressions of 'Islamic terrorism'. For Alexiev, to see the Tablighi Jamaat as a benign missionary movement is erroneous. Instead, he claims, 'Tablighi Jamaat actions and motives [have] serious implications for the war on terrorism'. He claims that the movement has 'always adopted an extreme interpretation of Sunni Islam, but in the past two decades, it has radicalized to the point where it is now a driving force of Islamic extremism and a major recruiting agency for terrorist causes worldwide', with al-Qaeda allegedly recruiting its cadres from among the ranks of the Tablighi (Alexiev, 2005).

Militant Islamic networks in East Africa

For observers such as Alexiev, the radicalization of the Tablighi can be seen in the context of the wider growth of Islamic extremism in parts of Africa, including East Africa. Al-Qaeda bomb attacks in Kenya and Tanzania in 1998 ushered in a new era of security concerns in East Africa linked to the perceived growth and interaction of domestic and transnational expressions of militant Islam. Since then, both local and Western governments and policy makers have frequently expressed concern over the potential of East Africa to be a new focal point for Islamic militant organizations. Sizeable Islamic communities live in the hinterlands and coasts of a broad band of East African countries – from Sudan to Tanzania. Earlier, developments in Somalia – involving serious clashes in 1993 between local Islamic militants and US troops – underlined the potential for growth in influence of transnational Islamic militancy, especially al-Qaeda, which has built contacts with local warlords.[4] Al-Qaeda was also implicated in the killing of 18 American peacekeepers in 1993, leading to the withdrawal of all US forces from the region. Contemporaneously, Somalia became a haven for Arab fighters expelled from Pakistan, where many underwent religious and guerrilla training. More recently, an Islamist movement, the Islamic Courts Union, has taken power in Somalia's capital, Mogadishu. There are fears that this will encourage the development of Somalia as a beachhead for al-Qaeda, an outcome that the US State Department is committed to fight (Tisdall, 2006; Rice et al., 2006).

Islamic militancy in Somalia

During the 1990s, Somalia was a key entry point for Islamic militants into East Africa. Infiltration was facilitated by the fact that Somalia has a lengthy border with Kenya, and an extensive, unguarded coastline with the Red Sea. At the same time, there was growth in expressions of Islamic militancy in, *inter alia*, Kenya, Tanzania and Uganda. Each of these countries has been characterized by: widespread political repression, economic crises, rapid social change, uneven industrialization and swift urbanization; and each country has experienced extensive economic, social and political problems. Many Kenyans, Tanzanians and Ugandans, including members of their minority Muslim communities, are at or near the bottom of the economic and political hierarchies, and some harbour deep feelings of disappointment and disillusionment in relation to economic and political outcomes (Haynes, 1996, 2005). According to Dagne, 'From 1991, when Osama bin Laden was based in Sudan, al-Qaeda has been building a network of Islamist groups in both the Horn of Africa (Eritrea, Ethiopia and Somalia) and East Africa (Kenya, Tanzania, and Uganda)' (Dagne, 2002: 5). Dagne also believes that, as in Afghanistan and Pakistan, al-Qaeda was able to exploit extant circumstances of widespread poverty, ethnic and religious competition and conflict, poorly policed state borders, and often corrupt and inefficient governmental officials to create a regional 'terror centre' in East Africa.

Concern with the growth of regional Islamic militancy was expressed by various sources, including the CIA: since 9/11 in particular, the Agency has taken the threat of Islamic militancy in East Africa very seriously, to the extent of withdrawing from Asia some of its best agents in charge of observing Islamist movements and reposting them to various countries in the sub-region (Tenet, 2002). Following the London bombings on 7 July 2005, UK security agencies also paid more attention to the 'Islamist threat' believed to emanate from East Africa.[5] Observers suggest that Kenya, Uganda and Tanzania are targets for the expansion of transnational Islamic militancy, seeking to exploit novel spaces for growth (McGrory et al., 2005). Ronfeldt and Arquilla (2001) contend that East Africa is the focal point for a 'war of networks', rather than a Huntingtonian 'clash of civilizations'. That is, rather than a traditional army, hierarchical political parties or guerrilla groups, there is instead a loose network of militant Islamic movements at work, whose operations are encouraged by the ease of communications provided by and via the internet. For Marchesin (2001), such Islamic networks comprise an important new realm of threats, especially to incumbent, unrepresentative governments: non-military phenomena of general, vague and flexible forms, embodied in a plethora of 'informal organizations', typically autonomous cells acting without any imperative contacts with an organizational head.

As already noted, this is not to claim that 9/11 was the starting point for such Islamic networks. Prior to September 11, there is evidence that both Kenya and Tanzania were already targets of transnational Islamic terrorism. For example, on 7 August 1998, al-Qaeda operatives used truck bombs against the US embassies in Nairobi, Kenya, and Dar es Salaam, Tanzania. The explosions killed 240 Kenyans, 12 Tanzanians, and 11 Americans, and injured over 5,000 people, mostly Kenyans. Four years later, on 28 November 2002, two simultaneous attacks were conducted against Israeli targets in Mombasa, Kenya. Suicide bombers drove a truck into an Israeli-owned hotel, killing 10 Kenyans and 3 Israelis, and injuring over 20 Kenyans. Around the same time, terrorists tried to shoot down an Israeli aircraft using surface-to-air missiles; had they succeeded they would have killed more than 200 passengers on board.

In sum, recent expressions of Islamic militancy in East Africa – primarily involving local operatives who may or may not be affiliated to al-Qaeda – are judged by both local governments and Western security agencies and governments to be a significant and growing threat to stability and Western interests in the East African sub-region. Kenya and Tanzania – both countries attract hundreds of thousands of Western tourists each year – represent soft targets for such attacks, with several factors – including, poor security, inadequate border controls, and the ability to 'blend in' to local populations – facilitating the infiltration of foreign Islamic militants, including al-Qaeda operatives (McGrory et al., 2005).

Further, there are suggestions – and, according to both government and academic sources in East Africa (see below), firm evidence – that some, among the burgeoning number of transnational and local Islamic NGOs, aid and abet the growth of Islamic militancy in the sub-region. They pursue this goal by blurring distinctions between social, economic, political and religious functions and goals in directions that are commensurate with the objectives of the militants. Typically, the goals of Islamic NGOs active in East Africa include:

- provision of relief and humanitarian assistance to poor (Muslim) communities during emergencies, natural disasters (prolonged drought and floods), famine and epidemics;

- improvement of medium- and long-term development outlooks, with a focus on community development, improving agricultural yields, clean water, and improved provision of health and education, especially in the least-developed African Muslim countries;

- *da'wa* (that is, Islamic call, an equivalent to Christian evangelism) and conversion to Islam, and

- publishing, broadcasting and disseminating Islamic teaching and values.

Salih argues that some Islamic NGOs in East Africa 'have been used as a vehicle for spreading political Islam at an accelerated rate combining faith and material rewards among the disfranchised Muslim poor . . . becoming cronies to militant Muslim groups, including an emergent tide of indigenous African Islamic fundamentalist movements' (Salih, 2002: 1–2). Ghandour (2002) contends that the characteristics of such Islamic NGOs include not only an exclusive reference to Islam and an often powerful social legitimacy, but also sometimes ambiguous bonds with militant Islamists. This may place them in conflict relationships with African governments, as well as Western NGOs and states. Ghandour (2002: 129) also claims that some Islamic NGOs act as intermediaries between

> Islamic financiers and recipients operating in the environment of Islamist activists. It is extremely difficult for Western intelligence services to identify, localise and block the financial flows towards violent [Islamic] groups, because the NGOs are very active mediators that cover their tracks. Practically there are no direct relationships between powerful Islamic financial backers and Islamic activist organisations.

Following the August 1998 Nairobi bombing, Kenya's government banned five Islamic NGOs – Mercy Relief International, the Al-Haramain Islamic Foundation, Help African People, the International Islamic Relief Organization and Ibrahim Bin Abdul Aziz Al Ibrahim Foundation – because of their (1) alleged sympathies towards the aims of local 'Islamic fundamentalists', and (2) alleged mediatory role in relation to the financing of local militant Islamic organizations (Achieng', 1998; Salih, 2002: 24–5). In addition, Kenyan police and FBI agents from the USA raided the offices of Mercy Relief International. According to John Etemesi, Director of the Coordinating Board for Kenya's NGOs, the government's actions were necessary as the NGOs had allegedly been 'working against the security interests of Kenyans' (Achieng', 1998).

Following 9/11, there was a clampdown on numerous Saudi Arabian, Sudanese and Gulf charities, businesses and NGOs in Tanzania; all were said to have active links with al-Qaeda. In late 2001, the country's central bank froze 65 bank accounts of such companies (Kelley, 2001). Sources in the banking industry in Dar es Salaam said the accounts belonged to several banks on the initial post-9/11 list issued by the US government of 20 globally sought-after international companies said to be al-Qaeda owned and run businesses. Most of the companies were said to have branches in both Tanzania and Kenya, having moved there when bin Laden left Sudan in 1996 (Jamestown Foundation, 2003b). In addition, Tanzania's government also expressed concern about what it regarded as several 'questionable' Islamic NGOs. These included the African Muslim Agency (a Kuwaiti organization, engaged in the construction of mosques, schools and hospitals) and the Community Initiative Facilitation Assistance Development Group (a joint Tanzanian–Saudi investment venture established in 1995), whose activities include a focus on gender-related poverty (Jamestown Foundation, 2003a: 3–4; Intermediate Technology Development Group – Eastern Africa, 2002).

As in Kenya and Tanzania, Islamic NGOs have also been active in Uganda, with similar concerns, including: relief assistance to refugees and homeless people; founding and running orphanages, health centres and vocational training centres; and dealing with displaced persons and victims of natural disasters. The International Islamic Relief Organization (IIRO) is one of the most active Islamic NGOs in Uganda; it also operates in Kenya. The IIRO was established in 1978 as a humanitarian NGO to provide assistance to victims of natural disasters and wars all over the world, because some 80 per cent of refugees and victims, it claims, are Muslims. The IIRO claims that its relief programmes are directed solely towards the provision of medical, educational and social support for those in desperate need. It also aims to encourage local entrepreneurs by sponsoring viable economic projects and small businesses that can help victims find employment and earn a living. To fulfil these objectives, the IIRO has established a wide network of national and international contacts with various Islamic and non-Islamic relief organizations, institutions and individuals, operating in several countries in Europe, Asia and Africa. The major part of IIRO's financial contributions comes from private donations in Saudi Arabia, and an endowment fund (Sanabil Al-Khair) was established to generate a stable income to finance IIRO's various activities. The NGO has several departments, including: Urgent Relief and Refugees; Health Care; Orphans and Social Welfare; Education; Agricultural Affairs; Architectural and Engineering Consultancy; andthe 'Our Children project' (www.islamic-knowledge.com/Organizations.htm). The European Intelligence Agency contends that assistance to Ugandan Islamists – both from al-Qaeda and the government of Sudan – was provided through various Islamic NGOs, including the IIRO, the Islamic African Relief Agency, the World Islamic Call Society, the International Islamic Charitable Foundation, Islamic African Relief Agency, and the Africa Charitable Society for Mother and Child Care (European Intelligence Agency, *Al Qaeda Infrastructure in Sudan*, p. 21, quoted in Marchesin, 2003: 4). Table 10.1 lists the Islamic NGOs that have been alleged to be supportive of Islamic militancy in Kenya, Uganda and Tanzania in recent years.

Many academic and Western intelligence sources agree that the growth of Islamic militant networks in East Africa is facilitated and promulgated by a shared sense of transnational Islamic identity that stems from long-established historical, cultural, linguistic and trade ties to the Arab world. They

TABLE 10.1 Islamic NGOs in Kenya, Uganda and Tanzania that are alleged to support Islamic militancy and terrorism

Islamic NGO (home country in brackets)	Where in Africa the NGO is active
The Africa Charitable Society for Mother and Child Care (Sudan)	Uganda
Help African People (Kenya)	Kenya
Islamic African Relief Agency * (Sudan)	Kenya, Uganda
Muslim World League * (Saudi Arabia)	Kenya, Tanzania, Uganda
World Islamic Call Society (Libya)	Uganda
International Islamic Charitable Foundation (Kuwait)	Kenya, Tanzania, Uganda
International Islamic Relief Organization (Saudi Arabia)	Kenya, Uganda
Ibrahim Bin Abdul Aziz al Ibrahim Foundation (Saudi Arabia)	Kenya
Mercy Relief International (USA)	Kenya
Al Haramain Islamic Foundation * (Saudi Arabia)	Kenya, Tanzania, Uganda
The African Muslim Agency (Kuwait)	Tanzania
Community Initiative Facilitation Assistance Development Group (Saudi Arabia)	Tanzania

Source: Salih, 2002

* These organizations were on the list of 25 Islamic charities and NGOs which, in January 2004, the US Senate Finance Committee had asked the US Internal Revenue Service (IRS) for records on their activities (for complete list, go to http://www.danielpipes.org/blog/164). This inquiry was part of an investigation into possible links between Islamic NGOs and terrorist financing networks. Committee Chairman Charles Grassley and senior Democrat Max Baucus stated in a contemporaneous letter to the IRS that 'many of these groups not only enjoy tax-exempt status, but their reputations as charities and foundations often allows them to escape scrutiny, making it easier to hide and move their funds to other groups and individuals who threaten our national security' (http://usinfo.state.gov/ei/Archive/2004/Jan/15-147062.html).

also accept that proselytizing of various Islamic militants – including but not restricted to bin Laden and his second-in-command, the Egyptian, Ayman al-Zawahiri – seeks to exploit popular dissatisfaction that has developed following decades of undemocratic rule, endemic and serious corruption, and growing poverty and developmental disappointments (Salih, 2002; Jamestown Foundation, 2003a, 2003b).

Concern with the influence of external Islamic militant groups was one of the *raisons d'être* of the US-sponsored East African counter-terrorism initiative (EACTI), announced by President Bush in June 2003. The stated purpose of EACTI was to root out local manifestations of 'Islamic terror groups' and to destroy their regional networks.[6] The inauguration of EACTI underlines how the US government believed that in recent years East Africa had become a 'safe haven' both for Middle East-based Islamic terrorist groups, as well as indigenous militant Islamic organizations.

In sum, explanations for the recent rise of Islamic militancy in East Africa suggest that its increased prominence is linked to the increased influence of regional networks with headquarters in various Arab countries that are known to be logistical hubs of Islamic militancy, including: Kuwait, Saudi Arabia, Yemen, and United Arab Emirates (Marshall, 2003; Salih, 2002). Various countries in the East African sub-region – including Kenya, Tanzania, and Uganda – provide new opportunities for the recruitment and mobilization of new members for militant Islamic organizations, including al-Qaeda, its affiliates and offshoots. Secondly, East Africa is said to offer favourable grounds for the spread of transnational Islamic militancy as a result of highly porous land and sea borders, widespread corruption, largely dysfunctional structures of law enforcement, endemic organized criminality (involving everything from drugs and people smuggling to weapons trafficking) and growing numbers of weak and failed states. These factors imply multiplication of 'grey zones' where state power is at best fragmentary.

Civil war in Sudan: Religious and international factors

In some African countries, including Sudan, Mauritania, Mali, Niger, Somalia, Chad and Eritrea, the issue of the relative religious, social and political positions of Muslims and non-Muslims is highly controversial. These African countries are located in what is often noted as the 'periphery' of Arab centres of political and commercial power, places that historically experienced long periods of Arab political and commercial dominance. They all straddle an African geographical and cultural Arab/non-Arab division located approximately 15–20 degrees north of the Equator.

The question of national identity and the socio-political role of Islam has long been a key focus of political competition and conflict in Sudan. Sudan is unique among African countries south of the Sahara, because it is only there that until recently Islam had the status of state ideology. Sudan has long been associated with a poor human rights regime, with certain non-Arab, partially Christian, ethnic groups – such as, the Dinka, Nuer and Nuba – victimized by successive regimes whose policy appeared to be both Arabicization and Islamicization of the entry country (Haynes, 1996: 157).

Islamic government in Sudan

Sudan achieved independence in 1956. Its population is about 40 per cent Arab, living mostly in the north. The remaining Sudanese are black Africans, living mostly in the south. Sunni Muslims overall comprise about 70 per cent of the population, Christians about 5 per cent, and the remainder (c.25 per cent) comprising followers of various local traditional religions. Until 2005, the National Islamic Front (NIF) government was in power, a northern- and Arab-based regime. Founded by Muslim Brotherhood leaders (particularly Hassan al-Turabi, who, as the late President Numeiry's attorney-general in the 1980s, played a key role in introducing *sharia* law), the NIF was the main political force behind the 1989 military coup that brought the NIF government to power. The National Congress, created in early 1999 by President Al-Bashir, served as a front for the NIF, and NIF members dominated the government until a change of regime in 2005.

Following the accession to power of the NIF regime, an Islamist government took over. Its stated ambition was to bring about a radical transformation of public life throughout north-eastern Africa, a notoriously unstable region long riven by multiple civil conflicts and traditional rivalries. During the 1990s, the Islamist regime helped create community associations, many of which were able to deliver much needed welfare and social services. Yet the regime also had fatal ideological flaws: it was too rigid and one-dimensional, lacking sufficient constructive direction to form an appropriate basis to rule a modern nation-state (de Waal, 2004). Instead, the lure of apparently permanent *jihad* was strong – leading the Sudanese government into a tragically pointless civil war with various ethnic groups, mainly in the south of the country, as well as destructive relations with its neighbours, including Uganda, to try to win that war.

Sudan's civil war began in the early 1970s, and over the next three decades more than two million people died, and over four million were displaced from their homes. The background to the long-running conflict was that at the time of Sudan's independence in 1956, the country's nationalist leaders did not regard Islamic ideas as progressive. They were primarily motivated by the fervour of anti-colonial success, looking to modernist, temporal ideologies, especially socialism, to express and convey national unity even in Sudan, a predominantly Muslim country. In other words, the preferred developmental model was not indigenously derived but drew on European models, whereby secularization was an integral part of developmental strategy. As a result, Islam remained culturally, socially and historically important, not judged to be significantly progressive to form a basis for the ideological, political and developmental advancement of post-colonial Sudan.

Things began to change in the early 1980s, following the failure of the country's post-colonial development programme. From this time until recently, governments attempted to emphasize their power by underlining what they saw as Sudan's Arab-Muslim identity, involving a concentrated process of attempted Arabicization. The then state president, Ja'far al-Numeri, adopted Arab-Islamic dress in public, with the *jellabiya* (robe) and *anima* (turban) worn for many public appearances. This served to jettison the military uniform that Numeri had previously preferred to wear in public. Numeri also supervised the issue of new currency at this time, with bank notes depicting him as resplendent in his new persona. In addition, *sharia* law was adopted as the country's national law from 1983 (although it was never made to stick in the largely non-Arab, partially non-Muslim, south). Such acts, Bernal notes, served to bolster 'Sudan's Muslim and Arab identity while associating Islam with power and nationalism' (Bernal, 1994: 48). Underlying the move towards Arabicization and Islamicization were both foreign and domestic pressures. In terms of the former, Sudan's then chief aid provider was the government of Saudi Arabia.[7] The Saudi government joined forces with the country's most important domestic Islamic movement, the Muslim Brotherhood, to demand more dynamic manifestations of Islam in public life. The result was that political discourse in Sudan became increasingly phrased in Islamic terminology, while Numeri's political opposition also adopted the language of Islam to press their case. Following Numeri's overthrow, the military Islamic regime of Omar Hassan al-Bashir, which achieved power following a military *coup d'état* in June 1989, sought to juxtapose a form of Islamic social control by use of the military's organizational skills. It attempted to use the *sharia* in a way reminiscent of Communist states' use of Marxist–Leninist dogma to justify policy.

The attempt at domination by mainly northern Arab-Muslims in Sudan, striving for control of the non-Arabs of the south was often portrayed as that rare phenomenon in Africa, a religious war. However, it is more appropriate to see the conflict as primarily informed by attempts by northern Arabs to dominate southern non-Arabs, not a conflict about religion as such, but with ethnic and cultural competition as the key focal point. In other words, the conflict was de facto a struggle for Sudan's national identity – should it be one based in Arab-Islamic domination or should it be secular and multi-ethnic pluralism? We can see this issue coming to the fore in the case of Sudan's Nuba people, non-Arab but mostly Muslim. The Nuba live in the area of the Nuba mountains in the north of the country, and have been consistently victimized by the Arab north for not being 'real' Muslims. However, the most significant issue is that the Nuba are not Arabs, but black Africans (Flint, 1993).

These factors – involving northern Arab attempts to Arabicize the south, including attempted countrywide imposition of *sharia* law; non-representative, authoritarian governments, backed by the military; and significant cultural differences between the Arab north and the predominantly non-Arab south – form the backdrop to Sudan's three-decade civil war. For 30 years, armed resistance to the state in the south was focused in the two wings of the Sudan People's Liberation Army (SPLA), led respectively by the late Colonel John Garang de Mabior and Riek Machar Teny-Dhurgon. The civil war dragged on for so long because while both sides could avoid defeat, neither was strong enough to impose its preferred outcome. The SPLA could prevent the victory of the Arab-dominated Sudanese army, but it could not defeat it. Similarly, the army could keep the SPLA confined to its strongholds but not beat it through force of arms. The result was a stalemate, until January 2004 when both the government and the SPLA signed a peace deal following foreign, especially, US pressure.

There was extensive foreign involvement in negotiations to end the conflict. Earlier, in the late 1990s and early 2000s, the civil war, once confined to the south, had spread to Sudan's north-east border with Eritrea. Sudan government forces encountered not only several thousand soldiers of the SPLA but also six other opposition armies, which had recently organized themselves to fight together under a single command. This threat of a wider regional conflict prompted peace initiatives from Libya and Egypt, and from Africa's intergovernmental Authority for Development. Later, in November 2002, a peace envoy from the US government, John Danforth, visited Sudan and met leaders of both the government and the SPLA. Danforth not only proposed a series of confidence-building measures to bring the warring parties together but also managed to broker a ceasefire allowing aid agencies to airlift supplies to the beleaguered Nuba mountains. On the other hand, as Danforth admitted, years of mutual distrust between the warring parties made reconciliation especially difficult.

It took fifteen months of extensive negotiations, until January 2004, before Sudan's government and rebel leaders signed a peace deal that appeared to mark the end to one of Africa's longest civil wars of modern times. It was expected that the south would henceforward enjoy considerable political autonomy, with an administration to be called the 'government of southern Sudan'. The late SPLA leader John Garang was not only to lead the southern government but also to become a national vice president. Garang was, however, killed in an air crash in August 2005. Immediately following his death, 36 people died in riots in Sudan's capital, Khartoum. Many of those involved were southern Sudanese living in Khartoum who believed that the crash was suspicious, probably carried out by the government in order to eliminate Garang and his influence. Most southerners had hoped that he would be able to lead them in the future, putting into effect policies to change their lives and end discrimination in favour of Arabs. Following Garang's death, Sudan's president, Omar al-Bashir, said he was determined to continue the peace process in which John Garang had played such a central role, ending more than twenty years of civil war. If this claim turns out to be true, it is highly likely that continued foreign pressure, especially that emanating from the powerful Christian evangelical lobby in the USA, will be influential in such an outcome.

Sudan and the evangelization of US foreign policy

In the 1980s, the US Jewish community had great success in helping Jews in the Soviet Union by highlighting their plight and lobbying the US government, encouraging the latter to address the issue in its foreign policy (US Department of State, 2005). Christian groups in the USA noticed this success, and as a result turned their attention to what they regarded as glaring international wrongs. The result was what has been called the 'evangelization' of US foreign policy, an issue we examined in Chapter 8. According to Allan Hertzke, author of *Freeing God's Children: The Unlikely Alliance for Global Human Rights* (Rowman and Littlefield Publishers, Inc., New York, 2004), two decades of civil war in Sudan came to an end, due in large measure to 'the activism of evangelicals and their alliance with others, including Jewish groups. It's an unheralded story, but it's also a historical fact' (Hertzke, quoted in LaFranchi, 2006).

The wider context was that, in recent years, evangelical churches in the USA have grown in significance in both demographic and financial terms. In addition, as noted in Chapter 8, many such churches have in recent years developed a focus on international concerns – from sexual trafficking to the persecution of Christians, to missionary activities in the Middle East and Israel. As a result, according to John C. Green of the University of Akron: 'There's no question that evangelicals, particularly religious conservatives among evangelicals, are broadening their political interests' (Green, quoted in 'Evangelicals and foreign policy: new religious might', 2002).

This is not a new focus, as such Christian activism in America's foreign affairs dates back to the early twentieth century. It included strong backing among establishment Protestant churches for the foreign policy idealism of Woodrow Wilson and Franklin D. Roosevelt. During this time, however, such support was often 'top-down' and 'elitist' without necessarily appealing to the ordinary church followers. According to Martin Marty of the University of Chicago, 'the genius of the evangelical movement today, in domestic and foreign affairs, is its grass-roots appeal . . . Evangelicals are much more ready to claim God's purposes as their own. If God calls us to be the "righteous nation" they act' (Waldman, 2004).

Alan Horowitz, a neo-conservative at the Hudson Institute think tank, has often focused the foreign policy activism of US evangelicals. Horowitz has encouraged US evangelicals to make common cause with the secular neo-conservatives whose mission is to spread both representative government and free trade. According to Horowitz, a 'tough-minded' Christianity drives many US evangelicals. As a consequence many are now embracing international causes with the same moral fervour that they have long brought to domestic matters. Since 1998, their influence has helped achieve federal laws to fight religious persecution overseas, to crack down on international sex trafficking and to help resolve one of Africa's longest and bloodiest civil wars, in southern Sudan. The influence of Horowitz and evangelicals in the making of US foreign policy was made clear when President Bush used a public forum to announce his support for a more robust international intervention in Sudan's Darfur region. According to LaFranchi, Bush's initiative caught even some of his senior aides off guard. 'This was a clear milestone for the rising interest of Christian evangelicals in US foreign policy' (LaFranchi, 2006). Earlier, in order to push for the Sudan Peace Act, Horowitz linked evangelical campaigners with African-American groups. The law, passed in 2002, threatened a series of diplomatic actions against Sudan's Islamist regime if it did not make serious attempts to end the decades of civil war against Christian and other non-Muslim and non-Arab ethnic groups, many of which are found in the south of Sudan (Waldman, 2004). Peace conferences in 2005 ended the 21-year civil war and produced an agreement under which state revenues, in particular oil money, would be shared between the government and the southern rebel groups.

Conclusion

The following points have emerged in this chapter, concerned with the role of religion in Africa's international and transnational relations.

- Both Christianity and Islam are of immense importance, informing many domestic and international political issues.

- In the late 1980s and 1990s, religion's political role in Africa – notably the influence of the Roman Catholic Church – was particularly manifested in involvement in democratization moves in several regional countries, including South Africa.

- US evangelical churches were important influences in founding thousands of American Independent Churches, although the latter mainly developed over time as indigenous churches with African characteristics.

- Both 'moderate' and 'extremist' transnational Islamic movements are active in Africa.

- The end of Sudan's long-running civil war was due in large part to the influence of US evangelical Christians who were influential in encouraging the Bush administration to enact a law in 2002 designed to punish severely Sudan's Islamist government if it did not make serious efforts to seek to end the conflict.

Overall, what emerged from our discussion was that external religious movements and traditions are of great significance in understanding Africa's transnational and international relations, in both historical and contemporary contexts. This should not, however, be taken to imply that such external actors were simply able to impose their policies and programmes on Africans. We saw important processes of indigenization of external religious tradition and ideas that leads to the conclusion that Africans are far from being passive accepters of foreign religious ideas, preferring instead to develop their own religious vehicles.

Notes

1   Our focus in this chapter is on sub-Saharan Africa, that is, Africa below the Sahara desert, which divides North Africa from the rest of Africa. However, for reasons of brevity, we shall often use the term 'Africa' in the chapter to refer to sub-Saharan Africa.

2   Data from the International Religious Freedom Report 2004 (http://www.state.gov/g/drl/rls/irf/2004/35383.htm).

3   According to the Brazilian educator, Paulo Freire (1921–97), conscientization is a process enabling people to develop an objective distance from reality, to conduct a critical analysis of that reality, and as a result fashion the necessary conditions enabling them to act upon and seek to change that reality. Freire did not claim that gaining critical awareness *necessarily* leads to positive social action, merely that it is an *essential* prerequisite for making that movement. For Freire, the final aspect of conscientization involves action towards the transformation of reality (Freire, 1999).

4   Infiltration of al-Qaeda into Somalia was said to be facilitated by the fact that the country had become a collapsed or 'failed' state by this time: that is, a polity without an effective central government and with a generalized breakdown of law and order.

5   The bombings were initially claimed by a previously unknown organization, 'The Secret Organization of al-Qaeda in Europe' (http://news.com.com/E-mail+traffic+doubles+after+London+bomb+blasts/2100-1038_3-5778088.html?tag=nl), although at the time of writing (mid-2006), it is still uncertain whether there was direct al-Qaeda involvement.

6   A US Department of Defense official, Vincent Kern, told more than 120 senior African military officers and civilian defence officials gathered at the Africa Center for Strategic Studies (ACSS) seminar on 10 February 2004, that in June 2003, 'President Bush announced a $100 million, 15-month Eastern Africa counter-terrorism initiative under which the United States is expanding and accelerating [US] counter-terrorism efforts with Kenya, Ethiopia, Djibouti, Uganda, Tanzania and Eritrea'. The programme, Kern said, was designed to counter terrorism by focusing on coastal and border security; police and law enforcement training; immigration and customs; airport/seaport security; establishment of a terrorist-tracking database; disruption of terrorist financing; and 'community outreach through education, assistance projects and public information'. Kenya, for example, was to receive training and equipment for a counter-terrorism police unit aimed at 'building an elite Kenyan law enforcement unit designed to investigate and react to terrorist incidents' (http://japan.usembassy.gov/e/p/tp-20040212-24.html).

7 Following the rupture of Sudan's relations with Saudi Arabia during the Gulf War of 1991, Iran became Sudan's most important patron and aid provider.

Questions

1 To what extent does religion influence international relations in Africa? Illustrate your answer by reference to one religion.

2 Assess the impact of transnational Islamic networks on Africa's international relations.

3 Describe and account for the significance of transnational ideas associated with Catholicism in relation to political change in South Africa from the 1980s.

4 Was the civil war in Sudan a religious war?

5 Assess the impact of international attempts to end conflict in Sudan in the early 2000s.

Bibliography

Achieng', J. (1998) 'Ruling on Muslim charities averts strike', International Press Syndicate, 18 September. Available at: http://www.hartford-hwp.com/archives/36/index-bfbc.html Accessed 5 January 2005.

Alexiev, A. (2005) 'Tablighi Jamaat: Jihad's stealthy legions', *The Middle East Quarterly*, 12, 1, May. Available at: http://www.meforum.org/article/686 Accessed 15 June 2006.

d'Antonio, M. (1990) *Fall from Grace: The Failed Crusade of the Christian Right*, London: Andre Deutsch.

Barrett, D., Kurian, G. and Johnson, T. (eds) (2001) *World Christian Encyclopedia: A Comparative Survey of Churches and Religions in the Modern World*, Oxford: Oxford University Press.

Bernal, V. (1994) 'Gender, culture and capitalism', *Comparative Studies in Society and History*, 36 (1), pp. 36–67.

Corten, A. and Marshall-Fratani, R. (eds) (2001) *Between Babel and Pentecost: Transnational Pentecostalism in Africa and Latin America*, Bloomington: Indiana University Press.

Dagne, T. (2002) 'Africa and the war on terrorism', Congressional Research Service Report for US Congress, Library of Congress. Document catalogue number: m-u 41953-1 no. 02-RL31247.

Diamond, L. (1993) 'The globalization of democracy', in R. Slater, B. Schutz, and S. Dorr (eds), *Global Transformation and the Third World*, Boulder, CO: Lynne Rienner, pp. 31–70.

Ellis, S. and ter Haar, G. (2004) *The Worlds of Power: Religious Thought and Political Practice in Africa*, London: C. Hurst.

'Evangelicals and foreign policy: new religious might' (2002) Religionlink.org ('Linking journalists to ideas and sources') Available at: http://www.religionlink.org/tip_020923c.php Accessed 2 June 2006.

Flint, J. (1993) 'Sudan cracks down on Muslim rivals', *The Guardian*, 11 June.

Freston, P. (2001) *Evangelicals and Politics in Asia, Africa and Latin America*, Cambridge: Cambridge University Press.

Freston, P. (2004) *Protestant Political Parties: A Global Survey*, Aldershot: Ashgate.

Friere, P. (1999) *The Paulo Friere Reader*, London: Continuum Publishing Group.

Gaborieau, M. (1999) 'Transnational Islamic movements: Tablighi Jamaat in politics', International Institute for the Study of Islam in the Modern World (ISIM) Newsletter, July, pp. 21–2.

Gaiya, M. (2002) 'The Pentecostal revolution in Nigeria', Occasional Paper, Centre of African Studies, University of Copenhagen, July.

Ghandour, A-R. (2002) *Jihad humanitaire: enquête sur les OGN islamiques*, Paris: Flammarion.

Gifford P. (1994) 'Some recent developments in African Christianity', *African Affairs*, 93 (373), pp. 513–34.

Gifford, P. (2004) *Ghana's New Christianity: Pentecostalism in a Globalising African Economy*, Bloomington: Indiana University Press.

Harris, I., Mews, S., Morris, P. and Shepherd, J. (1992) *Contemporary Religions: A World Guide*, Harlow: Longman.

Haynes, J. (1993) *Religion in Third World Politics*, Milton Keynes: Open University Press.

Haynes, J. (1996) *Religion and Politics in Africa*, London: Zed.

Haynes, J. (2005) 'Islamic militancy in East Africa', *Third World Quarterly*, 26 (8), pp. 1321–39.

Hoekema, A. (1966) *What about Tongue-Speaking*, Exeter: Paternoster Press.

Intermediate Technology Development Group – Eastern Africa (2002) Newsletter, December. Available at: http://www.itdg.org/html/itdg_eastafrica/kit_dec_02.htm Accessed 4 June 2005.

Jamestown Foundation (2003a) 'Tanzania: Al Qaeda's East African beach-head?, Part 1', *Terrorism Monitor*, 1, (5), pp. 1–4.

Jamestown Foundation (2003b) 'Tanzania: Al Qaeda's East African beach-head?, Part 2', *Terrorism Monitor*, 1, (8), pp. 1–3.

Janson, M. (2006) ''The Prophet's path: Tablighi Jamaat in The Gambia', *ISIM Newsletter*, No. 17, Spring, pp. 44–5.

Kelley, K. (2001) 'Somalia "next US target" after Taliban', *The East African*, 19 November.

LaFranchi, H. (2006) 'Evangelized foreign policy?', *The Christian Science Monitor*, 2 March. Available at: http://csmonitor.com/2006/0302/p01s01-usfp.htm Accessed 2 June 2006.

Marchesin, P. (2001) *Les nouvelles menaces: les relations Nord – Sud des anneés 1980 à nos jours*, Paris: Karthala.

Marchesin, P. (2003) 'The rise of Islamic fundamentalism in East Africa', *African Geopolitics* (no issue number). Available at: http://www.african-geopolitics.org/show.aspx?ArticleId=3497 Accessed 4 April 2004.

Marshall, R. (1991) 'Power in the Name of Jesus', *Review of African Political Economy*, No. 52, pp. 21–37.

Marshall, R. (1993) '"Power in the name of Jesus": social transformation and Pentecostalism in Western Nigeria', in T. Ranger and O. Vaughan (eds), *Legitimacy and the State in Twentieth Century Africa*, Basingstoke: Macmillan, pp. 213–43.

Marshall, P. (2003) 'Radical Islam's move on Africa', *The Washington Post*, 16 October.

Mbembe, A. (1988) *Afriques indociles: Christianisme, pouvoir et etat en societé postcoloniale*, Paris: Karthala.

McGrory, D., Ford, R. and Rice, X. (2005) 'Search for bombers centres on East Africa connection', *Times Online*, 26 July. Available at: http://www.timesonline.co.uk/article/0,,22989 1708386,00.html Accessed 6 August 2005.

Nolan, A. and Broderick, R. (1987) *To Nourish our Faith: The Theology of Liberation in Southern Africa*, Hilton, S. Africa: Order of Preachers.

Overton, S. (2005) 'The Yemeni arms trade: still a concern for terrorism and regional security', *Terrorism Monitor*, 3 (9), 6 May, pp. 6–7.

Pieterse, J. (1992) 'Christianity, politics and Gramscism of the right: introduction', in J. Pieterse (ed.), *Christianity and Hegemony: Religion and Politics on the Frontiers of Social Change*, Oxford: Berg, pp. 1–31.

Rice, X., Burkeman, O. and Carroll, R. (2006) 'Fall of Mogadishu leaves US policy in ruins', *The Guardian*, 10 June 2006.

Ronfeldt, D. and Arquilla, J. (eds) (2001) *Networks and Netwars*, Santa Monica, CA: Rand Corporation.

Rudolph, Hoeber S. (1997) 'Introduction', in S. Hoeber Rudolph and J. Piscatori (eds), *Transnational Religion and Fading* States, Boulder, CO: Westview Press, pp. 1–24.

Ryall, D. (1994) 'The Roman Catholic Church and socio-political change in South Africa, 1948–90'. Unpublished manuscript.

Salih, M.A. Mohamed (2002) 'Islamic NGOs in Africa: the promise and peril of Islamic voluntarism'. Occasional Paper, Centre of African Studies, University of Copenhagen, March.

Schoffeleers, M. (1988) 'Theological styles and revolutionary elan: an African discussion', in P. Q. van Ufford and M. Schoffeleers (eds), *Religion and Development: Towards an Integrated Approach*, Amsterdam: Free University Press, pp. 185–208.

Tenet, G. (2002) '"Worldwide threat – converging dangers in a post 9/11 world": Testimony of Director of Central Intelligence George J. Tenet before The Senate Select Committee on Intelligence'. Available at: http://www.cia.gov/cia/public_affairs/speeches/2002/dci_speech_0206 2002.html Accessed 4 August 2005.

Tisdall, S. (2006) 'The land the world forgot', *The Guardian*, 23 May.

US Department of State (2005) 'Report on global anti-Semitism'. Available at: http://www.state.gov/g/drl/rls/40258.htm Accessed 23 June 2006.

de Waal, A. (2004) 'Counter-insurgency on the cheap', *London Review of Books*, 5 August 2004. Available at: http://www.lrb.co.uk/v26/n15/waal01_.html Accessed 5 July 2005.

Waldman, P. (2004) 'Evangelicals give U.S. foreign policy an activist tinge', *The Wall Street Journal*, 26 May.

Walshe, P. (1992) 'South Africa Prophetic Christianity and the Liberation Movement, *Journal of Modern African Studies*, XXIX, (1), pp. 27–60.

Wilson, B. (1985) 'A typology of sects', in R. Bocock and K. Thompson (eds), *Religion and Ideology*, Manchester: Manchester University Press pp. 301–16.

Further reading

A. Corten and R. Marshall-Fratani (eds), *Between Babel and Pentecost: Transnational Pentecostalism in Africa and Latin America*, Indiana University Press, 2001. This book focuses on extraordinary recent growth of the Pentecostal movement in Africa and Latin America. The contributors focus both on its transcendental dimension, expressed through doctrine, and the religious experience it produces, while also assessing Pentecostalism's sociological and political impact in various countries, including Ghana, Nigeria, Kenya, Brazil and Peru.

S. Ellis and G. ter Haar, *The Worlds of Power: Religious Thought and Political Practice in Africa*, C. Hurst, 2004. The starting point of this book is that religious thought and political practice are closely intertwined in Africa. African migrants in Europe and America send home money to build churches and mosques; African politicians consult diviners; guerrilla fighters believe that amulets can protect them from bullets, and many ordinary people seek ritual healing. All of these developments suggest the frequent application of religious ideas to everyday problems of existence, at every level of society. Far from falling off the map of the world, Africa is today a leading centre of Christianity and a growing field of Islamic activism, while African traditional religions are gaining converts in the West.

P. Freston, *Evangelicals and Politics in Asia, Africa and Latin America*, Cambridge University Press, 2001. This book is a pioneering comparative study of the political aspects of the new mass evangelical Protestantism of sub-Saharan Africa, Latin America and parts of Asia. Freston examines 27 countries from these regions, examining specificities of each country's religious and political fields. He also looks at implications of evangelical politics for democracy, nationalism and globalization. This uniquely comparative account of the politics of global evangelicalism will be of interest to many students of international relations.

P. Gifford, *Ghana's New Christianity: Pentecostalism in a Globalising African Economy*, Indiana University Press, 2004. This book explores Ghanaian charismatic Christianity (or neo-Pentecostalism) in relation to economic and political processes. It has two goals: (1) to identify this new Christianity and its religious vision, and (2) to analyse its socio-political role in effecting modernity in Ghana, a country that in recent years has been developing relatively quickly, in part because of its willingness to take advantage of globalization in various ways. Gifford's study focuses on the country's capital, Accra, and assesses the range and diversity of the capital's new churches. Gifford's study is both extremely rich in data – on leaders, adherents, theology, discourse, practices, Bible use, media activities, music, finances and organization – and broad in range. It addresses the whole charismatic spectrum, from prophets and healers who focus on deliverance from demonic forces to teachers who stress human responsibility. It is of interest to international relations students as Gifford demonstrates that the original American-style Pentecostalism is transformed into a recognizably Ghanaian form of religion.

J. Haynes, Religion and Politics in Africa, Zed, 1996. This book provides an account of the ways in which politics and religious institutions and groups interact with governments in Africa. The emphasis is on Christianity and Islam, with a concern with both domestic and international political dimensions of these religions. The book is both thematic and comparative, locating the role of religion in politics in Africa in historical, social and international contexts. The approach adopted is based upon comparison within and between African states. This analytical framework allows a comparison and contrast between various religious and political factors, including the nature of the relationship between the African state and assorted religious actors. In short, the book is concerned with an examination of the roles of religion in politics in contemporary Africa with reference to the historical, especially colonial, past.

CHAPTER 11

The Middle East

This chapter focuses on the region commonly known as the 'Middle East', an area that for many people is one of the first that comes to mind when thinking about interactions between religion and politics, both domestically and internationally. Centred on the eastern Mediterranean basin, the Middle East is, however, a geographical region without clear or obvious borders, unlike, for example, sub-Saharan Africa which is bounded on east, west and south by oceans and to the north by the Sahara desert. The lack of obvious boundaries for the region of the Middle East has led to at least four extant versions of its geographic extensiveness, involving between 5 and 26 countries. First, in its most restricted form it comprises just 5 countries: Syria, Lebanon, Israel, Palestine and Jordan. A second, slightly more expansive, version adds Cyprus, Turkey, Egypt and Iraq, making a total of 9 countries. A third entity is larger still, and includes: Iran, Kuwait, Saudi Arabia, Bahrain, Qatar, United Arab Emirates, Oman and Yemen (17 countries in all). The fourth and largest version adds various North African countries, including: Libya, Tunisia, Algeria, Morocco, Mauritania, Sudan, Eritrea, Djibouti and Somalia, amounting overall to a Middle East region of 26 countries. In this chapter we focus on: Israel, Saudi Arabia and Iran, implying that the third version is our overall focus. This is for three main reasons. First, it enables us to examine the impact of three of the region's most important religious traditions in three of its leading countries: Israel (Judaism), Iran (Shia Islam) and Saudi Arabia (Sunni Islam). Secondly, in each of these countries various religious actors seek to influence foreign policies via the application of soft power, often in tandem with hard power wielded by the state in the form of military and economic leverage. Thirdly, these countries are a key source of international focus because of their importance to the stability of the Middle East, a concern underlined by the significant involvement of the USA in each country's foreign policy and international relations.

The religious context of this chapter is that, uniquely among regions of the world, the Middle East was the birthplace of 'three main world religions: Judaism, Christianity and Islam' (Korany, 2005: 72). Partly for this reason, and partly because there have been many recent examples of the interaction of politics and religion in the region, including the Iranian revolution in 1979 and the rise to power of Hamas in the Palestinian National Authority in 2005, many people now routinely associate the Middle East region with religious competition, tensions, and clashes, especially between Islam and Judaism. In this chapter, we examine the significance of religion in the foreign policies and international relations of Israel, Saudi Arabia, and Iran. In each case, we shall see attempts to influence foreign policy through wielding religious soft power, encouraging governments to apply religious principles, values and ideals. This is in line with what Fox and Sandler have noted: 'religion's greatest influence on the international system is through its significant influence on domestic politics. It is a motivating force that guides many policy makers' (Fox and Sandler, 2004: 168).

For many people, the relationship of religion and politics in the Middle East is contextualized by two key events: the 1948 founding of Israel as a homeland for the Jews and Iran's 1979 Islamic revolution. The latter was internationally significant in three main ways. First, unlike earlier globally resonant revolutions – such as the French Revolution (1789) and the Bolshevik Revolution in Russia (1917) – the dominant ideology, forms of organization, leading personnel, and proclaimed goals of the Iranian revolution were religious in both appearance and inspiration. Secondly, in Iran the key ideological sources and 'blueprint' for the post-revolutionary period were all Islamic, derived from the Muslim holy book, the Quran, and the *Sunnah* (the traditions of the Prophet Muhammad, comprising what he said, did, and what he approved of). Thirdly, there were fears expressed by Western governments – emphasized by the fact that approximately 70 US hostages were held in Tehran for 444 days by Islamic student militants following the revolution – that Iran's revolutionary regime would now aggressively attempt to utilize its Islamist ideology in order to export its revolution to radicalize further already restive Muslims in the Middle East and elsewhere.

Another key event in the Middle East to do with religion and politics was the founding of the State of Israel in 1948 as a homeland for the Jews after the horrific policy of attempted national extermination practised by the Nazis. Since its founding nearly 60 years ago, Israel's sense of identity has consistently been based on its 'Jewishness' (Korany, 2005: 72), although, as Smith notes, within Israel 'factions have always differed on what lands were essential to constitute the state of Israel' (Smith 2005: 220). The issue of the extent of the geographical area of Israel is at the centre of the continuing dispute with the Palestinians, a conflict that over the last six decades became internationalized, involving external involvement from various states and international organizations. The issue began as a secular security issue but evolved over time into a continuing political battle with significant religious dimensions.

In this chapter we focus on the following issues. First, we examine the political role of religious Jews in Israel. We also examine the influence of the 'Israel Lobby' and of Christian Zionists in the USA that are said to be collectively significant in helping mould US policy towards Israel. Secondly, we examine the soft power of religion in Saudi Arabia, with special reference to the country's foreign policy and international relations. Finally, we consider Iran's Islamic revolution, its post-revolutionary international relations and foreign policy, and the influence on the latter of influential religious actors, with special focus on Iraq and the competition with Saudi Arabia to achieve an influential position.

Voll suggests the context of these concerns. According to him, 'the structure of world affairs and global interactions is in the middle of a major change. Both in terms of actual operations and the ways that those operations are conceived and understood by analysts, the old systems of relationships are passing rapidly' (Voll, 2006: 12). In particular, 'across many political, economic, and military areas, international "soft power" is taking precedence over traditional, material "hard power"' (Arquilla and Ronfeldt, 1999). Often, however, in discussions of soft power, religion does not get much attention. For example, the US international relations expert, Joseph Nye, who originally coined the term 'soft power' over a decade ago, only briefly notes that 'for centuries, organized religious movements have possessed soft power' (Nye, 2004a: 98). Most of his attention, however, is on more secular sources of soft power.

But as we have already seen in this book, it is becoming difficult to ignore the soft power of religion as it is becoming increasingly visible in many parts of the world, linked to what is widely understood as a general resurgence of religion with international and foreign policy ramifications in some countries. For example, in the Middle East, much attention is devoted to militant transnational Muslim movements, including, but not restricted to, al-Qaeda. As Voll notes, 'the growing importance of soft power enhances the strength of these militant movements' (Voll, 2006: 15). Less often noted, however, is another use of religious soft power among many countries in the Middle East: attempts by domestic religious actors and organizations to influence their country's foreign policy and international relations. In this chapter we examine this issue in relation to Israel, Saudi Arabia and Iran.

Politics and religion in Israel: domestic and international factors

Religion, identity and Zionism

Israel is an ethnically and religiously mainly Jewish country, the only state in the world where a majority of citizens are followers of Judaism. Since the country's founding in 1948, a main goal of successive governments has been to maintain this aspect of Israel's character (Sandler, 2006). But Israel is not a theocracy.[1] In addition to Judaism, other religions, including Islam and Christianity, are respected. More than 75 per cent of Israelis classify themselves as Jews and 16 per cent characterize themselves as Muslims. The remainder – less than 10 per cent of the overall population – include Christians, Druze,[2] and the religiously unclassified.

Since its founding in 1948, there has been controversy over whether Israel is a modern, Western-style, essentially secular, state – that is, where religion is usually privatized, as in Britain, France and Germany – or a *Jewish* state, where Judaist laws and customs necessarily take precedence over secular ones. In 1969, Luckmann described the state of Israel as characterized by a process of bureaucratization along 'rational business lines'. This implied not only that Jewish religious interests were politically unimportant, unable to determine major issues of public policy, but also that there was overall an accommodation in Israel to an explicitly 'secular', 'Western' way of life (Luckmann, 1969: 147). Luckmann was implicitly referring to the well-known classificatory schema of the German sociologist Max Weber (1864–1920). Using Weber's terminology, Luckmann characterized Israel as both a 'modern' and 'rational' state with the following institutions: (1) a representative legislative body (the Knesset) to enact laws; (2) an executive authority – the government – to conduct the state's affairs; (3) a disinterested judiciary to enforce the law and protect individuals' rights; (4) a rational bureaucracy (civil service) to regulate and organize educational, social and cultural affairs; and (5) state-dominated security services – including, the police and the armed forces – to protect the state from both external and internal attack (Weber, 1978: 56). None of these institutions looked to religious bodies or organizations to fulfil their roles and duties.

Over time, however, Luckmann's conclusions would be increasingly contested. Six decades after its founding, can we say that Israel is 'just' another Western-style, secular state? One key source of doubt in this regard is the public role of Judaism in Israel, which many observers argue has become more prominent in recent years (Sandler, 2006). This is partly due to the fact that numbers of religious Jews have grown in recent years. Now Israel's Jews are almost evenly divided between the 'religious' and the 'secular'. Just under half – 49 per cent – classify themselves as 'religious'. Of these, 6 per cent define themselves as *haredim*, that is, 'ultra-orthodox', 9 per cent classify themselves as 'religious', 34 per cent as 'traditionalists', that is, they strictly adhere to *halakha* (Jewish law). The remaining 51 per cent of Israeli Jews regard themselves as 'secular', although half of them still profess to 'believe in God' (Elazar, n.d.).

Some secular Jews no doubt regard Israel's religious Jews as dangerous, intolerant fanatics, an opinion emphasized in November 1995 when the then prime minister, Yitzhak Rabin, was assassinated by Yigal Amir, a 25-year-old religious Jew. Amir killed Rabin because of the latter's willingness to negotiate with the Palestine Liberation Organization (PLO) to try to end the decades-long conflict between Israel and the Palestinians, a deal that involved allowing the Palestinians to control some of the land in the Gaza Strip and the West Bank (of the River Jordan) that Israel has occupied since its victory in the Six-Day War of 1967. For many religious Jews, including Amir, willingness to hand over territory to the Palestinians was unacceptable because they believed that it was God's will that present-day Israel should conform to the geographically larger size of the biblical entity, *Eretz Yisrael.* For many non-religious Jews, Rabin's murder appeared to be a clear manifestation of the willingness of 'Jewish fundamentalists [to] attack Jews with secularist leanings' in pursuit of their religious goals (Bealey, 1999: 140).

Religious Jews and 'Jewish fundamentalism'

Religious Jews are sometimes referred to as 'Jewish fundamentalists', characterized by their determination to follow the 'fundamentals' of Judaism and to work to get them observed in both private and public life (Silberstein, 1993). Contemporary Jewish fundamentalism – manifested by organizations such as the banned terrorist organization, *Gush Emunim* (see below) – has roots in Israel's remarkable victory, in just six days, over several Arab armies in the June 1967 war (Sprinzak, 1993). For religious Jews, this was a particular triumph as it led to the regaining of the holiest sites in Judaism from Arab control, including Jerusalem, the Temple Mount, the Western Wall and Hebron. The victory was taken as a sign of divine deliverance, an indication of impending redemption. At the time, even some secular Jews spoke of the war's outcome in theological terms (Sandler, 2006).

The nature of Jewish identity has long been understood as an overlapping combination of both religion and nation. Many Israeli, especially religious, Jews think of themselves as a nation inhabiting a *Jewish* state created by their covenant with God. The interpretation of the covenant and its implications gave rise to the characteristic beliefs and practices of the Jewish people. Vital to this covenant was the promise of the land of Israel. Following historical dispersions under first the Babylonians and then Romans, Jews prayed for centuries for the end of their exile and a return to the 'promised land': Israel. Except for relatively small numbers, Jews lived for centuries in exile, normally in separate communities. Awaiting divine redemption to return them to their homeland during the diaspora, many Jews' lives were defined by *halakha* (religious law), which served as a core, national component of their Jewish identity. Overall, the Jews' historical suffering during the diaspora was understood as a necessary continuation of their special dedication to God (Chazan, 1991).

Over time, a feeling grew among many Jews that they should seek to acquire their own national homeland. A mobilizing political ideology reflecting this aspiration – Zionism, focus of the endeavour to create a national home for the Jews – emerged in the second half of the nineteenth century. Fundamental to Zionism is the recognition of the national identity of the Jews, the rejection of exile and belief in the impossibility of assimilation. While the Jewish holy book, the Torah, is central to secular Zionists as a 'historical' document, many are uncertain about both the centrality of religious elements in Jewish cultural history and the extent of rejection of orthodox Jewish practices. As a result, the secular Zionism of Theodor Herzl's World Zionist Organization, founded 1897, was condemned as 'idolatry' by religious Jews, who believed that it sought to replace reverence for God and the Torah by secular nationalism and the 'worship' of the land. In response, religious Jews founded both the *Mizrahi* party (*Merkaz Ruhani* or Spiritual Centre in 1902) and *Agudat Israel* (Association of Israel, founded 1912), although many also supported Zionist efforts to establish a Jewish state. The result was that by the late 1930s and early 1940s there was growing support for the idea of the state of Israel even among religious Jews, stimulated by knowledge of the anti-Jewish Holocaust in Nazi-controlled Germany, during which the Nazis murdered around six million Jews.

Having established the religious and nationalist background to the formation of the state in Israel, next we examine religious Jews' influence on Israel's domestic and foreign policies.

Politics and religion in Israel

Since the country's founding in 1948, state policy in Israel has traditionally favoured the political centre ground; this means that neither religious nor secular political ideas have routinely been able to dominate the political agenda. Over time, however, religious Jews have become an increasingly significant political voice. They have not been collectively strong enough to govern alone via various political parties, although they have often been important components of successive coalition governments, the norm in Israel over time, reflective of the country's fragmented political society. Religious Jews are especially vocal in opposition to the policy of conceding parts of biblical Israel to the Palestinians, especially the West Bank of the River Jordan. The topic is a subject of intense controversy that divides the country. It has dominated the political agenda since the early 1990s, focused in the divisive Oslo peace accords of 1993, Prime Minister Rabin's assassination in 1995 and, following US pressure, the handing over of the Gaza Strip to the Palestinians a decade later (Smith, 2005; Ehteshami, 2002).

In national-level elections in recent years explicitly religious parties have achieved sigificant electoral success. In elections since the mid-1990s, religious parties have typically gained more than 20 seats of the total of 120, around 17 per cent. This has often been sufficient to give them a role in government. The current Knesset, elected in March 2006, has 27 members from three religious parties: *Shas* (12), *Ichud Leumi – Mafdal* (9),[3] Torah and Shabbat Judaism (6) ('Elections in Israel March 2006'). This means that nearly one-quarter of all Knesset seats were in the hands of religious parties following the 2006 election.

Religious political parties in Israel

Religious parties first entered government in 1949, but it was not until 1967 that they managed significantly to influence Israel's political life. Israel's decisive victory in the Six-Day War in 1967 suggested to many religious Jews that the messianic age had begun, leading inexorably to the recreation of the biblical kingdom of Israel. Various Jewish religious-political organizations, including *Edah Haredit* (God Fearful Community), *Neturei Karta* (Guardians of the City) and *Gush Emunim* (Bloc of the Faithful), also emerged at this time. *Gush Emunim* was formed in early 1974 in the West Bank settlement of Kfar Etzion. Its main concern was to achieve

(Continued)

conquest and settlement of what it regarded as the biblical land of Israel (*Eretz Yis-rael*). Over the next decade, *Gush* grew rapidly, especially after the 1978 Camp David agreement between Israel and Egypt that led to the return to the latter of the Sinai desert – grabbed by Israel in the 1967 war. Not only *Gush*, but also other such organizations, including the late Rabbi Meir Kahane's organization, *Kach* ('Thus') and *Kahane Chai* (Kahane Lives; founded after Kahane was assassinated in 1990), argue on religious grounds against giving back territory not only to Egypt but also to the Palestinians or any other non-Jewish entities. This is because they regard such a policy as in contradiction of God's will expressed in the Torah.

Religious zealots – organized in groups like *Kach* and *Kahane Chai* – were often mouthpieces of the mostly religious Jewish settlers who tried to influence Israeli policy in relation both to Egypt and the Palestinians: not to hand back land to non-Jews. Following the 1993 Oslo peace accords with the Palestinians, involving the latter receiving autonomy in the Gaza Strip from August 2005 and an area still to be ascertained around the West Bank city of Jericho, religious opposition to the accord with the Palestinians was manifested in mass murder. A Jewish religious zealot, Baruch Goldstein, linked to both *Kach* and *Kahane Chai*, murdered 29 people and injured approximately 100 more in a dawn attack on a mosque in the West Bank town of Hebron in February 1994. Following the massacre the Israeli government, in a sign of its commitment to crush Jewish extremist groups that were systematically using violence to try to achieve their objectives, banned both *Kach* and *Kahane Chai*.

The political significance of religious parties and movements on policy-making in Israel is unlikely to fade soon for several reasons. First, the basis of both nationality and the creation of the state of Israel remains a sense of religious identity, making the issue consistently vulnerable to the influence of religious Jews, some of whom are also political extremists. Secondly, there has been strong growth in numbers of religious Jews since the early 1970s. Now, it is claimed that up to a half of Israeli Jews 'respects the religious commands', while one in ten belongs to the *haredi* (ultra-orthodox) community. Around 60 per cent of the *haredi* population is under 25 years of age, and the proportion of the ultra-orthodox will grow because many have large numbers of children (Bhatia, 1996). Many such people form the core support and activist bases of the, sometimes extremist and banned, religious movements and parties. Thirdly, the latter will continue to have major political influence because of the nature of the country's political system based on proportional representation. As a result, such parties have the ability to acquire political rewards in return for supporting either of the two main secular political parties, Kadima and Labor-Meimad, in the context of the formation of coalition governments. Finally, in recent years there has been a dovetailing of secular security concerns (concerned with Israel's regional national interests and power) and religious interests (aversion to handing over land to the non-Jewish Palestinians, as it is believed to be against God's will). In tandem, the two constituencies amount to a powerful coalition of interests, often able to apply significant pressure on Israel's government both via the ballot box and other forms of leverage, including interaction with what Mearsheimer and Walt (2006) have identified as an extremely influential 'Israel Lobby' in the United States.

The Israel Lobby in the USA

How and under what circumstances might Israeli religious actors influence the foreign policy of the USA in relation both to Israel and more generally to the Middle East? We noted in Chapter 2 that, according to Telhami, 'religion plays an important role in politics in certain parts of the world' with 'greater prominence of religious organizations in society and politics' in some countries compared to others (Telhami, 2004: 71). As we have already seen in relation to Israel's domestic political scene, religious parties have been consistently influential in Israel's politics over time. As a result, it is also likely that they will have a voice in the country's foreign policy. However, religious actors' *potential* ability to wield such influence is not the same thing as saying that they will consistently be able to influence outcomes; ability in this regard will depend on various factors. Even if a religious organization or individual gets access to formal decision-making structures and processes it does not *guarantee* influence on either policy formation or execution. To have a policy impact, it will also be useful to establish and develop relations with key players in both society and politics, including influential print and electronic media. In sum, as Mearsheimer and Walt suggest, various 'interest groups', including religious ones, can acquire influence by lobbying elected representatives and members of the executive branch, making campaign contributions, voting in elections and by trying to mould public opinion in various ways (Mearsheimer and Walt, 2006: 6)

According to Mearsheimer and Walt, the Israel Lobby influences US policy towards the Middle East so significantly that 'the thrust of US policy in the region derives almost entirely from [US] domestic politics, and especially the activities of the "Israel Lobby"' (Mearsheimer and Walt, 2006: 1).[4]

Mearsheimer and Walt employ the term 'the Israel Lobby' as a shorthand expression to refer to a 'loose coalition of individuals and organisations who actively work to steer US foreign policy in a pro-Israel direction'. 'Hardliners' include the American–Israel Public Affairs Committee (AIPAC) and the Conference of Presidents of Major Jewish Organizations, important entities that support Israel's expansionist policies, while 'softliners' include Jewish Voice for Peace, bringing together groups that are inclined to make concessions to the Palestinians. Yet, despite their differences, according to Mearsheimer and Walt, both 'moderates' and 'hardliners' 'favour giving steadfast support to Israel' (Mearsheimer and Walt, 2006: 6). The Israel Lobby does not include only Jewish Americans but also conservative Christian evangelicals, such as: Gary Bauer, Jerry Falwell, Ralph Reed, Pat Robertson, Dick Arney and Tom DeLay, as well as various 'neo-conservative gentiles', including: John Bolton, Robert Bartley, William Bennett, Jeanne Kirkpatrick and George Will (Mearsheimer and Walt, 2006: 6). Some among the latter are also 'Christian Zionists', people who believe that Israel's rebirth in 1948 was the fulfilment of biblical prophecy, and support the government's expansionist agenda, as to do otherwise would be going against God's will (Clark, 2003). This belief is commonly, although not exclusively, associated with conservative evangelical Protestants in the USA. Christian Zionists also believe that the maintenance of a Jewish state in Israel is a precondition for the Second Coming of Christ and as a result advocate unwavering US support for the state of Israel. Finally, Christian Zionists consider that the return of the Jews to the Holy Land, and the establishment of the state of Israel in 1948, was in accordance with biblical prophecy, a necessary precondition for the return of Christ to reign on earth (Halper and Clarke, 2004). Note that Christian Zionist beliefs are different from those of Zionism, that is, the general principle that the Jews have a right to a national homeland in Israel. Christian Zionism is a specifically theological belief, not necessarily involving overt sympathy for the Jews, either as a national or a religious group. Christian Zionists believe that the Jews must eventually accept Jesus as the Messiah for biblical prophecy to be fulfilled. As a result, some Jews view Christian Zionism as a form of anti-Semitism.

Many Israelis recognize the Christian Right's political clout in the USA, especially during the period of the presidency of George W. Bush. For example, since 2001, 'Gary Bauer has met with several Israeli cabinet members and with [former] Prime Minister Ariel Sharon'. Another former prime minister Benjamin Netanyahu claimed that, ' "We have no greater friends and allies" than right-wing American Christians' (Zunes, 2004). It is not the case, however, that Israel's foreign policy is directed from outside by Christian

Zionists in the USA or any other external group. Instead, as Chazan explains, Israel's foreign policy and more generally the country's international relations are also strongly influenced by three domestic factors with significant religious elements: (1) the 'structure and composition of political institutions'; (2) 'social differentiation and the concern of specific groups'; and (3) 'substance of political debates and their relations to fundamental ideological concerns'. She also notes a key implication of these factors: Israeli reactions to stimuli from outside the country are 'filtered through a domestic political lens which operates according to its own distinctive rules' (Chazan, 1991: 83).

We saw in Chapter 2 that such an arrangement is quite common: foreign policy in at least some states – including, but not restricted to, the USA, India, Iran and Saudi Arabia – is affected, sometimes considerably, by domestic religious constituencies and organizations. In Israel, religious Jews' political significance derives from three main factors: (1) the nature of the country's political system: proportional representation, giving an influential voice to an array of small parties, including religious ones; (2) the ethnically and religiously fragmented nature of society; and (3) the country's conflict-ridden, ideologically diverse, political party system. When we add to the mix the fact that Israel's public life also reflects the consistently influential voice of public opinion, then we can conclude that Israel's foreign policy is heavily affected by the views of religious Jews. At times, this influence is significantly bolstered by the support of both secular nationalist constituencies within Israel and that of the 'Israel Lobby' in the USA, which brings together both Jewish American organizations and Christian Zionists (Walt, 2005; Mearsheimer and Walt, 2006; Halper and Clarke, 2004; Zunes, 2004; Clark, 2003).

Overall, the ambitions of religious Jews in Israel were strongly supported in recent years by lobby groups in the USA, including various Jewish American entities and non-Jewish Christian Zionists with strong representation in Congress. Yet such people were collectively unsuccessful in seeking Israeli retention of Gaza and removal of the Palestinians from both Gaza and the West Bank 'in order to fulfil Old Testament prophecy' (Smith, 2005: 220). This suggests that the combined soft power of Christian Zionists and Jewish American groups, while a major factor in current US Middle East policy, was insufficient to tip US foreign policy in the direction of not supporting Israel's pull-out from Gaza in August 2005.

In conclusion, in this section we have seen that the political involvement of religious Jews in Israel had an important impact over time on the country's policies, both domestic and foreign. However, it would be incorrect to see the issues in both contexts as simply reducible to religious concerns; it would be correct to see them as involving interaction of secular security and religious concerns expressed in a variety of political forms and contexts.

In the next section, we shift emphasis to examine religion's significance in the international relations and foreign policies of two important Middle Eastern Muslim countries: Saudi Arabia and Iran. We will see that in both cases significant political issues – respectively the 1990–01 Persian Gulf War and the 1979 revolution – led to a refocusing of the role of religion in politics, with important international ramifications. We also learn, however, that this did not necessarily imply that religious concerns dominated secular security concerns consistently in relation to either country. As with Israel, we conclude that in both Saudi Arabia and Iran, while religious actors and goals were politically significant, in terms of international relations this did not mean that religious concerns will always dominate secular concerns.

Saudi Arabia: religion and foreign policy

The monarchy is the central political institution in Saudi Arabia. The king's powers are in theory limited within the confines of Islamic (*sharia*) law and other Saudi traditions. He – never she – is chosen through a two-stage, informal process: the royal family chooses a candidate, and the decision is subsequently endorsed by the *ulama* (Muslim religious scholars trained in Islam and Islamic law). The current king is the 85-year-old Abdullah ibn Abdulaziz as-Saud who ascended to the throne in 2005, following the death of his brother, King Fahd.

The political role of the king in Saudi Arabia

In Saudi Arabia, the ruler should aim to rule in a consensual way in order to retain the support of important societal elements, especially the royal family and *ulama*. The overall political policy is enshrined in the Basic Law, adopted in 1992, that declared: (1) Saudi Arabia is a monarchy ruled by the sons and grandsons of King Abd Al Aziz Al Saud, and (2) the Muslim holy book, the Quran, is the country's constitution, and the basis of government is Islamic law (*sharia*). In addition, there have been several new laws in recent years, deemed necessary to seek to regulate the increasingly complex functions and concerns of modern Saudi society. However, the new laws are in addition to the *sharia*, and must not run counter to it. No political parties or national elections are allowed in Saudi Arabia, although a consultative council, the Majlis ash-Shura, with 150 members exists, albeit with little concrete power. Overall, the king enjoys absolute power, although the support of the *ulama* is central in upholding the legitimacy of his rule.

According to Hinnebusch, the king's position over time has grown stronger relative to the *ulama*. Thus, while Saudi 'decision-makers cannot wholly ignore political Islam in foreign policy making, no Islamisation of foreign policy has resulted' (Hinnebusch, 2005: 169). In addition, no influential international Islamic alliance has developed under Saudi auspices. There is a parallel here with an earlier, international ideology of significance in the Middle East: Pan-Arabism. Several factors – including the autonomy of separate state structures, the disorder of the international states system, the lack of economic interdependence involving Islamic countries, and the dependence of many on the most powerful countries in international relations, especially the USA – served collectively to undermine the ability of Pan-Arabism to serve as an effective international mobilizing ideology for the Arab states of the Middle East. The contemporary successor to Pan-Arabism is Pan-Islam. Pan-Islam originally emerged as a transnational Muslim movement during the second half of the nineteenth century. It called for Muslims around the world to come together, drawing on a belief not only that Muslims shared common interests based on religion but also that the great majority were being forced to live under European colonial rule. The idea of Pan-Islam is often credited to an individual, Jamal al-Din al-Afghani, the founder of Islamic modernism (Milton-Edwards, 2006). However, the concept of Pan-Islam was short-lived as, around the time of the First World War, it was replaced by Arab nationalism that quickly became more important among Arab states than the idea of transnational Muslim unity advocated by Afghani (Landau, 1990).

In recent years, however, there has been a resurgence of interest among Muslims in the idea of Pan-Islam, with numerous transnational groups forming. However, Pan-Islam is a useful idea for both rulers and their challengers. Many among the former, including the government of Saudi Arabia, have used it to try to solidify their rule. We saw in Chapter 5 that an important contemporary vehicle of Pan-Islam is the Organization of the Islamic Conference (OIC) – an organization that seeks to act as the main conduit of international Islamic concerns. We noted, however, that the ability of the OIC to act in this leadership role is undermined by the fact that its leading members, including Saudi Arabia and Iran, use the organization as a competitive vehicle for their national foreign policy concerns. Its cohesiveness is also impeded by the facts of the intra-Islamic division between Shia and Sunni versions of the faith. In addition, counter-elite revolutionary challengers, including al-Qaeda and its offshoots and imitators, find the concept of Pan-Islam to be a useful ideological referent when seeking to mount challenges to the status quo both internationally and in respect to various domestic governments, including that of Saudi Arabia.

Wahhabism and foreign policy in Saudi Arabia

Saudi Arabia is run ideologically under the aegis of Wahhabism, a very puritanical form of Sunni Islam that seeks to spread influence internationally by funding construction of mosques and Quranic schools around the world. Since the 1970s, the Saudis have sponsored an estimated 1,500 mosques and 2,000 schools worldwide, from Indonesia to France. As Nye notes, this Saudi funding is immensely important as a way of spreading its soft power. It is almost impossible to estimate the extent of financial largesse, emanating from both state and private sources, which is distributed in this way. Nye estimates that the Saudis have spent around $70 billion on aid projects since the 1970s' oil price hikes, channelled through both radical Islamic groups and mainstream Islamic charities. He also notes that even if this amount is heavily inflated, it still 'dwarfs the $150 million that the U.S. spends annually on public diplomacy in the Islamic world' (Nye, 2004b). The implication he draws is that US soft power loses out to Saudi soft power because the latter is bolstered by much greater financial rewards.

Like that of Israel, Saudi Arabia's foreign policy is partially based on religious considerations: for example, for religious reasons, the government opposed both Jewish Israel and the atheist Soviet Union. During the 1990s, as a result of both domestic and international pressures, the Saudi government, again like that of Israel, sought to reorientate its foreign policy. Partly as a result of American encouragement, Israel's government turned its attention to trying to find a political solution to the 'Palestinian problem'. The Saudi government was also encouraged by the USA to seek to redevelop its foreign policy towards a more 'pro-Western' focus, and this implied a reduction in religious influence and content of foreign policy, especially the funding of radical Islamist groups. This was a major shift in emphasis, as the religious component of Saudi foreign policy had been consistent in various ways, both financially and institutionally, for decades. As noted above, especially since the onset of oil prosperity in the early 1970s, the kingdom has donated tens of billions of dollars in a strategy which it views as necessary to support the spread of Sunni Islam and to back various Muslim nations and groups, especially those that adopt the Saudi religious ideology of Wahhabism (Hinnebusch, 2005: 156). Secondly, Saudi Arabia has consistently sought to exploit its position as guardian of the most holy places in Islam, Mecca and Medina, strongly encouraging Muslims around the world to make the pilgrimage (*hajj*), while also expanding arrangements to house and transport the millions of pilgrims who arrive annually. Thirdly, Saudi financial contributions have played a major role in building the World Muslim League (WML), a religious-prop-agation agency founded in 1962 with headquarters in Mecca. According to the WML documents published in Arabic on the WML website in 2005, Wahhabi clerics, backed by Saudi Arabia, 'are increasingly targeting Europe as an ideological recruiting ground' (Novikov, 2005: 8)

Saudi foreign policy was encouraged partially to change direction in the early 1990s. At this time, Saudi Arabia was faced with what appeared to be the strong possibility of invasion by Iraq, whose government had demon-strated aggressive intent by occupying Kuwait. It was by no means certain that a massive United States military presence in Saudi Arabia would deter Iraq from invading Saudi Arabia or withdraw from Kuwait. Consequently, the Saudi government was faced with a clear choice: openly side with the US government or risk invasion from Iraq on its own. In choosing the first op-tion, the Saudi government was compelled to join the United States-led anti-Iraq alliance to try to force Iraqi withdrawal from Kuwait. In response, Iraq tried to play the 'Islamic card', calling for Arab and Islamic solidarity against the USA and its allies. The Saudis noted, however, that a claimed shared Islamic orientation did not forestall Iraq's invasion of Kuwait. During the fighting, Iraq directed missiles against Saudi territory, with several strik-ing both the capital Riyadh and several other population centres. Saudi armed forces fought with anti-Iraq troops, most of whom were both non-Muslims and non-Arabs. Overall, the outcome of the war demonstrated to the Saudis that it was implausible to try to base the country's foreign policy alone in their vision of Islam. Instead, the king and his advisers became con-vinced that the kingdom's security interests necessitated a balancing of both secular security concerns and religious considerations (Hudson, 2005). As a result, Saudi policy shifted from its earlier focus – propagation of Sunni Islam and attempted containment of Shia Iran – to side with the USA in the anti-Iraq coalition.

The change in foreign policy orientation had serious political ramifica-tions domestically, resulting in a deepening – and by the time of writing (mid-2006) still unresolved political crisis dividing the country's ruling elite. On the one hand, there is King Abdullah – the 85-year-old leader of a group of reformers – who seeks closer links with the West, especially the USA, for security purposes. On the other side of the ideological divide is the interior minister, Prince Nayef, leader of the decidedly anti-American Wahhabi *ulama* (Ziyad, 2003). Internationally, the king has a higher profile, but domestically the prince is very influential. The division between the two men draws at-tention to the institution of the Saudi monarchy which has traditionally functioned as intermediary between two distinct political communities: a

Westernized elite that looks to Europe and the USA as models of economic and to some extent political development, and a Wahhabi religious establishment convinced that its interpretation of Islam's golden age serves as the country's most appropriate religious and ideological guide, including the view that giving a political voice to non-Wahhabis is idolatrous (Doran, 2004). The *ulama*, backed by Prince Nayef, strongly supports the principle of *Tawhid* (monotheism), epitomized by the ideas of Muhammad ibn Abd al-Wahhab, the eponymous founder of Wahhabism. The goal is to project an emphatically monotheistic version of Islam against the Wahhabi enemies, 'polytheists' and 'idolaters', including: Christians, Jews, Shi'ites, and even insufficiently devout Sunni Muslims. These four entities are collectively regarded as a grand conspiracy whose goal ultimately is to destroy 'true Islam' – that is, the Wahhabist form of Sunni Islam. The USA, referred to as the 'Idol of the Age', is said to lead the anti-Wahhabi conspiracy. This is because the US (1) attacked Sunni Muslims in both Afghanistan and Iraq, on both occasions making common cause with Shi'ites; (2) supports Israel against the Sunni Muslim Palestinians; (3) allegedly promotes Shi'ite interests in Iraq, and (4) encourages the Saudi government to de-Wahhabize the country's educational curriculum. More generally, US and Western culture is said to undermine Saudi societal values through its control of various media, including cable television and the internet. According to the Saudi Wahhabists, this tide of idolatry finds a focus in 'ultra-liberal', permissive attitudes toward sex, informed by Christian values, and supportive of previously unheard of female freedoms in Saudi Arabia (Novikov, 2005).

Tawhid and *jihad*

The ideas of *Tawhid* are closely connected to *jihad* or holy war, that is, the struggle by some Muslims – 'sometimes by force of arms, sometimes by stern persuasion' (Doran, 2004) – against idolatry. For many among the *ulama* there is little or no difference between seeking to eradicate un-Islamic cultural, social and political practices at home and supporting *jihad* against the USA in Afghanistan and Iraq. The position of the *ulama* on these issues in important in Saudi Arabia as the canon of *Tawhid* ensures they enjoy a uniquely important political status because of their privileged position, deriving from the fact that they alone have had the necessary education and training to identify and do away with anti- or un-Islamic behaviour and entities (Freeman, 2002). This underlines that *Tawhid* is not merely a set of religious ideas but also a set of political principles. Prince

(Continued)

Nayef, both interior minister and head of the secret security apparatus, is a strong supporter of the principle and practice of *Tawhid*, and of the *ulama* as a religious and political entity. The prince strongly defends Wahhabi puritanism in part because he depends politically upon the support of the conservative *ulama*. In foreign policy, Nayef's support for *Tawhid* includes championing *jihad*, and this is manifested in a concrete way through his control over the Saudi fund for the support of the Palestinian intifada (which the *ulama* perceive as a defensive jihad against a global anti-Islam, anti-Palestinian, Zionist–Crusader alliance) (Doran, 2004; Korany, 2005: 73).

Since 9/11 the battle for dominance in Saudi Arabia between 'moderates' and 'hardliners' has acquired a new international focus. On the one hand, there are the moderates, lead by King Abdullah, supported by the USA. The government of the latter sees itself engaged in a continuing war of ideas for the hearts and minds of moderate Muslims and Arabs. To win that war, according to Nye (2004b), the USA is going to have to become more accomplished in wielding soft power, especially in the Middle East. The biggest challenge to the USA in terms of soft power comes from radical Islamist ideologies, which in Saudi Arabia emanate from Wahhabist ideas, which have become increasingly significant internationally in recent years (Novikov, 2005). According to Nye, 'radical Islamists are expert in the use of soft power, attracting people to their ranks through charities that address basic needs and through religious institutions that form the backbones of communities' (Nye, 2004b). This highlights how difficult it is to control soft power, as Saudi Arabia's ruler has discovered. It can have unintended consequences – including attracting people to what many in the West see as intensely malevolent religious organizations and networks, including al-Qaeda.

Yet the soft power of Wahhabism is not a resource that the Saudi king and his allies can be sure of controlling, much less banking on to obtain favourable foreign policy results. Many among the *ulama*, as well as ordinary Saudis, regard the royal family as corrupt and in league with Western infidels. For some, the aim is to replace the current regime with a more authentically Islamic one, and some zealots are clearly not averse to the use of terrorism to try to achieve this goal, as indicated by attacks in 2003 on residential compounds and the bombing that ripped apart a police headquarters in Riyadh a year later. In sum, according to Nye, 'the royal family's bargain with the Wahhabist clerics backfired because the soft power of Islamic radicalism has flowed in the direction of Osama bin Laden and his goal of overthrowing the Saudi government' (Nye, 2004b).

In conclusion, Saudi Arabia's future ideological direction can ultimately be reduced to a single issue: can the state reduce the domestic and international soft power of the radical *ulama* and their Wahhabist ideas? We have seen that in Saudi Arabia, where such Islamists have access to the levers of power via Prince Nayef, they have not so far been able to direct Saudi Arabian foreign policy uniformly along the lines they would prefer. King Abdullah and his allies know that such a foreign policy direction would likely lead to serious conflict with the US government. Consequently, out of deference to Washington, the moderates aim to block Prince Nayef's support for al-Qaeda and other radical Islamists, albeit so far with limited success. Fear of offending Washington also prevented a Saudi/OIC stand against US sanctions against Iran and Pakistan for their development of nuclear capacities (Haynes, 2005).

Iran: Islamic revolution and foreign policy

The overthrow of the Shah of Iran in 1979 was one of the most significant, yet unexpected, political events of recent times, because of the pivotal role of Islamic actors in his downfall. Unlike earlier revolutions in other Muslim majority countries, such as Egypt, Iraq, Syria and Libya, Iran's was not a secular, leftist revolution from above, but one with massive popular support and participation from below that ended with an Islamic theocracy in power, with the state dominated by Muslim clerics under the overall leadership of Ayatollah Khomeini. It was also surprising that the Islamic revolution displaced the Shah's regime so easily, as it was not a shaky, fragile monarchy, but a powerful centralized autocratic state possessing a strong and feared security service (*Sazeman-i Ettelaat va Amniyat-i Keshvar*, National Organization for Intelligence and Security, known as SAVAK) and an apparently loyal and cohesive officer corps. The point, however, was that the forces that overthrew the Shah were united in their goal, derived from all urban social classes, the country's different nationalities and religious groups, and ideologically dissimilar political parties and movements. Following infighting that saw Muslim clerics eventually triumphant, an Islamic Republic was declared, with the Islamic Republican Party coming to power before promulgating an Islamic constitution.

The international significance of Iran's 1979 revolution

The Iranian revolution was internationally significant in three main ways. First, it was the first modern revolution where the dominant ideology, forms of organization, leading personnel, and proclaimed goals were all religious in appearance and inspiration. Secondly, the guiding principles of the revolution were derived from both the pages of the Muslim holy book, the Quran, and the *Sunnah* (the traditions of the Prophet Muhammad, comprising what he said, did, and of what he approved). While economic and political factors played a major part in the growth of the anti-Shah movement, the religious leadership saw the revolution's goals primarily in terms of building an Islamic state, publicly rejecting both 'Western' materialism and liberal democracy. Thirdly, there were immediate fears from Western governments that Iran's revolutionary regime would attempt to 'export' its revolution to radicalize already restive Muslims in the Middle East and elsewhere.

Radicals within Iran's ruling post-revolution elite lost ground following the death of Ayatollah Khomeini, the revolution's charismatic leader, in June 1989, a few months after the end of Iran's war with Iraq (1980–88). Iranians, like people everywhere, hoped for improving living standards. It was becoming increasingly clear to elements in the government that if Iran was to achieve this aim the country urgently needed foreign investment, technology and aid. A clear lesson was emerging: even a successful *Islamic* revolution would struggle to succeed when globally isolated. Over time, it also became clear that many, perhaps most, Iranians were not content with the policy of Islamicization, a process that for many amounted to little more than severe political and social repression, especially for women and non-Muslims, behind a religious façade (Ehteshami, 2002). Reflecting the weight of such concerns, in 1997 a self-proclaimed reformer, President Khatami, was elected to office in a landslide victory. Yet he found himself caught between the demands of, on the one hand, those wanting social and political liberalization and, on the other, the entrenched conservative religious leaders who did not. Ultimately, President Khatami was unable to assert himself sufficiently, and the result was a stalemate between reformers and conservatives, with the latter eventually returning to political pre-eminence (Barnes and Bigham, 2006; MacAskill and Tisdall 2006; Tisdall, 2006). In sum, nearly three decades after the event, Iran's Islamic revolution has managed to embed religious conservatives in power. The costs, however, were high: the government lost much of its initial popularity, failed to develop the country economically despite vast oil wealth, and did not manage to build a viable model of Islamic administration (Barnes and Bigham, 2006; Sohrabi, 2006).

What has been the impact of the revolution on the country's foreign policy and international relations more generally? The first thing to note is that few if any nations at the present time have so clearly articulated an official religion-based ideology and view of the state as an instrument of that ideology, as has Iran. Secondly, like Saudi Arabia, Iran's post-revolution foreign policies and activities have been the focal point of competition for influence by religious and non-religious interests. As a result, Iran's foreign policy has fluctuated between a focus on secular, especially security and economic, goals and religious objectives both regionally and internationally. The coming to power of President Mahmoud Ahmadinejad in 2005 led to a partial reassertion of religious concerns in Iran's foreign policy, although secular security matters were also pronounced including 'Iran's right to civil nuclear power, Iran's regional interests, [and] its attitude to the United States and Europe' (Barnes and Bignam, 2006: 33).

Public opinion, religion and foreign policy in Iran

It is often assumed that Iran is a closed society with little ability for most citizens to discuss matters of state. However, not only do foreign policy debates fill the Iranian press, but foreign policy is also a frequent topic of open deliberation in the Iranian parliament, the Majlis (Sarioghalam, 2001). The Ministry of Foreign Affairs is often the main promoter of Iran's secular state interests. In contrast, religious hardliners in Iran, like in Saudi Arabia, advocate Tehran's championing of Islamic causes and expressions of Muslim solidarity with co-religionists beyond Iran's borders, frequently attacking the Foreign Ministry's policies, especially in the pages of the Iranian daily *Jomhuri-ye Islami* (Afrasiabi and Maleki, 2003). This indicates that religion may have an impact on foreign policy, especially when the country's rulers find it useful to bolster support for a policy that it advocates, such as seeking to increase Iran's influence in neighbouring Iraq. This includes, more generally, propagation of (Shia) Islam and advancing the cause of other Muslim peoples. But such policies' significance will fluctuate dependent on the views of significant personnel, within government and outside it, both religious and non-religious, and their ability to influence government decisions (Afrasiabi and Maleki, 2003).

Following President Ahmadinejad's election in 2005, the former president, Mohammad Khatami, publicly criticized 'the "powerful organization" behind the "shallow-thinking traditionalists with their Stone-Age backwardness" currently running the country'. This was believed to be a covert reference to a radically anti-Bahai and anti-Sunni semi-clandestine society, called the Hojjatieh, said to be rapidly 'reemerging in the corridors of power in Tehran' ('Shi'ite supremacists emerge from Iran's shadows', 2005).[5] According to Barnes and Bigham, the chief ideologue of Hojjatieh is Ayatollah Mohammad Taqi Mesbah-Yazdi, a hardline Shi'ite cleric and key inspiration to Iranian 'messianic fundamentalists' (Barnes and Bigham, 2006: 2). Ayatollah Mesbah-Yazdi is a close ally of President Ahmadinejad, reflected in the claim that he issued a *fatwa* urging all 2 million members of the *bassij* Islamic militia[6] to vote for Ahmadinejad in the 2005 presidential elections ('Shi'ite supremacists emerge from Iran's shadows', 2005). This is evidence to bolster Sarioghalam's claim that 'Iran's foreign policy is shaped, not mainly by international forces, but by a series of intense post-revolutionary debates inside Iran regarding religion, ideology, and the necessity of engagement with the West and specifically the United States' (Sarioghalam, 2001: 1). Until the election of Ahmadinejad in 2005, there was often agreement that when the material interests of the state conflicted with commitments to 'Islamic solidarity', then Iran's government would usually give preference to secular security and economic considerations. Iran sought to use religion in pursuit of secular state interests – as a way of contending with neighbouring regimes or trying to force changes in their policies. For example, Iran's government has long promoted Islamic radicals and anti-regime movements when official relations with a Muslim country are poor, such as with Uzbekistan or Azerbaijan, but does not work to undermine secular Muslim regimes such as Turkmenistan if that regime's relations with Tehran are good (Kemp, 2005; Ramazani, 2004).

But the election of Ahmadinejad appears to have led to a change in the power balance in Iran, whereby religious soft power has emerged as an influential component of Iran's foreign policy especially in relation to Iraq and the competition there with Saudi Arabia for influence (Barnes and Bigham, 2006). Iran is 90 per cent Shi'ite and Iraq is between 60 and 65 per cent Shi'ite, while about one-third of Iraqis are Sunnis. These factors have facilitated the ability of Iran to achieve considerable power and influence in Iraq since the fall of Saddam Hussein in March 2003. From that time, Iran has actively supported the position of the USA in advocating elections in Iraq. The main reason was that by the use of its cultural and religious soft power, Iran had a practical way to try to facilitate the political dominance of Iraq's Shi'ite majority and, as a result, the government hoped to achieve an influential position in relation to the country's political future. The post-2003 position contrasts with the approach Iran adopted in the immediate aftermath of the 1979 revolution when the government focused efforts on hard power strategies, for example, seeking to export the revolution 'through the funding of Shiite resistance groups'. Now, however, 'current circumstances encourage Iran to use soft power to help create some sort of Islamic government in Iraq' (Kemp, 2005: 6). On the other hand, the use of Iranian soft power to appeal to co-religionists comes up against a bid from Saudi Arabia to extend its influence in Iraq. Both sides use a mix of hard and soft power, including religion. Iran is said to have a good intelligence presence and a better organized military capability in Iraq, while Saudi Arabia seeks both to use its financial largesse and to exploit the dissatisfaction of Iran's Sunni minorities. Iran's Sunni minorities live in some of the least-developed provinces and are under-represented in parliament, the army and the civil service. Iran's Kurds, who are Sunni, have rioted in the north, while the ethnic Arab south is another location that suffered both riots and a bombing campaign in 2005–06 (Kemp, 2005; Barnes and Bigham, 2006).

Iran is fighting in Iraq to win the hearts and minds of ordinary Iraqis, the majority of whom are Shi'ites. While Iran is believed to have a better intelligence presence in the country, Saudis are said to account for the majority of suicide bombers active in Iraq. Writing in *Newsweek* in August 2005, a former Central Intelligence Agency agent, Robert Baer, quoted an unnamed senior Syrian official who told Baer that more than 80 per cent of the 1,200 suspected suicide bombers arrested by the Syrians in the two years following the invasion of Iraq in March 2003 were Saudis. Baer then quoted Iran's Grand Ayatollah Saanei who responded by describing the Saudi Wahhabi suicide bombers as 'wolves without pity'. Iran, he declared, would 'sooner rather than later . . . have to put them down'. Saudi Arabian interests are thought to be behind the suicide bombing campaign. Saudi Arabia is also reported to be active in Iran in other ways, especially in the ethnically Arab, oil-rich south of the country. Riyadh is said to have offered financial incentives for local people to convert from Shi'ite to Sunni Islam (Baer, 2005).

Overall, it is probable that Iran will continue to promote democratic structures and processes in Iraq, as a strategy to help consolidate a strong Shi'ite voice in Iraq's government, and thus likely to help Iran increase and maintain its influence in the country. Iran is also likely to seek to continue to use its soft power as a key short- and medium-term means to try to facilitate its main objectives in Iraq: political stability and an accretion of Iran's influence. On the other hand, Iran's involvement in Iraq is also part of a long-term strategy that may involve exercise of both soft and hard power. Since 2003 Iran has opted for intervention through primarily soft power and religious ties, but it could choose to be a more significant and active (and violent) player should its strategic interests be challenged. 'Iran's capacity, capability, and will to influence events in Iraq are high in terms of both hard power and soft power' (Kemp, 2005: 7).

Conclusion

Focusing on the international significance of the interaction of religion and politics in the Middle East, this chapter has emphasized the following:

- In each of the country contexts we examined – Israel, Saudi Arabia and Iran – there were various issues of analytical significance in this regard.

- In Israel, Saudi Arabia and Iran, normative variables – such as, the concept of 'greater Israel', Sunni Islamic proselytization (Saudi Arabia) and attempts to export Islamic revolution (Iran) – have interacted with secular national interest concerns to produce foreign policy outcomes.

- In each country in relation to foreign policy and international relations, secular security concerns interacted with religious concerns in ways that were also linked to the salience of various expressions of soft power.

Overall, to understand the dynamics of the international involvement of religion and politics in the Middle East we must take into account how secular structures and processes interact with religious ones. We saw that the political involvement of religious Jews in Israel was important in helping mould the country's policies both in relation to the Palestinians in the Occupied Territories and the government of the USA. This emphasizes that over time secular Zionist concerns were augmented by religious Jews' concerns about the desirability of as large an Israel as possible in order to accord with God's will. However, it would be incorrect to see political struggles reducible to religious terms and issues; rather, they reflect interaction of both secular security and religious concerns. We also saw this in relation to Saudi Arabia and Iran, where in both countries various issues – including respectively the 1990–01 Persian Gulf War and the 1979 revolution – led to a refocusing of the role of religion in foreign policy and, more generally, international relations. More recently, however, the post-2003 conflict in Iraq, the election to power of President Ahmadinejad in 2005 and a corresponding rise in the influence of some religious individuals and organization, as well as recent attempts by Saudi religious interests to increase the country's influence in Iraq, all indicate that the soft power of religious interests in both countries, but especially Iran, is currently in the ascendant.

Notes

1   Theocracy is government by or subject to religious authority, where religious figures exercise political power, and where religious law is dominant over civil law. For example, led by Ayatollah Ruhollah Khomeini (1979–89), Iran was a theocracy under the Muslim Shi'ite clergy.

2   The Druze are a numerically small but distinct religious community. There are about 1 million Druze worldwide; most live in various Middle East countries – including Lebanon, Israel, Syria, Turkey and Jordan – while smaller communities live elsewhere, including the USA and Western Europe. Linguistically and culturally, the Druze are closely linked to Arabs and many Druze actually consider themselves to be Arabs (http://www.dailytimes.com.pk/default.asp?page=story_1-2-2004_pg3_5), although some Israeli Druze do not (http://news.bbc.co.uk/1/hi/ world/middle_east/3612002.stm). However, the Druze are not judged to be followers of Islam by most Muslims in the Middle East, although many Druze insist that their faith is actually authentically Islamic.

3   The Ichud Leumi (which is made up of the Moledet, Renewed National Religious Zionism, and Tekuma parties), ran together for the 17th Knesset in March 2006 with the National Religious Party (Mafdal) and won 9 Knesset seats (http://www.knesset.gov.il/faction/eng/FactionPage_eng.asp?PG=192).

4   The views of Mearsheimer and Walt were criticized by many following their publication in March 2006. The chief criticisms were that: they were being anti-Semitic, placing too much importance on Israel as a source of US foreign policy in the Middle East, and that Islamic terrorism was not only in response to US support for Israel but was also linked to other, more global factors to do with the colonial background, when British and French interests dominated the Middle East region. For a selection of critiques from the Letters page of the *London Review of Books*, where a shorter version of their article was published on 23 March 2006, go to: http://www.lrb.co.uk/v28/n07/letters.html. The original, and much longer, version of the piece, amounting to 82 pages, was a Working Paper (RWP06-011) published in March 2006 under the joint auspices of the University of Chicago and Harvard University, the institutions where Mearsheimer and Walt respectively were at the time employed.

5   Bahia is a religion founded in 1863 in Persia that emphasizes the spiritual unity of all humankind.

6   Islamic vigilantes loyal to Supreme Leader Ayatollah Ali Khamenei.

Questions

1   Why is religion an important factor in the Middle East's international relations?

2   Does the involvement of religion in the region's international relations make compromise more difficult to achieve in issues of competition and conflict?

3   What is the role of religion in Israel's foreign policy?

4   To what extent is it correct to see Saudi Arabia's foreign policy as a focal point of competition between 'moderates' and 'radicals'?

5   Why was Iran's revolution so significant internationally?

Bibliography

Afrasiabi, K. and Maleki, A. (2003) 'Iran's foreign policy after September 11', *The Brown Journal of World Affairs*, 9 (2), pp. 255–65. Available at: http://www.watsoninstitute.org/bjwa/archive/9.2/Iran/Afrasiabi.pdf Accessed 6 January 2006.

Arquilla, J. and Ronfeldt, D. (1999) *The Emergence of Noopolitik: Toward an American Information Strategy*, Santa Monica, CA: RAND.

Baer, R. (2005) 'The devil you think you know', *Newsweek,* 15 August. Available at: http://www.msnbc.msn.com/id/8853607/site/newsweek/ Accessed 13 June 2006.

Barnes, H. and Bigham, A. (2006) *Understanding Iran: People, Politics and Power*, London: The Foreign Policy Centre.

Bealey, F. (1999) *The Blackwell Dictionary of Political Science*, Oxford: Blackwell.

Bhatia, S. (1996) 'A dark shadow descends on Israel', *The Observer*, 2 June.

Chazan, N. (1991) 'The domestic foundations of Israeli foreign policy', in J. Kipper and H. H. Saunders (eds), *The Middle East in Global Perspective*, Boulder, CO: Westview Press, pp. 82–126.

Clark, V. (2003) 'The Christian Zionists', *Prospect*, July, Issue no. 88. Available at: http://www.prospect-magazine.co.uk/article_details. php?id=5643 Accessed 12 December 2005.

Doran, M. Scott (2004) 'The Saudi paradox', *Foreign Affairs*, January/ February. Available at: http://www.foreignaffairs.org/ 20040101faessay83105/michael-scott-doran/the-saudi-paradox.html Accessed 11 November 2005.

Ehteshami, A. (2002) 'The Middle East: Iran and Israel', in M. Webber and M. Smith (eds), *Foreign Policy in a Transformed World,* Harlow: Prentice Hall, pp. 255–86.

Elazar, D. (n.d.) 'The future role of religion in Israel'. Available at: http://www.jcpa.org/dje/articles2/relinisr.htm Accessed 5 June 2006.

'Elections in Israel March 2006', Israeli Ministry of Foreign Affairs. Available at: http://www.mfa.gov.il/MFA/History/Modern+History/Historic+Events/Elections+in+Israel+March+2006.htm#results Accessed 14 May 2006.

Fox, J. and Sandler, S. (2004) *Bringing Religion into International Relations,* Basingstoke: Palgrave Macmillan.

Freeman, C. (2002) 'Saudi Arabia's foreign and domestic dilemmas', Washington, DC: Middle East Policy Council.

Halper, S. and Clarke, J. (2004) *America Alone: The Neo-Conservatives and the Global Order,* Cambridge: Cambridge University Press.

Haynes, J. (2005) 'Al-Qaeda: ideology and action', *Critical Review of International Social and Political Philosophy,* 8 (2), pp. 177–91.

Hinnebusch, R. (2005) 'The politics of identity in Middle East international relations', in L. Fawcett (ed.), *International Relations of the Middle East,* Oxford: Oxford University Press, pp. 151–72.

Hudson, M. (2005) 'The Unites States in the Middle East', in L. Fawcett (ed.), *International Relations of the Middle East,* Oxford: Oxford University Press, pp. 283–306.

Kemp, G. (2005) *Iran and Iraq: The Shia Connection, Soft Power, and the Nuclear Connection,* Washington, DC: United States Institute of Peace.

Korany, B. (2005) 'The Middle East since the cold war: torn between geopolitics and geoeconomics', in L. Fawcett (ed.), *International Relations of the Middle East,* Oxford: Oxford University Press, pp. 59–76.

Landau, J. (1990) *The Politics of Pan-Islam: Ideology and Organization,* Oxford: Oxford University Press.

Luckmann, T. (1969) 'The decline of church-oriented religion', in R. Robertson (ed.), *The Sociology of Religion,* Baltimore, MD: Penguin, pp. 141–51.

MacAskill, E. and Tisdall, S. (2006) 'A year on, Ahmadinejad's popularity is soaring', *The Guardian,* 21 June.

Mearsheimer, J. and Walt, S. (2006) 'The Israeli lobby and U.S. foreign policy', *The London Review of Books*, 28 (6), 23 March. Available at: www.lrb.co.uk Accessed 6 April 2006.

Milton-Edwards, B. (2006) *Islam and Violence in the Modern Era*, Basingstoke: Palgrave.

Novikov, E. (2005) 'The World Muslim League: agent of Wahhabi propagation in Europe', *Terrorism Monitor*, 3 (9), 6 May, pp. 8-10.

Nye, J. (2004a) *Soft Power: The Means to Success in World Politics*, Washington, DC: Public Affairs.

Nye, J. (2004b) 'Sell it softly', *Los Angeles Times*, 25 April. Available at: http://www.ksg.harvard.edu/news/opeds/2004/nye_softly_lat_042504. htm Accessed 1 June 2006.

Ramazani, R. K. (2004) 'Ideology and pragmatism in Iran's foreign policy', *Middle East Journal*, 58 (4), pp. 549–59.

Sandler, S. (2006) 'Judaism and politics', in J. Haynes (ed.), *The Politics of Religion: A Survey*, London: Routledge, pp. 37–47.

Sarioghalam, M. (2001) 'Iran's foreign policy and US–Iranian relations: a summary of remarks by Dr. Mahmood Sarioghalam, National university of Iran, at the Middle East Institute, February 5, 2001'. Available at: http://209.196.144.55/html/b-sarioghalam.html Accessed 6 January 2006.

'Shi'ite supremacists emerge from Iran's shadows' (2005) *Asian Times Online*, 9 September. http://www.atimes.com/atimes/Middle_East/ GI09Ak01.html Accessed 13 June 2006.

Silberstein, L. (1993) 'Religion, ideology, modernity: theoretical issues in the study of Jewish fundamentalism', in L. Silberstein (ed.), *Jewish Fundamentalism in Comparative Perspective: Religion, Ideology, and the Crisis of Modernity*, New York and London: New York University Press, pp. 3–26.

Smith, C. (2005) 'The Arab–Israeli conflict', in L. Fawcett (ed.), *International Relations of the Middle East*, Oxford: Oxford University Press, pp. 217–36.

Sohrabi, N. (2006) 'Conservatives, neoconservatives and reformists: Iran after the election of Mahmud Ahmadinejad', 'Middle East Brief', Crown Center for Middle East Studies, Brandeis University, April, No. 4.

Sprinzak, E. (1993) 'Fundamentalism, ultranationalism, and political culture: the case of the Israeli radical right', in L. Diamond (ed.), *Political Culture and Democracy in Developing Countries*, Boulder, CO and London: Lynne Rienner, pp. 247–78.

Telhami, S. (2004) 'Between faith and ethics', in J. B. Hehir, M. Walzer, L. Richardson, S. Telhami, C. Krauthammer and J. Lindsay, *Liberty and Power. A Dialogue on Religion and U.S. Foreign Policy in an Unjust World*, Washington, DC: Brookings Institution Press, pp. 71–84.

Tisdall, S. (2006) 'Bush wrongfooted as Iran steps up international charm offensive', *The Guardian*, 20 June.

Voll, J. (2006) 'Trans-state Muslim movements in an era of soft power'. Paper prepared for the Conference on New Religious Pluralism in World Politics, Georgetown University, 17 March.

Walt, S. (2005) *Taming American Power: The Global Response to U.S. Primacy*, New York and London: Norton.

Weber, M. (1978) *Economy and Society*, Berkeley: University of California Press.

Ziyad, G. (2003) 'Saudi Arabia: lines in the sand'. Available at: http://www.worldpress.org/Mideast/1145.cfm Accessed 27 June 2006.

Zunes, C. (2004) 'Christian Right's grip on US foreign policy'. Available at: http://www.couplescompany.com/Features/Politics/2004/ChristianRight.htm Accessed 4 June 2006.

Further reading

L. Fawcett (ed.), *International Relations of the Middle East*, Oxford University Press, 2005. This textbook offers a historical framework and up-to-date analysis of contemporary events in the Middle East. The editor has brought together leading scholars in the field, and the book overall presents a balanced and comprehensive assessment of the international relations of the region.

R. Hinnebusch and A. Ehteshami (eds), *The Foreign Policies of Middle East States*, Lynne Rienner, 2002. This book adopts a country-by-country approach to explain the foreign policy dilemmas of each state. The contributions include: historical developments, domestic concerns, and both regional and global power structures, essential information for anyone trying to make sense of what is happening in the Middle East. Unlike some multi-author volumes, this book has a very useful common organization shared by each chapter. As a result, it is easy to read yet always informative and interesting.

S. Murden, *Islam, the Middle East and the New Global Hegemony*, Lynne Rienner, 2002. Murden examines the position of the Middle East in international relations by looking at 'free markets' and the 'Western hegemonic structure' in order to throw light on how the Muslim world in the region interacts with the USA, Europe and other manifestations of 'Western hegemony'. Murden argues that Western hegemony has changed its structure over time and has now become more diffuse, with its focus as much on the realm of cyberspace as the more traditional terrain of geopolitics.

C. Smith, *Palestine and the Arab–Israeli Conflict*, St. Martin's Press, 5th edn, 2004. This book is perhaps the most highly regarded volume on this topic. It analyses the role of both religious and secular issues in the evolution of the conflict.

S. Telhami and M. Barnett (eds), *Identity and Foreign Policy in the Middle East*, Cornell University Press, 2002. This book focuses upon how the formation and transformation of national and state identities among Middle Eastern countries has affected their foreign policy behaviour.

CHAPTER 12

South Asia

The South Asian region comprises five countries: Bangladesh, India, Nepal, Pakistan and Sri Lanka. They differ greatly in terms of size, geography, religious and cultural traditions, economic and political structures, forms of rule, and relations with external powers. The region has had a variable political history since its emergence from British colonial rule in the late 1940s: monarchical rule in Nepal; long-running civil war in Sri Lanka between the (Hindu) Tamil minority and the (Buddhist) Sinhalese majority; alternating military and civilian regimes in Bangladesh; periodic democratic interludes in Pakistan, with growing influence for Islamic political parties and movements; and a long-established, secular democracy in India, which has been influenced significantly in recent years by the growth of Hindu nationalism or 'fundamentalism'. In this chapter we focus on India, Pakistan and Sri Lanka. This is because in all three countries various religious actors are important politically, both domestically and in relation to regional foreign policies and international relations. In relation to these three South Asian countries, we conclude that: (1) domestic structures and processes throw up politically influential religious actors – and they may seek to influence international outcomes – yet their significance is relatively minor, and (2) religious goals do not take precedence over secular security concerns in regional states' foreign policies.

Religion and international relations: India, Pakistan and Sri Lanka

South Asia has been greatly affected by a changing international context in recent years, including: the upsurge in the influence of globalization in recent decades, the end of Cold War in 1989, the ramifications of September 11, 2001, and the subsequent war on terror. These factors interacted with domestic concerns – notably an increased political significance for religious concerns – in our three featured South Asian countries: India, Pakistan and Sri Lanka. The impact both of the end of the Cold War and increased influence of globalization can be seen in Rizvi's observation, that the 'democratic transformation of South Asia in the aftermath of the Cold War has been breathtaking' (Rizvi, 1995: 84). In addition, as Kumaraswamy notes, the 'end of the Cold War and the emerging new international order' were important factors in South Asia's recent international relations (Kumaraswamy, 1999: 175). There was increased pressure from the US government, directed against Pakistan's military regime to shift to take a full role in the post-9/11 'war on terror' against both al-Qaeda and Afghanistan's erstwhile rulers, the Taliban, in relation to India to improve relations more generally, and encouragement to the government of Sri Lanka to try to end the country's civil war.

India

Since independence in 1947, India has enjoyed long periods of democratic stability, initially under the rule of the secular Congress Party. However, India experienced sharpening political disputes from the late 1970s, characterized by a general decline in political stability and fragmentation of the hitherto stable political party system. At this time, numerous new parties emerged. Many sought to represent constituencies that until then were politically marginalized, including various religious (especially Hindu and Muslim), ethnic, caste and regional interests. The rise to political prominence of what is often referred to as Hindu nationalism or 'fundamentalism' dates from this time. The electoral success of the Hindu 'fundamentalist' Bharatiya Janata Party (BJP, 'Indian People's Party') began in the early 1980s, starting a process that saw the BJP become the most electorally significant party in India from the mid-1990s to the mid-2000s. During this time India had successive coalition governments led by the BJP. The increased political domestic influence of the BJP was built on a Hindu religious ideology known as Hindutva ('Hindu nationalism') (Bhatt, 2001). It was reflected in expressions of 'Islamophobia', as well as a move away from non-alignment towards closer relations with Israel and the USA. The influence of Hindutva was also reflected in relation to two specific foreign policy issues: the continuing dispute with mainly Muslim Pakistan over Kashmir and the civil war in Sri Lanka between Buddhist Sinhalese and Hindu Tamils. In short, Hindutva influenced India's foreign policy under BJP rule, although this was not the only factor of significance.

As Ganguly notes, 'the end of the Cold War and of the Soviet experiment shattered the long-cherished assumptions of India's foreign policy establishment and forced a radical realignment of its foreign policy'. Reflecting this, the late Narasimha Rao, a Congress prime minister between 1991–96, was the chief proponent of India's post-Cold War 'New Look' foreign policy (Ganguly, 2003/4: 41). This emerged as a result of two contemporaneous international developments that greatly affected India's international relations and foreign policy:

- a transformed global environment after the Cold War;

- collapse of India's key ally, the former Soviet Union, with subsequent impact on India's perceptions of the international power balance.

The BJP was in power between 1996 and 2004. Its tenure coincided with a phase of international relations which Kapila claims is characterized by the rise of 'United States unilateralism and new American policies of pre-emption and military intervention in global affairs without restraint' (Kapila, 2005). In addition, the collapse of the Soviet Union and the generally changed international environment as a consequence of globalization led to a reorientation of India's foreign policy. There were, however, competing influences. On the one hand there was Hindutva, a powerful domestic factor, and on the other there was the impact of globalization and the unilateral power of the USA. Indian governments from this time understood the desirability of forging new alliances and foreign policy directions. As a result, when the BJP came to power in 1996 there was not an abrupt shift in foreign policy direction, rather there was continuity, albeit with a significantly different ideological component: from non-alignment to Hindu nationalism. This was reflected in a BJP foreign policy focus concerned with 'US–India strategic cooperation, normalising and enlarging cooperation with both China and Israel' and a commitment 'to bring the "old foe", Pakistan, to the dialogue table' (Kapila, 2005).

Pakistan

Like India, the political situation in India's neighbour, Pakistan, was also characterized by both volatility and the pronounced influence of religious organizations – in this case, various Islamic entities. In the 1980s and 1990s, short-lived, democratically elected, civilian governments followed each other rapidly. Then, in October 1999, the military stepped in and terminated the democratic system. This was, however, a generally popular move that reflected a widespread view in Pakistan that when civilians were in power they tended to rule both poorly and corruptly. Many Pakistanis, disgusted at the inability of successive civilian governments to control the scale of corruption, were said at this time to be 'disillusioned, apathetic, weary . . . indifferent to the fate of the venal politicians . . . so busy lining their own pockets that they had little time to ponder the welfare of the country and its people' (Ali, 1999). Despite the unconstitutional nature of the military takeover, some prominent citizens openly called for a political system that would give the armed forces a permanent, institutionalized, 'supervisory' political role. The sustained political prominence of the military in Pakistan – still in place at the time of writing (mid-2006) – was bolstered by the support of influential Islamist parties and movements that – like their counterparts in India, the Hindu fundamentalists – sought to influence Pakistan's foreign policy and international relations, especially in relation to the Kashmir region, whose control has been disputed with India for six decades.

Sri Lanka

Sri Lanka's recent political history has been dominated for more than two decades by a still unresolved civil war between the majority Buddhist Sinhalese and the minority Hindu Tamils. Reoch calls the conflict the 'no mercy war' because it included suicide bombings and overall was fought with little apparent concern for civilian casualties: during the conflict there were more than 65,000 deaths on both sides. In addition, there have been serious human rights abuses by both sides, while an estimated one million people have been displaced from their homes (Reoch, 2001). Although the war has only intermittently received much attention from outside the region, when the conflict intensified in April 2000 it took on an international dimension with several external governments, including those of India, the USA and Norway, becoming involved in efforts to find peace between the two sides. India in particular has consistently sought to influence the outcome of the civil war, but not necessarily in favour of the Hindu Tamils. This preference might have been expected, given the religious make-up of India – over 80 per cent Hindu – and the presence of the Hindu fundamentalist BJP as the dominant force in government.

Religion and politics in India

India achieved independence in 1947 under the aegis of the Congress Party. Politically dominant for three decades, Congress later experienced

serious electoral decline. From the mid-1970s, its hegemony was undermined by the rise of various identity-based parties. During the 1980s and
1990s, the number of political parties increased from a handful to around
450 (Kohli, 1994: 89). Many of the new parties based their electoral appeal
on various identity factors, notably religion, ethnicity and caste. During
this time, communal tensions between, on the one hand, Sikhs and Hindus, and on the other, Hindus and Muslims, spread from the urban into
the rural areas where they were hitherto largely unknown. They became
pronounced in various southern parts the country, such as Tamil Nadu, as
well as in the north, including Punjab and Jammu-Kashmir. The conflict
between Sikhs and Hindus came to a head in the 1980s, rooted in the Sikh
demand for their own state in Punjab (putatively to be called 'Khalistan'),
characterized by various terrorist acts perpetuated by militant Sikhs, including the assassination of the then prime minister, Indira Gandhi, in
1984. Widespread destruction of Sikh-owned property and the murders of
Sikhs followed in several northern Indian cities, perpetrated by Hindu
gangs. Eventually, however, due to a combination of strong-arm tactics on
the part of the state and the political division of the Sikhs into various factions, Sikh demands for Khalistan diminished. During the 1990s, however,
a pronounced increase in tensions developed between India's Muslim minority, some 11 per cent of the population, and various Hindu fundamentalist movements.

Hindu–Muslim relations and the rise of the BJP

> India has its own homegrown brand of religious militancy – Hindu nationalism –
> which also enjoys close government ties. This militancy threatens to under-
> mine the religious impartiality (commonly known in India as 'secularism')
> upon which India's democratic constitution is based (Center Conversations,
> 2003: 1).

The issue of Hindu–Muslim relations has become a key political topic in
India, a concern highlighted by the growing significance of a political ideology known as Hindutva ('Hindu-ness'). Hindutva is a Hindi word, a neologism first presented by Vinayak Damodar Savarkar in his 1923 pamphlet
Hindutva: Who is a Hindu? Today the term refers to movements, primarily in
India, that advocate Hindu nationalism. The BJP, the ruling party in India
between 1996 and 2004, is closely linked with a variety of organizations and
movements that collectively promote Hindutva. Their collective name is the

Sangh Parivar ('family of associations'), and leading movements include the Rashtriya Swayamsevak (RSS), Bajrang Dal and the Vishwa Hindu Parishad (VHP) (Brass, 2005).

What is *Hindutva*?

Hindutva is an extreme right-wing ideology that grew in political and religious prominence during the twentieth century (Chiriyankandath, 2006). However, it did not play an important role in Indian politics until the late 1980s. From that time, largely because of two events, it attracted many formerly mainstream Hindus. The first was the use by the government of Rajiv Gandhi of a large parliamentary majority to overturn a Supreme Court verdict with which many conservative Muslims disagreed (the Shah Bano case). Secondly, there was the major quarrel between Hindus and Muslims over ownership of a sixteenth-century Mughal Babri mosque in Ayodhya. Some Hindus maintained that it was both birthplace and site of the original temple of Rama, a figure that Hindus believe was an avatar of God. Following growing frictions between Muslims and Hindus, the mosque was destroyed by a Hindu mob in 1992, leading to riots across India.

The overall aim of the Sangh Parivar is to increase the predominance of Hinduism in India, in relation to its societal, political and cultural presence. It seeks to pursue this goal through various means, including violence and terror (Human Rights Watch, 2002: 39–41; Ram-Prasad, 2000: 184). The Hindutva agenda included attempts to suppress or drive out Muslims and Christians, who together total around 17 per cent of India's population. This was because, for the Sangh Parivar, they were alien faiths, chronologically introduced into India by external conquerors. Islam was largely introduced by the Muslim Moghuls in the sixteenth century and Christianity by the British, mainly from the nineteenth century. At independence in 1947, the electorally victorious Congress Party reluctantly accepted partition (between India and East and West Pakistan), but decisively rejected the ideology of Hindutva. Later, however, in the 1980s, India saw tensions increase between Muslims and Hindus, a situation that facilitated the electoral rise of the BJP. The BJP is now a major force in the Indian political arena, a party that consistently emphasizes the ideology of Hindutva. This is said to amount to a serious challenge to traditional Indian understandings of, and commitment to, secularism (Chiriyankandath, 1996).[1]

The political rise of the BJP

The background to the rise of the BJP was that the party was initially a northern-based phenomenon popular only in certain Hindi-speaking areas, especially among certain urban constituencies, notably middle-class traders. Its political rise began in 1989 when the BJP won 85 seats in parliament (15.5 per cent of the total). Over the next decade the BJP built growing political support. It achieved a political breakthrough in the 1996 general elections, winning the most parliamentary seats of any party (161 of 545, 29.5 per cent). Falling well short of an overall majority, the BJP nevertheless headed the resulting short-lived coalition government. The BJP leader, Atal Bihari Vajpayee, became prime minister, but the new government soon fell after losing a confidence vote. However, this setback did not prevent the BJP from gaining the largest number of parliamentary seats in national elections in both 1998 and 1999; again it formed governments with Vajpayee as prime minister. From then, the BJP remained in power until losing the May 2004 elections to the resurgent Congress Party.

In power, the BJP energetically promoted economic reforms and avidly sought development goals, welcoming into the country as much foreign investment as possible. However, the BJP continued to be regarded as a serious challenge to traditional Indian understandings of, and commitment to, secularism. Marshall observes that in power the BJP remained close to the RSS and other Hindu nationalist organizations collected in the Sangh Parivar, effectively functioning as its 'political wing'. Prime Minister Vajpayee publicly praised the RSS and regularly attended its functions. Other high-level BJP figures, including the former Home Affairs minister L. K. Advani, also had close links with the RSS. In power, the BJP sought to pursue the objectives of Hindutva – that is, to try to 'Hindu-ize' Indian politics and society, by various methods, including: 'propaganda, the manipulation of cultural institutions, undercutting laws that protect religious minorities, and minimizing or excusing Hindu extremist violence. At the state level its functionaries have abetted and even participated in such violence' (Marshall, 2004).

Regarding what it sees as 'foreign' religions – notably, Christianity and Islam – as serious social and cultural threats, BJP officials not only sought to restrict minority religious groups' international contacts but also to reduce their domestic rights to build places of worship. The BJP government passed anti-conversion laws, as well as changing personal laws governing marriages, adoptions and inheritance. In addition, it practised legal discrimination against Christian and Muslim Dalits (the so-called 'Untouchables'), but not against those among the latter who classified themselves as Hindus. Marshall reports that 'with BJP support, laws were adopted in Tamil Nadu and Gujarat states restricting the ability of Hindus to change their religion, and proposals for national restrictions were made. In June 2003, the late pope, John Paul II, described these developments as "unjust" and said they prohibited "free exercise of the natural right to religious freedom"' (Marshall, 2004; Human Rights Watch, 2002).

Earlier, inter-communal relations between Hindus and Muslims had taken a serious turn for the worse. In December 1992, Hindu extremists, many of whom were said to be connected to various Hindu organizations, including the RSS and BJP, destroyed a historic mosque at Ayodhya (Chiriyankandath, 2006; Lall, 2005). Widespread communal riots followed, with huge loss of human life and destruction of property. Ten years later, in February 2002, Muslims in Gujarat experienced serious violence when between one and two thousand Muslims were massacred after Muslims reportedly set fire to a train carrying Hindu nationalists, killing several dozen people. Many Muslim victims were burned alive or dismembered while police and BJP state government authorities were said to have stood by or joined in the violence (Brass, 2005). The mobs are said to have had with them lists of homes and businesses owned by Muslims, lists that they could have acquired only from government sources. After the massacre, state BJP officials were accused of impeding the investigation into the events (Amnesty International, 2003).

Following the violence, a prominent Mumbai-based politician, Bal Thackeray, leader of the Shiv Sena, a political party based in Mumbai and allied to the BJP, stated that, 'Muslims are cancer to this country . . . Cancer is an incurable disease. Its only cure is operation. O Hindus, take weapons in your hands and remove this cancer from the roots' (MacFarquhar, 2003: 51). Gujarat's Chief Minister, Narendra Modi, a BJP member, called upon his supporters to 'teach a lesson' to those who 'believe in multiplying the population', implicitly referring to Muslims. Other Sangh Parivar officials were even more explicitly threatening (The Times of India, 2002). VHP International President Ashok Singhal described the Gujarat carnage as a 'successful experiment' and warned that it would be repeated all over India. After the December 2002 BJP election victory in Gujarat, VHP General Secretary Pravin Togadia declared, 'All Hindutva opponents will get the death sentence, and we will leave this to the people to carry out. The process of forming a Hindu rule in the country has begun with Gujarat, and VHP will take the Gujarat experiment to every nook and corner of the country' (Vyas, 2002).

In addition to anti-Muslim violence and outbursts, Christians were also targeted by Hindu militants, responsible for violent attacks in the late 1990s on Christian minorities in various states, including, Gujarat, Madhya Pradesh, and Orissa (Brass, 2005). The BBC ('South Asia: attacks on Indian, Christians continue, 1998) reported at this time that

> India's Home Ministry (internal security) and its National Commission for Mi-
> norities officially list over a hundred religiously motivated attacks against Chris-
> tians per year, but the real number is certainly higher, as Indian journalists
> estimate that only some ten percent of incidents are ever reported. These attacks
> include murders of missionaries and priests, sexual assault on nuns, ransacking
> of churches, convents, and other Christian institutions, desecration of cemeter-
> ies, and Bible burnings.

In order to maintain the political coalition that enabled it to rule at the national level, the BJP government sought to downplay such events and to portray itself as a moderate party. However, chiefly because of the anti-Christian attacks noted above, the US Commission on International Religious Freedom proposed in 2004 that India be included on the State Department's official shortlist of the worst religious persecutors for its 'egregious, systematic, and ongoing' violations of religious rights (Marshall, 2004).

In sum, India's commitment to secularism, written into the country's constitution after independence from British rule, appeared to many observers to be under serious threat, owing to the rise in prominence and significance of the Hindutva ideology. During the 1990s and early 2000s, there were numerous attacks on religious minorities, especially Muslim and Christians, and evidence of an increasingly overt and strident Hindu fundamentalism which seriously affected India's domestic politics (United States Commission on International Religious Freedom, 2004: 81–4).

Hindutva and foreign policy

To what extent, if at all, was the ideology of Hindutva projected into India's foreign policy and international relations, especially during BJP rule? According to Katalya (2004), following independence in 1947, India's foreign policy was characterized by both moderation and pragmatism, including:

- dialogue with Pakistan;
- expansion of trade and investment relations with China;
- strengthening of ties with Russia, Japan, Western Europe and the USA;
- attempts to help construct a regional organization, the South Asian Association for Regional Cooperation.

India's foreign policy changes

Ganguly asserts that there was a change in emphasis in India's foreign policy in the 1990s. This was not so much to do with the impact of Hindutva as the changed international circumstances of this time – including the end of the Cold War and the impact of globalization – which, he claims, was most important in explaining the shift in emphasis in India's foreign policy. Until this time, the main emphasis was on non-alignment between the two superpowers, the USA and the USSR, implying even-handed dealing with the governments of both countries. India also sought to project itself as a defender of the world's poor and powerless. In pursuit of the latter objective, India's political leaders demanded a 'global foreign aid regime designed to redistribute the world's wealth, an international trading order that favored the needs of the developing world, and the restructuring of such global institutions as the World Bank and the International Monetary Fund so as to give the weaker states a greater voice. These efforts produced little of substance' (Ganguly, 2003/4: 42).

The end of the Cold War and the onset of globalization coincided with the rise to power of the BJP and strident assertion of the ideology of Hindutva. What impact was there on India's foreign policy and international relations? MacFarquhar (2003) states that under the BJP, India's foreign policy shifted focus from a concern with non-alignment and development injustices to a pronounced concern with 'Islamist terrorism'. This implied a more abrasive stance towards Pakistan, which the Indian government claimed was the main sponsor of 'anti-Indian', Muslim terror groups fighting to wrest Muslim-majority Kashmir from Indian control (see below). More generally, the BJP government 'criticized nonalignment and advocated a more vigorous use of India's power to defend national interests from erosion at the hands of Pakistan and China. The BJP also favored the overt acquisition of nuclear weapons' (Federal Research Division of the Library of Congress, 1995).

Overall, Thirumalai (2001) claims that, following the BJP's ascent to power in the mid-1990s, 'the role of religion in India's foreign policy cannot be exaggerated. Hindus claim to be the most tolerant of all religious groups. But this claim has been continuously shattered, resulting in certain adverse reactions among various nations'. As a result

> India has to come to grapple with the fact that Hinduism is more or less a single nation religion, whereas Islam, Christianity and Buddhism are religions practiced and encouraged in many and diverse nations. The view the practitioners of other religions hold regarding Hinduism and Hindus certainly influences the foreign policy of these nations towards India. India's insistence on its secular credentials

may be appreciated in the academic circles all over the world, but India continues to be a Hindu-majority nation, a Hindu nation, in the minds of lay Christians, Muslims, and Buddhists all over the world. The foreign policy
formulations of other nations do not fail to recognize that India is a Hindu nation, despite India's claims to the contrary.

According to Marshall, perceptions of India as a Hindu nation were reinforced as a result of many incidents of Hindu extremism and terrorism in
the 1990s. Globally since 9/11, much attention has been paid to Islamic extremism and terrorism but relatively little attention to what some commentators see as increasingly violent trends towards Hindu extremism among
groups advocating Hindutva, including the RSS and VHP (United States
Commission on International Religious Freedom, 2004: 81–4). Such extremism, Marshall (2004) contends, was supported by 'allies in the Indian government, which until mid-2004 was led by the BJP'.

Bidwai suggests that 'if the ideologues of India's Hindu-supremacist
Bharatiya Janata Party and key policy-makers in the coalition government it
leads in New Delhi had their way, they would bring into being just such an
alliance or "Axis of Virtue" against "global terrorism"', involving the governments of India, USA, and Israel (Bidwai, 2003). India's then National Security Adviser Brajesh Mishra advanced the 'Axis of Virtue' proposal on 8
May 2003, in Washington. Mishra was addressing the American Jewish
Committee (AJC) at an event where there were also many US Congressmen
and women present. Mishra emphasized his desire to help fashion an 'alliance of free societies involved in combating' the scourge of terrorism.
Apart from the fact that the USA, Israel and India were all 'advanced democracies', each 'had been a significant target of terrorism. They have to jointly
face the same ugly face of modern-day terrorism'. The proposed 'Axis of
Virtue' would seek to 'take on international terrorism in a holistic and focused manner . . . to ensure that the global campaign . . . is pursued to its
logical conclusion, and does not run out of steam because of other preoccupations. We owe this commitment to our future generations' (Mishra, quoted
in Embassy of India, 2003). A month later, also in Washington, Deputy
Prime Minister Lal Krishna Advani spoke in glowing terms about the proposal. He stressed 'similarities' between India and the USA, calling them
'natural democracies'. He praised the relationship 'developing between our
two countries [that is, India and the USA], which is powerfully reflected' in
President Bush's latest National Security Strategy document. Obliquely referring to Pakistan, he added, 'it is not an alliance of convenience. It is a
principled relationship' (Bidwai, 2003). According to Bidwai, 'The BJP's

ideology admires people like [the then Israeli prime minister, Ariel] Sharon for their machismo and ferocious jingoism. It sees Hindus and Jews (plus Christians) as "strategic allies" against Islam and Confucianism. Absurd and unethical as it is, this "clash-of-civilisations" idea has many takers on India's Hindu Right'. Overall, according to Bidwai (2003), there were three main reasons why the BJP wished to move India closer to Israel and its ideology of Zionism:

- a wish to build closer relations with Israel's main ally, the USA, and thus try to isolate Pakistan;

- shared 'Islamophobia' and anti-Arabism;

- shared commitment to an aggressive and dynamic nationalism.

Owing to a change of government in India in May 2004, the 'Axis of Virtue' proposal did not make it past the planning stage. Following the election, the Congress Party and its allies had the largest number of seats in parliament (216, compared to the BJP's 186) but it did not achieve enough to rule with an overall majority (273 seats). As a result, the new Congress government had to heed the wishes of its main coalition partners, the Communists and the Muslim League, while the Congress government itself featured committed secularists averse to the 'Axis' proposal. In the next section we turn to examine India's major regional rival, Pakistan, and the political influence of its Islamist actors both at home and abroad.

Religion and politics in Pakistan

As a country, Pakistan is an entirely artificial creation. It was created as a homeland for India's tens of millions of Muslims following serious communal conflict in the late 1940s that left an estimated one million people dead. Carved out of India, initially in two territories (East and West Pakistan) separated from each other by thousands of kilometres, the country became independent in August 1947. A republic was established in 1956. Fifteen years later, Pakistan's national territory was confined to former West Pakistan following the de facto independence of Bangladesh (formerly, East Pakistan). After a military coup in July 1977, martial law came into operation until 1985 when a semi-democracy emerged. Constitutional democracy followed in 1988, surviving until October 1999 when a military government took over (Nasr, 2001).

Pakistan started life with a number of inauspicious structural characteristics that militated against the establishment of a workable democratic
system. In addition, there was no sustained external encouragement to democratize. This was largely because Pakistan was a key regional ally of the USA
during the Cold War, a time when American governments preferred stable
allies rather than democratic ones. In other words, the long-term support
of US governments for 'stable' – that is, in Pakistan's case, military – governments not only undermined chances of democratization in Pakistan
but later encouraged Islamic groups in a bid to counter the influence of
secular political parties that wanted democratic rule (see below).

In 1997, fifty years after independence, Diamond characterized Pakistan
as being at 'the edge of political chaos, with massive political corruption
and heavy-handed presidential intervention forcing out one elected government after another' (Diamond, 1999: 29). At this time, many Pakistanis
were very condemnatory of their political leaders, a position explained in
part by recent corruption scandals involving senior politicians (Diamond,
1999: 92). Sizeable majorities of the Pakistani public considered that the
country lacked an impartial judiciary (62 per cent), freedom of the press (56
per cent), or a government free of corruption (64 per cent). 'The bottom
line: nine years into civilian government, half do *not* consider Pakistan a
democratic state (about a quarter do)' (Diamond, 1999: 50). Diamond described the extant political system a 'hollow democracy, rife with semiloyal
and disloyal behavior on the part of important political actors. No one
should confuse its persistence with consolidation or with liberal democracy'
(Diamond, 1999: 73). This dismal political context helps to explain the rise
of Islamic organizations and parties in Pakistan in the 1990s and early
2000s, in part because they tended to be seen as relatively uncorrupt and
untainted by the failures of secular governments.

Islamism in Pakistan

Pakistan was founded on the idea that the Muslims of India formed a secular
nation and, as a result, they were entitled to a territorial homeland of their
own, in much the same way that the Jews (and especially Zionists) in the
diaspora considered that they could only flourish within their own nation-
state: Israel. Initially, Pakistan was constituted in two halves, East and West,
separated by India, and with practically no history of shared national unity.
The members of the Pakistani 'nation' did not speak a common language,
have a common religion (although most were Muslims), homogeneous culture, or share the same geographical or economic space. As a result, Pakistan
was emphatically not a nation in the traditional Western sense of a group of

people living in a contiguous territory believing they have the same ethnic origins, and sharing linguistic, religious and/or other cultural attributes. Over time, lack of shared characteristics proved fatal to the pursuit of national unity: following a civil war, the independent state of Bangladesh (initially, East Pakistan) was created in 1971 with India's help (Nasr, 2001).

At the time of the establishment of East and West Pakistan, the country's rulers faced two main problems: first, how to create a sense of national identity to suit the reality of the new boundaries and, secondly, how to devise a workable system of government for a populace divided by huge geographical distances, as well as religious, ethnic, cultural, regional, economic, linguistic and ideological differences. Initially, it was assumed that the umbrella of a presumed common 'Muslim identity' would take care of these differences. Consequently, the new political leaders espoused an Islamic form of nationalism as the country's unifying symbol. The appeal to their heterogeneous people's shared Muslim heritage was initially enough to overcome the immediate differences, but not sufficient over time to suppress or eradicate within the new state contradictions of Muslim religious feeling, regional nationalisms and class antagonisms. As Lapidus put it: 'Pakistan was born as an Islamic state to differentiate it from the rest of the [Indian] subcontinent, but Muslim identity [did] not prove adequate to unite the country internally' (Lapidus, 1988: 742). In sum, the founding circumstances of Pakistan were not conducive to long-term national, political or religious unity.

Initially, after the break from India in 1947, Pakistan's leaders enjoyed a high degree of popular, albeit 'inverse legitimation'. That is, the new government was widely regarded as legitimate primarily because it was the regime that came to power following what most Pakistanis no doubt saw as unconscionable and incomprehensible Indian aggression (Nasr, 2001). But the benefits of the honeymoon period soon disappeared. Governmental legitimacy declined due to: poor economic performances, the use of political repression to stifle opposition forces, and serious state-level corruption. Democracy did not become institutionalized in the early years of independence and, as a result, it became impossible to establish a workable democratic system.

Pakistan's political system

Pakistan's political system is notable for personalistic, rather than institutional, wielding of power, facilitated by three developments. First, Pakistan's federal system was designed to supply provincial legislatures and governments to check the power of the state at the national level. However, these important

(Continued)

checks and balances soon became filled with cronies of figures at the centre and, as a result, the ability to check the power of the national government diminished. Secondly, religious, ethnic and regional divisions helped make Pakistan's politics both volatile and violent. Thirdly, when the Muslim League government gained power after partition it was at the cost of abandoning its political hinterland in Northern India, a development that served, more generally, to blight the growth of a competitive party system. Instead, political leaders, both civilian and military presided over a political system rooted in populism, with power heavily personalized and frequently abused.

Pakistan failed to develop a viable political party system. Under military rule, all political parties were banned in the late 1950s, and even during the periods they were allowed to function the state sought closely to control them. Following a brief period of relative freedom in the 1970s and first half of 1980s, the then military dictator, General Zia, banned political parties again, claiming that the very concept of pluralistic parties was 'non-Islamic'. When they were allowed to operate, parties were essentially sectional – that is, ethnicity-, religion-, or region-orientated – in character, largely ineffectual at mobilizing citizens and prone to enter, and quickly leave, unstable multi-party alignments. In sum, the characteristics of Pakistan's political system, reflecting the characteristics of its inauspicious founding and alternating between military and civilian rule, were not encouraging for the development of democracy but did serve to focus political issues within secular/religious divisions.

Following General Zia's death in a mysterious plane crash in 1988, an event that precipitated a return to democracy, numerous political parties and groups emerged or re-emerged. The main contenders for political power at this time were two broad-based coalitions, one dominated by secular, the other by religious, parties. The former was the Pakistan Democratic Alliance (PDA), dominated by the left-of-centre Pakistan People's Party, led by Benazir Bhutto, allied to several smaller parties. Its opponent was the Islam-e-Jamhoori Ittehad (IJI, Islamic Democratic Alliance), a coalition whose main components were the Pakistan Muslim League and the Jamaat-i-Islami (Pakistan Islamic Assembly). Other significant parties at this time included Altaf Husain's MQM, representing the *mohajir* community in Sind, that is, refugees from India who entered Pakistan in the late 1940s, and the regionally-based Awami National Party, with roots in the North-West Frontier

Province and northern Baluchistan. The overall point is that these coalitions comprised parties representing a variety of sectional interests, including ethnic, religious and regional interests. However, their very diversity meant that the winning coalition would comprise a conglomerate of competing groups whose main aim would be to acquire as much power as possible and to deny it to their rivals (Haynes, 2001: 124–32; United States Commission on International Religious Freedom, 2004: 85–7).

Islamism and foreign policy

Although Pakistan emerged as a homeland for India's Muslims, this did not mean that there was only one concept of the idea of a Muslim state: in fact, there were at least two. On the one hand, the secularized political elite considered Islam a communal, political and national identity that could be stripped of its religious content. On the other hand, a sizeable segment of the populace, led by Muslim religious leaders, expected – and later, when it was not forthcoming, demanded – a state whose constitution, institutions and routines of daily life would be governed by Islamic law and norms. The importance of the struggle – over both the political role of Islam and the ethnic and regional rivalries between West and East Pakistan – can be gauged by the fact that no constitution could be devised until 1956, a decade after the founding of the state. The constitution declared Pakistan to be 'an Islamic state', and made all parliamentary legislation subject to review by an Islamic Research Institute.

Following a military coup in 1958, the constitution was abolished and the Republic of Pakistan was declared. The aim was to try to curb the power of the religious leaders and organizations. Over the following decades, however, the issue of the nature of the state in Pakistan was not resolved. Various rulers, such as General Zia ul-Haq (1977–88), sought to Islamicize the state further. Secular civilian political leaders, such as Zulfikar Ali Bhutto (prime minister, 1972–77) tried to reduce Islam's political influence. Later, attempting to increase support from the conservative Islamic establishment, the government of Nawaz Sharif (1988–93) achieved passage of an Islamic law bill in 1991. While for many religious Muslims the law did not go far enough in seeking to Islamicize the country, many secular-minded Pakistanis feared that a theocracy was being established (Cohen, 2004; Malik, 2002).

In foreign policy terms, the political significance of Islam in Pakistan is reflected in the existence of a number of influential Islamist organizations whose chief concern is a resolution of the Kashmir conflict with India in

Pakistan's favour. While many such organizations have existed for many years, their numbers grew during the period of rule by General Zia (1977–88). This was because he sought to use such organizations as a political instrument to support his rule, and this policy led to a growth in their numbers and political significance. There are three main Islamist groups explicitly seeking Kashmir's 'liberation' from India: Lashkar-e-Taiba, Jaish-e-Mohammed and Harakat ul-Mujahidin. Lashkar-e-Taiba (LeT, 'Army of the Righteous') is the armed wing of Markaz-ud-Dawa-wal-Irshad, a pro-Sunni, anti-US Islamist group founded in 1989. LeT fights India in the disputed territory of Kashmir. In recent years, several LeT operatives were convicted of terrorist charges by the United States government. A second group, Jaish-e-Mohammed ('JeM, The Army of Mohammed') was formed in 1994. It is a militant Islamist group based in Pakistan but largely funded from the United Kingdom, especially Birmingham. Like LeT, JeM carries out armed attacks on Indian armed forces and civilians in the Indian state of Jammu and Kashmir. Both JeM and LeT are said to canvass 'for supporters at British universities and mosques', and have done so for decades. 'Although both are outlawed in Britain they still collect around £5 million a year from UK donors, most of whom believe they are giving to humanitarian causes in Kashmir when some of that money is diverted to terror cells'. Ahmed Omar Sheikh, a former English public schoolboy, was one of their more notorious recruits. He 'abandoned his degree course at the London School of Economics in 1992' (McCarthy, 2002) and at the time of writing (mid-2006) is on death row in Islamabad for masterminding the kidnap and murder of the *Wall Street Journal* reporter, Daniel Pearl.

The third organization, Harakat ul-Mujahidin (HuM, 'Movement of Holy Warriors') is an Islamist militant group based in Pakistan but operating primarily in Indian-controlled Kashmir, where it undertakes insurgent and terrorist activities. In mid-February 2000, the deputy leader of the HuM, Farooq Kashmiri, a well-known Kashmiri commander, replaced the organization's head, Fazlur Rehman Khalil. The group has a presence in several Pakistani cities, including Rawalpindi and Muzaffarabad, as well as in Afghanistan. It is believed that HuM has a few thousand, mostly armed followers, situated primarily in Azad Kashmir (part of the former princely state of Jammu and Kashmir now controlled by Pakistan), Pakistan, and the Kashmir and Doda regions of India. Due to defections to Jaish-e-Mohammed, HuM lost some of its membership, although it is said still to be capable of carrying out operations in Kashmir against both Indian troops and civilian targets. HuM has also been linked to an indigenous Kashmiri Islamist group, al-Faran, which in 1995 kidnapped and murdered five Western tourists in Kashmir. In addition, in December 2000, HuM was involved in hijacking an Indian airliner. Several of its militant followers managed to gain agreement for the release of Masood Azhar. Azhar had been imprisoned by the Indian government in 1994 for terrorist activities; he had led the HuM's forerunner, the Harakat ul-Ansar. On his release, Azhar chose to form a new group – the Jaish-e-Mohammed (see above) – rather than return to HuM (Katzman, 2002).

Similarities in world-view between *Hindutva* organizations in India and Islamist entities in Pakistan

There are similarities in the strategic world-view of Pakistan's Islamist groups described above and those of some of India's Hindutva organizations, including the RSS and VHP. Each is concerned with three overlapping areas of concern: the local, the regional and the global. The advocates of Hindutva see the world in bifurcated terms – that is, a universe essentially divided between themselves and Others, that is, non-Hindus – while Pakistan's Islamists see the world as polarized between Muslims and non-Muslims. Followers of Hindutva identify a key enemy, Pakistan, said to be the main supporter of militant Islam not only in India generally but in Kashmir in particular. For Pakistan's Islamists, the governments of India and the USA are the main enemies, followed by those of Israel and Russia: all are perceived as inherently 'anti-Muslim' (Council on Foreign Relations, 2003). The USA and India are the main adversaries for the following reason. The government of the USA is believed to have a clear and aggressive anti-Muslim strategy, manifested in punitive actions in Afghanistan and Iraq since 9/11, where co-religionists – that is, Sunnis – have been on the receiving end of US military actions. India, on the other hand, especially under BJP rule, is regarded as being in general terms 'anti-Muslim', but especially excoriated for its unwillingness to concede control of Kashmir to the Muslim majority population, for reasons associated with its ideology of Hindutva (Chiriyankandath, 2006).

Finally, within Pakistan, the United States government is heavily criticized by the Islamist organizations for being willing to ally itself with the 'corrupt' regime of General Musharraf, in order, it is claimed, to try to dominate the region. As a result, Pakistan's Islamist militants believe that every 'good Muslim' should join a holy war against the USA and its local allies, the

Musharraf government. In its place, they want an Islamic state, looking to the model established by the Taliban in neighbouring Afghanistan during 1996–2001. Overall, Pakistan's Islamists would like to see Pakistan's international relations characterized by the following: (1) abandonment of Pakistan's association with the USA and replacement by a strategy of enhancing links with Muslim countries in order to achieve 'strategic depth'; (2) a deepening of confrontational relationship with India in order to force a resolution of the Kashmir issue; and (3) the use of Kashmiri Islamist militants to try to undermine India's resolution to hold on to Kashmir, as it is accepted that Pakistan's military capability cannot match that of India's (Council on Foreign Relations, 2003).

As noted above, the General Zia government in the late 1970s and the 1980s encouraged the formation and development of some of Pakistan's Islamist entities, including, Sipah-e-Sahaba and the Shia Tehrik-e-Jafria. However, it is not clear to what extent the current Musharraf government, which took power in 1999, still seeks their support (Harrison, 2001). The US Council on Foreign Relations claimed in 2003 that the Islamist groups had 'achieved substantial autonomy'. Indeed, since 9/11 and the subsequent global 'War on Terror', President Musharraf has repeatedly promised to crack down on Pakistan's domestic Islamist groups *if* they support the use of terror to achieve their objectives – although it is not clear that he has made much progress in this regard (Harrison, 2001). Following the war in Afghanistan (2001–02) and the US-led invasion and subsequent occupation of Iraq in March 2003, Pakistan's Islamist groups became increasingly vociferous both in their anti-US and anti-Musharraf statements. On the other hand, an alliance of Islamic political parties – known as the Muttahhida Majlis-e-Amal and consisting of the Jamaat-e-Islami, Jamiat Ulema-e-Islam, Jamiat Ulema-e-Pakistan and Tehrik-e-Islami – is the third largest bloc in the current government and this serves as a further limiting factor on Musharraf's actions in this regard. Finally, it is unclear to what extent (1) Pakistan's Islamist entities form linkages and networks with similar groups in other countries, (2) their proposed Islamic state stretches beyond the territorial borders of the present Pakistan state, and (3) they believe 'their goals are realisable' (Council on Foreign Relations, 2003).

In the next section, we focus upon Kashmir, the issue that serves as a cause célèbre for both Pakistan's Islamists and India's supporters of Hindutva, in order to assess the importance of religious factors in the conflict. Following that, we shift focus to the continuing civil war in Sri Lanka for two reasons. First, to gauge the extent in which the conflict is informed with religious factors and, second, to examine reasons for India's interventions in the civil war. The key question is: did India intervene for religious and ethnic reasons, that is, to support the claim of the Sri Lanka's Tamil minority for a separate state?

Religion and the India–Pakistan dispute over Kashmir

At the heart of the current conflict between nuclear-armed India and nuclear-armed Pakistan is religious militancy. If South Asia is a nuclear powder keg, religious militancy is the match that threatens to set it off. As is widely known, militant Islamic groups that Pakistan has long supported and is only now beginning to restrain attacked India's Parliament in December 2001 and attacked a Christian church in Islamabad, Pakistan's capital, in March 2002. Then in May 2002 Islamic militants slaughtered more than thirty Indians, most of them women and children, in the disputed state of Kashmir, precipitating a renewal of severe tensions between these two nuclear powers and longtime rivals (Center Conversations, 2003: 1).

Conflict over Kashmir has involved the governments of India and Pakistan for six decades. During British colonial rule, Kashmir was an anomaly: a Muslim-majority state ruled by a Hindu prince. The origin of the dispute is that at the time of British withdrawal in 1947, the departing colonialists did not leave a precise prescription for how to divide the roughly 500 princely states of British India, including Kashmir, between India and Pakistan. In many cases, there was no problem as such states were usually physically located clearly within the borders of post-colonial India or Pakistan. But the Kashmir valley, part of the state of Jammu-Kashmir, was a particularly intractable issue between the two countries. This was because Muslims were a clear majority in the Kashmir valley, although ruled by a Hindu prince.[2] Following the division of India in 1947, hostilities broke out between the two sides over the issue of who would rule in Kashmir, leading to the involvement of the United Nations (UN) in, so far unsuccessful, efforts to arrive at a resolution of the 'Kashmir question'. Now, sixty years on, the UN position is still that the political status of Kashmir should be settled by a referendum among its people. Yet, the vote has never been held. Fighting between India and Pakistan, including that involving militant Islamist groups supported by Pakistan, some of which are mentioned above, continues.

Conflict between India and Pakistan over Kashmir has not, however, been continuous. During the late 1970s and early 1980s there was a period of relative calm and stability between the two sides. It was, however, during this period that Pakistan's government under the leadership of General Zia-ul-Haq came to power in a *coup d'état*. He was instrumental in helping to create the Islamist groups discussed above. Over time, however, they achieved a high degree of independence although it is possible that the current regime of General Musharaff continues to use them to advance policy objectives. Contemporaneously, in India, the Congress governments of Indira Gandhi and her son, Rajiv, began to shift the country away from secular nationalism towards Hindu nationalism, a policy later pursued by the BJP regimes of the 1990s and early 2000s (Haggerty, 2002). The impact on the Kashmir question was not only to sharpen the conflict in general terms but also to make religion, rather than nationalism, the key issue at stake in the status of Kashmir (Smock, 2006).

In 1989 there was a local revolt in Kashmir led by local Muslims directed against both the Indian government and the Hindu ruler of the state, which attracted both political and material support from Pakistan. Since that time, there has been an inability to resolve the Kashmir issue, alternating between periods of relative calm and outbreaks of conflict. Haggerty notes that from the late 1990s the Kashmir issue became complicated by the fact that both India and Pakistan were nuclear weapons possessors, a situation that led to 'a vastly increased level of international interest and involvement' (Haggerty, 2002). This was also a time of growing political salience in India of the ideology Hindutva and in Pakistan of the political position of various Islamist groups, including the alliance known as the Muttahhida Majlis-e-Amal.

Hindutva and the Kashmir conflict

The rise of *Hindutva* in India in the 1980s and 1990s influenced the country's conflict with Pakistan over Kashmir in two main ways. First, Hindutva became a significant issue in relation to India's domestic concerns, especially during the 1990s when the country was under BJP control. Hindutva was also an influential factor in relation to foreign policy in two ways: (1) the relationship with Pakistan, and (2) more generally in relation to Muslim countries and fears of Islamic extremism. While Ram-Prasad notes that in India in recent years 'religious ideology in itself has played virtually no *direct* role in major political and economic decisions' (Ram-Prasad, 2000: 153, my emphasis), it seems clear that as a soft-power factor – especially in relation to Kashmir – *Hindutva* has been important, in tandem with traditional secular nationalist concerns

(Continued)

(Chiriyankandath, 2006; Ram-Prasad, 2000). Note, however, that this implies salience of Hindutva soft power especially when it is linked to hard power. Ram-Prasad claims that 'there is very little even in a "hard" Hindu nationalism which could translate into an ideology of expansion' (Ram-Prasad, 2000: 188), yet as we have seen, when *Hindutva* ideas are linked to hard power it bolsters India's resolve not to allow Kashmiri Muslims – in association with the government of Pakistan – to control the state, regarded by many Indians as the 'jewel in the crown' of 'Hindu India'. This underlines what we have repeatedly noted in this book in relation to various other countries, including the USA, Iran and Israel: a nation's foreign policy does not take place in isolation but from a combination of domestic factors, including: 'geo-strategic location, economic health, military strength and domestic stability' (Kapila, 2005), and, we might add, in some cases the soft power of religion.

Religion and conflict in Sri Lanka

Apart from the issue of Kashmir, there was a second regional conflict that significantly engaged India's foreign policy from the 1990s: the Sri Lankan civil war. Like Kashmir, this conflict was also linked to religious issues, as the civil war was between the majority, the Buddhist Sinhalese, and minority Hindu Tamil people. Sri Lanka's conflict attracted the attention of successive Indian governments, for two main reasons: (1) it was regionally destabilizing, and (2) it centrally involved Tamils, a people which in the Indian context had been agitating for independence (Allen, 1992; Jayawardena, 1992).

Ceylon became independent in 1948, changing it name to Sri Lanka (in Sinhalese, 'resplendent land') in 1972. In 1978, the country's legislative and judicial capital was moved from Colombo to nearby Sri Jayewardanapura Kotte, and the national flag was also changed: orange and green vertical bars were added, representing the Hindu Tamil[3] and Muslim minority populations. Despite this attempt to indicate that Sri Lanka was not solely a Buddhist nation, it remained the case that 'Buddhist nationalism' played a pre-eminent political role in Sri Lanka, serving as a unifying force among the Sinhalese majority (Young, 2000). Buddhist Sinhalese comprise three-quarters of the population, while Hindu Tamils make up around 18 per cent of the population. The remaining people, less than 10 per cent, are mainly Muslims and Christians (Jayawardena, 1992).

Religion, ethnicity and civil war in Sri Lanka

The civil war in Sri Lanka pits Sinhalese Buddhists against Tamil Hindus. It is a conflict about identity, an issue that includes both ethnicity and religion. As Young notes, 'religion plays a role in the conflict, [although] most Sri Lankans view its origins more in ethnic rather than religious terms'. There is also a pronounced developmental dimension. While Sri Lanka was once hailed for its impressive developmental indicators, including 'a high literacy rate and life expectancy, and low rates of infant and maternal mortality', the civil war, which erupted in 1983, saw these indicators deteriorate greatly. The war had a 'devastating impact . . . on demography, health, education, and housing', while highlighting 'wide disparities within ethnic and regional groups' (Young, 2000: 1). Believing that they will not ever get a fair deal because of demographic reasons, many Tamils now demand their own independent state.

Many Sri Lankans and foreign commentators regard the conflict in Sri Lanka as having roots in the British colonial period, with inherited political and economic grievances following independence in 1948 that were not adequately addressed by successive governments (Young, 2000). Following the end of British rule, Sinhalese majority governments in Ceylon/Sri Lanka sought to overturn what they regarded as British colonial favouritism towards the Tamil minority, especially in relation both to education and distribution of government jobs. As a result, successive Sinhalese-majority governments effected policies that favoured the Sinhalese over the Tamils, including giving Buddhism a privileged position constitutionally. Over time, Tamil grievances grew, escalating to the point that civil war broke out in 1983 following the killing in the city of Jaffna of 13 mostly Tamil soldiers. Over the next quarter century the conflict was often extremely violent, a wide-ranging struggle between the two ethnic/religious groups over political, developmental, religious and ethnic concerns. The civil war has so far resulted in more than 65,000 deaths on both sides, while a resolution to the conflict still seems far away (Young, 2000: 1).

During the 1980s and 1990s, successive governments officially did away with some of the policies discriminating against Tamils and, in addition, recognized Tamil as one of the country's official languages. But for many Tamils this was inadequate and the fighting continued until a ceasefire in December 2001, signed between the Tamils' military wing – the Liberation Tigers of Tamil Eelam (LTTE) – and the government. It is likely that the changed international climate after 9/11 influenced the Tamils' decision to enter into the ceasefire: various influential governments – including that of India, as well as those of the USA, Britain, Canada and Australia – declared the LTTE to be a terrorist organization. This meant that henceforward the Tigers found it very difficult to build international links and support for their struggle.

The 2001 ceasefire was not, however, followed by an overall resolution of the conflict, although Norway led determined international mediation attempts to try to achieve that objective (Støre, 2006). Several major obstacles to peace remained, notably:

- intense rivalry between the two main (secular) Sinhalese political parties, the Peoples Assembly (PA) and the United National Party (UNP);
- fierce opposition from sections of the Buddhist clergy, opposed to any accommodation to the Tamils and their grievances, concessions which they viewed as threatening to the dominant position of Buddhism in Sri Lanka;
- governmental reluctance to accept the mediation of external parties;
- apparent unwillingness of the LTTE to entertain any settlement short of a separate state (Young, 2000).

From this list of barriers to a settlement to a conflict that is now twenty-five years old, we can note both secular nationalist and religious concerns. This combination of factors appears to make the situation particularly difficult to resolve. As a result, the period from the time of the signing of the ceasefire has seen a diminution in the ferocity of the conflict, but no clear cessation. Four years later, in August 2005, a sniper assassinated Sri Lanka's Sinhalese foreign minister, Lakshman Kadirgamar, an act that led to a reignition of the conflict.

We noted above that the Sri Lankan civil war was a conflict that drew the attention of successive Indian governments, and which at times led to India's overt involvement in the war. India's government was keen to resolve the conflict, for three main reasons:

- to underline India's credentials as South Asia's leading regional power,
- to try to undermine the claims of India's own Tamils for autonomy or independence, through denial of the demands of Sri Lanka's Tamil separatists;
- to emphasize the Indian government's stated belief that Sri Lanka's Tamils were unacceptably discriminated against by the Sinhalese majority (Pal, 2006).

The major point to emphasize, however, is that there was no knee-jerk support of the Sri Lankan Tamils simply because most were, like more than 800 million Indians, followers of Hinduism. In fact, Indian involvement in the civil war has largely been seen as a secular national interest concern, because of the close geographical position of Sri Lanka to India. This point can be illustrated by reference to the 1970s and early 1980s, a period when India was often controlled by secular Congress governments led by Indira Gandhi. At this time, India's key foreign policy goal in relation to Sri Lanka was to prevent its government building closer ties not only with various Western countries, including Britain and the USA, but also with neighbouring countries, including Pakistan and China (Pal, 2006). For the Indian government this posed an unacceptable challenge to India's position as South Asia's chief regional power. According to Krishna (2001), on various questions – including 'the Soviet invasion of Afghanistan [1979], declaring the Indian ocean a zone of peace, the issue of broadcast facilities to the Voice of America, the use of Trincomalee harbour, [and] membership in ASEAN [Association of South East Asian Nations]' – Mrs Gandhi believed that, in relation to India, Sri Lanka's government was acting too independently and provocatively. Seeking an issue to help her focus India's concerns and as a result to deal with Sri Lanka, she focused upon the situation of the Tamil minority in Sri Lanka. She declared that the Tamils' fate was a crucial issue for India's national security. In sum, at this time, India's foreign policy under Mrs Gandhi was pursued 'for reasons having to do with assertion of India's hegemony over Sri Lanka' (Pararajasingham, 2004). India trained and armed Tamil militants, not in order to achieve a Tamil state ('Tamil Eelam'), but to complement diplomatic pressures already being exerted on Sri Lanka's government to compel it to toe the line and bend to India's will.

Following unsuccessful attempt to get Sri Lanka to bend to India's will, in the late 1980s, India's government negotiated an agreement with the government of Sri Lanka on the Tamils' behalf, but without consulting the LTTE (Jayawardena, 1992). India promised Sri Lanka's government military support if needed to enforce Tamil compliance with a deal that gave the Tamils a few political concessions, including constitutional changes to grant them more local power, but certainly not the independence being demanded. Perhaps unsurprisingly, the initiative did not resolve the conflict, although it did achieve India's foreign policy aim of bringing Sri Lanka's government firmly under its influence if not control. Later, in 1991, when a government led by Indira Gandhi's son, Rajiv, tried to flex India's muscles by intervening in Sri Lanka militarily – both to exercise India's new-found influence and to overturn the earlier policy to arm the LTTE – he was assassinated by a Tamil extremist. This suggests that India seriously underestimated the depth of feeling underpinning Tamil nationalism in Sri Lanka that by this time had grown to be a major force of such potency that even applied Indian firepower could not obliterate it. Indeed, as Bose (1994) argues, India's physical intervention appears to have achieved the opposite effect to that intended: it served significantly to help consolidate Tamil nationalism in Sri Lanka. Overall, however, the situation was made more complex by a lack of agreement among Indian governments over the direction and thrust of India's policy. Under Congress Party rule, the issue was viewed in secular nationalist and national interest terms. The government consistently supported Sri Lanka's (Sinhalese) government, as it was seen as the best means to curtail regional instability because of the war. BJP administrations, on the other hand, saw the conflict more through a *Hindutva* focus. This led them to make statements supporting the Tamils on religious grounds, a stance that also gained the backing of the regional government of Tamil Nadu, which had long backed the LTTE on ethnic ground (Shankar, 2006).

Conclusion

In this chapter we focused on the influence of religion in the international relations of South Asia, with particular focus on India, Pakistan and Sri Lanka. We saw that:

- in each of the three countries, various political issues have long been associated with religious factors;
- this was often in the context of competition or conflicts over identity, land or other resources;
- in each case, identifiable religious constituencies – including, Hindu fundamentalists in India, Islamists in Pakistan, and Sinhalese Buddhists and Tamil Hindus in Sri Lanka – sought to influence their country's foreign policy and international relations.

Our surveys of the political roles of religious actors in the three countries enables us to conclude that religious actors' influence in relation to the international relations of India, Pakistan and Sri Lanka is at times significant. Their chief tactic is to try to influence government policy, augmented, when they are available, by attempts to build transnational networks of religious believers, for example in relation to Kashmir. This implies more generally that the soft power of religion is a variable that should not be overlooked. On the other hand, this is not to suggest that religious soft power is *always* the most influential factor in the region's international relations. But it does underline how in each of the regional countries we examined, domestic structures and processes throw up politically influential religious actors that seek to influence international outcomes, although they are by no means guaranteed success. They are, however, likely to be most successful when religious soft power works together with 'secular' hard power.

Notes

1   According to Marshall (2004), 'Until the nineteenth century, the word "Hindu" had no specific religious meaning and simply referred to the people who lived east of the Indus River, whatever their beliefs. (The Indian Supreme Court itself has held that "no precise meaning can be ascribed to the terms 'Hindu' and 'Hinduism.'") It was only when the census introduced by the British colonial authorities in 1871 included Hindu as a religious designation that many Indians began to think of themselves and their country as Hindu'.

2   Mahmud (2005) explains that the state of Jammu-Kashmir, of which the Kashmir valley is a part, is not religiously homogeneous. Jammu is two-thirds Hindu and one-third Muslim, while the Kashmir valley is about 80 per cent Muslim. Azad Kashmir (the Pakistan-controlled) portion is 'almost entirely Sunni Muslim, including 1.5 million refugees settled in various cities of Pakistan'.

3   Tamils are an ethnic group, predominantly Hindu, whose language is also Tamil, a Dravidian language. In Sri Lanka, Tamils are mostly located in the country's Northern and Eastern provinces. Tamils are in the majority in the Indian state of Tamil Nadu, in the south-east of the country; there are strong links between the two communities. Some Tamils are indigenous, others are descendants of estate labourers imported under British colonial rule.

Questions

1   To what extent has the end of the Cold War and deepening globalization affected the role of religion in conflict in South Asia?

2   What is 'Hindu nationalism' and how does it affect political outcomes in India?

3   'Pakistan is a Muslim state and so we should expect a leading role for Islam in both domestic and foreign policy'. Discuss.

4   Was the civil war in Sri Lanka a religious war?

5   To what extent has international involvement in South Asia helped to resolve religious conflicts?

Bibliography

Ali, T. (1999) 'The panic button', *The Guardian*, 14 October.

Allen, D. (1992) *Religion and Political Conflict in South Asia: India, Pakistan and Sri Lanka*, London: Greenwood Press.

Amnesty International (2003) 'India: Best Bakery case – concerns for justice'. Amnesty International Press Release. AI Index: ASA 20/018/2003 (Public) News Service No: 165, 9 July. Available at: http://web.amnesty.org/library/Index/ENGASA200182003?open&of=ENG-IND Accessed 9 January 2006.

Bhatt, C. (2001) *Hindu Nationalism: Origins, Ideologies and Modern Myths*, Oxford: Berg.

Bidwai, P. (2003) 'Critical moment for India', *Frontline*, 20, 13, 21 June. Available at: http://www.tni.org/archives/bidwai/critical.htm Accessed 6 September 2005.

Bose, S. (1994) *States, Nations, Sovereignty, Sri Lanka, India and the Tamil Eelam Movement*, New Delhi: Sage Publications.

Brass, P. (2005) *The Production of Hindu–Muslim Violence in Contemporary India*, Seattle: University of Washington Press.

'Center Conversations, 2003. An Occasional Publication of the Ethics and Public Policy Center', No. 17, February 2003, 'Hindu nationalism vs. Islamic jihad: religious militancy in South Asia. A Conversation with Cedric Prakash, Teesta Setalvad, Kamal Chenoy, Sumit Ganguly, Sunil Khilnani, and Jonah Blank'. Available at: http://www.eppc.org/docLib/20030503_CenterConversation17.pdf Accessed 1 September 2005.

Chiriyankandath, J. (1996) 'The 1996 Indian general election'. Briefing paper 31, London: Royal Institute of International Affairs.

Chiriyankandath, J. (2006) 'Hinduism and politics', in J. Haynes (ed.), *The Politics of Religion: A Survey*, London: Routledge.

Cohen, S. (2004) *The Idea of Pakistan*, Washington, DC: The Brookings Institution.

Council on Foreign Relations (2003) 'The role of Islamic groups in Pakistan's foreign policy'. Available at: http://www.cfr.org/publication. html?id=5773 Accessed 10 October 2005.

Diamond, L. (1999) *Developing Democracy: Towards Consolidation*, Baltimore, MD: Johns Hopkins University Press.

Embassy of India (2003) 'Address by Shri Brajesh Mishra, National Security Advisor of India at the American Jewish Committee Annual Dinner', 8 May 2003. Available at: http://www.indianembassy.org/indusrel/ 2003/nsa_ajc_may_8_03.htm Accessed 6 September 2005.

Federal Research Division of the Library of Congress (1995) 'India: the role of political and interest groups'. Country Studies Series. Available at: http://www.country-data.com/cgi-bin/query/r-6130.html Accessed 9 January 2005.

Ganguly, S. (2003/4) 'India's foreign policy grows up', *World Policy Journal*, Winter, pp. 41–7.

Haggerty, D. (2002) 'Ethnicity and religion in international politics: the Middle East, the Balkans, and India–Pakistan', Consortium of Social Science Associations Congressional Briefing, 19 September. Available at: http://www.cossa.org/ethnicity.htm Accessed 10 January 2006.

Harrison, S. (2001) 'Pakistan: the destabilisation game', *Le Monde Diplomatique*, October, pp. 17–18.

Haynes, J. (2001) *Democracy in the Developing World*, Cambridge: Polity.

Human Rights Watch (2002) '"We have no orders to save you": state participation and complicity in communal violence in Gujarat', New York: Human Rights Watch.

Jayawardena, L. (1992) *Buddhism Betrayed?: Religion, Politics and Violence in Sri Lanka*, Chicago: University of Chicago Press.

Kapila, S. (2005) 'India's foreign policy challenges 2005: a perspective analysis', *South Asia Analysis Group*, 17 January. Available at: http://www. saag.org/papers13/paper1223.html Accessed 10 January 2006.

Katalya, K. (2004) 'Issues and trends in Indian elections', *South Asian Journal*, 5 (July–September). Available at: http://www.southasianmedia.net/ Magazine/Journal/previousissues5.htm Accessed 9 January 2006.

Katzman, K. (2002) 'Terrorism: Near Eastern groups and state sponsors, 2002'. 'Congress Research Service Report for Congress', 13 February. Available at: http://www.fas.org/irp/crs/RL31119.pdf Accessed 9 January 2006.

Kohli, A. (1994) 'Centralization and powerlessness: India's democracy in a comparative perspective', in J. Migdal, A. Kohli and V. Shue (eds), *State Power and Social Forces: Domination and Transformation in the Third World*, Cambridge: Cambridge University Press, pp. 93–136.

Krishna, S. (2001) *India's Role in Sri Lanka's Ethnic Conflict*, Colombo: Marga Institute.

Kumaraswamy, P. R. (1999) 'South Asia after the cold war', in L. Fawcett and Y. Sayigh (eds), *The Third World Beyond the Cold War: Continuity and Change*, Oxford: Oxford University Press, pp. 170–99.

Lall, M. 2005 'Indian education policy under the NDA government', in K. Adeney and L. Saez (eds), *Coalition Politics and Hindu Nationalism*, London: Routledge, pp.153–70.

Lapidus, I. (1988) *A History of Islamic Societies*, Cambridge: Cambridge University Press.

MacFarquhar, L. (2003) 'Letter from India: the strongman', *The New Yorker*, 26 May, pp. 50–7.

Mahmud, E. (2005) 'The missing intra-Jammu and Kashmir dialogue'. Available at: http://www.stimson.org/southasia/?SN=SA20050301780 Accessed 12 January 2006.

Malik, I. (2002) *Religious Minorities in Pakistan*, London: Minority Rights Group International.

Marshall, P. (2004) 'Hinduism and terror', *First Things: A Monthly Journal of Religion and Public Life*, 1 June. Available at: http://www.freedomhouse.org/religion/country/india/Hinduism%20and%20Terror.htm Accessed 24 April 2006.

McCarthy, R. (2002) 'Pearl trial told how Briton drove off with journalist', *The Guardian*, 23 April.

Nasr, S. (2001) *The Islamic Leviathan: Islam and the Making of State Power*, Oxford: Oxford University Press.

Pal, A. (2006) 'Sri Lanka on verge of civil war – again' *The Progressive*, May, p. 1.

Pararajasingham, A. (2004) 'India's Sri Lanka policy: need for a review', South Asia Analysis Group, Paper no. 1187, 13 December. Available at: http://www.saag.org/papers12/paper1187.html Accessed 1 September 2005.

Ram-Prasad, C. (2000) 'Hindu nationalism and the international relations of India', in K. Dark (ed.), *Religion and International Relations*, Basingstoke: Macmillan.

Reoch, R. (2001) 'The "no mercy war" in Sri Lanka', Asian Human Rights Commission. Available at: http://www.hrsolidarity.net/mainfile.php/1999vol09no05/968/ Accessed 9 January 2006.

Rizvi, G. (1995) 'South Asia and the new world order', in H.-H. Holm and G. Sørensen (eds), *Whose World Order?*, Boulder, CO: Westview, pp. 69–88.

Shankar, S. (2006) 'The tiger towards its territory', *South Asia Monitor*. Available at: http://www.southasiamonitor.org/2006/apr/news/10view1.shtml Accessed 27 June 2006.

Smock, D. (ed.) (2006) *Religious Contributions to Peacemaking*, Washington, DC: United States Institute of Peace.

'South Asia: attacks on Indian Christians continue' (1998) BBC News, 30 December. Available at: http://news.bbc.co.uk/1/hi/world/south_asia/244653.stm Accessed 23 May 2006.

Støre, J. (2006) 'Managing conflict and building peace: Norwegian policy for peace and reconciliation'. Speech delivered by Norway's Minister of Foreign Affairs, Jonas Gahr Støre, at the Real Instituto Elcano, Madrid, 13 March.

Thirumalai, M. S. (2001) 'Language and culture in India's foreign policy – Part 1', *Language in India*, 1(3). Available at: http://www.languageinindia.com/may2001/foreign.html Accessed 2 September 2005.

The Times of India (2002) 'Venkaiah to Modi: no anti-minority remarks please', 10 September. Available at: http://www1.timesofindia.indiatimes.com/cms.dll/articleshow?art_id=21793227 Accessed 9 January 2006.

United States Commission on International Religious Freedom (2004) 'Annual report', May, Washington, DC: United States Commission on International Religious Freedom.

Vyas, N. (2002) 'Hindutva opponents to get death: VHP', *Daily Times (Pakistan)*, 19 December. Available at: http://www.dailytimes.com.pk/default.asp?page=story_19-12-2002_pg4_23 Accessed 9 January 2006.

Young, M. (2000) 'Sri Lanka's long war', *Foreign Policy in Focus*, 5(35), pp. 1–4.

Further reading

C. Bhatt, *Hindu Nationalism: Origins, Ideologies and Modern Myths*, Berg, 2001. Bhatt's book is clearly written and stimulating. It is both reasoned and succinctly argued, an analysis that delves into the history of the phenomenon and provides an illuminating account of the issues that will shape it in the future.

P. Brass, *The Production of Hindu–Muslim Violence in Contemporary India*, University of Washington Press, 2005. In recent years, serious Hindu–Muslim rioting in India created a situation where communal violence became a common event. Brass, one of the world's pre-eminent experts on South Asia, looks back at more than 50 years of riots in the north Indian city of Aligarh. Brass exposes the mechanisms by which endemic communal violence is deliberately provoked and sustained. He offers a compelling argument for abandoning or refining a number of widely held views about the supposed causes of communal violence, not just in India but throughout the rest of the world. An important addition to the literature on Indian and South Asian politics, this book is also an invaluable contribution to our understanding of the interplay of nationalism, ethnicity, religion, and collective violence, wherever it occurs.

L. Jayawardena, *Buddhism Betrayed: Religion, Politics and Violence in Sri Lanka*, University of Chicago Press, 1992. Jayawardena traces the emergence and development of inter-societal conflict in Sri Lanka, stresses that the civil war has multiple roots and causes, with religion an important source of friction between Sinhalese and Tamils.

S. Nasr, *The Islamic Leviathan: Islam and the Making of State Power*, Oxford University Press, 2001. Nasr manages to balance sophisticated political theory and effective historical analysis in his case studies of Pakistan and Malaysia. He challenges the prevailing assumption that Islam is against or is incompatible with secularism and modernization.

CHAPTER 13

Pacific Asia

Pacific Asia comprises 14 states, 4 in East Asia (China, Japan, Korea and Taiwan) and 10 in South-East Asia (Brunei, Cambodia, Indonesia, Laos, Malaysia, Myanmar (Burma), the Philippines, Singapore, Thailand and Vietnam). McCargo explains that, 'unlike the more ambiguous phrase 'Asia-Pacific', 'Pacific Asia' clearly excludes Australia and North America' (McCargo, 2001: 141). Many of the major religions of the world are found in the Pacific Asian region, including: Buddhism (both Theravada and Mahayana),[1] Confucianism (in various forms, often mixed up with Taoism[2] and/or Buddhism), Islam (Indonesia is the world's most populous predominantly Muslim country, with a population of more than 200 million people), Christianity (often Catholicism, primarily in the Philippines, although both China and South Korea also have significant Catholic minorities), Hinduism (principally in Bali, an Indonesian island), Taoism, Shintoism (Japan),[3] as well as numerous localized traditional religions.

Religious diversity is augmented by economic, historical and political differences. Economically, Pacific Asia ranges from 'the high-tech capitalist economies of Taiwan and Singapore, to the predominantly agricultural societies of Laos and Vietnam'. Historically, the region has a complex and dissimilar colonial background and influences: no colonial control in Thailand or China, and British administrations in Burma, Hong Kong (now part of China), Malaysia and Singapore. In addition, the Dutch controlled Indonesia and the French what was called 'Indochina' (Laos, Cambodia, Vietnam). Moreover, the Spanish had a long-term colonial presence in the Philippines, and the Japanese in Korea and Taiwan. Some regional countries (Cambodia, China, Japan) had very old civilizations, while others (such as the Philippines) were newly created. Finally, there are many kinds of political systems in Pacific Asia. These include an absolute monarchy in tiny Brunei, a constitutional monarchy in populous Thailand

and a long-established military regime in Myanmar. There are also well-established regional democracies, including Japan, South Korea and Taiwan. In addition, Indonesia and the Philippines have more recently democratized, and Malaysia and Singapore have well-established 'illiberal democracies', that is, political systems with both democratic and authoritarian characteristics (McCargo, 2001: 141–2).

Pacific Asia and 'Asian Values'

Pacific Asia is a region with religious, economic, historical and political diversity. In recent years, there has been a continuing debate between two groups – 'Orientalists' and 'reverse Orientalists' – over what constitute the region's most politically and culturally important characteristics. While the Orientalists refer to the region's various indigenous forms of authoritarian rule which are said to be 'culturally appropriate', reverse Orientalists cite various recent rulers – including Muhammad Mahathir (Malaysia) and Lee Kuan Yew (Singapore) – who, it is claimed, turn old stereotypes into useful claims of cultural distinctiveness (Barr, 2002). This issue has been a key factor in the controversy over whether there are, in fact, distinctive 'Asian Values'. Some contend that 'Asian Values' are actually linked to some of the region's religious traditions, leading 'value system[s] most congruent with Oriental authoritarianism' (King, 1993: 141). For example, Fukuyama sees Confucianism as both 'hierarchical and inegalitarian', characteristic of 'the community-orientedness of Asian cultures' (Fukuyama, 1992: 217). The overall concern here is that, according to the proponents of a distinctive 'Asian culture', including former rulers and current intellectuals, such as Jiang Qing, liberal democracy is 'culturally alien' to the Pacific Asian region (Ommerborn, n.d.). This is because many of the region's countries are said to have political cultures and histories that, while differing from country to country in precise details, nevertheless reflect an important factor: a societal emphasis on the collective or group, not the individual. This in turn emphasizes 'harmony', 'consensus', 'unity' and 'community', all cornerstone values of Confucianism that are said to differ significantly from 'Western culture' and its allegedly individualistic, self-seeking values (Deegan, 2005: 26).

In this chapter we focus primarily on two religions, Confucianism in relation to China, and Buddhism in relation to Thailand, Myanmar and Cambodia. For comparative purposes, we also examine the role of transnational Islam in relation to ethnic struggles for autonomy in Thailand and the Philippines.

The structure of the chapter is as follows: First, we examine Confucianism in relation to China, focusing on what has been called the country's 'post-Communist' foreign policy which is referred to as being 'New Confucian' or 'Neo-Confucian' in orientation. Secondly, we consider the political impact of Buddhism in relation to Thailand, Myanmar and Cambodia, three Buddhist-majority regional countries. We discover that there are no influential regional Buddhist networks that influence those countries' foreign policies or international relations more generally. This is because in each country, nationalism has 'secularize[d] national identities that were historically rooted in religion'. This implies that 'each nation adopted [Buddhism] in a unique way according to its national characteristics (Tepe, 2005: 287, 297). For example, unlike Cambodia or Myanmar, Thailand was never colonized by a Western country. As a result, Buddhism developed as the core of the country's national ideology. In recent years, 'new Buddhist movements' have emerged, some with overtly political goals and aspirations, emphasizing that Buddhism is still of great importance in Thailand. In Myanmar, there was a different position regarding the social and political role of Buddhism. Buddhist monks (*sangha*) played a leading role in the country's attainment of freedom from British colonial rule after the Second World War. However, more recently there has been intermittent political conflict between some sections of the *sangha* and state, with the former playing the role of chief political opposition. Once again, however, we see the political role of Buddhism in the context of domestic concerns rather than international issues. Unlike in Thailand or Myanmar, in Cambodia, Buddhism had to contend with serious attempts to snuff it out. During five years of rule by the murderous Khmer Rouge in the 1970s, the regime tried energetically to exterminate religion, including Buddhism, while killing millions of Cambodians. However, following the Khmer Rouge's overthrow in 1979 by a Vietnamese invasion, an initially hesitant state recognized the continuing popular appeal of Buddhism and allowed it a resurgent voice in national affairs.

Overall, the chapter makes the following points:

■ While both Buddhism and Confucianism have political roles in Pacific Asia, it is only in relation to China that we see a significant role in foreign policy and international relations.

■ The Chinese government emphasizes what it describes as a 'culturally authentic' 'New Confucianism' as a prescriptive policy to try to balance the power of the USA and to achieve greater cultural and moral influence for China.

■ Buddhism does not play a significant international or transnational role in Pacific Asia's politics.

■ Important regional networks of dissident Muslim minorities are in conflict with the state in Thailand and the Philippines.

China: Confucianism and foreign policy

Confucianism is an ancient religious and philosophical system. It has developed over the last 2,500 years from writings attributed to a Chinese philosopher, Confucius (the latinized version of Kung Fu-tzu (that is, Master Kung), a teacher in China who lived between c.551–479 BCE). His key teachings were concerned with principles of good conduct, practical wisdom, and 'proper' social relationships, and focused upon relationships between individuals, between individuals and their families, and between individuals and general society. The German sociologist Max Weber noted that, in China, Confucianism was historically 'the status ethic of prebendaries, of men with literary educations who were characterized by a secular rationalism' (Weber, 1969: 21). This underlines how important it was in China to belong to the *cultured* stratum; if one did not, he (much less she) did not count; and an adhesion to Confucianist values was an important element. As a result, Confucianism was a status ethic of the 'cultured' stratum that in turn not only helped determine the way of life in China itself but also influenced neighbouring areas that historically came under Chinese influence or control, including present-day Korea, Japan, Singapore, Taiwan and Vietnam. In Korea, for example, Confucianism grew in significance from the seventh century to become not only the traditional ideological core of the governing system but also of 'a religious or philosophical system which affected the social and cultural aspects of the nation's life' (Barr, 2002: 157–74).

Over time, however, countries influenced by Confucianism diverged politically. On the one hand, China, North Korea and Vietnam are three of the few remaining Communist countries. On the other hand, from the time of the Cold War, Japan, South Korea, Singapore and Taiwan have been closely allied with the USA and more generally the West. This suggests that while these countries may share cultural characteristics that highlight the importance of the community or the collective over the individual, a shared background in Confucianism does not dictate similar political developments or international relations. In China, Confucianist cultural and religious factors can be seen in relation to a 'post-Communist' ideology that emphasizes certain patterns of living and standards of social value, while also providing an important backdrop to recent developments in political thinking and foreign policy (Barr, 2002: 46–63; Kim, 1998; Ross and Johnston, 2006).

Confucianism: The core of Chinese civilization?

A leading Chinese intellectual, Jiang Qing, has recently argued that the 'Confucian religion is the core of Chinese civilization, including political, cultural and religious aspects'. As the de facto Chinese state religion, he claims that 'it should be the cultural consensus and spiritual belief of the whole nation' ('Confucianism will never be religion', 2006). For Jiang Qing, government is legitimate only when it clearly reflects the values associated with the community's cultural traditions and principles, and in China, he contends, this is Confucianism. He also claims that the so-called 'universal' appropriateness of Western-style, political and social values is simply wrong, as he believes it inevitably leads to undesirable outcomes, including 'social Darwinism or poverty of the third world etc.' (Ommerborn, n.d.). Instead, national political institutions and practices in China should reflect local cultural values ('Confucianism will never be religion', 2006). Critics contend, however, that Jiang Qing 'negate[s] the generalisation of Western principles like democracy, freedom, and human rights etc.' (Ommerborn, n.d.).

These concerns have risen to prominence in response to the stresses and strains that globalization has placed on China's hitherto inward-looking political, social and developmental concerns (Barr, 2002: 46–63). To try to deal with the domestic impact of globalization, China's rulers have sought to draw ideologically on Confucianist ideas and values (Jacques, 2006). This was evident in the visit of Hu Jintao to the USA in May 2006 when in a speech at Yale University he set out, for the first time in such a forum, the Chinese view of 'a harmonious world based on the idea of Chinese civilisation'. This Confucianist focus dovetails with an important strand of domestic concern established in the mid-1990s: an interlinked social, political and economic programme designed to 're-educate' and 'reinform' the Chinese people in Confucian values. The campaign was accompanied by officially sponsored excursions into political philosophy with Confucianism harnessed to desirable prescriptions for politics and economic growth, based on principles of harmony, consensus and order. The overall aim was to try to eliminate or at least reduce the kinds of adversarial activity associated by at least some of China's leaders with economic liberalization characteristic of economic globalization (Yu, 2004).

As a result of the government's initiative, Hwang notes, 'the dormant seeds of a long-buried debate are beginning to sprout in China, with implications that could shape the future of the world's most rapidly developing society' (Hwang, 2005). Both scholars and state officials are now busy re-examining China's Confucian past, attempting to devise strategies both to deal with domestic internal social and political conflicts, and to help provide a suitable, post-Communist ideological content for the country's foreign policy and international relations. What are referred to as 'New Confucianist' or 'Neo-Confucianist' ideas significantly inform the current debate 'about values and morality, expressed in questions about how the country should legitimately be ruled'. In the likely absence of meaningful democratic reforms at home, the Chinese government was said to be experimenting with Confucianism as a state ideology of control. The government's aim was said to be to try to reinforce its hold on power through a focus on the cultural and societal appropriateness of Confucianism as a way of uniting the Chinese at a time of economic polarization (Tamney and Chiang, 2002).

This is not to suggest that the government's current focus on Confucianism is entirely cynical or self-serving. As Naím (2005) notes, Confucian ideas have 'long persist[ed] in the minds of Chinese politicians'. A noted China scholar, John King Fairbank, wrote in 1948 that even at the time of the Communist revolution, Confucianist ideas informed the ideas of revolutionary leaders, including Mao Zedong. This was because 'Confucianism began as a means of bringing social order out of [political] chaos . . . . It has been a philosophy of status and consequently a ready tool for autocracy and bureaucracy whenever they have flourished' (Naím, 2005). Six decades later, China's current leaders are again seeking to draw on 'whatever Confucian instincts remain in the population to contain the social upheaval that is coming with the country's rapid modernization' (Pan, 2004). Social and political stresses and strains are reflected in official data, indicating that there were around 87,000 protests and incidents of social unrest in China during 2005 – an average of more than 230 a *day*, an increase of 6.6 per cent on 2004 (Watts, 2006). Many of the clashes between 'the masses' and the police had their roots in either property disputes, 'pollution' or 'corruption' issues, while others focused on 'deadly ethnic' conflict, especially in Central China. A key problem occurred when the state tried to take land from local people for major developmental projects. During 2003, for example, 'tens of thousands of rice farmers fighting a dam project staged a huge protest in the western part of the country. The same day, authorities crushed a strike involving 7,000 textile workers . . . The Communist Party has indicated it is worried that these outbursts of discontent might coalesce into large-scale, organized opposition to its rule' (Pan, 2004). Despite these clear manifestations of popular protest, the government seems unwilling to establish democratic reforms, while seeking to try to contain popular agitation in other ways. These include trying to make the ruling Communist Party more accountable and popularly-based, giving in to some protests but cracking down hard on others, and trying strictly to control the flow of information which has increased as a result of globalization, including via the internet and email. On the other hand, growing popular access to foreign news media, coupled with greatly increased ownership of mobile telephones in recent years, has made state attempts at censorship difficult to accomplish fully (Tamney and Chiang, 2002).

Part of the problem, the government acknowledges, is that China is now increasingly affected by globalization and wider changes in the post-Cold War world, including China's often-problematic relationship with the USA (Ross and Johnston, 2006). After the Cold War ended in 1989, the US government sought to get to grips with China by advancing a policy of what it called 'constructive engagement'. This portrayed the USA as a superpower with only benign intentions, whose main goal was to find common ground with the (then mostly authoritarian) countries of Pacific Asia, including China. China's government saw the US initiative as useful because it implied a lessening of the need to respond to external pressures in areas where it was vulnerable: democracy and human rights. And, along with US 'constructive engagement', there seemed to be a growing international willingness to accept the belief that there was something called 'the Asian way' that justified different, less than fully democratic, development patterns (Kim, 1998). As already noted, such ideas are currently linked in China both to traditional Confucianist ideas and to a modern expression, known as 'New Confucianism'.

Ideas associated with New Confucianism can be seen to dovetail neatly with US views on economic development: both share a belief that capitalism and free markets – the 'theology of the marketplace' – will solve the world's developmental problems, including those of China. President Clinton embraced this principle in 1996, declaring that 'freer enterprise will fuel the hunger for a more free society'. For many authoritarian leaders in Pacific Asia, including the government of China, this was a comforting thought, 'since even the most dictatorial regimes in Asia now embrace free-market capitalism' (Miller, 1997: 1–2). However, as Zhou (2005: 105) notes,

> there is no doubt that different political systems are the essential reason for the conflicts between the United States and China. However, more profound causes of the disagreement between the United States and China on human rights issues

lie in the different levels of economic development and the divergent cultures and basic values of the two countries. The notion of the responsibility of the state for individuals, the lack of the concept of rights in traditional Chinese thought, and humiliation in recent history and corresponding sensitivity to sovereignty, count for the ordinary Chinese attitudes toward US policies on human rights towards China.

This suggests that, since the mid-1990s, a shared belief in the dogma of capitalism has not been sufficient to remove sources of friction between the USA and China, especially the issue of an alleged lack of political and religious freedoms in the latter. In particular, there is the issue of the persecution of the Falun Gong religious sect. Falun Gong (also known as Falun Dafa) means 'Law of the Wheel Breathing Exercise', and is a largely spiritual movement that incorporates Buddhist and Taoist principles, Qigong (body, mind and physical exercises) and healing techniques. The aim is to cleanse both mind and body and simultaneously make better moral character through a regime of exercises, meditation and study. Falun Gong exercises are believed to be both relaxing and energizing, with practitioners often performing them as a group. Li Hongzhi, also known as 'The Master' or 'Master Li', introduced Falun Gong to China in 1992. His teachings and philosophy are set forth in two books *Falun Gong* and *Zhuan Falun* (*Turning the Law Wheel*), available in a variety of languages. Falun Gong is practised all over the world and Li Hongzhi claims to have a following of more than 100 million people.

Falun Gong in China

Followers of Falun Gong in China have experienced high levels of persecution in recent years (Human Rights Watch, 2002). The Chinese government initiated a general campaign against spiritual and religious groups in 1999, including Falun Gong practitioners. As a result, in April 1999, some 10,000 Falun Gong practitioners took part in an unauthorized silent protest against the Chinese government actions outside Zhongnanhai, the Chinese leadership's official residence. Three months after the protest, the Chinese government reacted by outlawing Falun Gong because it allegedly practised 'evil thinking' that threatened China's social stability. From that time, Falun Gong practitioners have been arrested throughout China. Many have been interrogated and forced to sign letters rejecting the practice. The Chinese government has also destroyed more than two million Falun Gong books and instructional tapes and has placed Li Hongzhi on a list of wanted criminals (Human Rights Watch, 2002: 15–18.)

China's rulers have various concerns linked to international attention on the alleged lack of religious freedoms in the country. The government has 'uneasy connections with foreign religious groups active in China', including various Christian churches, both Catholic and Protestant. Reacting to China's religious repression, the Vatican placed its ambassador in Taipei, Taiwan, not Beijing (Waldron, 1999). In addition, the influence of conservative Protestant evangelical groups on US government's foreign policy (see Chapter 8) helped increase the pressure on the Chinese government, which has faced tough questions 'on matters of religious persecution' (Waldron, 1999). Collectively, these issues emphasize that China's rulers must now seek to deal with various serious problems simultaneously: demands for religious and political freedoms; developmental concerns, including how to feed and employ the vast, and growing, population of more than one billion people; maintenance of the considerable flow of foreign investment; and, above all, how in the long run to retain their hold on power. In this context, the government regards New Confucianism as an important ideological referent in relation to both domestic and foreign policy. As Waldron notes, however, 'religion may well turn out to be a more important factor in foreign policy than in domestic policy' (Waldron, 1999).

A Chinese intellectual, Jiang Qing, contends that China, 'challenged by Western civilization in its broadest sense', should now seek to deal with current political and social problems by reference to the 'Confucian religion' ('Confucianism will never be religion', 2006). For Jiang 'remaking the Confucian religion' would 'enable Chinese people to launch a "dialogue between Chinese civilization and Western civilization"', that is, including a 'dialogue between the so-called Confucian religion and Christian religion' ('Confucianism will never be religion', 2006). Raja Mohan explains that 'besides providing the ethical glue at home, Confucius has become the emblem of a new Chinese foreign policy initiative'. In recent times, the Chinese government has begun 'offering support to build "Confucius institutes". The purpose of the Confucius institutes is to teach Chinese language and culture to the world'. This is an attempt, Raja Mohan contends, to support China's position as arguably the second most globally powerful country behind the USA, a recognition of the importance of 'soft power'[4] – that is, the power of attractive ideas – to underpin and extend China's 'growing hard power. The British Council, Alliance Française and Max Mueller Bhavan might as well make space for the new cultural juggernaut from China. Beijing hopes to set up at least a hundred Confucius institutes around the world in coming years' (Raja Mohan, 2005). They are already established in the USA, affiliated with the University of Maryland, the Chicago public school system and San

Francisco State University, and in the United Kingdom, where the prestigious London School of Economics is building links with Beijing's Qinghua University (Jain and Groot, 2006).

The background is that ever since 2003 and the accession to power in China of Hu Jintao and Wen Jaibao, China has sought to alleviate international concerns about its increasing economic, diplomatic and military power with a new policy slogan: 'China's Peaceful Rise' evolved into 'China's Peaceful Development', in case the word 'rise' was seen as a threat both to China's neighbours and the USA (Schmitt, 2006). According to Jain and Groot, this is manifested in China's current '"soft power" offensive'. The concept of soft power advocacy is said to have made a strong impression in China, especially after 'some agitation by at least one Shanghai think-tank' to influence China's Communist Party leaders to try to enhance China's soft power and thus China's global and regional influence (Jain and Groot, 2006).

We can see that a concern with a China's New Confucian values in relation to its foreign policy provides a useful foundation for construction of a post-Communist ideological framework. In November 2005, on the occasion of the opening of the first Confucius Institute in Japan, Wang Yi, Chinese ambassador to Japan, defined New Confucian values in relation to current Chinese foreign policy, what he called 'an independent foreign policy of peace'. The concept of peace, he asserted, was seen in Chinese foreign relations, in 'friendly neighboring policy', 'virtuous treatment' and 'happy relation with close neighbours and distant friends alike' (http://english. hanban.edu.cn/market/HanBanE/426610.htm).

Such concerns are undoubtedly a factor in the government's declared aim to underpin China's 'peaceful rise' to great power status, seeking through the use of New Confucian tenets not only to balance the USA globally but also regionally in relation to both Japan and India. The policy is rooted in a strategy of increasing civilizational dialogue, which for the Chinese government is an attempt to underpin and extend its attempts to help build world peace (Pan, 2004). Such concerns were manifested at a national conference in August 2005 in Beijing, devoted to a focus on the contemporary salience of Confucianist ideas.[5] A Shandong University professor, Ding Guanzhi, argued that the Confucian concept of seeking the 'golden mean' meant keeping a balance. A righteous government should use power to maintain the mean, he said, and power between nations should be kept in balance (Hwang, 2005). The implication seemed clear: China's international economic and military rise was henceforward to be focused on what the government regarded as a fundamental geopolitical imbalance. In this view, the position of the USA as the sole global superpower needed rectifying, and

Confucianist ideas were useful to inform China's rise to a comparative level of power and influence. At the same conference, Ren Ziyu, 'a scholar on world religions and the recently retired director of the [Chinese] National Library', averred that 'Confucianism lasted for 2,000 years because new content was constantly added . . . The core teachings had undergone two major waves of change in history . . . Today, with economic globalization and cultural polarization, it is time for a third surge of Chinese culture. Not just academic thought, we both need conscious power' (Hwang, 2005). In sum, it is clear that both the Chinese government and various scholars now seek to focus New Confucianist ideas in a novel foreign policy focus that would not only build more productive international relations, but also improve relations with the USA, and more generally, to help build 'world peace'. Attempting to use ideas associated with China's oldest and most famous philosopher – Confucius – has the added advantage of avoiding overt reference to the USA's traditional *bête noire*: the continuing official state ideology in China: Marxism–Leninism. It is also especially useful that Confucius, both teacher and quasi-religious figure, is best known for championing peace and harmony, and unsurprising that China's government now proclaims adherence to similar values, eager to try to dispel regional and international concerns about its rapid global economic rise.

In sum, it is useful to think of China's attempt to project soft power in the context of recent and current attempts to win influence by persuasion and appeal rather than by expressions of hard power, that is, economic leverage and (threats of) military force. Elizabeth Economy, director of Asian Studies for the US-based Council on Foreign Relations,[6] contends that Chinese soft power is a mix of 'culture, education and diplomacy', while Bruce Gilley, expert on contemporary Chinese politics at New School University, contends that China wields soft power alongside hard power, such as its military threat and ability to impact, especially in the developing world, on other nations' political and/or economic security (Pan, 2004).

Buddhism and politics in Pacific Asia: Thailand, Myanmar and Cambodia

We noted at the outset of the chapter that the Pacific Asian region has a variety of religions. As we have seen, New Confucianism influences both China's contemporary foreign policy and international relations, although opinions differ regarding how this should be understood in terms of both soft and hard power. Like Confucianism, Theravada Buddhism is a significant religious tradition in Pacific Asia.[7] The use of the Pali term 'Theravada' (Doctrine of the Elders) to define the particular school reflects the fact that Theravadins present themselves as belonging to the branch of Buddhism which they believe preserves the 'orthodox' or 'original' teaching of the Buddha, Prince Siddhartha Gautama, born 2,500 years ago in what is now northern India. Theravada Buddhism is the form of Buddhist culture that is highly significant in Sri Lanka's religious, political and social life, as we saw in Chapter 12. In Pacific Asia, this form of Buddhism is the leading religion in Myanmar (Burma) and Thailand, and, until their Communist takeovers in the 1970s, Laos and Cambodia. Since the demise of the Communist Khmer Rouge in Cambodia in 1979 there has been a partial return of Theravada Buddhism (henceforward referred to in this chapter as 'Buddhism'). This is also the case in Laos where the government, which remains Communist in orientation, has tentatively allowed Buddhism to return to social prominence in recent years.

Buddhism in Thailand, Myanmar, and Cambodia

Buddhism has permeated the life of the nations of the region's Buddhist countries, leaving its distinctive mark on social, cultural and individual activity. The result is that, as in relation to Confucianism in China, Buddhism has long served as one of the main socializing, acculturating and unifying forces in several Pacific Asian countries. As a result, Buddhism has profoundly influenced cultural, economic, and political development of several Pacific Asian nations, and at the current time it continues to influence many regional people's cultural, social and political values. In Thailand, Myanmar, and Cambodia in particular, Buddhism is the root from which national identity and political and social heritages have for centuries developed.

During the post-Second World War era, a period characterized for many Pacific Asian countries by an assault from two secularizing influences – Western-style modernization and Communism – Buddhism showed both tenacity and adaptability. However, like many other religious traditions, Buddhism found itself increasingly subject to the eroding influences of foreign secular ideas. Both secularism (the idea that the government, societal morals, education, and so on, should be independent of religion) and secularization (a significant decline in the prestige and influences of religious institutions, personnel, and activities and a change in the overall character of human thought and action, such that they become less governed by mystical or transcendental criteria) were important. Both secularization and secularism undermined traditional Buddhism-orientated world-views in Thailand, Myanmar and Cambodia. In response, Buddhist practitioners sought to make major efforts to shore up Buddhism's traditions, institutions, scriptural integrity, monastic discipline and moral values. As a result, both Buddhist renewal and reform have taken place, significantly involving sustained activism on the part of the Buddhist laity in Thailand, Myanmar and Cambodia (Haynes, 1998: 188–206). Buddhist monks (the *sangha*) also found it necessary to reinterpret traditional Buddhist teachings to seek to appeal to increasingly modernized, urbanized and educated citizens in each country.

This train of events began when colonialism was overthrown in the Pacific Asian region following the Second World War. In the various national struggles for independence, Western notions of equality, liberty, self-determination and so forth were commonly employed by nationalist leaders seeking to legitimize their quest for national freedom with unifying ideas that were also seen as attractive and modern (Acharya and Stubbs, 1999: 118). Notions of representative government were particularly important here, forming a focal point of political attacks on traditional religious-political modes of government. The result was that by the time of the Second World War there was a small but influential group of Western-educated elites who had developed comprehension of, and commitment to, new secular values. Later, however, attempts to impose secularization on traditional cultures and societies often led to tensions and conflicts (McCargo, 2001: 143–5; Cady and Simon, 2006).

Post-colonial state policies towards religion in Buddhist Thailand, Myanmar and Cambodia[8] were shaped not only by rulers' goals of Western-style modernization but also by their need to legitimate their rule and to unify often ethnically and religiously divided peoples. Their main problem was that the two goals – modernization and building nation-states – were often mutually exclusive. This is because while striving for modernization entails rejection of those aspects of a society's traditions deemed impediments to a rationalized bureaucratic order, often including religious principles, nation-building depends on the very opposite. What is necessary here are successful attempts to identify what is basic to national identity, which might well include religion, and more generally community values rooted in a common history. Under prevailing circumstances of conflict and tension, political leaders in Thailand, Myanmar and Cambodia eventually (re)turned to religious values for assistance. The concept of 'national religion' – in each case, Buddhism – was invoked to try to initiate, explain and legitimize political actions, institutions and programmes, albeit with varying degrees of success (Stuart-Fox, 2006).

Buddhist 'passivity' and politics in Pacific Asia

It is sometimes alleged that Buddhist countries are characterized by political 'passivity' (Huntington, 1991; Fukuyama, 1992). Critics of this view point to various high-profile political struggles involving Buddhists in Thailand, Myanmar and Cambodia in recent years (Stuart-Fox, 2006). In addition since the 1970s, there have been frequent popular protests against authoritarian rule both in Thailand and, most prominently, in Myanmar, where Aung San Suu Kyi has led them for over a decade.[9] There has also been the rise and fall of the murderous Khmer Rouge regime in Cambodia. Overall, this political volatility undermines claims of 'passivity' that are said to be central to Buddhist beliefs.

Claims of 'Buddhist passivity' are especially prominent when commentators refer to the alleged political proclivities of rural dwellers in the Buddhist countries of Pacific Asia (McCargo, 2001). However, it is by no means certain that it is their Buddhist culture that impels such people towards political passivity. Apparent Buddhist 'passivity' may merely reflect both a general lack of political influence for the mass of ordinary people, as well as a rational response to heavy-handed, often military based, state power. 'Passive' Buddhists may sensibly decide that it would be foolhardy to confront the state openly, assessing that realistically they have no chance of success in such a confrontation. But this is hardly a unique trait of rural Buddhist people! In other words, rather than alleged passive Buddhist culture being the cause of political passivity, it may well be much more important that powerful, unrepresentative governments, often closely backed by the military, create and embed political passivity by showing ordinary people that resistance to state power is not only futile but also highly dangerous. The implication is that the religion of such 'politically passive' people is not that important; yet, we never read of 'Muslim' or 'Christian' passivity in, for example, the Middle East or Africa. It is just as likely, however, that often powerless rural people in both regions are just as politically 'passive' as their counterparts in the Buddhist countries of Pacific Asia when confronted by overwhelming state power that is underpinned by the power of the military.

Pacific Asia: Religious networks and international relations

We saw in earlier chapters that some religious expressions – notably, Protestant evangelicals of various kinds, Roman Catholics, and various interpretations of Islam, including 'moderate' and 'extremist' entities – have developed geographically extensive transnational religious networks. In some cases, they have been politically and/or developmentally significant. We have noted various examples, including the influence of Roman Catholics, in helping countries to democratize in Eastern Europe, Latin America and Africa, the role of US Protestant evangelicals, credited with 'evangelizing' US foreign policy under President George W. Bush, leading to more emphasis on development and religious freedom goals and, in relation to Islam, the centripetal influence of 'moderates' and 'extremists'. So far in the current chapter, we have examined the international relations and foreign policy influence of New Confucianism. In relation to the latter we noted that there is in this context what might be seen as a coming together of both soft and hard policy concerns in the Chinese government's reorientation of foreign policy away from Communism, in response to changing international conditions, including the influence of globalization (Yahuda, 2005). There are, however, no notable regional or international Confucian networks independent of government that would enable us to identify transnational or international dimensions to New Confucianism's current significance in China.

Turning to Buddhism, however, we have already noted not only that it is the most significant religion in three regional countries – Thailand, Myanmar and Cambodia – but also that it has a presence in several other regional countries, including Laos, Singapore, Japan and Taiwan. This suggests that potentially there are necessary conditions for the development of transnational religious networks of the kind that we have seen in relation to Islam and Christianity: that is, followers of a religion that are in contact with co-religionists in foreign countries. In the next section we focus on two questions:

- Does Buddhism inform the foreign policies of regional countries with significant Buddhist populations?
- Are there politically influential transnational Buddhist groups?

What would a Buddhist foreign policy look like? We noted above in relation to China's New Confucianist foreign policy that one of the key goals is said to be 'world peace'. A key Buddhist religious goal is 'universal peace' ('The common goal of universal peace in Buddhism and the Bahá'í Faith', 1990). So if Buddhism was a key component of a regional country's foreign policy, we might expect to see signs of it in a pronounced focus on regional and international peace. However, the lack of significance of such a key tenet of Buddhism in regional countries' foreign policies and international relations can be shown negatively: researching for this book, I could find very few relevant analyses highlighting Buddhism's foreign policy significance.

I found that one of the very few attempts to examine a Buddhist country's foreign policy was not concerned with a Pacific Asian country but the tiny Himalayan kingdom of Bhutan, where three-quarters of the population is Buddhist. According to Upreti, foreign policy in Bhutan 'is an important instrument of Gross National Happiness, the alternative model of development that Bhutan has pursued over the last two decades . . . A balanced foreign policy approach is required to attain the objectives of GNH'. This intriguing idea does not, however, appear to manifest itself in anything more profound than a statement regarding the importance of attempting to engage with globalization and foreign influences in such a way as not to undermine Bhutan's existing Buddhist culture while increasing the country's economic and human development. In addition, Bhutan's government seeks to 'regulariz[e] foreign policy in a way that the external influences do not affect [Bhutan's] traditional cultural fabric' (Upreti, 2005: 5). In sum, there is little significance in Upreti's account that would enable us to ascertain concrete Buddhist ingredients to Bhutan's foreign policy.

Mongolia is another Asian country with a Buddhist majority, in relation to which the influence of Buddhism in foreign policy has been briefly noted (US Library of Congress, 1986). During the Cold War, Mongolia's Buddhist beliefs were thought to encourage a certain foreign policy direction: to try to link the Communist and non-Communist states of Asia, including Pacific Asia. Mongolia's capital, Ulan Bator, was at this time headquarters of the Asian Buddhist Conference for Peace (ABCP), an organization that held conferences for Buddhists from various Asian countries, including Japan, Vietnam, Cambodia, Sri Lanka and Bhutan. It also published a journal for international circulation, while maintaining contacts with such groups as the Christian Peace Conference, the Afro-Asian People's Solidarity Organization and the Russian Orthodox Church. The Asian Buddhist Conference for Peace also sponsored the Dalai Lama's visits to Mongolia in 1979 and 1982. Finally, the ABCP, headed by the abbot of the Gandan Monastery in Mongolia, was said more generally to support the foreign policy goals of the Mongolian government, which during the Cold War were in accord with those of the Soviet Union (US Library of Congress, 1986). Since the demise of the Cold War, however, both the influence of the ABCP and an alleged Buddhist focus of Mongolia's foreign policy seem to have diminished.

In relation to mainly Buddhist Thailand's foreign policy, a theme of regional and international cooperation has also been periodically highlighted. Thailand participates in various international and regional organizations, including the Association of South East Asian Nations (ASEAN), whose member states, in addition to Thailand, include: Indonesia, Malaysia, the Philippines,

Singapore, Brunei, Laos, Cambodia, Myanmar and Vietnam. ASEAN foreign and economic ministers hold annual meetings, with cooperation focused on economic, trade, banking, political and cultural matters. In neighbouring Myanmar during the Cold War, foreign policy was notable not for regional cooperation but for a pronounced neutrality. Since the end of the Cold War, however, Myanmar has been less isolationist, attempting to strengthen regional ties. Like Thailand it is a member of both ASEAN and BIMSTEC (Bangladesh, India, Myanmar, Sri Lanka and Thailand. But neither country appears to have a demonstrable Buddhist element to foreign policy goals.

Our brief survey of the few extant references to Buddhist inputs to foreign policy among regional Buddhist countries in Asia makes it clear that there is not anything particularly 'Buddhist' in the foreign policies of Bhutan, Mongolia, Thailand or Myanmar (Cady and Simon, 2006). This observation underlines the fact that Buddhism lacks a unifying ethos that can transcend the influence of regionally more dynamic ideologies, especially that of nationalism. In the case of all the Buddhist Asian countries we have noted in this regard, the post-colonial ideology of nationalism has been much more influential than Buddhism in focusing attentions of both governments and citizens (McCargo, 2001; Stuart-Fox, 2006). While, as we have noted, Buddhism has periodically played an often important *domestic* political role, when it comes to regional countries' foreign policies and international relations, its influence seems at best negligible and more often non-existent. This is partly because Buddhism lacks an institutionalized church which, as we saw in the case of Roman Catholicism, was crucial for development of both regional and international networks under the aegis of the Pope in the Vatican and which was able to link together the numerous national churches in pursuit of shared goals. In addition, certain non-religious factors significantly, perhaps fatally, undermine the ability of Buddhists to form and develop transnational networks: Pacific Asia is a disparate region, perhaps the world's 'most complex and diverse region', with numerous languages, civilizations, ethnicities and races (McCargo, 2001: 142). Collectively, these factors undermine the likelihood of Buddhism playing a significant role in the international relations of Pacific Asia, not least because regional Buddhists lack a lingua franca to communicate.

Before closing, however, it is important to examine a significant regional radical Muslim network because of its influence on domestic politics in both Thailand and the Philippines as well as in the wider context of the US-led 'war on terror'. Islamist networks have developed in the Pacific Asian region, in the context of the anti-Soviet Union war in Afghanistan that also led to the development of al-Qaeda and other radical groups in many parts of the Muslim world (Frost et al., 2003; Abuza, 2005). During this conflict, *mujahidin* guerrillas supported by the US government fought the Soviet occupation forces. During the 1990s, a nucleus of Islamist fighters in Afghanistan formed the first cadres of a network that developed in Pacific Asia. Frost, Rann and Chin (2005) note several important factors in relation to its development:

■ *The Afghan experience was central to the recent development of more radical Islamic groups in South-East Asia.* Like Muslims nearly everywhere, most of Pacific Asia's more than 200 million Muslims (around one-fifth of the global total) are characterized by their moderate and tolerant views. This has typically enabled them to live in relative harmony with other religious groups and secular institutions. Now, however, more aggressive and anti-pluralist versions of Islam have been imported from various centres of Islamic militancy, including Saudi Arabia, Pakistan and Afghanistan. While extremist Islamic arguments have only appealed to small but often significant minorities in the region, some Muslims from Pacific Asian countries joined the anti-Soviet resistance in Afghanistan in the 1980s. In addition, many leaders of the region's radical Islamic groups served or trained in Afghanistan. Others studied in *madrasas* (religious schools) either within the region or in foreign countries, including Pakistan; in such cases, many individuals came into contact with radical interpretations of Islam.

■ *The Afghanistan conflict added a new dimension to already existing demands for autonomy or independence from some Muslim minority peoples in the some Pacific Asian countries.* The influence of aggressive and/or extremist versions of Islam was noticeable in relation to some already disaffected regional Muslim ethnic groups in some Pacific Asian countries, including in southern Thailand, Aceh in Indonesia and the southern Philippines. The Afghanistan war afforded many both additional religious and ideological inspiration as well as in some cases foreign assistance and/or funding.

■ *Socio-economic factors have encouraged regional radical Islamic groups to organize and develop strategies to try to achieve their goal of independence.* Most such radical Islamic groups demand independence, an outcome strongly resisted by central governments of affected countries. Even when demands for autonomy falling short of independence were accepted, for example, in relation to Muslim demands in the southern Philippines, they were not properly put into effect. In addition, the 1997 Asian financial crisis led to new or increased economic and financial pressures on all regional governments; as a result, state spending on sensitive welfare areas, including education, was often cut back. This

helped lead to an increase in Muslim schools, which in turn were sometimes focal points for independence demands. Finally, often well-
funded Islamic radical movements were in a position to offer and
provide financial support when those they recruited were killed in combat. This was an attraction for many poor Muslims already enthused by
the religious programmes of the radical groups.

■ *Regionally, national borders are often porous with weak immigration controls.*
For example, until recently, Malaysia did not require an entry visa for
entrants from Muslim countries that are members of the Organization
of the Islamic Conference (OIC), while the Philippines has an
underdeveloped, ineffective immigration system which can often be
circumvented by the use of bribes. Such circumstances facilitate the
entry of people, including Islamic radicals, into regional countries.

■ *Long-standing economic and trade links between South-East Asia and Middle
Eastern and South Asian countries.* Many such links operate outside state-
controlled channels, and governments find them difficult to monitor
and control. Such networks can facilitate the transfer of funds from the
Middle East and South Asia to regional radical Muslim groups.

Muslims in Pacific Asia no doubt see themselves as part of the global
Muslim community, the *ummah* (Esposito, 1987). In some cases, they also
identify themselves as disadvantaged minorities who see their membership
of the *ummah* as an opportunity to draw upon its strengths in relation to
various issues, including in some cases autonomy or independence demands
(Hooker, 1997; Islam and Chowdhury, 2001). For example, the Philippines is
home to more than 100 ethnic groups. Most Filipinos are Roman Catholics,
and the country's Muslim minority is concentrated in the southern islands,
amounting to more than four million people in the southern population of
over 14 million, that is, about 5 per cent overall. Thirteen ethno-linguistic
groups comprise the country's Muslim population, among them the
Tausugs, Maranaos and Maguindanaos; all are active in a Muslim secession-
ist movement. The Muslim separatists contend that their people have been
forcibly included in a state that is dominated both by domestic Catholics
and by foreign and domestic capitalists (Encarnacion and Tadem, 1993:
152). But the Muslim separatists of the Philippines are divided among themselves in relation both to tactics and organizational matters. The largest
separatist group, the Moro Islamic Liberation Front (MILF), had to deal
with other groups with differing agendas. During the 1980s, the Muslim
struggle for autonomy in the Philippines became internationalized, with
Libya supplying military equipment to the MILF. Later, in the 1990s, the

MILF adopted an effective cease-fire and maintained it until 2000 when renewed heavy fighting broke out. However, in 2001 the MILF signed a cease-fire with the authorities, leaving only the Abu Sayyaf group still fighting ('Attention shifts to Moro Islamic Liberation Front', 2002).

Abu Sayyaf: Religious terrorism in the Philippines

Abu Sayyaf ('the sword bearer') was formed in 1990 in the southern Philippines and attracts a fluctuating number of recruits, numbering between 250 and 600 people at any one time (Country Reports on Terrorism, 2004). The Philippine authorities suspect that Abu Sayyaf receives funds from Islamist groups in the Middle East (Council on Foreign Relations, 2005). From April 1992 the group unleashed a number of terrorist assaults beginning with a hand-grenade attack on the Roman Catholic cathedral in Iligan city that killed five and wounded 80 people. Three years later, in 1995, 200 alleged Abu Sayyaf activists attacked the southern town of Ipil, killing 53 people. In 2000, Abu Sayyaf militants were implicated in the kidnapping of a party of foreign tourists, most of whom were freed by the end of the year following the payment of large ransoms. Later, 'in February 2004, the group planted a bomb in a passenger ferry docked off the coast of Manila killing more than 100 people'. Following this incident, the Philippine government conducted a sustained military offensive against 'Abu Sayyaf rebels in the south in efforts to quell the group's attacks against civilians' (Council on Foreign Relations, 2005).

As in the Philippines, both religion and ethnicity have played a crucial political role in the demands of Muslim separatists in southern Thailand. Many among the Malay-Muslim minority – around three million people or 4 per cent of the national population of over 70 million – were alienated from the mainstream of predominantly Buddhist Thailand, because of their 'strict adherence to Islam' and the perception that Thailand is a Buddhist state (Encarnacion and Tadem, 1993: 153). Muslim estrangement was exacerbated by the fact that many among the Malay-Muslim minority engage in non-lucrative small-scale farming which serves to marginalize and impoverish them in a national economic situation dominated by Thai Buddhists and ethnic, non-Muslim Chinese (Braam, 2006).

One result of Muslim alienation was armed conflict with the state over a long period of time. Muslim rebels have fought Thai authorities for more than forty years in a conflict that has still not been resolved. Two groups, the Pattani National Liberation Movement and the Path of God, have long been at the forefront of separatist demands. Over time, many Muslim militants have been incarcerated, usually around 200 at any one time. In the late 1990s, the Thai authorities claimed that there were less than 200 Muslim fighters in the field compared to around 2,000 twenty years earlier. The government also claimed that it had tried to meet the Muslim demands by increasing government services and by greater local participation in state political activities. It asserted, however, that its attempts had been thwarted because of encouragement from foreign Muslim governments to the Muslim separatists, including those of Iran and Libya, which has helped to keep the flame of revolt alive (Russell and Jones, 2004).

After a brief lull, there was a resurgence in militant Islamic activity in the early 2000s. Abuza notes the existence of four distinct organizations, 'two of importance, while two others are more fringe groups'. The most significant organizations are 'the Gerakan Mujahideen Islamiya Pattani (GMIP) and the outgrowth of the old Barisan Revolusi Nasional (BRN) organizations now known as BRN Coordinate (BRN-C)'. There are also two smaller fringe groups: Jemaah Salafi and New Pulo (Abuza, 2005: 5).

The GMIP was founded in 1986 but quickly degenerated into a criminal gang until 1995 when two Afghan veterans consolidated power. Since then, the rural-based GMIP has led attacks on police and army outposts. The group has close relations with a Malaysian militant organization, the Kampulan Mujahideen Malaysia (KMM), also founded by Afghan war veterans in 1995. The Thai National Security Council acknowledged that there is 'a new Islamic grouping' which, 'through increasing contacts with extremists and fundamentalists in Middle Eastern countries, Indonesia, Malaysia and the Philippines, they have metamorphosed into a political entity of significance [sic]' (Crispin, 2004). A key concern for the Thai government is whether any of these new Islamic groups have established contact with the notorious Jemaah Islamiyah of Indonesia.

Jemaah Islamiyah and regional religious terrorist networks

Jemaah Islamiyah ('Islamic Group' or 'Islamic Community') is often abbreviated to JI. It is a militant Islamic separatist movement in Indonesia, suspected of killing hundreds of civilians, dedicated to the establishment of an Islamic state in South-East Asia, to include Indonesia, Singapore, Brunei, Malaysia, and the south of Thailand and the Philippines. Analysts have identified financial and organizational links between Jemaah Islamiyah and other terrorist groups, such as Abu Sayyaf and al-Qaeda (Crispin, 2004). It is likely that JI cadres undertook the Bali

(Continued)

car bombing of 12 October 2002 when suicide bombers killed 202 people in a nightclub and wounded many others. Following this outrage, the US Department of State designated JI as a foreign terrorist organization. Jemaah Islamiyah is also alleged to have perpetrated further bombings, including the Zamboanga and the Metro Manila explosions, as well as the bombing of the Jakarta Embassy in 2004. However, the Thai government denies that there are links between local groups and JI. A Thai Foreign Ministry spokesman said that, 'The causes of the situation [are] domestic. It's not part of any international terrorist network but of course we are concerned about the introduction of extremist ideologies among the youths. We are concerned about the possibility of extremist groups in the region connecting together and this could become a serious problem [sic]' (Abuza, 2005: 5).

In conclusion, Islamist groups in both the Philippines and Thailand justify anti-government struggles by use of a similar argument: they are coerced into conforming to the requirements of the dominant religious/national groups in each country and are regarded as second-class citizens, with no legitimate way to improve their condition under the present circumstances. In other words, Muslim separatists in both countries do not see themselves as part of the nation, instead believing their ethnic, religious, political and economic rights are consistently and comprehensively violated. However, none of the separatist groups were powerful enough to achieve their objectives and were eventually encouraged to seek peace with the state authorities. But since the end of the war in Afghanistan in the 1980s between Islamists and Soviet troops, development of a regional Islamist militant network has manifested itself. The result appears to have been to stiffen the resolve of some Muslim militants to seek independence or at least significant levels of autonomy for Muslim minorities. In addition, al-Qaeda has sought to exploit and benefit from pre-existing disaffection of Muslim minority peoples in both countries, not only in relation to their national governments but also to the perceived aggressive intrusion of Western capitalist interests (Abuza, 2005; Russell and Jones, 2004). As a result, there is now a collection of regional Islamist groups that, while for the most part operating relatively autonomously, are collectively informed by shared ideological convictions deriving from the ideas of various figures, including Sayyid Qutb, one of the key ideological figures informing al-Qaeda. As Frost, Rann and Chinn (2003) note:

It is increasingly evident that Southeast Asia has become an important arena for international terrorism, notably Al Qaeda. Al Qaeda is a highly decentralised and

elusive transnational terrorist network that is difficult to identify and combat. . . .
In Southeast Asia, Al Qaeda's activities appear to have been concentrated in the
Philippines, Malaysia, Singapore and Indonesia. Al Qaeda established contacts in
Southeast Asia from 1988 and established a logistics base in the Philippines in
the early 1990s.

Conclusion

The chapter makes the following general points:

- Both Buddhism and Confucianism are politicized in Pacific Asia but
  only the latter in relation to China has a significant role in the country's foreign policy and international relations.

- The Chinese government emphasizes a 'culturally authentic' 'New Confucianism', regarded as a prescriptive policy to balance the power of the
  USA, to increase Chinese influence and, more loftily, to try to build
  world peace.

- Buddhism does not play a significant international or transnational political role in Pacific Asia.

- There is a regional network of dissident Muslim minorities. Some cadres
  draw on the radical ideas of al-Qaeda, which are linked to ethnic demands for autonomy or independence in what are seen as unrepresentative and illegitimate states. Our examples were from Thailand and the
  Philippines, where restive Muslim minorities have engaged in political
  conflict with the state for decades.

In the chapter, we focused on two religious expressions – New Confucianism
in relation to China, and Buddhism in the context of Thailand, Myanmar
and Cambodia. We saw that in relation to China, New Confucianism has
supplied a clear ideological focus to recent foreign policy that now informs China's external interactions both regionally and in relation to the
USA, and the government's stated aim to help build 'world peace'. Secondly, we considered the political impact of Buddhism in relation to the
foreign policies of various Asian Buddhist countries, including Bhutan,
Mongolia, Thailand and Myanmar. We noted that there does not appear
to be any significant input from Buddhism in relation to any of them. In
addition, there are no transnational Buddhist networks with regional political significance. The main reason for this is the importance of singular
nationalist ideologies for regional countries. This secular ideology has

created and maintained national identities that in many cases have deep historical roots. In this context it is not surprising that each regional country has in its own way adopted and adapted religious traditions in accordance with national characteristics and state policies, and has been uninterested in creating and developing transnational networks of religious believers. Finally, we noted and briefly examined the regional impact of radical Muslim networks that were able to draw on religious, ethnic, social and political grievances that have had an impact on the region's religious and national stability.

Notes

1   Lacking a god to worship, Buddhism is sometimes regarded as a philosophy based on the teachings of the Buddha, Siddhartha Gautama, rather than a religion. Siddhartha Gautama lived between c.563–483 BCE. Buddhism began in India, and gradually spread throughout Asia to Central Asia, Tibet, Sri Lanka and South-East Asia, as well as to China, Mongolia, Korea, and Japan in East Asia. Buddhism is both a philosophy and a moral practice, whose purpose is to work towards the relief of suffering, characteristic of human existence, by ridding oneself of desire. In the early 2000s, there were an estimated 350 million Buddhists around the world, divided into three main schools: Mahayana (56 per cent), Theravada (38 per cent) and Vajrayana (6 per cent).

2   Taoism (sometimes written as Daoism) 'refers both to a Chinese system of thought and to one of the four major religions of China (with Confucianism, Buddhism, and Chinese popular religion)'.

3   'A religion native to Japan, characterized by veneration of nature spirits and ancestors and by a lack of formal dogma.'

4   Employed in international relations, 'soft power' is used to describe ability of both states and non-state entities indirectly to influence what other states and non-state actors do through cultural and/or ideological measures. An international relations scholar, Joseph Nye, coined the term in 1990.

5   According to Hwang (2005), over 200 'scholars gathered at a Beijing hotel for a two-day conference sponsored by the government-backed China Confucian Foundation and three other organizations'.

6   According to its website, the Council on Foreign Relations is a 'nonpartisan resource for information and analysis' (http://www.cfr.org/).

7   Theravada Buddhism of South-East Asia differs from both Mahayana Buddhism – of Mongolia, Tibet, Bhutan and various East Asian countries – and the Tantric Buddhism of parts of Central Asia. The overall purpose

and aim of Buddhist practice is to liberate the individual from suffering (*dukkha*). While some interpretations stress stirring the practitioner to the awareness of *anatta* (egolessness, the absence of a permanent or substantial self) and the achievement of enlightenment and nirvana, others (such as the 'Tathagatagarbha' sutras) promote the idea that the practitioner should seek to purify him/herself of both mental and moral defilements that are a key aspect of the 'worldly self' and as a result break through to an understanding of the indwelling 'Buddha-Principle' ('Buddha-nature'), also termed the 'True Self', and thus become transformed into a Buddha. Other Buddhist interpretations beseech bodhisattvas (that is, enlightened beings who, out of compassion, forgo nirvana in order to save others) for a favourable rebirth. Others, however, do none of these things. Most, if not all, Buddhist schools also encourage followers to undertake both good and wholesome actions, and consequently not do bad and harmful actions. There can be very large differences between different Buddhist schools of thought.

8   Thailand is over 90 per cent Buddhist, as is Myanmar and Cambodia.

9   The military dictatorship in Myanmar has detained Aung San Suu Kyi, a Nobel Prize-winning peace activist, periodically since 1990, when her party, the National League for Democracy, won the country's only democratic election. She is the daughter of Burmese General Aung San, a popular hero instrumental in helping to win national independence from the British in 1948.

Questions

1   Are transnational religious networks in Pacific Asia politically important?
2   To what extent is China's foreign policy now characterized by New Confucianist ideas?
3   Why is Buddhism in Pacific Asia largely confined to individual countries?
4   Are separatist movements in Thailand and the Philippines motivated more by ethnic demands than religious grievances?
5   Is there a regional religious terrorist network linked to Al-Qaeda?

Bibliography

Abuza, Z. (2005) 'A conspiracy of silence: who is behind the escalating insurgency in Southern Thailand?', *Terrorism Monitor*, 3(9), pp. 4–6.

Acharya, A. and Stubbs, R. (1999) 'The Asia-Pacific region in the post-cold war era', in L. Fawcett and Y. Sayigh (eds), *The Third World Beyond the Cold War*, Oxford: Oxford University Press.

'Attention Shifts to Moro Islamic Liberation Front' (2002) *Jane's Intelligence Review*, April, pp. 20–23.

Barr, M. (2002) *Cultural Politics and Asian Values: The Tepid War*, London: Routledge.

Braam, E. (2006) 'Travelling with the Tablighi Jamaat in South Thailand', *ISIM Review*, no. 17, Spring, pp. 42–3.

Cady, L. and Simon, S. (eds) (2006) *Religion and Conflict in South and South-East Asia: Disrupting Violence*, London: Routledge.

'Confucianism will never be religion' (2006) *China Daily*, 6 January. Available at: http://www.chinadaily.com.cn/english/doc/2006-01/06/content_509753.htm Accessed 17 January 2006.

Council on Foreign Relations (2005) 'Abu Sayyaf Group (Philippines, Islamist separatists)', New York: Council on Foreign Relations.

Country Reports on Terrorism (2004) United States Department of State, April 2005. Available at: http://library.nps.navy.mil/home/tgp/asc.htm Accessed 18 June 2006.

Crispin, S. (2004) 'Thailand's war zone', *Far Eastern Economic Review*, 11 March.

Deegan, H. (2005) 'Culture and development', in S. Hunter and H. Malik (eds), *Modernization, Democracy, and Islam*, London: Praeger.

Encarnacion, T. and Tadem, E. (1993) 'Ethnicity and separatist movements in South-East Asia', in P. Wignaraja (ed.), *New Social Movements in the South*, London: Zed Books, pp. 152–73.

Esposito, J. (1987) 'Islam in Asia: an introduction', in J. Esposito (ed.), *Islam in Asia: Religion, Politics, and Society*, New York: Oxford University Press, pp. 3–19.

Frost, F., Rann, A. and Chin, A. (2003) 'Terrorism in Southeast Asia', *Parliament of Australia – Parliamentary Library*. Available at: http://www.aph.gov.au/library/intguide/FAD/sea.htm Accessed 16 January 2006.

Fukuyama, F. (1992) *The End of History and the Last Man*, Harmondsworth: Penguin.

Haynes, J. (1998) *Religion in Global Politics*, London: Longman.

Hooker, M. (1997) *Islam in South-East Asia*, Leiden: Brill.

Human Rights Watch (2002) 'Dangerous meditation. China's campaign against Falungong', New York/Washington/London/Brussels: Human Rights Watch.

Huntington, S. (1991) *The Third Wave: Democratization in the Late Twentieth Century*, Norman: University of Oklahoma Press.

Hwang, K. (2005) 'Analysis: China resurrects Confucius', *Washington Times*, 12 August. Available at: http://www.washingtontimes.com/world/20050825-104920-5524r.htm Accessed 26 August 2005.

Islam, I. And Chowdhury, A. (2001) *The Political Economy of East Asia: Post-Crisis Debates*, New York: Oxford University Press.

Jacques, M. (2006) 'This is the relationship that will define global politics', *The Guardian*, 15 June.

Jain, P. and Groot, G. (2006) 'Beijing's "soft power" offensive', *Asia Times Online*, 17 May. Available at: http://www.atimes.com/atimes/China/HE17Ad01.html Accessed 2 June 2006.

Kim, S (ed.) (1998) *China and the World: Chinese Foreign Policy Faces the New Millennium*, Boulder, CO and London: Westview.

King, A. Y. C. (1993) 'A nonparadigmatic search for democracy in post-Confucian culture: the case of Taiwan, R. O. C.' in L. Diamond (ed.), *Political Culture and Democracy in Developing Countries*, Boulder, CO Lynne Rienner, pp. 139–62.

McCargo, D. (2001) 'Democratic consolidation in Pacific Asia', in J. Haynes (ed.), *Towards Sustainable Democracy in the Third World*, Basingstoke: Palgrave, pp. 141–62.

Miller, M. (1997) 'Asia/Pacific', *Foreign Policy in Focus*, 2(5), March, pp. 1–6.

Naím, M. (2005) 'Three wise men', *Foreign Policy*, January–February. Available at: http://www.foreignpolicy.com/story/cms.php?story_id=2741 Accessed 2 September 2005.

Ommerborn, W. (n.d., probably 2003) 'The importance of universal principles in Confucianism and the problems connected to Jiang Qing's concept of political Confucianism and his theory of particular principles'. Available at: http://www.eko-haus.de/menzius/universal.htm#_ftnref 3]%20 Accessed 16 January 2006.

Pan, P. (2004) 'Civil unrest challenges China's party leadership. Protests growing larger, more frequent, violent', *Washington Post*, 4 November.

Raja Mohan, C. (2005) 'The Confucian Party of China', *The Indian Express* (Mumbai), 19 December. Available at: http://www.indianexpress.com/full_story.php?content_id=84219 Accessed 17 January 2006.

Ross, R. and Johnston, A. (eds) (2006) *New Directions in the Study of China's Foreign Policy*, Stanford, CA: Stanford University Press.

Russell, S. and Jones, E. (2004) 'Islam in Southeast Asia: a summary', Center for Southeast Asian Studies, Northern Illinois University, December.

Schmitt, G. (2006) 'Confucius say – Caveat emptor: What China means by "peaceful rise"', *The Weekly Standard,* Vol. 11, Issue 31, 1 May. Available at: http://www.weeklystandard.com/Content/Public/Articles/000/000/012/129bywdp.asp?pg=1 Accessed 2 May 2006.

Stuart-Fox, M. (2006) 'Buddhism and politics in Laos, Cambodia, Myanmar and Thailand'. Paper presented at the Cambodia, Laos, Myanmar and Thailand Summer School, Asia Pacific Week 2006, The Australian National University, Canberra, 30 January.

Tamney, J. and Chiang, L. Hsuch-Ling (2002) *Modernization, Globalization, and Confucianism in Chinese Societies*, Wesport, CI: Greenwood.

Tepe, S. (2005) 'Religious parties and democracy: a comparative assessment of Israel and Turkey', *Democratization*, 12(3), pp. 283–307.

'The common goal of universal peace in Buddhism and the Bahá'í Faith' (1990) 'A paper delivered to the Asian Buddhist Conference for Peace', Ulan Bator, Mongolia 16–25 September. Available at: http://statements.bahai.org/90-0916.htm Accessed 3 May 2006.

Upreti, B. C. (2005) 'Gross national happyness (sic) and foreign policy of Bhutan: interlinkages and imperatives'. Paper presented at the conference, 'Rethinking Development: Local Pathways to Global Wellbeing', St Francis Xavier University, Antigonish, Nova Scotia, Canada, 20–24 June.

US Library of Congress (1986) 'Buddhism', *Area Handbook for Mongolia,* 2nd edn. Available at: http://countrystudies.us/mongolia/47.htm Accessed 19 September 2005.

Waldron, A. (1999) 'Religious revivals in Communist China', *Foreign Policy Research Institute – FPRI Wire*, 7(3), February. Available at: http://www.fpri.org/fpriwire/0703.199902.waldron.religiousrevivalscommunist china.html Accessed 18 January 2006.

Watts, J. (2006) 'Land seizures threaten social stability, warns China's leader', *The Guardian*, 21 January.

Weber, M. (1969) 'Major features of world religions', in R. Robertson (ed.), *Sociology of Religion*, Baltimore, MD: Penguin, pp. 19–41.

Yahuda, M. (2005) *The International Politics of the Asia Pacific*, 2nd edn, London: Routledge.

Yu, Keping (2004) 'From the discourse of "Sino-West" to "globalization": Chinese perspectives on globalization', Working Paper GHC 04/1, Institute on Globalization and the Human Condition, Hamilton, Ontario, Canada, March.

Zhou, Qi (2005) 'Conflicts over human rights between China and the US', *Human Rights Quarterly*, 27(1), February, pp. 105–24.

Further reading

L. Cady and S. Simon (eds), *Religion and Conflict in South and South-East Asia: Disrupting Violence*, Routledge, 2006. This book seeks to advance comparative and multidisciplinary scholarship on the issue of the alignment of religion and violence in the contemporary world, with particular attention to South and South-East Asia. Both regions are characterized by: recent and emerging democracies, a high degree of religious pluralism, the largest Muslim populations in the world, and several well-organized terrorist groups, making understanding of the dynamics of religious conflict and violence particularly urgent. The contributors ask whether there is an intrinsic connection between religion and violence. Is religious terrorism rooted in religion, or is it cloaked by religion? Is religious violence a misnomer, an indication that authentic religion has been hijacked? What difference, if any, does this make for policy interventions? Bringing scholars together from religious studies, political science, sociology, anthropology and international relations, the book brings a sustained focus on the role of religion in fostering violence in both regions.

S. Kim (ed.) *China and the World: Chinese Foreign Policy Faces the New Millennium*, Westview, 1998. This book is a well-regarded survey of China's foreign policy in the context of the rise of globalization and a changing world order. It provides essential background information to help explain the shift to a New Confucian focus in the early 2000s.

R. Ross and A. Johnston (eds) *New Directions in the Study of China's Foreign Policy*, Stanford University Press, 2006. This book brings together several generations of specialists in Chinese foreign policy to present readers with current research on both new and traditional topics. The authors draw on a wide range of new materials – archives, documents, memoirs, opinion polls and interviews – to examine traditional issues such as China's use of force from 1959 to the present, and new issues such as China's response to globalization, its participation in several international economic institutions, and the role of domestic opinion in its foreign policy. The book also offers a number of suggestions about the topics, methods, and sources that the Chinese foreign policy field needs to examine and address if it is to grow in richness, rigour and relevance.

M. Yahuda, *The International Politics of the Asia Pacific*, Routledge, 2nd edn, 2005. Yahuda's book is a useful survey of the region's international relations, tracing its development in terms of both historical and contemporary concerns, including globalization and the post-Cold war order.

CHAPTER 14

Conclusion

We have seen in this book that, compared to the past, there is now much more awareness of the cross-border dimensions of religion and effects on international relations. Undeniably, September 11, 2001 (9/11) was an important event in this regard, as it was significantly responsible for raising governmental, academic and public awareness. But it is important to recognize that 9/11 was but one, albeit highly important, issue: a murderous attack by a transnational religious extremist organization, al-Qaeda, against the world's most conventionally powerful country, the USA. This unexpected attack, indicative of a wider conflict between the USA – and by extension, the West – and Islamic extremism, did not, however, by any means exhaust all the ways that religion can affect outcomes in contemporary international relations.

We examined two key ways that religion affects outcomes in international relations: (1) transnational religious actors, and (2) domestic religious actors that impact significantly on state foreign-policy formation and execution. In relation to the first category, we saw that various transnational religious actors, notably various Islamic, Roman Catholic and Protestant evangelical groups, collectively bring a renewed religious dimension to international relations. In the second category, we examined religious actors that seek to influence state foreign policy in a number of countries, including the USA, India, Pakistan, Saudi Arabia and Iran.

Because of its potentially vast subject matter, this book did not set out to examine each and every area where religion has an impact on international relations. Instead, we were mainly concerned with examining how religion affects two sets of issues of great significance in current international relations: (1) social development and human rights, and (2) conflict and conflict resolution. The starting point for the book was the fact of a widespread religious resurgence, a deepening of globalization and a changed international environment after the Cold War came to an end in the late 1980s. The collective impact of these developments, as many analysts of international relations would now agree, is that we cannot any longer ignore religion's international influence. One key area of concern is: what are the implications for international relations of religious resurgence in many parts of the world? While there are no definitive answers, a budding literature devoted to this theme is now appearing (Thomas, 2005; Fox and Sandler, 2004; Norris and Ingelhart, 2004).

Our starting point in this book was a question: how do religious actors affect outcomes in international relations? We noted that there are two main ways by which they might do this. First, they might seek to pursue objectives via expansion of transnational networks, a development that has received increased attention over the past two decades, a period during which the Cold War ended and globalization deepened. The result was that 'the structure of world affairs and global interactions is in the middle of a major change. Both in terms of actual operations and the ways that those operations are conceived and understood by analysts, the old systems of relationships are passing rapidly' (Voll, 2006: 12). Significant changes in this regard are notable 'across many political, economic, and military areas, [where] international "soft power" is taking precedence over traditional, material "hard power"' (Arquilla and Ronfeldt, 1999: ix). Secondly, there are numerous attempts by religious actors to influence state foreign policies. The result, according to Fox and Sandler, is that 'religion's greatest influence on the international system is through its significant influence on domestic politics. It is a motivating force that guides many policy makers' (Fox and Sandler, 2004: 168). Overall, in both cases, the main tool that religious actors seek to utilize is their soft power, especially by encouraging others to accept and apply religious principles, values and ideals.

Given the burgeoning interest in how religion affects international relations, it is surprising that to date few discussions of soft power in international relations have focused on religion. Joseph Nye (1990), who originally coined the term 'soft power' over fifteen years ago, only briefly refers to religion, noting that 'for centuries, organized religious movements have possessed soft power' (Nye, 2004a. 98). Instead, he focuses on secular sources of soft power and their effects on international relations. Nye has employed the term over the years especially in relation to the waxing and waning of US soft power. For Nye (2004b),

> The basic concept of power is the ability to influence others to get them to do what you want. There are three major ways to do that: one is to threaten them with sticks; the second is to pay them with carrots; the third is to attract them

or co-opt them, so that they want what you want. If you can get others to be attracted, to want what you want, it costs you much less in carrots and sticks.

This suggests that a useful way to understand the concept of 'soft power' is to perceive it as the capability of an entity, not necessarily a state, to influence what others do through direct or indirect influence and encouragement. We saw that soft power co-opts people: it does not coerce them. Certain attributes – such as, culture, values and ideas – represent different, not necessarily lesser, forms of influence compared to 'hard' power: more direct, more forceful measures typically involving (the threat or use of) armed force and/or economic coercion. In international relations, a country's power is often regarded as a quantitative measure derived from various material attributes, including: gross national product (GNP), military capability and natural resources. However, seeking to measure a country's potential hard-power assets is not necessarily a good guide to understanding whether it will be able to achieve its foreign-policy goals. The problem is that even when a country seems to have sufficient relevant material assets 'to get the job done' *and* the will to use them, this does not always translate into success. For example, the USA was not able to achieve its main goal in the Vietnam War (1954–75) – to prevent a Communist regime taking power – nor, so far, in relation to Afghanistan and Iraq, to establish secular, pro-Western regimes, built on democratic foundations. In each case, US foreign policy sought unsuccessfully to apply its hard power.

In short, soft power is neither 'sticks nor carrots', but a 'third way' of seeking to achieve objectives. Soft power is more than influence, since influence can also rest on the hard power of (military or diplomatic) threats or (financial) payments. On the other hand, while soft power is not entirely synonymous with cultural power, it is the case that 'exporting cultural goods that hold attraction for other countries can communicate values and influence those societies' (Nye, 2004c) – for example, US efforts during the 'third wave of democracy' in the 1980s and 1990s to undermine authoritarian governments in many parts of the world (Haynes, 2001).

Economic strength is usually not soft power. This is because responding to an economic incentive or sanction is not the same as aligning politically with a cause that is admired or respected. We can see this in relation to the influence of foreign-aid donors, collectively of great importance in encouraging some economically poor authoritarian regimes to democratize in the 1980s and 1990s. This followed significant oil price rises in the 1970s and associated international indebtedness, when the ability of many such regimes to maintain adequate programmes of political and economic development dropped sharply in the 1980s and 1990s. The result was that it became increasingly difficult, especially for many developing countries without oil, for them to balance their budgets. Many became increasingly dependent on loans and aid from the West. Aid donors argued that the situation would be remedied by democratization, part of a general process of improving governance. Increasingly, the continuity of foreign aid was made dependent on aid-hungry regimes agreeing to democratize. In this way, many economically poor, authoritarian regimes were encouraged to shift to democracy via the use of a range of inducements, including both sticks and carrots. In addition, in a linked move, several Western governments, including those of the USA and Britain, encouraged the installation of market-based economic programmes to the extent that they were 'intrinsic' to democratic openings in economically impoverished Africa and Central America (Haynes, 2001). In short, recent external encouragement to democratize, linked to the supply of aid and loans, was often of major significance for poor countries; but it was not soft power, because normally overt economic leverage was used.

Soft power is not necessarily humane. For example, the soft-power activisms of various significant political figures – including the Indian nationalist, Mohandas 'Mahatma' Gandhi, the US civil rights leader, Martin Luther King, and South Africa's anti-apartheid activist par excellence, Nelson Mandela – were uniformly informed by universal humanist ideas, while those of others – including the German Nazi leader, Adolph Hitler, the Russian Communist head, Josef Stalin, and the mastermind of the 9/11 attacks, Osama bin Laden – are said by Nye to be reliant on twisting people's minds (Nye, 2004c). This suggests that the exercise of soft power not only relies on persuasion or the capacity to convince people by argument but also is a sign of an ability to attract, and attraction often leads to acceptance of associated ideas. As Nye (2004c emphasis added) puts it,

> If I am persuaded to go along with your purposes without any explicit threat or exchange taking place – in short, if my behavior is determined by an observable but intangible attraction – soft power is at work. *Soft power uses a different type of currency – not force, not money – to engender cooperation. It uses an attraction to shared values, and the justness and duty of contributing to the achievement of those values.*

Religion may be a form of soft power. We can see this in relation to the post-9/11 'war on terror', when competing conceptions of soft power have vied for supremacy, and religious values are often central to this competition. Lacking an influential soft-power, hearts-and-minds policy that would demonstrably persuade all Muslims not to follow extremist groups who encourage violence, US foreign policy has found it very difficult to convince many Muslims that its objectives in both Afghanistan and Iraq are not simply self-serving (Shlapentokh et al., 2005). In addition, both 'extremist' and 'moderate' Islamic ideas and movements have competed post-9/11 for the support of ordinary Muslims by offering differing soft-power visions. Casanova (2005), Voll (2006) and Appleby (2006) have recently discussed the international impact of various Muslim transnational networks. Some – al-Qaeda is an obvious example because of the events of September 11, 2001 – can have a greater impact on the world stage and receive more foreign-policy attention from the great powers than many 'weak' states in the international system.

More generally, in the chapters of this book we examined a variety of transnational religious phenomena – including, the Roman Catholic Church, various Protestant evangelical entities (often conservative and American-based), as well as several Islamic transnational entities, both 'militant' and 'moderate' (Voll, 2006; Casanova, 2005). The main purpose was to try to understand how cross-border religious networks affect outcomes in international relations. But, as already noted, it took 9/11 to put transnational religious actors into the foreground of concern for international relations analysis. Before 9/11 international relations interest in transnational phenomena was often linked to questions of 'conventional' – that is, political and economic – security. Religious actors were often regarded as interesting phenomena, although remote from central questions affecting states and state power in international politics. Now, however, it is widely accepted that various religious actors can not only directly affect the *internal* politics of states and thus qualify state power, as conventionally understood, but also have significant ramifications for outcomes in *international* relations.

Examining a more general and complex relationship – that between religion and globalization – we saw that, apparently, irrespective of which religious tradition we are concerned with, many religious ideas, experiences and practices are all significantly affected by globalization. The impact of globalization is encouraging many religions to adopt new or renewed agendas in relation to a variety of religious, social, political and economic concerns. It is also stimulating many religious individuals, organizations and movements to look beyond local or national contexts to regional or international environments. Finally, we saw that in many cases such concerns are focused in two main areas: *social development and human rights*; and *conflict and conflict resolution*.

Most analyses of globalization focus primarily on economic, social or cultural issues, including the economic range and social and cultural significance of the activities of transnational corporations (TNCs). This often leads to the perception that TNCs are taking economic power both from governments and from citizens. This comes in the context of what is often understood as significant downsides to economic globalization: the apparent mass impoverishment of already poor people, especially in the developing world. These circumstances have led to a new focus for numerous religious organizations, concerned with trying to redress these imbalances, reflecting more generally a concern with multiple – social, economic and human rights – concerns. This focus is manifested in various ways, including: new religious fundamentalisms, support for anti-globalization activities, such as anti-World Trade Organization protests, and North/South economic justice efforts (Spickard, 2001). In sum, recent religious responses to globalization have often included a stress on social interests, manifested in various ways, which together go way beyond the confines of what might be called 'church' or more generally 'religious' life.

These concerns are now increasingly pursued within inter-faith contexts. We saw that various inter-faith religious forums are trying to bring collective and sustained concern to social development issues – and by extension, human rights issues – through an interfaith focus. The key example we noted in this regard was the World Faiths Development Dialogue (WFDD), an initiative that, encouraged by the World Bank, has recently sought to map areas of convergence among development agendas of various separate religious faiths. Many shared a focus on relationships of service and solidarity, harmony with the earth, and the vital – but necessarily limited – contribution of material progress to human development and satisfaction (World Faiths Development Dialogue, 1999).

A senior World Bank figure, Katherine Marshall, delivered a speech in June 2005 that seemed to be especially significant in emphasizing that the World Bank no longer believed 'that religion and socio-economic development belong to different spheres and are best cast in separate roles – even separate dramas'. This observation was based on a concern that was examined in the pages of this book: recognition that around the world both religious organizations and (secular) development agencies often share similar concerns: how to improve (1) the lot of materially poor people, (2) the societal position of those suffering from social exclusion and (3) unfulfilled human potential in the context of glaring developmental polarization within and between countries, which the World Bank now accepts has arisen in part because of the polarizing impact of globalization (Marshall, 2005). Marshall's speech also emphasized that while in the past religion was understood by the World Bank to be primarily concerned with 'otherworldly' and 'world-denying' issues, it now accepted that religion can play a significant role in seeking to achieve developmental goals for millions of people, especially in the developing world. The Bank also now recognizes that issues of 'right' and 'wrong', as well as those linked to social and economic justice, are central to the teachings of *all* the world religions (that is, Buddhism, Christianity, Hinduism, Islam and Judaism). This realization is influential in highlighting: (1) how relatively marginal most current manifestations of religious fundamentalism are, yet (2) at the same time, potentially increasingly the likelihood that disadvantaged people might turn to various religious fundamentalisms, compared to people who are happy and confident in their developmental positions.

Reflecting such concerns, recent years have seen regular 'leaders' meetings', convened to enable religious leaders to try to address these issues. A recent meeting was held in Canterbury, England in October 2002, hosted by James Wolfensohn, then president of the World Bank, and Dr George Carey, at the time head of the worldwide Anglican communion of around 70 million people. The main purpose of the meeting was to bring together an important group of leaders 'from the world's faith communities, key development organisations, and from the worlds of entertainment, philanthropy and the private sector'. Linked to the Millennium Development Goals announced in 2000, with the goal of achieving them by 2015, key themes addressed at the meeting included: poverty, HIV/AIDS, gender, conflict and social justice. Participants accepted that poverty, HIV/AIDS, conflict, gender concerns, international trade and global politics explicitly link all the world's countries and peoples, rich and poor, into a global community. Another main theme was the dualistic impact of globalization, with its differential impact on rich and poor countries. The meeting revealed a growing sense of religious solidarity that highlights the urgency of developing shared responsibility and partnership to deal with collective problems facing humanity. Yet it is crucial to move from talk to action, as much more needs to be done to progress from expressions of shared religious solidarity in response to shared development problems to a realization of practical plans involving collaboration between the worlds of faith and development in confronting major development issues (Marshall and March, 2003).

The second issue that informed many of the chapters of this book was also linked to the impact of globalization: religion's involvement in both conflict and conflict resolution in various parts of the world. A starting point for our analysis in this regard was to note that globalization both highlights and encourages religious pluralism. But religious responses may well be different. This is because some religions, including Judaism, Christianity and

Islam (sometimes known as the 'religions of the book', because in each case their authority emanates principally from sacred texts, actually, similar texts) claim what Kurtz calls 'exclusive accounts of the nature of reality', that is, only *their* religious beliefs are judged to be *true* by adherents (Kurtz, 1995: 238).

As globalization results in increased interaction between people and communities, the implication is that not only are encounters between different religious traditions likely to be increasingly common but also that there will be various outcomes as a result: some will be harmonious, others will not. Sometimes, the result is what Kurtz has called 'culture wars' (Kurtz, 1995: 168). These can occur because various religious world-views encourage different allegiances and standards in relation to various areas, including the family, law, education and politics. As a result, conflicts between people, ethnic groups, classes, and nations can be framed in religious terms. Such religious conflicts seem often to 'take on "larger-than-life" proportions as the struggle of good against evil' (Kurtz, 1995: 170). We noted this in relation to religious minorities who may regard their own existential position – for example, Muslim minority communities in Thailand, the United Kingdom, France, the Philippines and India – to be unacceptably weakened because of actual or perceived pressure from majority religious communities – Buddhists in Thailand, Christians in Britain, France and the Philippines, and Hindus in India – to conform to the norms and values of the religious and cultural majority.

We also saw many examples of religious involvement in recent and current international conflicts in the book's various chapters. For example, we learned that stability and prosperity in the Middle East is a pivotal goal, central to achieving general peace and the elimination of poverty. Yet the Middle East is particularly emblematic in relation to religion, in part because the region was the birthplace of the world's three great monotheistic religions (Christianity, Islam and Judaism). This brings with it a legacy not only of shared wisdom but also of conflict – a complex relationship that has impacted in recent years on countries as far away as Thailand, the Philippines, Indonesia, the USA and Britain. A key to peace in the region may well be achievement of significant collaborative efforts among different religious bodies, which along with external religious and secular organizations, for example from Europe and the USA, may through collaborative efforts work towards developing a new model of peace and cooperation to enable the Middle East to escape from what many see as an endless cycle of religious-based conflict. Overall, this emphasizes that religion may be intimately connected, and not only in the Middle East, to international conflicts and their prolongation as well as attempts at reconciliation of such conflicts. In other words, in relation to many international conflicts, religion can play a significant, even a fundamental role, contributing to conflicts in various ways, including how they are intensified, channelled or reconciled. In addition, we also saw that religion has a key part to play in resolution of conflicts in other parts of the world, including South Asia (notably India/Pakistan) and Africa (for example, in relation to the recently ended civil war in Sudan). We also noted its involvement in the still simmering civil war in Sri Lanka, between the minority (Hindu) Tamils and the majority (Buddhist) Sinhalese.

In sum, in various ways religion is becoming a more and more important factor in international relations, yet it would be incorrect to focus only on the links with conflict. To do so, would mean that we would be likely to overlook the many recent and current examples of religious involvement in attempts at conflict resolution. On the other hand, the fact remains that many current international conflicts have religious aspects that can exacerbate both hatred and violence and make the conflicts themselves exceptionally difficult to resolve. Hans Kung, an eminent Roman Catholic theologian, claims that

> the most fanatical, the cruelest political struggles are those that have been colored, inspired, and legitimized by religion. To say this is not to reduce all political conflicts to religious ones, but to take seriously the fact that religions share in the responsibility for bringing peace to our torn and warring world (Hans Kung, quoted in Smock 2004).

We saw in the introductory chapter the concern in international relations analysis with the concept of the 'clash of civilizations'. This thesis is built upon the belief that there is a serious 'civilizational' threat to global order that has become especially apparent after the Cold War. It is rooted in the idea that there are competing 'civilizations' that engage in conflict that affects outcomes in international relations in various ways. On the one hand, there is, the 'West' (especially North America and Western Europe) with values and political cultures deemed to be rooted in liberal democratic and Judaeo-Christian concepts, understood to lead to an emphasis on tolerance, moderation, and societal consensus. On the other hand, there is supposedly a bloc of allegedly 'anti-democratic', primarily Muslim, countries, believed to be on a collision course with the West.

We saw, however, that a key problem with this thesis is that there are no 'civilizations' that actually act in international relations in a uniform and single-minded way. Wherever we look – to the USA, to Europe, to Israel, to the Muslim countries of the Middle East – what is most notable is the *plurality* of beliefs and norms of behaviour that are apparent, even in allegedly cohesive and uniform civilizations. It is useful to bear these concerns in mind when we are seeking to examine the role of religion in relation to international conflict under the circumstances of globalization. We saw that religion is often implicated in both domestic and international conflicts. On the other hand, it is important not to overestimate religion's potential for and involvement in large-scale violence and conflict, especially if that implies ignoring or underestimating its involvement and potential as a significant source of conflict resolution and peacebuilding. It is important to recognize that, especially in recent years, numerous religious individuals, movements and organizations have been actively involved in attempts to end conflicts and to foster post-conflict reconciliation between formerly warring parties (Bouta et al., 2005). This emphasizes that various religions collectively play a key role in international relations and diplomacy by helping to resolve conflicts and build peace. The 'clash of civilizations' thesis oversimplifies causal interconnections between religion and conflict, in particular by disregarding important alternate variables, including the numerous attempts from a variety of religious traditions to help resolve conflicts and build peace. When successful, religion's role in helping to resolve conflicts is a crucial component in wider issues of human development because, as Ellis and ter Haar note: 'Peace is a precondition for human development. Religious ideas of various provenance – indigenous religions as well as world religions – play an important role in *legitimising or discouraging violence*' (Ellis and ter Haar, 2004, my emphasis).

Finally, the book makes clear that religion has now reappeared as an important domestic and international political actor, in part because of the impact of deepening globalization, which has led to an expansion of channels, pressures and agents via which norms are diffused, and interact through both transnational and international networks and interactions. As a result, religious actors now pursue a variety of goals in international relations that in many cases links their concerns to the economic, social and political consequences of globalization.

Bibliography

Appleby, R. Scott (2006) 'Building sustainable peace: the roles of local and transnational religious actors'. Paper presented at the conference on 'The New Religious Pluralism in World Politics', Berkley Center for Religion, Peace and World Affairs, Georgetown University, 16–17 March.

Arquilla, J. and Ronfeldt, D. (1999) *The Emergence of Noopolitik: Toward an American Information Strategy*, Santa Monica, CA: RAND.

Bouta, T., Kadayifci-Orellana, S. Ayse and Abu-Nimer, M. (2005) *Faith-based Peace-Building: Mapping and Analysis of Christian, Muslim and Multi-faith Actors*, The Hague: Netherlands Institute of International Relations.

Casanova, J. (2005) 'Catholic and Muslim politics in comparative perspective', *Taiwan Journal of Democracy*, 1 (2), pp. 89–108.

Ellis, S. and ter Haar, G. (2004) *Religion and Development in Africa.* Background paper prepared for the Commission for Africa.

Fox, J. and Sandler, S. (2004) *Bringing Religion into International Relations*, Basingstoke: Palgrave Macmillan.

Haynes, J. (2001) *Democracy in the Developing World*, Cambridge: Polity.

Kurtz, L. (1995) *Gods in the Global Village*, Thousand Oaks, CA: Pine Forge Press.

Marshall, K. (2005) 'Religious faith and development: rethinking development debates'. Paper presented at the 'Religious NGOs and International Development Conference', Oslo, Norway, 7 April.

Marshall, K. and March, R. (2003) *Millennium Challenges for Development and Faith Institutions*, Washington, DC: The World Bank.

Norris, P. and Inglehart, R. (2004) *Sacred and Secular: Religion and Politics Worldwide*, Cambridge: Cambridge University Press.

Nye, J. (1990) *Bound to Lead: The Changing Nature of American Power*, New York: Basic Books.

Nye, J. (2004a) *Soft Power: The Means to Success in World Politics*, Washington, DC: Public Affairs.

Nye, J. (2004b) 'Edited transcript, 04/13/04 Carnegie Council Books for Breakfast'. (Nye discussing *Soft Power: The Means to Success in World Politics* with Joanne Myers.) Available at: http://www.carnegiecouncil. org/viewMedia.php/prmTemplateID/8/prmID/4466 Accessed 10 April 2006.

Nye, R. (2004c) 'The benefits of soft power', *Harvard Business School Working Knowledge*, 2 August. Available at: http://hbswk.hbs.edu/item. jhtml?id=4290&t=globalization Accessed 10 April 2006.

Shlapentokh, V., Woods, J. and Shirav, E. (eds) (2005) *America: Sovereign Defender or Cowboy Nation*, Aldershot: Ashgate.

Smock, D. (2004) 'Divine intervention: regional reconciliation through faith', *Religion*, 25 (4). Available at: http://hir.harvard.edu/articles/1190/3/ Accessed 1 September 2005.

Spickard, J. (2001) 'Tribes and cities: towards an Islamic sociology of religion', *Social Compass*, 48, pp. 103–16.

Thomas, S. (2005) *The Global Transformation of Religion and the Transformation of International Relations: The Struggle for the Soul of the Twenty-First Century*, New York/Basingstoke: Palgrave Macmillan.

World Faiths Development Dialogue (1999) *Poverty and Development: an inter-faith perspective*. Available at: http://www.wfdd.org.uk/documents/publications/poverty_development_english.pdf Accessed 2 March 2006.

Voll, J. (2006) 'Trans-state Muslim movements in an era of soft power'. Paper presented at the conference on 'The New Religious Pluralism in World Politics', Berkley Center for Religion, Peace and World Affairs, Georgetown University, 16–17 March.

Index